BEYOND MOTHERING EARTH

BEYOND MOTHERING EARTH
Ecological Citizenship and the Politics of Care

SHERILYN MacGREGOR

UBCPress · Vancouver · Toronto

15 14 13 12 11 10 09 08 07 06   5 4 3 2 1

Printed in Canada on ancient-forest-free paper (100 percent post-consumer recycled) that is processed chlorine- and acid-free, with vegetable-based inks.

Library and Archives Canada Cataloguing in Publication

MacGregor, Sherilyn, 1969-
   Beyond mothering earth : ecological citizenship and the politics of care / Sherilyn MacGregor.

Includes bibliographical references and index.
ISBN-13: 978-0-7748-1201-6 (bound); 978-0-7748-1202-3 (pbk.)
ISBN-10: 0-7748-1201-X (bound); 0-7748-1202-8 (pbk.)

   1. Ecofeminism. 2. Caring. 3. Women – Social conditions.
I. Title.

HQ1194.M32 2006   305.42082   C2006-902217-8

Canadä

UBC Press gratefully acknowledges the financial support for our publishing program of the Government of Canada through the Book Publishing Industry Development Program (BPIDP), and of the Canada Council for the Arts, and the British Columbia Arts Council.

This book has been published with the help of a grant from the Canadian Federation for the Humanities and Social Sciences, through the Aid to Scholarly Publications Programme, using funds provided by the Social Sciences and Humanities Research Council of Canada.

Printed and bound in Canada by Friesens
Set in Arrus and News Gothic by Artegraphica Design Co. Ltd.
Copy editor: Joanne Richardson
Proofreader: Stephanie VanderMeulen
Indexer: Christine Jacobs

UBC Press
The University of British Columbia
2029 West Mall
Vancouver, BC V6T 1Z2
604-822-5959 / Fax: 604-822-6083
www.ubcpress.ca

To my parents, Nancy and George MacGregor,
for everything

Contents

Acknowledgments   ix

1 Introduction: Earthcare or Feminist Ecological
Citizenship?   3

PART ONE: THEORETICAL INTERROGATIONS

2 The Roots and Rhetoric of Ecomaternalism   19

3 "Down among the Women": Ecofeminism and
Identity Politics at the Grassroots   33

4 From Care to Citizenship: Calling Ecofeminism Back
to Politics   57

5 The Problems and Possibilities of Ecological
Citizenship   81

PART TWO: CONVERSATIONS

6 Conversations with Activist Women:
Towards a Counter-Narrative   123

7 The Private, the Public, and the Planet:
Juggling Care and Activism in Daily Life   145

8 Activist Women Theorize the Green Political   180

9 No Motherhood Issue:
The Project of Feminist Ecological Citizenship   217

Appendix: Research Process and Methods   238

Notes   249

References   265

Index   281

Acknowledgments

My research and this book would not have been possible without the cooperation of the thirty women who took time out of their busy lives (from the autumn of 1999 to the summer of 2000) to tell me about their activist and caring work. I first want to express my thanks and appreciation to them.

I owe thanks to many other people for their support and assistance at different stages of the research and writing process. I am most indebted to Catriona Sandilands whose mentorship, incisive and rigorous criticism, and commitment to conversation over the past nearly ten years are the reasons I was able to see this project through to fruition. Her book *The Good-Natured Feminist: Ecofeminism and the Quest for Democracy* (1999) was an inspiration for my research and continues to inform my thinking in important ways. Ilan Kapoor, Lorraine Code, and Margrit Eichler each helped guide me through the research and writing process and gave excellent advice on how to work through and present my various conflicting arguments. Lorraine Code deserves special thanks for her careful reading and editing of my early drafts. I also appreciate Lee Quinby's critical feedback and encouragement.

I am grateful for the support and friendship of many of my colleagues in the Faculty of Environmental Studies at York University, especially the members of the Democracy Reading Group (namely, Nick Garside, Navin Nayak, Cheryl Lousley, Kim Fry, and Pablo Bose) who helped me think and talk through what ecological citizenship might and might not mean. Ellie Perkins, Gerda Wekerle, Deborah Barndt, Barbara Rahder, Roger Keil, and Engin Isin contributed in different, yet equally valuable, ways to the different stages of the process. Students in my Environmental Politics and Advocacy course provided inspiration, though they probably didn't know it at the time. And many of my good friends in Toronto gave much needed moral (and sometimes IT) support for which I am very thankful, especially Olga Kits, Jen Cypher, Kara Lysne-Paris, Richard Milgrom, John Sandlos, and Adrian Ivakhiv.

Several people have helped and encouraged me more recently as I was completing this book, a task that has largely taken place at Lancaster University and in my new home in the English Lake District. Thanks especially to Andy Dobson and Derek Bell for welcoming me into the UK environmental politics and citizenship loop, and to Richard Twine for keeping at least one of my feet firmly planted in the field of ecofeminism. I owe a great deal of thanks to Randy Schmidt, my editor at UBC Press, for supporting the manuscript with enthusiasm from the beginning and for being generous with encouragement while I was preparing the book. Holly Keller and Joanne Richardson at UBC Press also deserve thanks for their skilled and sympathetic editing. I am grateful to Maureen Reed and John Barry who reviewed the manuscript and gave extremely helpful comments and advice on how to improve it. I owe John Barry a special note of thanks for supporting my book even though he disagrees with some of my arguments about "green men." I have taken his comments seriously and I look forward to future conversations.

Finally, I want to thank my family for caring *for* and *about* me throughout my many years of academic work, and my partner Simon Pardoe, not only for his love, patience, and good humour (which seem remarkably limitless) but also for making swift walks up the hill non-negotiable during the final stages of this project.

My research has been generously funded by the Social Sciences and Humanities Research Council of Canada. I held a doctoral fellowship from 1996 to 1999 and a Postdoctoral Fellowship from 2002 to 2004. An earlier version of Chapter 4 was published (with the same title) in *Ethics and the Environment* 9 (1), 2004. Parts of Chapter 5 appear in "No Sustainability without Justice: A Feminist Critique of Environmental Citizenship," in *Environmental Citizenship*, edited by Derek Bell and Andrew Dobson (MIT Press, 2006). An excerpt from Chapter 6 appears as "A Matter of Interpretation: The Place of 'Lived Experience' in Ecofeminist Research" in *Women and Environments International* (Fall 2001). My chapter entitled "The Public, the Private, the Planet and the Province: Women's Quality-of-Life Activism in Urban Southern Ontario," which appears in *This Elusive Land: Women and the Canadian Environment*, edited by Melody Hessing, Rebecca Raglan, and Catriona Sandilands (UBC Press, 2005), is based on material that appears in Chapters 7 and 8 of this book.

BEYOND MOTHERING EARTH

1 Introduction: Earthcare or Feminist Ecological Citizenship?

> Women have had no voice, but ecofeminism is a radical
> new language. Women must provide the moral energy
> and determination for both the First and Third Worlds.
> They are the future and hope in the struggle over life.
>
> – *Carolyn Merchant,* Earthcare: Women and the
> Environment

Ecological feminism has a history of deliberating such difficult questions as: Are women more "naturally" connected to nature than men? Do women's gendered roles and experiences give them unique insight into human-nature relationships? Why is it that women around the world seem to demonstrate relatively more concern for the quality of their environments than men? Where do the roots of this concern lie? These questions, and the answers they provoke, are the focus of *Beyond Mothering Earth*, in which I critically interrogate "ecofeminist" discourses that make connections between *women's caring* and *ecological politics*. I question why it is that many ecofeminists assert a special role for women as environmental caretakers without considering their lives as political subjects or what it might mean for women in inegalitarian societies to bear such an enormous responsibility. The position that animates the discussion that follows is that *feminist ecological citizenship* is a more promising, and more radical, language for articulating the goals of ecofeminist politics than the language of care.

In 1996 Berkeley historian and pioneering ecofeminist theorist Carolyn Merchant published *Earthcare: Women and the Environment*. Since Merchant is a big-name environmental scholar, it is not surprising that the book quickly made its way onto environmental studies and women's studies reading lists.

Earthcare contains numerous examples of women's efforts to protect the environment and human health throughout history and around the world. From the "moral mothers" of nineteenth-century New England to the "hysterical housewives" at Love Canal in the 1970s, to the *Planeta Fêmea* tent at the 1992 Earth Summit in Rio de Janeiro, Merchant celebrates the contributions of women to the struggle for ecological sustainability. In fact, her dedication reads: "To the women who will care for and defend the earth in the third millennium from those who have done so in the recent and deep past." The book offers an important glimpse into discourses of ecofeminism and has inspired my ten-year-long engagement with a dominant line of ecofeminist argumentation about women's role in grassroots environmental movements.

Like many ecofeminist scholars, Merchant places great hope in the myriad material and moral connections that women qua women seem to have to nature. This hope is translated into an ethico-political prescription for change founded on the "intimate knowledge of nature" (Merchant 1996, 16), which comes out of women's daily caring practices and leads Merchant to call for a "partnership ethic of earthcare." The "daily caring practices" part of this assertion is important for many ecofeminists who want to avoid making "essentialist" claims about women's biological nature (i.e., that there are essential qualities that all women share by virtue of being female). Aware that charges of essentialism have long undermined ecofeminism, these theorists emphasize that the link they make is a socio-material and experiential one: women's mothering and caregiving work mediates the relationship between people and nature and thereby engenders a *caring stance* towards nature. This rhetoric of "ecomaternalism," as I call it, is pervasive in much of the contemporary ecofeminist discourse. Some of the best-known ecofeminist scholars draw upon a similar connection between women's caring for people and their environmental concern. For example, Maria Mies and Vandana Shiva (1993) write of the "subsistence perspective" and the "feminine principle"; Ariel Salleh (1997) celebrates the "barefoot epistemology" of Southern "re/sisters"; and Mary Mellor (1992, 1997, 2000) calls for a "Women's Experience (WE) world" and for the development of "materialist ecofeminism" or "deep materialism." Each of these writers presents a picture of ecofeminism that is built not on abstract theorizing but, rather, on what women do – indeed, *have always done* – to survive the vicissitudes of capitalist-patriarchal-colonial development. Explaining her own version, Mellor (2000, 114) argues that "women are not closer to nature because of some elemental physiological or spiritual affinity, but because of the social circumstances in which they find themselves." Merchant defends against the charge of essentialism by claiming her position to be gender inclusive; that is, under the right conditions, men can be earthcarers too. Others contend that even if they may in some ways be problematic, assertions about a feminine socio-material connection to nature are both inspirational and *strategically useful* for the development of ecofeminism as a political movement (Sturgeon 1997).

Social research provides empirical evidence to support the claim that women typically demonstrate a higher level of concern for environmental issues than men (e.g., Tindall, Davies, and Mauboulès 2003; Hunter, Hatch, and Johnson 2004). Many feminist scholars make much of the fact that women are often drawn into environmental activism because as mothers they fear for their children's health and feel a sense of duty to protect and restore their environments. Joni Seager (1993, 269) argues, for example, that "women's environmental activism occurs within the context of, and as a result of, their particular socially assigned roles – roles that in many key ways do transcend boundaries of race, ethnicity, and class." Merchant (1996, 13) quotes one activist as saying that women are "'mothers of the earth' who want to take care of it." Examples can be found in the media: a 1999 edition of *Homemakers* magazine featured an article entitled "Nature Made It, Women Saved It" (Bossin 1999); the spring 2001 issue of the Canadian feminist magazine *Herizons* carried the front-page headline "Will Women Save the Earth?" (illustrated by a photographic image of female arms handcuffed around a tree) (Felesky 2001). Both make celebratory links between women's environmental activism and their feminine or maternal instincts.

But what does it mean for a woman to invoke the identity of "mother" to explain her participation in the political sphere? Why see activism as an extension of women's private roles rather than as a conscious choice to engage in public life? Few ecofeminists have addressed these questions because, in spite of their interest in women's grassroots activism, few regard what women activists do as an expression of citizenship. I contend that this is precisely what ecofeminist scholarship ought to do.

Why citizenship? Since the 1990s, for a number of reasons relevant to ecofeminist politics, there has been a renaissance of feminist interest in citizenship. First, in joining conversations about citizenship that have been growing in the social sciences in recent decades, feminists make the important argument that this ostensibly gender-neutral concept is actually deeply gendered (Voet 1998). Second, many feminists analyze the gendered nature of citizenship within the context of societies in which capitalist globalization and a right-wing backlash against the welfare state have led to a decrease in social rights and an increase in individual duties. Rather than accept a right-wing definition of citizenship, some feminist theorists want to reinvigorate citizenship as a political location from which to destabilize the boundaries between public and private and to argue for the collective provision of social goods like care (see, for example, Lister 1997). Third, some feminist political theorists see citizenship as a response to the feminist embrace of an essentializing identity politics that obliges women to present themselves as women in politics (e.g., Voet 1998). Recognizing that "woman" is an internally diverse concept and that women have multiple and shifting identities, these theorists argue that the political construct of citizen should be seen as an "articulating principle" (Mouffe 1992b, 378) because it can be at once pluralistic and yet unifying enough to foster a politics of "solidarity in difference" (see also Yuval-Davis 1997; Benhabib 1992). From this feminist perspective, fixing a feminine (or maternal) foundation for politics is undemocratic and apolitical because by defining one identity as authentic it shuts down debate among women. Citizenship, on the other hand, provides an inclusive space for the public performances of political subjectivity that destabilize and resist dominant ideologies of gender.

Informed by these feminist approaches to citizenship, and drawing on those ecofeminists who have considered its merit for ecological politics (e.g., Plumwood 1995b; Gaard 1998; Sandilands 1999a, 1999b), I argue for a project of *feminist ecological citizenship*. I believe that it is a project worth pursuing because citizenship, defined in feminist terms, offers a way to develop ecofeminist positions that are non-essentialist, democratic, and oppositional. As a theoretical project it will not provide definite answers, but it may point to a way out of the kinds of questions and debates that Seager (2003) has declared to be counterproductive to ecofeminism.[1] Feminist citizenship has the potential to be a positive political identity that allows women to express their gender-related concerns for environmental quality but that does not forever tie women (in general) to the private sphere of care and maternal virtue. The cultivation of a democratic public culture in which to debate issues of environmental justice – which includes the collective responsibility for human and non-human well-being – is central to this project. Feminist citizenship discourse also provides a common ground upon which ecofeminists may engage in much needed encounters with other branches of ecopolitical scholarship – branches that share their interest in sustainable human-nature relationships and yet have understandings of citizenship that are woefully gender blind.

In addition to arguing for feminist ecological citizenship,[2] I explain why over-reliance on the discourses of care, mothering, and subsistence labour is not a good strategic move for ecofeminism. Citing feminist and ecofeminist scholarship from a range of disciplines, I provide reasons why ecomaternalist rhetoric offers little hope for the development of a democratic or feminist ecopolitical movement. One reason is that it does not take into account the cultural baggage of the ethics of care discourse, which claims to be rooted in a feminized and different moral voice. In agreement with feminist moral philosophers (e.g., Bowden 1997; Card 1989; Tronto 1993), I argue that, within the context of a white male-dominated society that constructs and enforces women's capacity to care, ecofeminism should not romanticize but, rather, *politicize* this capacity. Ecomaternalist arguments that celebrate women's caring for people and the planet without condemning its implication in oppressive political economic systems risk affirming sexist notions about women's place in society. And I think they are particularly dangerous in an era during which unpaid caring work is increasingly exploited in order to facilitate economic restructuring and the dismantling of the welfare state. An ecofeminist approach to citizenship, on the contrary, recognizes care as a form of work and a moral orientation that has been feminized and privatized in Western societies and that must be distributed fairly within and between societies if gender equality and sustainability are to be realized.

Nor are ecofeminist claims about women's "earthcare" particularly reliable: they are based on selective readings of a narrow list of empirical examples. For example, the Chipko movement is inaccurately held up by ecofeminists as a women-led conservation movement, while women's involvements in pro-development activism are almost never mentioned, nor are examples of earthcare in which men and women have worked together as equal partners (Agarwal 1998b; Reed 2000, 2003). That women engage in environmental activism at great cost to themselves and often under circumstances that are not of their own choosing is seldom discussed. Because many ecofeminist academics want to downplay the privileged place of Western theory in ecofeminism by listening to voices from the grassroots, the experiences of women activists in grassroots environmental struggles are often appropriated and treated as "truth." But, paradoxically, by invoking experientially and epistemologically based women-nature connections, *even when they are said to be based in material conditions*, many ecofeminists falsely universalize private feminine identities and roles, ignore the complex and shifting contexts within which caring and environmental activism take place, and tread dangerously close to perpetuating racism, sexism, and colonialism. They avoid biological essentialism but fall into the trap of "sociological essentialism" (Sandilands 1999a), or what I would call experiential reductionism.

Overview of the Book
In 1987 British feminist Lynne Segal offered some "troubled thoughts" on a contemporary feminism that appeared to be in the midst of a "maternalist revival" (145). Her critique of cultural feminism in *Is the Future Female?* figures prominently in my thinking about ecofeminism. There are some interesting parallels between the arguments I present in what follows and those that frame Segal's book.

I have already highlighted one similarity: both Segal and I are troubled by essentialism. While hers is a socialist feminist critique of the essentialism and psychological determinism of 1980s cultural feminism, mine is an interdisciplinary critique – informed in part by postmodern feminism and feminist political economy – of the experiential reductionism in the ecofeminism of the 1990s.[3] The persistence of essentializing rhetoric in various branches of feminist theorizing suggests that too much weight is placed on private identities and experiences and not enough on the public and political dimensions of women's lives – or on how private identity and public appearance are related. Segal contends that the most significant contribution of feminist politics is to put hitherto private issues on the public agenda and to demand that "caring, sharing, and loving" no longer be regarded as sentiments exclusive to the family. In agreement with Segal and other feminist scholars, I think ecofeminism, too, needs a "calling back to politics" (Dietz 1991, 250). I present this argument in three stages, in Chapters 2, 3, and 4.

In Chapter 2, "The Roots and Rhetoric of Ecomaternalism," I provide an overview of some of the antecedents of contemporary ecomaternalist discourse. Two periods in the history of feminist movements are particularly interesting to my discussion: (1) when maternalist arguments were used to justify women's demands for equal citizenship in the late nineteenth and early twentieth century, and (2) when these arguments were invoked by 1970s cultural feminists to promote women's special – that is, morally superior – approach to politics. In Chapter 3 I provide examples of celebrated grassroots activism in the South (the Chipko movement) and in the North (the Love Canal Homeowners' Association) in order to demonstrate how ecofeminists regard women's private identities as the bases for public engagement and political empowerment. This chapter, which is entitled "'Down among the Women': Ecofeminism and Identity Politics at the Grassroots," also provides a critical interrogation of what looks to me like a "grassroots turn" by locating it within the debates over identity politics and strategic essentialism. I then argue in Chapter 4, which is entitled "From Care to Citizenship: Calling Ecofeminism Back to Politics," that there are political risks in celebrating women's association with caring (as both an ethic and a practice) and in reducing women's ethico-political life to care. While there are important aspects to ecofeminist valuations of women's caring, I think a greater degree of scepticism is in order. I develop this position by drawing on the work of feminist philosophers, political economists, and political theorists who have argued that the positive identification of women with caring ought to be treated cautiously for it obscures some of the negative implications of feminized care and narrows our understanding of women as political actors (e.g., Dietz 1985, 1998). In Chapter 4 I also explain why ecofeminists would be better served by using feminist theories of citizenship to understand and interpret women's engagement in ecopolitics.

One of the reasons Segal criticizes the essentialist discourse of cultural feminism is that it stands in the way of much needed solidarity between feminist women and men in the labour and socialist movements. Troubled by the sexism of leftist men and by how women's caring and community service work is taken for granted by socialist thinkers, Segal (1987, 242) calls for a rethinking of politics that begins with the question: "How do we provide for the needs of all, and not at the expense of women?" "Unless and until" the left starts to take this feminist question seriously, she argues, there will be little hope of building an inclusive counter-hegemonic coalition or creating a society that allows all people to live full and creative lives. But it will be difficult for men to take feminism seriously if it relies on "us versus them" identity politics and female supremacist arguments that call on women to save the world while blaming men for endangering it.

I too find reason to question the new (and greening) left's receptivity to ecofeminist analyses at the same time as I am dissatisfied with ecofeminists' response to being left out. I have been frustrated on many occasions by the disregard of gender inequality as a relevant issue in left-green discussions about ecopolitical alternatives to unsustainable capitalist and political systems. Therefore, in Chapter 5, "The Problems and Possibilities of Ecological Citizenship," I place my analysis of ecofeminist discourse against a backcloth of current green political (or ecopolitical) thought, a field that is at once exciting and unimaginatively patriarchal in its visions. Within this body of literature, "sustainability" and "environmental citizenship" have become popular concepts throughout the 1990s and into the 2000s. The growing awareness of environmental degradation and the belief that human societies are fast approaching the biophysical limits of our inhabitation of the planet has prompted environmental scholars and policy makers to focus their attention on what it means to live sustainably (or less unsustainably).[4] Concerns about sustainability have informed proposals for a range of dramatic changes to current systems – economic, regulatory, and political – that would improve the quality of life of current populations while ensuring similar chances for survival of subsequent ones. However, because sustainability is a contestable concept, and because moving towards a sustainable society will require such dramatic and sweeping changes in individual human behaviour and collective and institutional social practices, many ecopolitical theorists argue that it is necessary to democratically involve people in the process not only in order to promote justice but also in order to ensure the consent and ongoing active participation of all concerned. In addition to positing it as the most appropriate means of articulating this green democratic involvement, many see citizenship as a way to change individual behaviour, to foster values of stewardship and ecological virtue in local places and in global civil society (e.g., Curtin 1999; Dobson 2003). This green writing on citizenship offers valuable challenges to those theorists (feminists included) who make little room for ecological questions in their understandings of citizenship. Hartley Dean (2001, 491) sums up these challenges nicely:

> Green thinking has impacted on our understanding of citizenship in
> at least three different ways. First, environmental concerns have en-
> tered our understanding of the rights we enjoy as citizens. Second, the
> enhanced level of global awareness associated with ecological thinking

has helped to broaden our understanding of the potential scope of citizenship. Third, emergent ecological concerns have added fuel to a complex debate about the responsibilities that attach to citizenship.

In the second part of Chapter 5 I critique ecopolitical approaches to citizenship from a feminist perspective. My assessment leads me to conclude that, as in many periods before this one, blind spots where gender is concerned significantly weaken contemporary left-green analyses. It seems that the new linkage of environmentalism and democracy leaves many questions unanswered and often unasked. As Carole Pateman (1988) would say, "only half the story is told" in ecopolitical discourse: there is silence in this androcentric (or male-centred or masculinist) discourse about the specificity of gender. And once again there is denial of the inescapable relationship between the realm of politics and the *realm of necessity* – the foundations of political analysis upon which most feminist political theorists stand. I argue that blindness to gender specificity and gender asymmetries undermines the promise of ecological citizenship, for a society that has not addressed the unequal division of responsibility for sustaining life will surely not be very "sustainable" – socially, politically, or ecologically. Although only a few ecofeminists have engaged in conversation (in print, at least) with the "green men" (they are predominantly men, as I show in Chapter 5), ecofeminist critiques of ecological citizenship provide important contributions to this project.

I am in agreement with Segal's argument in *Is the Future Female?* that one of the biggest problems with a feminism based on women's moral superiority is that it does as much to support a right-wing as it does a left-wing vision of social change. Segal notes that, throughout the 1980s, socialist men in Britain were not the only ones to take women's caring labour for granted: the Conservative government of Margaret Thatcher called on women to resume their place in the so-called traditional family and turned left-wing discourse of self-reliance back on itself to support the dismantling of the welfare state. Thatcher even called upon "women's special qualities to suggest *her own* greater integrity, sincerity and depth of feeling" (Segal 1987, 246, emphasis mine). As Steven Best and Douglas Kellner (1991, 198) point out: "under the direction of Thatcher and Reagan/Bush, the right has appropriated and monopolized moral and political discourse to its own advantage, defining democracy in a way compatible with the destruction of the welfare state and a return to *laissez-faire* capitalism and atomistic individualism." Similar neoliberal policy developments have become increasingly evident in Canada in the 1990s and into the first decade of the 2000s (the temporal and cultural context of this book). So, just as Segal observed in 1980s Britain, in 1990s and present-day Canada women are being implicated in the campaign to remove responsibility for social service from the state and put it back into the household where it purportedly belongs.

Simply put, the 1990s were a period of neoliberal economic and political restructuring within nation-states – a restructuring that was seen as part and parcel of the increasing globalization of capitalism.[5] As multinational corporations grew less loyal to national economies, national and subnational (e.g., provincial) governments in the developed world were prompted to implement neoliberal economic policies that could attract investment back from the more investment-friendly countries of the South. This move amounted to a race to the bottom, in that the lowest common denominator of minimal regulation became the international standard by which competitiveness was judged. In advanced capitalist countries like Canada, this shift has resulted in the dismantling of the welfare state and the gradual privatization of social services, the deregulation of industries, the erosion of environmental and labour standards, the weakening of local governments, and the creation of free-trade agreements (e.g., the North American Free Trade Agreement) (Teeple 1995). All of these changes have occurred in the province of Ontario (where my research takes place), spearheaded by the new right government of Premier Mike Harris, whose Progressive Conservative Party was elected in the summer of 1995, re-elected in 1999, and then, after a brief post-Harris period under Premier Ernie Eves (Harris' minister of finance), defeated by the equally neoliberal Liberal Party in 2003. My research for *Beyond Mothering Earth* was completed before the Liberal Party, led by Premier Dalton McGuinty, came to power late in 2003. At the time of writing it is impossible to say what impact this new Ontario government will have on a province still coping with the legacy of Harris' Common Sense Revolution. There are thus far few signs of real changes in economic or social policy. I shall therefore refer to the neoliberal agenda in the present tense.

While feminist scholars generally accept this explanation of the dominant forces guiding global economic restructuring, they are critical of analyses that focus strictly on changes in the relations and modes of production, retaining the male worker as the main protagonist and overlooking the realm of social reproduction (including caring and necessary labour) and gender divisions altogether. Many feminists have noted that there has been a lack of attention to the deeply gendered aspects of changes in the global economy (e.g., Bakker 1996a, 1996b; Adam 2002). Looking at new economic realities through a feminist lens gives rise to several concerns about recent changes in the conditions of women's lives and their role in the organization of caring labour both within and among nations. These concerns include the dismantling of social welfare and a redefinition of citizenship.

Canadian political theorist Janine Brodie (1995, 1996a, 1996b) observes that, with the dismantling of the welfare state, feminists are in the paradoxical position of having to defend a system about which they are ambivalent (to say the least) because the immediate implications of cutbacks in social spending for women's lives are severe. Feminist researchers have documented the impacts of cuts to all aspects of social welfare on women as recipients or clients of state-funded services (Cohen 1995; Calder 2003). The erosion of social programs has resulted in increased rates of poverty and decreased quality of life among women and, if they are parents, their children. Perhaps the most notable theme in feminist literature on social policy and economic restructuring in the 1990s is the analysis that women are expected to act as the "shock-absorbers" (Brodie 1995, 19) of privatization by filling in for lost state-provided services with their own unpaid, caring labour in private households and through volunteer work in communities. The feminist critique of the concept of "community care" was especially prominent in the early 1980s in Margaret Thatcher's Britain (Finch and Groves 1983; Finch 1984, 1990) and has become highly relevant in the Canadian context since the mid-1990s (see, for example, Brodie 1996a; Bakker 1996b; Evans and Wekerle, eds. 1997). Governments often promote this strategy as a way to provide better, more personalized care to dependent people while at the same time saving taxpayers millions of dollars per year. The basic feminist criticism of community care policies is that the state is exploiting and intensifying unpaid caring labour ostensibly in order to reduce social spending at the same time that it is obscuring this reality with the euphemistic language of "community." It has been established, in numerous feminist studies, that women do the vast majority of unpaid caring labour. As a result, it is clear that community care policies promise to further entrench the unequal gender division of caring labour and women's social subordination (Stinson 2005). Brodie (1996a) refers to this as the "'re'-privatization of care" to highlight the underlying assumption that it is being returned to its rightful place in the home and in the hands of mothers, daughters, and wives.

The globalization of capitalism and the progressive erosion of the nation-state (as it is conventionally understood) have contributed to a redefinition of citizenship. Brodie (1996b, 130) observes that "it has become increasingly apparent that the new neoliberal state marks a distinct shift in shared understandings of what it means to be a citizen and what the citizen can legitimately ask of the state." Her work is part of a growing body of feminist public policy research that seeks to uncover the gender subtext of recent changes in shared understandings of citizenship (see also Pateman 1992; Jenson 1996).[6] Under the Keynesian welfare state social citizenship entitled people to a basic standard of living regardless of personal status because it was recognized that structural forces could constrain opportunities and create economic instability. Further, there was a consensus that the state had a responsibility to safeguard the basic well-being of individuals. Feminists in the West have long supported an approach to citizenship that emphasizes social rights so that women may participate equally and avoid being burdened with an unfair share of responsibilities. However, with the implementation of a new right agenda there has been a marked shift away from social citizenship towards a definition of citizenship that is conditional and exclusive. Janine Brodie (1996a,

19) writes: "The rights and securities universally guaranteed to citizens of the Keynesian welfare state are no longer rights, universal, or secure. The new ideal of the common good rests on market-oriented values such as self-reliance, efficiency, and competition. The new good citizen is one who recognizes the limits and liabilities of state provision and embraces the obligation to work longer and harder in order to become more self-reliant" (quoting Drache 1992, 221).

In addition to criticizing the effects of this shift on women, feminists have noted that the new right's reassertion of community responsibility and the virtues of self-reliance and volunteerism as conditions of citizenship coincides dangerously with the left's focus on an increased role for civil society. The progressive left-wing discourse that sees self-help, mutual aid, and civic participation as foundational to the democratic system (with which the paternalistic and disempowering welfare state interferes) dovetails neatly with a neoliberal disdain for government intervention. An analysis of the co-optation of left discourse in facilitating economic restructuring is important in light of my interest in ecological citizenship and in light of my examination of the role women's caring labour plays in the search for sustainability. The analysis becomes especially challenging when one notes the similarity between the ecopolitical discourse of green virtue and the "environmentality" of governments that seek to discipline people into being good green citizens in order to shift the focus away from the state's responsibility for environmental quality (Darier 1996; Luke 1997). Recognizing the disciplinary power of the notion of "care for future generations" leads me to wonder whether women are more implicated than men in the ecopolitical discourse of sustainability. I address this issue in Chapters 5, 7, and 9.

Feminist critics have argued that the most significant overlap between left-wing and right-wing visions of welfare reform involves their blindness to gender. They are rightly sceptical of these visions on the grounds that few are based on an understanding of the gendered division of unpaid caring labour or on an adequate assessment of the diverse needs and interests that exist in families and communities. For example, Fiona Williams (1989, 124) notes that, like neoconservative governments, when the left ascribes a significant role for "informal networks of care," they assume "the availability of women to provide not only the unpaid informal care, but probably also the voluntary work and the low paid domiciliary work." Few have acknowledged the possibility that a greater role for civil society will intensify demands on women (who in many countries make up the majority of unpaid community volunteers and activists), and few have considered the social implications of doing caring work without pay.

Given that neoliberal governments are downloading the responsibility and work of caring onto the private sphere at the same time as ecological citizenship proponents are envisioning a greater role for individuals, what does this mean for caregivers who participate in the public domain as citizens? Perhaps changes in social policy have resulted in an intensified burden of caring responsibilities while making it more difficult for citizens to find time for civic engagement. In Canada the final report of the 2000 National Survey of Giving, Volunteering, and Participating (released in 2001 to coincide with the International Year of the Volunteer) found that about one million fewer people reported volunteer activities in 2000 than in 1997, and it recorded a noticeable decline in the rate of civic participation in Ontario. Although the report does not provide a detailed analysis of the change, it does conclude that volunteering and civic participation have been affected by a "deepening time-crunch within Canadian families" (Hall, McKeown, and Roberts 2001, 55). In other words, the demands of work and family, combined with other economic and social factors, make it difficult for people to find time for civic activities. This point leads to the second part of *Beyond Mothering Earth*, where my theoretical analysis of ecopolitical and ecofeminist scholarship in Part One is complemented by empirical research. I empirically explore the implications of the convergence of new right and new greening left agendas through in-depth, qualitative research into the lives of thirty Ontario women. These women engage in public caring work through being active volunteers in environmental campaigns and organizations, and they engage in private caring work through being mothers. I interviewed them from September 1999 to July 2000, at the beginning of the Harris government's second term.

I begin Part Two with Chapter 6, "Conversations with Activist Women: Towards a Counter-Narrative," which introduces my empirical research and the context within which it took place. I explain the feminist methodological principles that informed my research and then provide a brief overview of the research process. (Readers with an interest in qualitative research can turn to the appendix for a more detailed account of the research design and methods.) I think it is important to include a discussion of methodology in any work that includes empirical inquiry so that readers may gain insight into the researcher's motivations and commitments. In Chapter 6 I make clear that my aim is to disrupt the approach, common in many ecofeminist texts, that places "lived experience" in a privileged position vis-à-vis theorizing in a way that both reifies experience and fails to see theorizing as a political activity. I argue that it is important to grapple with, rather than dismiss, the problems associated with theorizing the contested concepts of "women," "identity," and "experience" that have been discussed by postmodern feminist scholars (e.g., Riley 1988; Alcoff 1988; Scott 1992; Sandilands 1999a). My research critically interrogates the activist-academic relationship and takes a provisional and conversational approach towards the interpretation of women's experiences. I call for the development of a different kind of theoretical politics for ecofeminism, one that forges a democratic and reflexive relationship between women who, as activists and theorizers, work on environmental issues. There is much to learn from those feminist scholars of epistemology who recommend less reductionistic ways of interpreting women's experiential knowledge. Modelling this approach in my interviews with thirty women activists in the greater Toronto area I show that the women's analyses of their own experiences "speak back" to ecofeminist scholarship in interesting ways.

In Chapter 7, "The Private, the Public, and the Planet: Juggling Care and Activism in Daily Life," and Chapter 8, "Activist Women Theorize the Green Political," I present an analysis of my interviews with women who juggle multiple roles in their everyday lives. My conversations with them were animated by two interrelated questions, both of which come out of my analysis of ecofeminist and ecopolitical literature: First, what is life like for women who combine the work of caring in the private sphere with that of active civic participation on issues of environmental quality? Second, what is the relationship between the prescriptions and portraits found in ecofeminist and ecopolitical literature and the perceptions of the women who come close to emulating them? The accounts given by the women are significant to the development of both ecofeminist and ecopolitical theory because they help highlight relationships among gender, care, citizenship, and environmental change. Drawing on direct quotations from the women I interviewed, I discuss numerous findings that complicate the profiles of the "housewife activist" and the "eco-citizen" that are offered in the academic literature to which I am responding.

A focus on women's grassroots activism on quality-of-life issues provides a link to another body of literature that has informed the development of my argument. There is a growing political movement that addresses the environmental quality of inner-city neighbourhoods and low-income communities: the environmental justice movement (Hofrichter 1993; Taylor 1997; Gosine 2003). Such struggles have been on the rise throughout the 1990s as increasing evidence is found to support the analysis of "environmental racism" (Bullard 1990). The globalization of capitalism has meant that multinational corporations are not held responsible for the clean-up of industrial pollutants that contaminate the local environments inhabited largely by poor and racialized people. Paradoxically, the very people who are most active in the struggle for environmental justice face the greatest obstacles to citizen participation. It has been well documented that women constitute the majority of activists in local anti-toxics struggles. They are the ones who have made the links between environmental contamination and health problems such as cancer and asthma (Taylor 1997). As some researchers have argued, the prevalence of women leaders in the environmental justice movement has a great deal to do with "the gendered division of environmental risks" (Rocheleau, Thomas-Slayter, and Wangari 1996). The women in my study also find that women dramatically outnumber men in local quality-of-life campaigns, which, for them, include such issues as pesticide use, lead and water contamination, waste management, and industrial emissions. I suggest that their work in urban and suburban communities comes under the rubric of environmental justice, even though many of the women do not use the terminology or resemble the environmental justice activists typically celebrated in the literature.

Finally, both Segal and I argue as we do because we want to contribute to moving an important intellectual and political movement in a more promising direction. Segal, a long-time feminist activist and academic, offers an immanent critique that she hopes will strengthen rather than undermine feminist politics. Although I have not been involved in an "ecofeminist movement" per se, I am committed to many of the goals and analyses of an ecologically oriented feminism. I have been involved in urban environmental issues since my graduate studies in urban planning and take an active role in raising feminist-environmental concerns within activist-academic circles. Insofar as my theoretical perspective is informed by Canadian traditions in feminist sociology and political economy and feminist urbanism, I consider it to be distinct from, and certainly having no particular loyalty to, American ecofeminist scholarship.[7] And I am less interested in whether it is called ecofeminism, feminist environmentalism, feminist political ecology, and so on (there may be more varieties by the time this book goes to print) than I am in the kinds of debates that the convergence of feminism and environmentalism can inspire. My theoretical perspective, activist-academic involvements, and social location as a white middle-class, fifth-generation Scots-Canadian (once a Torontonian but now living in rural northwest England) come together to inform an analysis that comes from within, but goes against the grain of, contemporary ecofeminism. As I explain in my concluding chapter, "No Motherhood Issue: The Project of Feminist Ecological Citizenship," the central point of *Beyond Mothering Earth* is to create a space for fruitful consideration of issues that need more discussion and debate among ecofeminists and between ecofeminists and other green theorists. I hope that it will contribute to the ongoing development of these theories and practices in ways that foster new arguments and that offer possible resolutions to some long-standing contradictions.

PART ONE

Theoretical Interrogations

Women are emerging as leaders
and guardians of life-centred cultures, economies and
policies. Movements to defend water are being led by
women. Movements to defend biodiversity are being led
by women. Movements for food and water rights are being
led by women. While overcoming their marginalisation,
women are emerging as guardians of life and the future.

> – *Vandana Shiva, "Women and Religion in the Context
> of Globalization"*

Having stood up to fight
for a sexless society, we now find ourselves entrapped
in the familiar deadlock of "woman is wonderful."

> – *Monique Wittig,* One Is Not Born a Woman

2 The Roots and Rhetoric of Ecomaternalism

It's Time for Women to Mother Earth.

– Women's Environment and Development
Organization slogan, circa early 1990s

Most books on ecofeminism begin with an explanation of its history and a delineation of its various types. Because there are already many published accounts from which to choose, I shall resist providing one here.[1] It is important, however, to begin this discussion by noting that ecofeminist discourse is made up of so many complex positions and ongoing debates that generalizations about ecofeminism can be dangerous. It is difficult to make arguments about particular trends in ecofeminist scholarship while being fair to the internal diversity that exists within its different fields. With this caveat noted, my interrogation of ecofeminist discourse is organized around the debate between two broad camps: the one that celebrates women as "the future and hope in the struggle over life" (Merchant 1996, 23) and the one that sees this as disconcertingly essentialist. This dichotomy mirrors Linda Alcoff's (1988) reduction of second-wave feminist theories into (1) the "female essentialists" (including liberal, socialist, and cultural feminists) who celebrate a distinctive femaleness and (2) the "poststructuralists" (anti-universalists and posthumanists) who seek to deconstruct subjectivity and show how it is produced within a range of social and political contexts. Regardless of their positioning, what ecofeminists add to feminism is an analysis of relationships between "women" and "environments" (or "nature").

Without delving too deeply into the messiness of the debates between so-called essentialists and anti-essentialists, I want to carefully consider whether the use of gender-specific care metaphors is, all things considered, a strategic move for ecofeminism. The starting point of my analysis is a sense of discomfort with a tendency in ecofeminist discourse to naturalize women's caring and to celebrate, uncritically, their life-sustaining and mothering labours. The purpose of this chapter is to set up the historical and theoretical context within which my research is situated. In it, I trace a narrative through (predominantly American) feminist theory that documents the development of maternalist rhetoric in ecofeminist texts.[2] I map out the shifts I see in the discourse, a shift from proclaiming women's moral authority on environmental issues, to asserting their spiritual, biological, and/or psychic closeness to nature; and then to a contemporary celebration of women's social and material connections to nature (and their concomitant understanding of ecological crisis), which is manifested in grassroots quality-of-life activism motivated by a maternal sense of responsibility and care.

Situating Ecomaternalism

Despite there being significant historical antecedents that are less well recognized (I touch on some of these below), the contemporary linkage of feminism and environmentalism in the West is attributed to French feminist writer and activist Françoise d'Eaubonne, who coined the term *eco-féminisme* in 1974. In an article entitled "Le temps de l'ecoféminisme," d'Eaubonne explains that this new global movement of feminists draws upon the "specifically feminine" power to combat the ecological crisis and the systems of male dominance that have given rise to it. Women are not only more morally outraged than men by the scale of environmental destruction, she argues, but, because they give birth to new generations, women are also more aware of what needs to be done to ensure a future world for them to inhabit. While d'Eaubonne (1974, 52) does not suggest that patriarchal power be replaced by an earth-loving matriarchy, she does make it clear that there is something special about women's biologically based knowledge that offers great hope: "the planet placed in the feminine will flourish for all."

The word "ecomaternalism" appropriately describes the rhetoric that makes explicit links between women's mothering and caring disposition and their unique propensity to care for nature. Describing what she calls "motherhood environmentalism," Canadian ecofeminist theorist Catriona Sandilands (1999a, xiii) writes that, in this discourse, "women's concerns about nature, even if they have eventual public appearance and impact, boil down to an obvious manifestation of natural protective instincts towards home and family. It is all about threats to children and self-sacrifice for the sake of future generations." For many ecofeminists, this assertion comes with a claim for women's moral superiority and for a need to revalue and recognize women as "the future and hope" in the search for sustainability (Merchant 1996). Recent publications contain numerous examples of this kind of discourse, and there are many contemporary cases of women using their maternal identities as a way to frame and authorize their political campaigns all over the world (e.g., Mothers of

East LA, Mothers against Genetic Engineering in Food and the Environment, Mothers for Clear Air, Mothers against Drunk Driving, Mothers for Natural Law, Madres de la Plaza del Mayo, to name just a few). The evolution of Western feminism (and ecofeminism) shows that this is not a new strategy. Maternalism has been integral to women's political campaigns since well before the first wave of feminist movements.

In one of the first anthologies of ecofeminist writings, Charlene Spretnak (1990) offers an account of the roots of ecofeminism. She names three paths (or "three well-trodden paths into our garden") through which ecofeminism travelled before reaching its "flowering" in the early 1990s. These paths, in her view, are radical/cultural feminist dominance theory (a distinct branch of feminism that rejects the analyses of domination offered by Marxism and critical theory because they ignore or minimize the existence and/or effects of patriarchy), nature-based goddess religions, and environmentalism or green politics (for Spretnak deep ecology is the most relevant influence). While Spretnak's account is probably accurate in tracing the evolution of the ecofeminism of her time, a more up-to-date history looks quite different. A more recent version by Greta Gaard (1998), for example, demonstrates that ecofeminism at the turn of the twenty-first century has a much more complex root system than that indicated by Spretnak. Focusing almost exclusively on her own American context, Gaard counts animal rights activism, anti-toxics activism, anti-nuclear activism, feminist spirituality, womanism, and the "lived experience"[3] of women as important streams flowing into the vast "lake" of ecofeminism. In the years since Spretnak's article appeared, ecofeminism has indeed been through a period of growth, change, and reassessment. The focus in more recent ecofeminist writings has moved away from theory and towards activism and what is called "lived experience." I would argue that this shift has been very much influenced by internal debates within feminism as well as by the entry of environmentalism into mainstream culture and the emergence of the environmental justice movement. I explain these latter developments in subsequent chapters. Here it is helpful to place the evolution of ecofeminism and its continued, yet changing, use of maternalist rhetoric within the broader context of feminist movements.

Invoking maternalism as a justificatory rhetorical strategy for (white, middle-class) women's entry into politics has been apparent at most stages of the history of Western feminism. Recognizing this point, I offer a brief history of the roots and rhetoric of contemporary ecofeminism, which begins in the "civic maternalism" of women reformers in the first wave of feminism, is rekindled with the emergence of cultural feminism in the late 1970s and throughout the 1980s, and then undergoes some significant shifts as a result of the "identity politics" of the 1990s.[4] This last period, in which the validity of feminism and the very category of "woman" itself are called into question, brings us to the rather curious situation of today, in which the grassroots activism of women who do not identify with feminism or environmentalism, much less with ecofeminism, has come to be paradigmatic of ecofeminist practice.

Moral Mothers Clean Up Politics [5]

Feminist histories of women's community-based activism in the nineteenth century offer insights into the different ways in which women have acted as political agents out of care and concern for the interests of others. They show that contemporary perspectives that celebrate women's caring for their communities and environments, seeking to extend their life-affirming values beyond the intimacy of the private household, have obvious antecedents in first-wave women's movements (Koven and Michel 1993). Although many accounts of ecofeminism (typically looking only at American ecofeminism) locate its roots in the cultural feminism of the 1980s, some ecofeminist scholars have recently claimed connections to women's quality-of-life struggles in urban communities. If one were to trace the evolution of feminist-environmental perspectives in Canada, for example, it would become obvious that turn-of-the-twentieth-century urban environmental reform movements are a more significant antecedent than the American-styled cultural feminism of the 1970s and 1980s.[6]

Conventional histories of feminism begin with the so-called "first wave" that took place in North America and western Europe roughly between the 1870s and the 1920s. A common theme in the rhetoric of a significant subsection of first-wave feminism is the celebration of maternal identity, traditional female roles (based on the Anglo-American tradition of a gendered division of labour in a heterosexual family), and "special nurturing qualities ... common to all women" (Kealy 1979, 8). During the period known as the progressive era (circa the late 1800s and early 1900s) in the United States, middle-class and elite women formed organizations aimed at redressing a range of social ills and bolstering public morality through their campaigns for "temperance, religious instruction, improvements in the workplace, better housing, facilities for single women, and state-run public health and child welfare programs" (Errington 1988, 65). Women's activism on quality-of-life issues has been named "civic maternalism" by feminist historians because it involves projecting the values of the private sphere into the realm of public politics (Cott 1989; Birch 1983; Koven and Michel 1993). Also called "municipal housekeeping," women's advocacy of sanitation programs, urban beautification projects, and immigrant settlement houses was instrumental in establishing an environmental and social justice ethos that underpins modern professions like city planning and social work. Daphne Spain (2000, 108) writes that "the ideology of municipal housekeeping helped women justify their participation in city affairs. It was a logical extension of a woman's duties to her family and home, because it emphasized her responsibilities for clean streets, clean sidewalks, and clean air." Spain's research helps challenge the popular notion that it was only white middle-class women who were involved in civic maternalism. She notes that African American women were also very active in club work in the early years of the twentieth century, informed by what was known as the "social gospel."

In their book *Mothers of a New World: Maternalist Politics and the Origins of Welfare States*, editors Seth Koven and Sonya Michel (1993, 4) use "maternalism" to describe the deployment by middle-class women activists in the nineteenth century (in North America, Australia, and western Europe) of "ideologies and discourses that exalted women's capacity to mother and applied to society as a whole the values they attached to that role: care, nurturance, and morality." This discourse implicitly appeals to the virtues of motherhood and domesticity to challenge the boundaries between the public and private spheres. In addition to applying private values to public spaces, middle-class women activists' engagement in the public sphere eventually led them to question their own relegation to the private sphere and their secondary status in society. Maternalist rhetoric was invoked explicitly to justify women's suffrage, the right to vote and to become full citizens. Since mothers raised the next generation of men who fought in wars (even though women could not fight themselves, a key reason – almost as important as their lack of property ownership – for their being denied citizenship), their "nurturant labour" ought to be rewarded with the status of citizenship. Such was the vision of maternal citizenship. While some women opposed female suffrage on the grounds that getting involved in politics would "pollute women by implicating them in the violent business of wars and empire" (Koven and Michel 1993, 11), the dominant position of this era was that citizenship would give women equal rights to protection by the state, equal access to education and other public institutions, and a respectable status in the public sphere (see also Voet 1998). Moreover, by bringing the particular values of the private sphere into the public realm of politics, women would in effect humanize (or feminize) politics and improve society for all. Maternalism shaped women's struggle for citizenship, and, as a result, motherhood and women's citizenship (as distinct from men's citizenship) are conceptually and politically linked to this day.[7]

A few ecofeminists have recognized historical antecedents of ecofeminism in nineteenth-century Anglo-American women's political engagements.[8] Carolyn Merchant (1996), for example, profiles women's conservation activism from the turn of the twentieth century. She includes chapters in *Earthcare* on historical examples of women's involvement in environmental issues in which maternalist rhetoric was employed. Her chapter on "corn mothers" and "moral mothers," for instance, tells stories about how Native American women's role in horticulture, especially in growing corn, gave them a privileged position in their societies until the invasion of European colonists in the seventeenth century. "Moral mothers" is her name for American farming women

in the late colonial period (the mid-1800s), who, in keeping with the dominant ideology of the era, upheld the morals of the family by keeping their
home environments healthy and their gardens fertile. Merchant also includes
a chapter in which she presents women's role in wilderness conservation at
the turn of the twentieth century as an example of women's earthcare. She
describes the efforts of hundreds of thousands of American women who were
members of elite women's clubs and leagues dedicated to studying and lobbying government on environmental issues such as water quality, forest protection, and the preservation of bird and wildlife habitat. Much of this work was
buttressed by a belief that conservation was a moral standpoint specific to
women because of their roles as mothers and domestic managers. Women
believed it was their responsibility as women to ensure the quality of life for
their children and for the next generation. Merchant writes that by the 1920s
women naturalists outnumbered men in organizations like the Sierra Club
and the National Parks Association. Men eventually challenged women's authority on matters ecological, however, and went on to replace them as experts
with the advent of professionalization in resource fields like park and forestry
management in the first half of the twentieth century.

Another important precursor to contemporary ecofeminism that has been
celebrated in ecofeminist literature is in the work of early "material feminists"
who sought to improve unhealthy environments in industrial Western European and North American cities.[9] The most celebrated example for ecofeminists
is Ellen Swallow Richards, an American water chemist and the first female
instructor at the Massachusetts Institute of Technology (MIT). Her work at
MIT was devoted to demonstrating connections between daily life in the domestic sphere and environmental conditions. Swallow Richards argued that
because women were intimately acquainted with the care and use of basic
resources like water and food (as well as with their by-products: sewage, waste,
and air pollution), they were the ones who needed to be educated in and
entrusted with environmental management. Consequently, she started educational programs for women so they could become experts in "home economics." Swallow Richards is credited by some with founding the science of ecology
in the 1870s (Merchant 1996; Mellor 1997).[10] Viewed in this historical light,
it is not surprising that much has been made by contemporary ecofeminists of
the fact that the word "ecology" comes from the Greek word *oikos*, meaning
"household." The connection is important for ecofeminists because it suggests
that women's traditional responsibility for taking care of the household – and
the people who reside there – gives them insight into how to care for the earth
(e.g., Salleh 1996; Shiva 2004).[11]

Cultural Feminism and the Ethics of Care

The second wave of feminism, which began in the early 1970s after a forty-
year period of political marginalization in the West, is understood to have

emerged out of the ranks of activist women who were disenchanted with the sexism of men in the anti-war, environmental, civil rights, peace, and student movements (Echols 1989). Decades after the formal, if not substantive, achievement of citizenship rights, some feminists realized the limitations of a universal political identity (i.e., citizen) that was inherently masculine. This realization inspired a move among many feminists towards a feminism "unmodified" by established androcentric theories like Marxism and liberalism (MacKinnon 1987). Generally speaking, second-wave theorizing and activism was informed by explicitly feminist analyses of patriarchy and by political commitments to liberate women from their subordinate status in society.[12] Unlike many of their first-wave predecessors, who sought entry into mainstream politics and lobbied for citizen status (largely by deploying a sense of maternal "difference"), second-wave feminists emphasized the radical goal of uniting women into a new social movement that would offer an alternative to the male-dominated politics of the day.[13] Thus they rarely addressed notions of citizenship (Voet 1998).

A dominant characteristic of this second wave was a drive to make women's oppression as women – the result of sexism and patriarchal values in both public and private spheres – visible to the general public and to insert feminist analyses into mainstream theories, policy making, and research. In the 1970s the feminist slogan "the personal is political" conveyed a twin message: that there are no strictly "personal" problems that should be off limits to state intervention or public concern and that the "personal" (i.e., the sphere with which women traditionally have been associated) is a source that can enrich politics and public life (Voet 1998; Mack-Canty 2004). Second-wave approaches to political activism included, but were not limited to, demands for women-specific changes in government policy and legislation; increasing access to and more equitable pay in the workforce; increasing control over women's own reproductive health; and increasing public awareness of and attention to male violence against women and girls. Feminists of this era also worked to set up separatist women's health centres and refuges for victims of sexual violence (such as rape crisis centres).[14]

Feminists who applied their arguments to environmental issues took up causes like nuclear weapons proliferation and the use of chemical pesticides. Origins of a link between radical feminism and environmentalism can be found, in particular, in the anti-militarism movement. This link also developed out of women's dissatisfaction with the environmental movement, in which male domination was a source of frustration (Mellor 1992). As problems within these movements emerged it became necessary for women to assert their differences from men in order to achieve their political goals. Among the strategies chosen for the task was the deployment of maternalist rhetoric.

Most ecofeminist scholars agree that it is out of this milieu that ecofeminism emerged as a distinct movement, largely based in the United States. Spretnak, being primarily a scholar of religions, finds many links between ecofeminism and the feminist spirituality movement, which advocates a feminine reverence for nature – a reverence that she believes prevailed in prehistoric times. The most important texts are those that make explicit links between symbolic and mythical representations of women and women's potential, rooted in transhistorical and cross-cultural practices, to model an alternative relationship between human beings and nature (e.g., Merlin Stone's *When God Was a Woman* [1976] and Starhawk's *The Spiral Dance* [1979]). It is the link to the cultural feminism of the second wave of the women's movement, however, that most scholars agree has shaped ecofeminism and its attendant praxis.[15] Here two of the key scholars are Mary Daly and Susan Griffin, authors who believe in women's unique connections to nature and their possession of "natural" moral goodness due to their separation from the depravity of male culture. These feminists look to fields such as anthropology and cultural history, which offer evidence for the historical existence of a distinctively feminine culture based in women's experience and wisdom, and free from patriarchal exploitation (e.g., Gimbutas 1974; Eisler 1988).

Many feminists attribute women's morality and propensity to care to their psychological development and/or socialization as women. This group of "difference theorists" tends to focus more on ideas and individuals than on material conditions and social structures (some do consider class to be relevant, however). Cultural feminists argue not only that women possess special qualities of nurturance, cooperation, and altruism due to their socialization as women but also that feminine ways of being offer a better model for society than masculine ones. As a result, they sought ways of reclaiming women's traditional culture and finding avenues for making the political personal. Much of this so-called "gynocentric" thinking is related to mothering: both to the experience of being mothered and to the experience of being a mother. Judith Grant (1993), who is a critic, refers to this as "mothering theory." In explaining that women have a greater propensity for caring than men, feminist psychologists and psychoanalysts look at the processes through which feminine gender identity, an integral part of which is the urge to mother, is acquired and reproduced in early childhood.

The most recognized and influential among these feminist scholars is Carol Gilligan (1982) who, after studying women's moral development, argues that women speak "in a different voice" from men and hold a different set of moral values from men. Her research suggests that women's moral decision making is based on caring in context rather than on the notions of abstract rights and justice that characterize a male approach to moral dilemmas. In order to explain this difference, Gilligan draws from the object-relations analysis (an adaptation of Freudian psychoanalysis) of Nancy Chodorow (1978) and Dorothy Dinnerstein (1976), which explains how women's capacity for mothering is reproduced through the pre-oedipal development of self in infant girls. In *The Reproduction of Mothering*, Chodorow (1978) argues that because girls form their sense of self and subjectivity in relation to a female (i.e., their mother) whom they are culturally expected to emulate, they never develop a truly separate identity as a subject, acquiring instead qualities of connectedness, dependence, care, and empathy that ultimately prepare them for mothering. This argument is significant for Gilligan because it suggests that women have an approach to relationships that is less hierarchical and more responsive to others than that of men. For this reason it is important to begin to hear this different voice. According to Gilligan (1982, 173): "As we have listened for centuries to the voices of men and the theories of development their experience informs, so we have come more recently to notice not only the silence of women but the difficulty in hearing what they say when they speak. Yet in the different voice of women lies the truth of an ethic of care, the tie between relationship and responsibility."

Gilligan's work sowed the seeds for subsequent discourse among ecofeminists on the ethics of care and, arguably, the ethic of earthcare.[16] Ethics of care proponents, interpreting Gilligan, do not see women's unique ways of knowing as simply *different* from men's but, in fact, as *superior* to them: if we listened to this different and better voice, then we would learn to create a healthier and more harmonious world. This appears to be a tacit argument for women's entry into the public domain, and it is similar to those heard in the late nineteenth century. However, because cultural feminists were less interested in joining patriarchal politics than their liberal first-wave predecessors, they favoured the language of care and "maternal thinking" over the language of citizenship. New and distinctively feminine approaches to politics were needed. It is therefore not surprising that the work of Sara Ruddick has been influential among ecofeminists. For example, in "Maternal Thinking" (1980, 1989) Ruddick discusses the importance of maternal practice (characterized by three key aspects of motherhood: the preservation, growth, and social acceptability of children) not only for individual women's ways of knowing but also for a feminist theory of peace and justice that has significance for society in general. Such a maternalist theory of justice would be based on responsibilities rather than rights, on interdependence rather than autonomy, on "the morality of love," and on other fundamental aspects of maternal thinking (Ruddick 1989; see also Noddings 1984). Ruddick argues that mothering is a practice (as opposed to a biologically based status) in which everyone, even men, can engage. She claims, in her more recent work as well, that inherent in the practices and processes of mothering are "preservative love" and qualities of life enhancement and protection that can form the basis of a peaceful society. Mothering, in short, is *the* model upon which a non-violent society can be built; maternal thinking should therefore become "an instrument of peace politics" (Ruddick 1989). So although citizenship does not figure prominently in these discussions, connections between mothering and women's unique approach to politics are clearly made.

Discussions of ecofeminist ethics have tended to emphasize the different, gendered approach to ethical thought and behaviour taken by women, which, presumably, entails a greater sense of responsibility than that felt by men. Marti Kheel (1993, 254-55), for example, writes that "research by Carol Gilligan suggests that women's ethical conduct and thought tend to derive more from a sense of connection with others and from feelings of care and responsibility that such connection entails." She goes on to suggest that it is "natural" for women to "behave in moral ways" and that most women are confounded by "how and why compassion and moral behaviour fail to be sustained" in social relationships and institutions (255). An alternative ecofeminist ethic, she argues, would begin with women's "instinctive responses" to ethical dilemmas, such as whether human beings are justified in killing animals for meat (257). Referring to Ruddick, Ynestra King (1990, 116) writes of a need to emulate the mindful social and ethical nature of mothering: "in bringing up their children, mothers face ethical and moral choices as complex as those considered by professional politicians and ethicists." She argues that the importance of ecofeminism lies in its ability to arrive at a "genuine ethical thinking" that is based on "ways of knowing the world that are not based on objectification and domination":

> Here, potentially, we recover ontology as the ground for ethics. We thoughtful human beings must use the fullness of our sensibility and intelligence to push ourselves to another stage of evolution. One where we will fuse a new way of being on this planet with a sense of the sacred, informed by all ways of knowing – intuitive *and* scientific, mystical *and* rational. It is the moment where women recognize ourselves as agents of history – yes, even as unique agents – and knowingly bridge the classic dualisms between spirit and matter, art and politics, reason and intuition ... This is the project of ecofeminism. (King 1990, 120-21)

In her 1992 book *Breaking the Boundaries* British sociologist Mary Mellor includes a chapter called "Caring for the World: Making and Taking Time," which contains numerous examples of how cultural feminist theories are used to support ecofeminist political visions. Mellor (1992, 270) invokes the work of Gilligan to support her call for a distinctively female-oriented world: "Gilligan calls upon us to reclaim women's morality." She also draws upon such notable cultural feminists as Andrée Collard (1988) and Adrienne Rich (1976) to argue that in women's lives the left can find a way forward and a way out of the destruction of our time. Mellor writes (1992, 249):

Socialists have long sought a world in which people offer mutual support to each other without demanding cash payment or profit. Greens
look for a sustainable, decentralized world of face-to-face interaction
... Programmes and blueprints for a new society are constructed to
take us "forward" or bring us "back" to a green or socialist world. It is
odd that they do not see that this world exists already. Most of wom-
en's lives are spent in a decentralized world beyond the market where
basic needs prevail. Women, particularly in subsistence economies,
are rooted to the Earth and the reproduction of life in their daily work.

In arguing for a shift from a world based on male experience (a ME-world)
to one based on women's experience (a WE-world), Mellor repeatedly says
that these differences do not reflect a biological division. However, making
reference to Ruddick, she claims that only those who have gone through the
experience of mothering – which, by her definition, involves caring for children and living in "biological time" – are capable of bringing about the WE-
world. She states, "Women who do not have any caring responsibilities or
anyone emotionally dependent upon them can operate independently according
to the rational principles of the ME-world" (255), whereas "women, moving
at the pace of the slowest child or the most needy adult, are closer to the
sustainable pace of the planet" (281). Moreover, it is their inability to mother
that leads men to oppress and to exploit women and nature. Here Mellor
echoes the claims of Chodorow (1978) and Dinnerstein (1976), who suggest
that unless men share in the joys of child-rearing "we risk the end of civilisa-
tion" (267).

Influenced by Ruddick's arguments, ecofeminist theory in the 1980s and
early 1990s frequently refers to and deploys maternal thinking. In direct action campaigns against militarism, for example, women activists played on the
popularly accepted connections between women and nature as well as on the
moral superiority attributed to mothers. Mother's Day was a popular time to
hold rallies in the United States: in 1987 there was a Mothers and Others Day
Action at a Nevada nuclear test and a Mother's Day protest against a land
development in Vermont.[17] In western Europe feminist peace activists and
ecofeminists regularly made arguments premised on the natural peacefulness
of women in opposition to the natural aggressiveness of men. The British
women who protested the siting of Cruise missiles at Greenham Common and
the group called Women Oppose the Nuclear Threat (WONT) in the early
1980s, for example, took the position that war is an inherently male activity
that women's morality must be enlisted to overcome. They pinned baby clothes
to the fence encircling the military base as a show of maternal concern for
their children's future. Petra Kelly (1984), a founder and leader of the German Green Party, claimed in her book *Fighting for Hope* that the hegemony of
masculine values ("materialism, waste, alienation, domination, possession")

threatened the existence of men, women, and nature. Similar sentiments are found throughout an early British ecofeminist collection entitled *Reclaim the Earth: Women Speak Out for Life on Earth* (edited by Caldecott and Leland 1983, with foreword by Susan Griffin), although dissenting voices can be heard as well.

Rumblings of discontent with maternalist approaches to ecofeminism were apparent in the early 1990s. In a 1991 special issue of *Hypatia: Journal of Feminist Philosophy*, the first collection of articles on ecofeminism from an explicitly philosophical perspective, several authors discuss their discomfort around the association of ecofeminism with stereotypically feminine identities and practices. Although the language of poststructuralism does not figure prominently, many of the criticisms take up the issue of universalism and call for greater attention to the social, political, and cultural contexts within which femininity is constructed and expressed. Interestingly, it is the male contributors who have the most to say about ecofeminism's relationship to mothering and care. American philosopher Deane Curtin, for one, wonders about the promise of ethics of care discourse for ecofeminism. He writes: "while an ethic of care does have an intuitive appeal, without further development into a political dimension, Gilligan's research may be turned against ecofeminist objectives ... In a society that oppresses women, it does no good to suggest that women should go on selflessly providing care if social structures make it all too easy to abuse that care" (Curtin 1991, 66). In the same journal Roger J.H. King (1991) challenges the simplistic use of the "vocabularies of caring" and "lived experience" in ecofeminist literature, which he finds inappropriate for the development of environmental ethics. In particular he criticizes essentialist invocations of women's caring for being ignorant of the diverse kinds of relationships to nature and other beings experienced by women within different contexts and social positions. And Patricia Jagentowicz Mills (1991, 167) criticizes ecofeminism's "abstract pro-nature stance," reminding readers that, amid the move to reclaim motherhood, ecofeminists should not forget the political origins of feminist discourse on reproduction: "the liberatory roots of the attempt to reclaim and reconstruct motherhood *began* with women who found themselves suffering from the alienation of enforced motherhood ... feminists must remain committed first and foremost to a woman's right to choose *not* to reproduce, the right *not* to mother, because the compulsory motherhood that results from seeing pregnancy as merely 'natural' maintains the domination of women within a patriarchal society."

Also evident in the *Hypatia* collection is a sense that ecofeminist theorists are at a loss when it comes to finding empirical examples of ecofeminist practice. In her article "Ecofeminist Theory and Grassroots Activism," for example, Stephanie Lahar (1991) observes that ecofeminism needs to find a politically potent activist emphasis. While ecofeminism as critique or as a conceptual framework is (or has the potential to be) remarkably powerful, she argues, it lacks examples of how its ideas, visions, and principles may be put into practice in communities and local places. Ecofeminism should "remain accountable and connected to the people who have developed it in the past and who carry it now, imperatives for change must also be translated into political action at the grassroots level" (40). Lahar asks : "Can we afford not to have an action-oriented philosophy at a crisis point in social and natural history ... ?" (35-36). Perhaps her vision has been realized: since the early 1990s it seems that the main goals of ecofeminism, like those of feminist scholarship generally, have been focusing on everyday life, listening to the narratives of diverse and marginalized women, and (re)discovering women's grassroots struggles. According to Sandilands (1999a), however, the official emphasis on diversity and experience has not upset the place of women's caring nature as the central narrative of ecofeminism; instead, identity has gone underground as ecofeminists have participated in the discourse of identity politics.

Maternalist justification for women's political engagement has been a central theme in the evolution of feminist movements. The deployment of maternalist rhetoric was a key strategy of both the first and second wave of Western feminisms, but with an important difference. Progressive-era reformers sought to secure women's status as citizens by arguing not only that women's motherhood is a contribution to society for which they should be recognized but also that their private sphere values have the potential to clean up the corrupt political sphere of men. They challenged the public-private divide by showing how the political could not survive without the private. Thus citizenship itself was reconfigured not only by admitting (some) women into its ranks but also by undermining the notion that citizens were independent, disembodied, and strictly public actors. At the same time, they affirmed the value of citizenship as a respectable status offering "individual equal political and civic rights with all other citizens" (Voet 1998, 21). In the late 1970s and 1980s, in contrast, cultural feminists had little to say about citizenship but a great deal to say about women's special contribution to the public sphere. They did not seek entry into men's politics on men's terms or a blurring of the separate spheres; rather, they accepted and called for a reversal of the public-private dichotomy by offering a vision of politics based on moral insights achieved through the private experience of mothering. In both cases, feminists celebrated women's motherhood and caring as traits that made women different from, and morally superior to, men at the same time that they offered critiques of gender inequality in patriarchal societies that devalued all things feminine.

Perhaps it is the case that ecofeminists (particularly in the United States) have been influenced more by cultural feminist scholarship than by first-wave arguments for maternalist citizenship, although some have acknowledged similarities between women's activism in the progressive era and contemporary women's quality-of-life struggles. It is interesting that very few ecofeminists have addressed the concept of citizenship, given that so many are concerned about women's participation in environmental struggles. There is interest in the transformation many women seem to make from apolitical housewives and mothers concerned about their local environments to empowered activists operating in the political sphere, but rarely is there sustained, critical analysis of this process, of how it might inform theoretical ideas about citizenship, or, indeed, of women's own understanding of themselves as citizens. The desire to celebrate the "unsung heroines" (Solnit 2005) of an increasingly familiar environmental narrative seems to outweigh the desire for a democratic and political ecofeminist vision. It is, I would argue, *a maternalism without citizenship*. I reflect on this observation in Chapter 3 by discussing the shift to identity politics, strategic essentialism, and women's grassroots activism in "third-wave" (eco)feminism, and by illustrating how this shift has shaped ecofeminist rhetoric in the 1990s and early 2000s.

3 "Down among the Women": Ecofeminism and Identity Politics at the Grassroots[1]

> The first lesson is the view from below. This means that
> when we look at reality, when we want to gain clarity about
> where to go and what to do, we start with the perspective
> of women, particularly rural women and poor urban women
> in the South. Further, we start with everyday life and its
> politics, the strategies of women to keep life going.
>
> – *Maria Mies and Veronika Bennholdt-Thomsen,*
> The Subsistence Perspective

Feminist movements, like many new social movements at the beginning of the twenty-first century, are in a period of transition and uncertainty. Since the mid-1980s, due to sustained criticism by working-class women, lesbians, racialized women, and women living with disabilities, there has been a trend in feminist thinking and theorizing towards analyses of multiple oppressions. Critics have argued that the second-wave feminist discourse of "sisterhood," wherein gender is foregrounded and "woman" is conceptualized as a unitary category of analysis, is inappropriate for addressing the complex experiences that shape most women's lives. This situation has brought about a phase in feminism's history in which "identity politics" – where the aim is to reclaim the experiences, knowledges, languages, and cultures of marginalized people – reigns supreme. Susan Hekman (1999, 4) defines identity politics as "taking one's identity as a political point of departure, a motivation for action and a delineation of one's politics." According to Judith Squires (1999, 134), during the identity politics phase the response of those excluded by feminist assumptions about women's experience generally has been "to assert the specificity of their own experiences and demand recognition for the particularity of their own identities. The identifications of sexuality, race, and class were all high-lighted as central to the personal experiences and political identity of most women. Attention shifted from an exclusive focus on gender difference to an exploration of the question of the differences among women."

In the wake of postmodern and postcolonial critiques of and debates over identity – that is, over to whom and for whom feminism speaks – some feminists have become pessimistic about whether there is any point in retaining the feminist label at all. It is common to hear that we have entered a "post-feminist" period. Others, however, suggest that ecofeminism is itself the third wave in feminist politics for two reasons: first, ecofeminism undertakes a critical analysis of the underlying *logic of domination* (Warren 1990; Plumwood 1993) and, hence, has the intellectual potential to problematize all forms of oppression based on dualistic thought. Second, it has the potential to be a vision around which diverse types of movements of grassroots activists and privileged academics might coalesce in a public conversation about how to create a just and sustainable world. As I explain in Chapter 2, I am interested in the fact that few use the language of citizenship to communicate this potential vision.

In this chapter I elaborate on these third-wave claims first by situating ecofeminism within recent feminist scholarship on women's grassroots organizing and then by providing examples of the maternalist rhetoric used in some of the most commonly given examples of ecofeminist activism. I show how many ecofeminists claim women's private identities (e.g., as mothers), rather than their status and practice of citizenship, as the bases for their public, political engagement. In the final part of the chapter I critically interrogate this discourse by framing it within the debate over identity politics and strategic essentialism. After discussing some postmodern feminist critiques of identitarian rhetoric in feminism and ecofeminism, I ask: "Is strategic essentialism an oxymoron?" and answer that, in the end, "Yes, it is."

The Rise of a Third Wave?

Ecofeminism appears to respond to women's movement historian Johanna Brenner's (1996) call for a third wave that is driven by women's grassroots organizing and a renewed attention to women's practices and identities in everyday life.[2] Some have claimed that, while it can be considered as part of a third wave, ecofeminism has always been a grassroots political movement inspired by pragmatic concerns (Warren 2000; Mack-Canty 2004). Maria Mies and Vandana Shiva (1993, 13) contend that ecofeminism has the potential to ignite a common global politics, to unite social movements in the North and the South around subsistence needs that are common to "all people irrespective of culture, ideology, race, political and economic system and class." However, the pursuit of ecofeminism as a philosophical critique of domination and a political movement has, arguably, been eclipsed by a trend towards positioning women's environmental activism rather than women's theorizing at the heart and future of ecofeminism. One of the central themes in this kind of writing is the valorization of women's "grassroots movements" and subsistence struggles as models of politics from which ecofeminist theorists ought to learn. This change in the theory-practice balance runs parallel to the shift in feminism from traditional feminist theorizing, which, at times, has been both abstract and exclusionary, to a contemporary focus on the community activism of non-elite women who may, but usually do not, identify as feminists.

It may be a result of identity politics that there has been an intensified emphasis in feminist research on profiling the diversity of grassroots women's movements. One explanation is that some feminist scholars are responding to (and trying to rectify) a very narrow understanding of women's political engagements within Western/Northern feminist scholarship. As postcolonial, lesbian, and anti-racist feminists have suggested, it is due to white-Western/Northern-heteronormative (and so on) feminism's exclusive yet universalized concept of "woman" that insufficient attention has been paid to the "real life" experiences of women who work to improve the living conditions of low-income and marginalized people. Too much of the research on feminist politics, the critics say (rightly or wrongly), has focused on struggles over reproductive rights (rights that have been systematically denied to lesbians, poor women, disabled women, and women of colour in the North and the South); politicizing the private sphere (in ways that deny the possibility that homes can feel as safe for women under siege by systemic racism as they can for those who are not), and employment equity (for women who have the privilege of being admitted into select professions). In response to these criticisms, there is a growing trend in feminist research towards uncovering old and documenting new examples of the community organizing efforts of working-class women, disabled women, lesbians, and women of colour around the world.[3] These practices offer examples of different, yet equally valuable, forms of political action and resistance.

This project includes a recovery and feminist analysis of the long and multi-layered history of women's collective action in trade unions and anti-poverty organizing and other examples of working-class, immigrant, and racialized women's struggles to survive in classist, (hetero)sexist, able-ist, and racist capitalist societies.[4] For example, feminist historians have written about women-led food riots, neighbourhood-based welfare rights organizing, and cost-of-living protests that took place during the Depression years in North America and Europe (see, for example, Frank 1985; Orleck 1993; Kaplan 1982). Feminist historian Sherna Berger Gluck (1997) cites examples of racialized women's protests against police violence and forced sterilization in the 1960s. Note that many of these examples come from between the first and second waves, which suggests that there is also something exclusionary in the accepted periodization of the women's movement. Jeri Dawn Wine and Janice Ristock (1991, 3) observe that "the concerns of women more marginalized from the centres of power have been surfacing in recent years in the grassroots activism of poor and working-class women, lesbians, Native women, immigrant women, women of colour, disabled women, elderly women and rural women." Their 1991 book *Women and Social Change: Feminist Activism in Canada* is an example of the effort made at that time to raise the profile of non-traditional activism by women living at the intersections of multiple oppressions and identities.[5]

Patricia Hill Collins' (1990) book *Black Feminist Thought* was arguably a wake-up call for those feminists who had undertheorized the intersections of (hetero)sexism, racism, and classism and who had tended to falsely universalize women's experiences of oppression. She uses research on Black women's experiences (drawing heavily on first-person narratives) to ground the analysis rather than research on feminist principles developed by and for white middle-class women. Her epistemological approach is rooted in the belief that each group of people – African American women, Latina lesbians, Puerto Rican men – has and speaks from unique standpoints and that these "unique standpoints" (236) are situated and partial. Collins has also played a pivotal role in showing that the activist work of racialized (in her case African American) women takes on different meanings within their particular contexts and serves to destabilize conventional feminist understandings of politics. Interestingly, mothering remains central to the analysis, albeit in different ways than those seen in white middle-class feminist writings. Her discussion of "community othermothers" (129-32) and women-centred networks illustrates that a dominant theme in Black women's political activism is the interconnectedness of family survival and institutional transformation. "Community othermother" is a term Collins uses to explain the role that a generalized ethic of care and feelings of responsibility for the children of an entire community plays in African American women's activism. In contrast to studies that portray racialized women as victims of oppression, Collins' work celebrates the power of women in African American communities and the many ways in which Black women practise political resistance in their everyday lives.

Some Latin American feminist theorists have also shown how maternalist politics have been dominant in Latina community organizing. Motherhood, combined with the meaning and significance of mothering in "traditional" cultures, often forms the basis for a political identity that inspires community activism among Latin American women (e.g., Pardo 1995; Alfaro 1994). An oft-cited example of Latin American maternalist politics involves the Madres de la Plaza del Mayo, a group of Argentinean women who held public vigils to demand justice for their "disappeared" family members, using their motherhood identity to place moral pressure on the military regime (Jaquette 1994). Similarly, in her book *Grassroots Warriors: Activist Mothering, Community Work and the War on Poverty*, Nancy A. Naples (1998) presents the narratives of women activists (mostly African and Latin American) in a way that reveals a more complex set of motivations and a wider range of issues taken up by "activist mothers" than those presented in most feminist research on women's organizing. "Activist mother," a term Naples coins, refers to a woman who believes it is her duty as a mother to fight on behalf of her children and her "defined racial-ethnic and geographic community" (329). Her "grassroots warriors," the name she gives to women community workers in low-income neighbourhoods, clearly see their role as protectors and caretakers of communities that they experience as being in a poverty-induced state of crisis. Naples' discussion of the intersections of class, race, and gender, and their relationships to mother-work and activism, is important in challenging the simple explanations of maternalist politics offered by Ruddick and others (discussed in Chapter 2). It is interesting to examine how, and to what extent, this kind of feminist research and theorizing has shaped contemporary discourses of ecofeminism.

Ecofeminism at the Grassroots Today

It is within the context of a shift in feminist scholarship towards non-elite, non-feminist women's organizing that the current grassroots focus in ecofeminism should be seen. Before giving specific examples of this focus, I think it is useful to take a brief closer look at what is meant by "grassroots" and why it has become rhetorically necessary to distinguish women's grassroots activism from expressions of ecofeminism. The *Oxford English Dictionary* defines "grassroots" as "fundamental level or source, ordinary people, the rank and file of a political party." In social movement literature the origins of the term appear to lie in the language of left-wing participatory democracy and signal a move away from old state-centred politics towards an expanded role for citizens in civil society (Held 1987; Barber 1984; Young 1990). To be working "at the grassroots" implies the spontaneous convergence of active citizens on common interests in ways that subvert or circumvent, and hence challenge, the dominant political system. For example, in *Wild Politics* Susan Hawthorne (2002, 2) argues that "a world structured from the ground up, from grass roots, through a wild politics, founded on a culture inspired by biodiversity ... could lead western global culture away from the vicious cycles of violence that are perpetrated in international politics, in communities, and inside family homes."

In recent years the concept of grassroots organizing has also taken on less positive connotations. For example, NIMBYism (NIMBY=Not In My Back Yard) has manifested itself in effective "ordinary people's" opposition to local change, such as the establishment of homeless shelters and halfway houses in their communities. In Canada right-wing spin doctors often claim that their political parties have been forged by grassroots movements and that their candidates speak for ordinary people with common sense ideas.[6] With regard to the environmental movement, it is well known that the "wise use movement" in the United States (called the SHARE movement in Canada) claims to be the result of a mobilization of "ordinary people" living in resource industry towns but was, in fact, created with the help of public relations firms hired by the forestry and mining industries (Beder 1997). In their book *Toxic Sludge Is Good for You*, John Stauber and Sheldon Rampton (1995) describe how public relations firms manufacture phony grassroots groups to create the impression that there is a groundswell of "real people" supporting a particular corporate agenda. Perhaps having more democratic participation by regular folks does not, of itself, result in progressive (i.e., socially just and ecologically sound) outcomes; rather, it is as important to pay attention to the content of democratic movements as it is to observe the rate and range of participation. Such attention leads to awareness that the rhetoric of politics "at the grassroots" has been co-opted by right-wing governments and big businesses to challenge the legitimacy of so-called special interest groups with opposing political agendas. Scepticism about grassroots discourse does not rule out the possibility that organized efforts by citizens' groups may effect change in political and economic systems, but it does demonstrate the malleability of the concept of "grassroots" in political rhetoric and its ability to support different ends.

Despite the evidence of a shadow side to this concept, for many feminists and ecofeminists the discursive move of defining organizing by women as "grassroots" signals opposition to other, more institutionalized or elite forms of feminist politics. Writing about "a new generation of women leaders [who are] carrying out an invisible revolution ... to protect their children against pollution, disease, and homelessness," feminist historian Temma Kaplan (1997) gives several examples of women's grassroots struggles (e.g., against toxic contamination at Love Canal, New York, and Warren County, North Carolina) in her book *Crazy for Democracy*. She defines "grassroots" as follows: "To the women claiming its provenance, being from the grassroots generally means being free from any constraining political affiliations and being responsible to no authority except their own group. Though such women generally recognize their seeming powerlessness against corporate and governmental opponents, *they also assert their moral superiority, their right to be responsible citizens, not according to official laws, but on their own terms*" (2, emphasis mine).

While Kaplan demonstrates some interest in connections between grassroots activism and citizenship, ecofeminists have tended to move in a different direction. Given the history of identity politics, it is possible that the grassroots label is used strategically to counter a perceived hierarchy in which academics, the majority of whom are located in "first world" universities, speak for and define feminism. In recent ecofeminist writing one can sense an expectation that efforts at theorizing will be invalid unless accompanied by examples (and sometimes empirical case studies) of women's organizing in non-elite and peripheralized places. I would argue that, although the inclusion of grassroots activism in feminist scholarship stems from a desire for greater democratization, ecofeminists do violence to this desire when they equate "grassroots" with "authentic" in a way that reifies and accepts uncritically the experiences and knowledges of activist and non-academic women. To call something "grassroots" in an ecofeminist conversation is very often to distance it from (Western/Northern) feminism as a political ideology or body of theory.[7] I discuss this observation further in Chapter 6. Here I illustrate this practice with a quotation from Australian ecofeminist Ariel Salleh (1996, 271), taken from an article that appeared in the journal *Environmental Politics* in 1996: "It is plain from women's ecological actions across the globe – the 300-year-old tradition of Chipko tree huggers, the peasant mothers of Seveso, Australian Koori women anti-base activists – that *it is empathic nurture rather than any sophisticated social theory* that guides these sound and genuinely universalised political stands" (emphasis mine).

In her 1997 book *Ecofeminism as Politics*, Salleh (an ecofeminist who has been exceptionally successful, along with Vandana Shiva, in having her academic work included in scholarly environmental publications like *Environmental Politics*) sets out an argument for why ecofeminism should move away from feminism, weakened as it has become by "a postmodern academic retreatism," and take up the kind of "womanist politics" found in the movements of women of colour (1997, 105).[8] For her, womanist politics offers a way out for ecofeminism when academic feminism (also labelled "professional metropolitan feminism" [107]) fails, as it inevitably will. One of her book chapters is entitled "When Feminism Fails." What might it mean to be a womanist? "A 'womanist' woman is responsible, flexible, courageous, wilful, preferring feminine culture yet committed to the whole community's well being. The key here is a transvaluation of 'feminine' experiences and, in particular, the relational sensibility often gained in mothering labours" (104). Maria Mies and Veronika Bennholdt-Thomsen (1999) have also taken aim, in *The Subsistence Perspective*, at the alleged dominance of postmodernism in women's studies departments and among "middle-class feminists" in "the Anglo-Saxon world." The alternative approach they propose involves celebrating the everyday life-sustaining knowledge of rural and peasant women in the global South.

This rhetorical strategy appears in a notable proportion of ecofeminist literature, where it is implied that the knowledges and experiences of "ordinary women" offer a more authentic political identity for ecofeminism than those offered by ecofeminist academics. Several ecofeminist theorists have, from their chosen case studies, extrapolated a series of assertions about the meanings of women's and grassroots survival struggles not only for ecofeminism but also for the search for an alternative environmental-political paradigm (e.g., Shiva 1989; Mies and Shiva 1993; Mies and Bennholdt-Thomsen 1999;

Brú-Bistuer 1996; Hawthorne 2002). Increasingly, it seems that they want to rewrite the multidimensional history of ecofeminism so that it centres specifically on the life-sustaining work that women around the world have always done. According to Salleh (1997, 107): "ecofeminism has a history of its own, shaped by the day-to-day efforts of ordinary women to survive with their children in an era of excess."

It is not my intention to provide a detailed examination of the numerous examples of ecofeminist references to women's grassroots struggles; rather, I want to cite a few specific examples to demonstrate that there is an observable pattern in the ecofeminist literature that places these paradigmatic examples at the centre of ecofeminist conversations. This pattern consists, I believe, in drawing a single line from "the grassroots" to the development and affirmation of theory on the page. In a circular move, many ecofeminist scholars tend to define ecofeminism, look for an example to label as ecofeminist, and then use it to affirm the definition. I shall provide two sets of examples.

Romantic Re/sisters: "Third World Women" and Their Subsistence Work
My first set of examples comes from the women, environment, and development (WED) literature, which contains perspectives on women's relationships to their environment but that has a different history and set of concerns from those of ecofeminism. The relationship between WED and ecofeminism is a contestable one. WED literature has become increasingly important to ecofeminist theorizing, yet insofar as feminism is a product of Western/Northern political and intellectual traditions and struggles, it is debatable whether, strictly speaking, ecofeminism exists in developing countries at all. Carolyn Merchant (1996, 18) lists "women in the Third World" as a separate category in her typology of ecofeminism, and Vandana Shiva (1989, 1993), who is an Indian physicist and environmental activist, has for many years affirmed a connection between Southern women and ecofeminism. In contrast, Salleh (1997) has argued that the more feminism moves towards postmodernism and away from the "womanist politics" of marginalized women, the less it has to offer "re/sisters" in the South. There are instead, as Salleh and others illustrate, many examples of women's practices and political mobilization around environmental concerns in postcolonial (and still colonized) countries that bear a basic resemblance to Northern/Western ecofeminism in that vast numbers of women are becoming politically active in order to build better lives for themselves and for their communities. Another important contributor to this debate is Bina Agarwal (1992, 1998b, 2001), who writes about Indian women's environmental work but uses the term "feminist environmentalism" rather than "ecofeminism," precisely because she finds the underlying assumptions of the latter problematic.

Feminist scholars in the North and South have long argued that women bear a disproportionate burden of imperialist-capitalist-patriarchal development and its concomitant social and ecological consequences. Although it has antecedents in the fields of feminist political economy and international development and resource management (Boserup 1970), WED has only been around as a recognized approach since the mid-to-late-1980s. The focus of WED literature, as illustrated in the works of Shiva (1989, 1993, 1994), Gita Sen and Caren Grown (1985), and Irene Dankelman and Joan Davidson (1988), is to critique development policies that are oblivious to women's needs and concerns and that fail to value women's indigenous knowledge. Efforts have since been made to substantiate the notion of women's special understanding of environmental degradation (and how to prevent it) by showing that women do a disproportionate amount of subsistence work (e.g., farming, gathering fuel and water, tending to the health of children and elders, and so on) in the developing world. Empirical studies, such as those conducted in the 1980s by Aotearoa/New Zealand economist Marilyn Waring (1988), have documented and quantified women's leadership in the informal economies that serve to keep people alive in the face of the crushing impacts of structural adjustment programs (see also Elson 1995).

Throughout the 1990s publications on women's relationships to their environment in developing countries demonstrate a trend towards including, in edited collections, case studies of women's grassroots struggles around basic subsistence needs such as securing land, retaining rights to seeds, and managing forests (e.g., Rocheleau, Thomas-Slayter, and Wangari 1996).[9] A common theme in these texts is that those hurt most by ecological degradation are those "closest" to natural resources in the South and that these people are primarily women. In addition to naming a range of ways in which women suffer more from ecological problems than men, this literature makes a point of including tales of triumph and resistance. In women's survival struggles there is hope for the future. Merchant (1996, 19) demonstrates this position clearly when she writes:

> Women of the South have born [sic] the brunt of environmental crises resulting from colonial marginalization and ecologically unsustainable development projects. As subsistence farmers, urban workers, or middle-class professionals, their ability to provide basic subsistence and healthy living-conditions is threatened. Women in the Third World, however, have not remained powerless in the face of these threats. They have organized movements, institutes and businesses to transform maldevelopment into sustainable development. They are often at the forefront of change to protect their own lives, those of their children, and the life of the planet.[10]

The WED perspective is most clearly expressed as a normative (and some would argue liberal [e.g., Gaard 1998]) political position in the work of the

Women's Environment and Development Organization (WEDO). Several ecofeminist texts use it as an example of ecofeminism, even though its members do not use the term (Sturgeon 1997; Gaard 1998; Salleh 1997). WEDO was formed in 1989 in order to provide a voice for women's "unique and important perspective" on environmental issues (Ransom 1999, 132). A conference held in 1991 called the World Women's Congress for a Healthy Planet brought together a diverse group of 1,500 women ("including many from the grassroots level") to report on the impacts of environmental degradation that affect their lives and to recount their strategies (and "success stories") for coping with them (Ransom 1999).[11] The outcome of the conference was the Women's Action Agenda 21, which was to be a submission to the United Nations Earth Summit in Rio de Janeiro. According to Pamela Ransom (1999, 132), director of environmental health and biosafety at WEDO, the Women's Action Agenda 21 represents a broad vision for the twenty-first century "rooted in women's values and concerns." An argument for the legitimacy of such a statement being made by women is that "it is women who suffer most from environmental degradation because they are closest to home and land, and are often the first line of defence against threats to the family and community" (ibid.). Those who are closest to the earth's processes because of their daily activities are best suited to ensure their sustainability for future generations. The assumption is that, when it comes to the quality of their environment, caring is the natural position for women. And the logic goes on to suggest that, therefore, women ought to play a much more significant role in policy making and leadership on international environmental issues than they do now. As WEDO founder Bella Abzug explains: "We do regard ... a clean environment, a healthy society, the preservation of the earth as being a very fundamental thing for any society, and we feel that women particularly have a very essential role to play" (quoted in Sturgeon 1997, 159).

WEDO is an organization that has been oriented towards more mainstream political strategies (directing its efforts at the UN level) while drawing its legitimacy from grassroots women. And it has been relatively successful: some claim that WEDO's lobbying efforts have forced the UN to give more than a passing glance to gender issues in its recent policy documents like Agenda 21 (Sturgeon 1997; Littig 2001). Chapter 24 of Agenda 21 is entitled "Global Action for Women towards Sustainable Development" (United Nations 1992). It is surprising, given their goals and rhetoric, that the language of citizenship is nowhere to be found in connection with the work of WEDO.

In that it is a global non-governmental organization (with headquarters in New York City) engaged with global institutions, WEDO occupies one end of a spectrum of women's organizing to address the particular concerns of non-academic, non-Western women about development-related environmental degradation. Without a doubt the most celebrated case examples of WED come from the opposite end of the spectrum, and these, like the Chipko movement and the Greenbelt movement, are cited in a number of WED as well as ecofeminist texts. Noël Sturgeon (1997, 125) notes that the Chipko women especially are presented as "the ultimate ecofeminists" and claims that the movement has attained "talismanic status" in certain kinds of ecofeminist writings.[12]

Based on a three-centuries-old tradition, and more recently linked to Gandhianism, this "women-led tree-embracing movement" (as Merchant [1996, 20]) calls it) is an organized effort to save local forests from commercial logging. The movement gained international renown among ecofeminists in large part due to the writings of Vandana Shiva (especially *Staying Alive*, published in 1989) who names it a symbol of women's resistance to "maldevelopment" (her term for bad development). Colleen Mack-Canty (2004, 169) suggests that the Chipko movement is "most often specifically cited as the beginning of ecofeminism" itself. Shiva and others make much of the Chipko women's methods: by hugging the trees the women use their bodies to protect the trees from the logger's axe, much as they would protect an endangered child. Shiva (2004, 54) has recently turned Chipko into a verb to describe other Indian women's protests, such as that against a dam project near Tehri on the Ganges River: "Kusumji the organizer of the [Tehri] women's dharna told me about how they had to do a Chipko in order to save their sacred pipal and bel trees." In her much cited *Staying Alive*, Shiva (1989, 67) argues that "environmental movements like the Chipko have become historical landmarks because they have been fuelled by the ecological insights and political and moral strengths of women." She and Maria Mies (1993) hold up the Chipko movement as the clearest example of the subsistence perspective available today and as embodying an alternative conception of freedom that is unique to women. "Because of their responsibility for daily survival," they write, "women are more concerned about a survival subsistence perspective than men are, most of whom continue to believe that more growth, technology, science, and 'progress' will simultaneously solve the ecological and economic crisis; they place money and power above life" (Mies and Shiva 1993, 304).[13]

Taking the Chipko women as a starting point, Salleh devotes a considerable portion of *Ecofeminism as Politics* to listing a range of ecofeminist actions from around the world. She states that the actions of "re/sisters" – the term she uses to describe women activists who have made "an intuitive historical choice ... to put life before freedom" (Salleh 1997, ix-x) – "express *a materially embodied standpoint grounded in working women's commonsense understanding of everyday needs*" (17, emphasis mine). Salleh makes the move from grassroots struggles to political theory in developing her "barefoot epistemology" as a counterpoint to the Eurocentric, anthropocentric, and androcentric theories that have resulted in the current ecological mess. Invoking Sara Ruddick's (1989) explanation of maternal thinking, Salleh (1997, 144) asserts that her argument for ways of knowing grounded in women's caring labour is not linked to biology: "rather, the argument makes a materialist epistemological claim about cognitive capacities derived from certain skills: a unity of body and mind found in those who work with head and hand in a self-directed way."

So for Salleh, and for several other ecofeminist writers, women's ways of knowing, which are linked to reproductivity – from labour pains to laundry loads – are unequivocally foundational for a new and more authentic approach to environmental change. Salleh (1997, 136) calls it "a yet invisible but universal public caring." As I have noted, in their book *Ecofeminism*, Mies and Shiva (1993) write about these kinds of examples of women's grassroots struggles as evidence of a "subsistence perspective" unique to women whose lives are devoted to ensuring the survival of their families and communities. Mies writes: "Subsistence work as life-producing and life-preserving work in all ... production relations was and is a necessary precondition for survival; and the bulk of this work is done by women" (in Mies and Shiva 1993, 298). Mies has since co-written *The Subsistence Perspective: Beyond the Globalized Economy* (1999), in which she and Veronika Bennholdt-Thomsen further develop the approach. This perspective envisions the creation of societies based on a set of values and practices different from those that support capitalism, patriarchy, and white supremacy. Mies writes that "a new life for present and future generations, and for our fellow creatures on earth ... can only be found in the survival struggles of grassroots movements" (in Mies and Shiva 1993, 297). Shiva (2004, 64) has more recently affirmed this view: "while men in power redefine religion on fundamentalist terms in support of market fundamentalism, women in diverse cultures mobilize their faith, their spirituality, their power to protect the earth and life on earth." The aim is to translate women's subsistence labour, traditional knowledge, life-sustaining practices, and care of the earth through activism into an alternative, theoretical model for sustainability.

Love Canal Legacy: Quality-of-Life Activism and Environmental Justice

> In the North, it is grassroots housewives, as opposed to so-called emancipated feminist women, who are generally the strongest fighters. They are less affected by the masculinist privilege that can so readily compromise professionals. (Salleh 1997, 136)

A second set of examples of women's grassroots activism that is important to ecofeminism comes out of feminist research on women's quality-of-life and environmental justice activism, predominantly in North America (but see Rocheleau, Thomas-Slayter, and Wangari 1996 for examples from western Europe). Here again it may be that critiques of Northern ecofeminism's exclusivity have taken the search for political identity to the streets. Or perhaps it is simply the popularity of case studies of women activists in the South that has led several recent feminist texts to feature similar stories of Western/Northern women working in local communities to ameliorate the effects of the environmental crisis. In any case, it is as if no ecofeminist text is complete – or legitimate – without voices from the grassroots. That these voices almost never utter the word "ecofeminism" (or feminism) is a matter I take up in the second part of this chapter and again in Chapter 6.

Just as more inclusive research on women's activism has occasioned a reassessment of feminist theories of politics, several writers have noted that an increase in the numbers of urban environmental justice organizations in which women form the majority of activists challenges the dominant understanding of "environment" and "environmentalism" (e.g., Miller, Hallstein, and Quass 1996; Rocheleau, Thomas-Slayter, and Wangari 1996; Di Chiro 1998; Taylor 1997). I draw on this literature in Chapters 7 and 8, in which I present an analysis of my conversations with women activists in the Toronto area. Readers will find, however, that my research departs from and complicates the approaches taken in many accounts of environmental justice activism.

The environmental justice movement (EJM) emerged in the late 1980s out of anti-racist critiques of mainstream and radical environmental movements, including ecofeminism (Bullard 1990; Guha 1994; McAdams 1996). Similar to the challenge that women's grassroots activism presents to feminism, the emergence of environmental justice is described by Dorcetta Taylor (1977, 40) as a new stage of environmentalism that marks "a radical departure from the traditional ways of perceiving, defining, organizing around, fighting, and discussing environmental issues." Whereas the mainstream North American environmental movement has historically (or at least until the 1980s) tended to identify with wilderness preservation issues, environmental justice activists have argued for an expanded definition of "environment" to include social, political, economic, and built environments – in other words, the places "where we live, work and play" (Gottlieb 1993). This argument gets at the fact that a majority of people in the world live in urban environments and that many never have the luxury of experiencing the wilderness or the bucolic rural settings that many environmentalists revere. It also serves to highlight the fact that some people bear the costs of environmental degradation more than others and that this inequality depends largely on race and class. Many scholars who are critical of environmentalism have accused it (and ecofeminism) of being a white middle-class movement that has ignored the plight of the poor and of people of colour in all regions of the world (Guha 1994; Bullard 1990, 1994).

People of colour in the environmental justice movement have criticized the mainstream environmental movement for being predominantly white and

Anglo-European, just as ecofeminists have challenged the domination of men in both the "eco-establishment" and the "eco-fringe" (Seager 1993). Two of the most prominent writers about women in the EJM in the United States, Dorceta Taylor and Giovanna Di Chiro, have empirically documented the leadership of women in groups organized around local environmental concerns. Taylor (1997) reports that, in stark contrast to groups in the traditional environmental movement, well over 50 percent of the environmental justice organizations in the United States is led by women, many of whom are women of colour. Di Chiro (1998, 104) says that "the vast majority of activists in the environmental justice movement are low income women and predominantly women of color." She makes a point of distancing environmental justice activists from those in the mainstream movements, stating that they are not really environmentalists (or feminists) at all:[14] "Activists in the EJM are unlikely to identify themselves as the 'new environmentalists' because they do not view themselves as an outgrowth of the 'old' environmental movement together with its 'save the whales and rainforests' sloganeering" (107).

Interestingly, Di Chiro calls the EJM an "unmarked women's movement" that is distinct from ecofeminism in that it is about activism rather than theorizing, about quality-of-life issues rather than feminist issues. Among the examples of women's environmental justice activism she cites are the Mothers of East Los Angeles, a Mexican American organization founded in 1985 to tackle a number of community quality-of-life issues, one of which was the siting of a hazardous waste incinerator in its neighbourhood. She tells the story of these hitherto apolitical women becoming motivated to organize because they feared for the health and safety of their children. Di Chiro argues that, while maternal identity and the experience of mothering are central to women's environmental activism, "mother" is simply a symbolic identity. Echoing Ruddick (1989), she notes that "the concept of 'mother' stands in for the protector of the community, the family ... no matter which gender" uses it (Di Chiro 1998, 119).

As the Indian Chipko movement has come to symbolize women's environmental resistance in the developing world, so the struggles of working-class (mostly white) women against the Hooker Chemical Company, a large petrochemical company with a plant in Love Canal, New York, have become the paradigmatic (if not the original) case of environmental justice activism in the United States. The environmental justice movement is believed to have started at Love Canal in the late 1970s. It was there that Lois Gibbs and a group of women "who preferred being homemakers to being activists" (Kaplan 1997, 17) came together after discovering that their community was contaminated by toxic waste. A chemical soup of polychlorinated biphenyls (PCBs) and dioxins was causing reproductive problems among neighbourhood women and making their children sick. As working-class residents in an industry town, many of whom had husbands employed as chemical workers, the women realized the risks of taking on a large corporation. But after years of living with the health effects of environmental contamination, the women believed that the risks of not taking action were too great. They formed the Love Canal Home-owners Association and embarked on a three-year fight to force Hooker Chemical to take responsibility for the contamination and to get compensation for having to move away from the neighbourhood (see Newman 2001).

The Love Canal story is celebrated as an example of women's grassroots environmental activism, and the women involved in these struggles have been called "mother environmentalists" or "homemaker citizens." Kaplan (1997) calls them "prophets" and describes lead organizer Lois Gibbs as a "Chicken Little" (that Cassandra-like character in the children's story whose warning that "the sky is falling!" was ignored by the other farmyard inhabitants). Gibbs has since established the Citizens' Clearing House for Hazardous Waste and is credited with "almost single-handedly shap[ing] the nature of grassroots environmental activism in the US" (Seager 1993, 265). Yet the emphasis is on the private bases of women's efforts rather than what it might mean to use (when they do) the language of citizenship. Joni Seager (1993) makes reference to the Love Canal case, and others like it, arguing that "the everyday knowledge of ordinary housewives" offers more hope for an alternative environmental vision than that thus far offered by ecofeminist theorists. She makes a point of using this case as a more "authentic" example of women's connections to the environment than that provided by ecofeminism, with its apolitical undercurrents, its essentialism, and its false universalism. Rejecting the "motherist politics" in ecofeminism in one chapter of *Earth Follies*, Seager goes on to argue that we may be witnessing "the emergence of a women's voice on the environment" that "derives from materially grounded facts about women's social location" as housewives (269). She refers ironically to the Love Canal women as "hysterical housewives," who, like most women but unlike most "rational men," have been socialized to listen to "their gut feelings." Because they were mothers responsible for their children's health and well-being, these women were the first to notice the effects of toxic contamination in their neighbourhood. Although she seeks to distance herself from maternalism and points out some of the dangers in maternalism-based activism, Seager cannot escape the fact that "maternalism brings many women into environmental politics ... and that women can often bring attention to their cause if they speak as mothers" (278).

The Love Canal case lends support to another theme in the ecofeminist literature that is also related to maternalist rhetoric: connections between women and environmental health. Much is made in ecofeminist literature of the impacts of toxic pollution on women's reproductivity, such as dioxin in breast milk, miscarriages, birth defects, and infertility. There is also concern over increases in environmentally related illnesses that require women to spend more time caring for their children: asthma, food allergies, chemical sensitivities, and childhood leukemia and other types of cancer. The conflation of women's and children's health, and the political implications thereof, are interesting aspects of ecomaternalism that have yet to be taken up; instead, there is an unquestioned alignment of women's and children's interests – indeed women's responsibility for children's interests – where environment and health are concerned. For example, Shiva (in Mies and Shiva 1993, 82) writes: "The patriarchal systems would like to maintain silence about ... poisonous substances, but *as mothers women cannot ignore the threats posed to their children*" (emphasis mine).[15]

The idea that women possess special knowledge of the way their own bodies and the bodies of others are affected by toxic substances is often used to bolster the argument that they are also more capable of solving the ecological crisis than men. Salleh (1997, 17), for one, notes that "women's ecological commitment is fed by an intimate biocentric understanding of people's survival links into the future of the planet at large" and gives examples of women's long-standing commitment to exposing links between health and ecological contamination. The contributors to *Sweeping the Earth: Women Taking Action for a Healthy Planet* (note the housework metaphor) document a range of women's struggles to expose and redress the effects of environmental contamination on human health. In her introduction, the book's editor, Miriam Wyman, draws inspiration from Rachel Carson's pioneering efforts to show links between the use of pesticides and the growing epidemic of cancer in North America. Wyman's (1999, 4) interpretation is that femaleness had a great deal to do with Carson's understanding of these links, just as it does for many women working against the odds to affect change today: "for her efforts, Rachel Carson was accused of being hysterical and emotional, and to this day it is a considered a crime to be passionate, to care, to take things personally – all the things that women know are needed to change the world." The articles in the collection report on the actions and experiences of women dealing with the harmful impacts of environmental contamination, and breast cancer is by far the dominant concern.

There is a popular observation in this literature that women, rather than trained doctors or epidemiologists (many of whom are, of course, women), discover the links between environmental contamination and health. For example, Seager (1993, 277) argues that, despite the fact that they are typically ignored or labelled as hysterical, women possess an "expertise [about environmental health that is] grounded in daily experience, not externally ratified knowledge." Moreover, she claims that, because they are caregivers attuned to the welfare of others, women are the first to recognize the effects of environmental pollution (see also Shiva 2004). This canary in the coal mine imagery also serves to affirm women's epistemic privilege in ecological matters. Not only does mother know best but she also often knows first. Seager writes (1993, 272): "Women are the first to notice when the water they cook with and bathe the children in smells peculiar; they are the first to know when the supply of water starts to dry up. Women are the first to know when the children come home with stories of mysterious barrels dumped in the local creek; they are the first to know when children develop mysterious ailments."

What can we make of this pattern in ecofeminist research and, especially, of the persistence of maternalist rhetoric in ecofeminism? Why has it continued in spite of a growing uncertainty that surrounds efforts to identify the universal and naturally occurring traits of women? Why retain such a focus in the face of feminist arguments that maternalism limits the ability of ecofeminism to be inclusive and democratic? Why has the concept of citizenship played little or no part in discussions of women's grassroots action? In the next part of the chapter I respond to these questions with a discussion of whether "strategic essentialism" is a persuasive justification for ecofeminist discourse to uncritically celebrate women's caring.

Strategic Essentialism and the Politics of Ecofeminist Identity

Contemporary feminists have been far more concerned with identity politics than with other kinds of political questions, for example, those regarding citizenship. In a 1988 essay entitled "Cultural Feminism versus Post-Structuralism: The Identity Crisis in Feminist Theory" philosopher Linda Alcoff spells out a central dilemma of feminist theory: what to do about the concept of woman, a concept that is at once the "necessary point of departure" for feminism and *overdetermined*[16] by patriarchal culture. This dilemma became a "crisis" when feminists no longer felt certain about what identity or identities to adopt in political discourse. Alcoff (1988, 405-6) describes the situation as follows:

> In attempting to speak for women, feminism often seems to presuppose that it knows what women truly are, but such an assumption is foolhardy given that every source of knowledge about women has been contaminated with misogyny and sexism. No matter where we turn – to historical documents, philosophical constructions, social scientific statistics, introspection, or daily practices – the mediation of female bodies into constructions of woman is dominated by misogynist discourse. For feminists, who must transcend this discourse, it appears we have nowhere to turn.

Alcoff goes on to explain that there have been two main responses to this identity crisis among feminist theorists. Cultural feminists, as we have seen, respond by reappropriating and revalidating devalued feminine nature. Poststructuralist and postmodern feminist theorists seek to deconstruct the category "woman" as well as to deny that there are essential natures at all. Finding both approaches lacking, Alcoff (1988, 422) suggests her own, third way out of the dilemma, which is to transcend it with a new alternative that uses the strongest elements of both cultural and poststructuralist feminism to explore "the possibility of a gendered subject that does not slide into essentialism." A balance must be struck between the need to talk about "women" and the need to resist masculinist definitions of "woman." She calls this balance positionality: "woman is a position from which a feminist politics can emerge rather than a set of attributes that are 'objectively identifiable'" (435).

In response to the discomfort of being caught between rocks and hard places, other feminists have argued for a third position, which they call strategic essentialism. Strategic essentialism can be defined as the use of common identities for the strategic, political purposes of oppositional social movements (Spivak 1987). It goes hand in hand with identity politics in responding to constructivist and poststructuralist critiques of essentialized group identities by, according to Diana Fuss (1989, 31), "deploy[ing] essentialism as a provisional gesture" in order to be able to speak about the kinds of subjects who have been hitherto invisible.[17] In other words, the use of essentialized identities can be a conscious political strategy to let the subaltern speak (Spivak 1985). In the case of feminism, it provides a way for feminists to simultaneously acknowledge that their rhetoric plays into universalizing and reductionist ideas about women and use it anyway – for a good cause.

The topic of strategic essentialism in ecofeminism is most directly taken up by Sturgeon (1997, 5) in her book *Ecofeminist Natures*, in which she argues that "ecofeminism seems to be situated in a history of feminism in such a way that it is required to solve the mystery of how to create an anti-essentialist coalition politics while deploying a strategic politics of identity." She is referring to the situation in which feminists want to avoid using "woman" as a universal category – because the word can obscure differences among women – but still need to talk about "women" in order to engage in feminist politics. And in order to assert an ecofeminist politics, it is necessary to talk about and to justify the particular stance that "women" take on the environment. In ecofeminism, which she defines as a growing social movement, Sturgeon finds the use of essentialist rhetoric acceptable if it contributes to an oppositional consciousness and political collectivities. She calls the common identities that ecofeminists often deploy (such as "indigenous woman," "third world woman" and "moral mother") "essentialist constructs," or "ecofeminist natures," and defines them as "notions of women, nature, and certain racially defined groups that use biological, universal, ahistorical, or homogenizing ways of definition" (ibid.). Despite the problems inherent in these essentialist constructs, which she admits and explains, Sturgeon defends ecofeminism against its anti-essentialist and postmodernist critics by arguing that certain ecofeminist deployments of essentializing rhetoric are "part of creating a shifting and strategic identification of the relation between 'women' and 'nature' that has political purposes" (11). Such deployments are necessary and valuable in the development of a radical political movement, and they seem to resonate with many women. "Particular strategic essentialisms may have positive oppositional ends, even while they may limit radical results; [and] ... politically well-intended anti-essentialism may have destructive consequences for a promising radical social movement" (10).[18]

In many cases, ecofeminists use ecomaternalist arguments to establish (i.e., to create, strategically) *non-biological links* between women and nature or women and environmental knowledge by focusing on the material conditions and types of work that are part of women's socially prescribed roles in society (e.g., Mellor 2000). Sturgeon explains this as a particular ecofeminist position that argues for a special relationship between women and nature using historical, cross-cultural, and materialist analyses of women's work. As we have seen, by looking at women's role in agricultural production and the managing of household economies worldwide, this position maintains that environmental problems are more quickly noticed by women than men and affect women's subsistence work more seriously than they do men's work. This position is accompanied by claims that women's knowledge and sense of moral responsibility about the environment – products of their everyday subsistence work as mothers, caregivers, and provisioners – are what we need in order to move towards a more sustainable society. Looking to Merchant (1996, 16) again: "As producers and reproducers of life, women in tribal and traditional cultures over the centuries have had highly significant interactions with the environment. As gatherers of food, fuel, and medicinal herbs; fabricators of clothing; preparers and preservers of food; and bearers and caretakers of young children, women's intimate knowledge of nature has helped to sustain life in every global habitat."

Such rhetoric is found in international policy debates, for example, where the strategic use of women's "traditional knowledge" is seen as a way to gain women a place at the table (if not as citizens, then perhaps as lay experts). Like the suffragettes in the late 1800s and early 1900s, groups like WEDO deploy maternalist rhetoric as a justificatory strategy for their entry into public discourse (e.g., "It's time for women to Mother Earth"). WEDO seems to have been successful in making a place for women in high-level environmental policy meetings like the Rio Summit, but what are the longer-term effects of this strategy? How do policy makers, the majority of whom do not make gender part of their political platform, regard women's concerns? Does the strategy foster critical discussions of gender relations and the impacts of environmental change on women's lives? Or are gender roles taken as given? No one seems to have asked these questions. It is my position that an effort to address them will lead to the conclusion that essentialist arguments are not a good strategy for a feminist politics that values democracy and that seeks to destabilize existing gender codes.

Is Strategic Essentialism an Oxymoron?

> My point is not that everything is bad, but that everything is danger-
> ous, which is not exactly the same thing as bad. (Foucault, 1984, 343)

As Judith Squires (1999, 133) observes, in this era of identity politics, "the equality/difference debate is displaced by political activism, not destabilized by theoretical reflection." Theoretical reflection might lead us to wonder whether emphasizing women's maternal sense of responsibility to care for people and the planet is a strategic move for ecofeminism at this point in history. I am sympathetic to Sturgeon's desire to understand and explain rather than to critique outright: understanding is just good practice for a social critic. And certainly the hyperbolic exchanges among ecofeminists over essentialism suggest that greater understanding and generosity are needed. But I disagree with Sturgeon when she argues that the invocation of "essentialist natures" is valuable for ecofeminism *in spite of the particular dangers it presents:* "these mo-ments of essentialism, these ecofeminist natures, are historically contingent, contradictory and contested. They remain politically important even when they have particular political costs" (Sturgeon 1997, 111). This seems to me an instrumentalist argument that loses sight of the principles of justice and de-mocracy. For example, how can one argue that *despite* the implicit racism involved in categorizing "third world women" as the ultimate ecofeminists (to which she devotes an entire chapter) this kind of strategic essentialism can help unite women in common struggle?[19] Others might find this ethically and politically indefensible. Chandra Talpade Mohanty (1991), for example, makes it clear that homogenizing categorizations and romantic portrayals of women in "the South" do much more harm than good. It is also questionable to sug-gest that, despite the poverty of women who are stuck in underpaid care-related jobs and the exploitation of women's caring labour for new right agendas, celebrating women's ethic of earthcare might be a good way to get an ecofeminist argument heard (I say more on this in Chapter 4). Others might see it as a dangerous affirmation of sexism and an acceptance of roles borne out of op-pression. I am left wondering why, after noting the fundamental problems that obtain in the deployment of essentialized natures, we would accept it as a useful strategy rather than take up the challenge of finding another.

Feminist critiques of the kind of identity politics in which many ecofeminists are engaged point to these and many other pitfalls associated with rhetorical claims about women's common experience. An important one is the risk of falsely universalizing the meaning of these experiences, which take place within different contexts and at different times. Mothering means different things to differently situated women, and some women (e.g., "single mothers" and les-bian parents) routinely have their practice of motherhood questioned. Another problem is that when knowledge and subjectivity are reduced to "lived experience" women are perceived as being incapable of abstract thought and reasoning, an assumption that has justified their exclusion from the category of knowing subject (Code 1991). These problems are evident in ecofeminist theory, although the number of available critiques is thus far very limited. One theorist who has discussed problems associated with strategic essentialism and identity politics in ecofeminism is Catriona Sandilands. Her book *The Good Natured Feminist: Ecofeminism and the Quest for Democracy* (1999a) is an in-depth exploration of the relevance of postmodern theory to ecofeminism, in which she finds ample reason to be wary of motherhood environmentalism. From her writings I take the following arguments against strategic essentialism as well as a set of challenges for ecofeminism that I shall keep in mind throughout the following chapters, wherein I develop my argument against strategic deployments of "care" as a metaphor for women's approach to environmental change.

First, Sandilands examines the myriad ways in which identitarian rhetoric occurs in ecofeminist texts and, unlike Sturgeon, finds that its denial of democracy is a significant limitation for ecofeminism as a social movement. The quest for an "authentic" political identity that is distinct from a putatively reified feminist one (that may or may not have been based solely on white middle-class women's experiences) has led some ecofeminists to create other kinds of identities that are so fixed and closed-ended that they give rise to the same kind of "not me problem" (Grant 1993) that ecofeminists had wanted to redress in the first place. This move closes off the democratic potential of ecofeminism. Sturgeon (1997, 1999a) wonders whether "academic feminists" can afford to dismiss ecofeminist arguments as essentialist when they have such popular resonance among women. But who are these women? Salleh (1997) makes no secret of the women in which ecofeminists are interested when she celebrates "re/sisters" and makes a point of excluding middle-class women (especially feminist academics) living in Northern industrialized urban areas. Significantly, it seems that what women do and think or how they are connected to the environment is no longer debatable in much ecofeminist writing. Political subjectivity seems to be something that most ecofeminists have undertheorized: to me this is obvious in their neglect of the concept of citizenship.

Sandilands (1999a, xx) suggests that one way out of ecofeminism's identity crisis is to explore "a more flexible, open-ended version of subjectivity, such as the one offered in Lacanian-inspired psychoanalysis, in which a subject is constituted imperfectly *in* discourse rather than transparently prior *to* discourse." In other words, instead of clinging to "women" as subjects with inherent qualities that are pre-political, ecofeminists might take a perspective that acknowledges the multiplicity of subject positions and the "discursive spaces describing shifting moments of symbolic representation derived from temporary common understanding" (ibid). (This is not to say that essentialist moments are not, at times, powerful, as Sturgeon [1997, 1999] has argued.) Ecofeminists might also recognize that conflicts as well as coalitions are possible between and within subject positions. Such open-endedness and willingness to embrace tensions are necessary if ecofeminism is to realize its democratic potential. Denise Riley (1988) argues that, in their efforts to decentre feminism's definition of women by focusing on diversity of experiences, some feminists have failed to challenge the notion that these are uniquely "women's experiences," hence maintaining a core of gender identification (the fiction of femininity) rather than contesting it. According to Riley:

> Perhaps it is not so much the "experience" that is the puzzle which persists after the pluralizing correction had been made but the "women's experience." The phrase works curiously, for it implies that the experiences originate with the women, and it masks the likelihood that instead these have accrued to women not by virtue of their womanhood alone, but as traces of domination, whether natural or political. And while these may indeed pertain uniquely to one sex, they can hardly be used to celebrate or underwrite the state of being a woman without many gloomier qualifications. (99)

Closely related to Riley's point is a second important criticism of ecofeminist uses of strategic essentialism. Sandilands (1999a) argues that some ecofeminist scholars who try to avoid biological essentialism by asserting the material or experiential roots of women's superior knowledge about the environmental crisis and how to solve it fail to avoid fixing a particular identity that rests on *an unproblematized notion of gender*.[20] It is as if, for some ecofeminists, the desire to justify a particular set of political claims has overshadowed the "interrogative element" (Quinby 1994) in feminism, whereby assumptions are continuously questioned and the power relations that underlie discursive practices are subjected to critical analysis. "Throughout my interactions with ecofeminism," Sandilands (1999a, xix) writes:

> I have chafed – as I have seen many others do – against the narrow construction of identity (maternal and otherwise) that underlies ecofeminist attempts to combine a feminist with an environmental politics to provide a route to the liberation of both. While I think it is crucial to recognize and act from moments of political affinity grounded in the relation between the oppression of women and the domination of nature, I find it misguided to consider their coalition (as some ecofeminists have tended to do) in a way that reduces both women and nature to a very particular point of connection. Such a reduction essentializes women and domesticates nature, *as if gender were a natural*

product and as if nature were describable in terms of particular cultural conventions of femininity. (Emphasis mine)

I find the concept of reductionism significant here; perhaps it offers a way to sidestep the question of essence altogether.[21] (As Seager [2003] has noted, getting bogged down in this debate is counterproductive to ecofeminism's more pressing aims.) It is very likely that Fuss (1989) is right: we will never reach a conclusion on the matter of "what" women are, and essence is not inherently a bad concept to have around. But we may be able to agree that reducing women to putatively pre-political, yet actually overdetermined (and perhaps mythical), elements of feminine gender identity or experience is a practice inimical to feminism. Quinby (1997, 154) notes that "avowals of an eternal feminine can also simply renew age-old constraints on women." If feminism is, among other things, about upsetting gender codes in order to liberate women from prescribed roles, then we may look at the strategic deployment of "moral mother" rhetoric, see that it reaffirms rather than challenges femininity, and declare it to be profoundly un-strategic, even un-feminist (Davion 1994).

It is important to note the irony that the identities and experiences that women have embraced in the practice of identity politics are not new, feminist-created identities but, rather, exactly the ones imposed on them by the society they seek to change. I conclude this chapter by noting another reason why it is problematic that Sturgeon neglects to address an important shadow side of strategic essentialism: ecofeminists have little control over how the deployment of maternal identity and values will be regarded in the realm of the political. In making this point, I am echoing Sandilands' (1999a, 114) critique of Carlassare's defence of strategic essentialism: "what Carlassare fails to address is the fact that strategic essentialism is never simply strategic but contains within it the potential to create a perception of essence despite the supposedly ironic nature of the stance." Sandilands suggests (in Judith Butler 1990, 1993) that this recognition might lead ecofeminists to consider the politics of gender performativity as a better use of irony.

As I discuss in greater detail in Chapter 4, this position also requires a thorough investigation of the ways in which care and motherhood represent a paradox for feminists: they can be both personally rewarding and oppressive. Since there has always been tension in feminist scholarship between celebrating and seeking to overcome women's association with caring, it follows that the tension would persist in ecofeminist discourse. Deane Curtin (1999, 87) captures this dilemma succinctly when he argues that "depictions of women's 'proper' role create a dilemma for ecofeminists: while such labour is often experienced as an oppressive demand, the environment and the human community cannot survive without it." Conversely, grassroots efforts to improve the quality of life in communities and households may be a source of political and personal empowerment for women; however, insofar as they are *naturalized and privatized*, celebrating these efforts uncritically can come dangerously close to accepting the unfair and unsustainable gendered politics of care. (To invoke Foucault's famous line again: not bad, but dangerous.) I explore these dangers and dilemmas further in Chapter 4, in which I argue that citizenship offers a superior framework for understanding and representing women's ecopolitical engagements.

4 From Care to Citizenship: Calling Ecofeminism Back to Politics

> What of ecofeminism? Is its analysis so irrevocably
> grounded in misrecognition, standpoint epistemologies
> and identity politics, so strongly committed to a trans-
> parent speaking nature, that it cannot be recalled from
> the edge of the democratic cliff?
>
> — *Catriona Sandilands*, The Good-Natured Feminist:
> Ecofeminism and the Quest for Democracy

One of the themes in contemporary ecofeminist literature is that women's care-related perspectives on human-nature relations should be adopted as a generalized normative stance, a form of ecological civic virtue or "a universal public caring" (Salleh 1997). This argument is supported by those ecofeminist theorists who portray caring relationships as models for sustainable living and as important sources of political empowerment for women in the larger social sphere. As described in Chapter 3, the women who appear in the narratives that inform ecofeminist alternative visions are variously referred to as grass-roots women, housewife activists, and "re/sisters" who work voluntarily to sustain life and to fight against the powers that jeopardize life. The vision their experiences inspire consists of an integration of diverse political struggles into one overarching movement for survival that is grounded in everyday material practices at the local level. So grounded, it is a vision that is fundamentally different from right-wing ideologies, which embrace global capitalism, as well as from the philosophies of postmodernism, which are said to privilege discourse and to discourage activism.

While there are important aspects of ecofeminist valuations of women's caring – particularly in light of the way non-feminist ecopolitical discourse ignores the work of care (which I discuss in Chapter 5) – I argue that there are also political risks in celebrating women's association with caring, both as an ethic and as a practice, and in reducing women's ethico-political life to care. In view of these risks, I think a degree of scepticism is in order. I question whether care – as in earthcare – is a wise choice of metaphor around which to create a feminist political project for social and ecological change. How can societal expectations that women be caring and the exploitation of women's unpaid caring labour under capitalism be challenged at the same time as women's caring stance towards the environment is held up as an answer to the ecological crisis? What does it mean, moreover, for women to enter the realm of the political through a window of care and maternal virtue? How is this *feminist?* And how, if at all, is it political?

It is my position that ecofeminists should see caring through less-than-rosy-glasses, as a paradoxical set of practices, feelings, and moral orientations that are embedded in particular relations and contexts and that are socially constructed as *both feminine and private*. Revaluing care in the way many ecofeminists seem to do results in affirming gender roles that are rooted in the patriarchal dualisms that all feminisms, by my definition at least, must aim persistently to resist and disrupt. I support my position by drawing on the work of some of the feminist philosophers, political economists, and political theorists who have argued that the positive identification of women with caring ought to be treated cautiously because it obscures some of the negative implications of feminized care and narrows our understanding of women as political actors. In the first part of the discussion I cast doubt on ecofeminist ideas about the "feminine principle" (Mies and Shiva 1993) by highlighting some of the critiques of care ethics made by feminist moral philosophers. I then subject ecofeminist celebrations of caring labour to questions raised by feminist political economists about its exploitation in globalizing capitalist societies. I also question whether claims that women are empowered through their care-inspired eco-activism have been accompanied by a sufficient consideration of feminist political transformation. That discussion leads into the final part of the chapter, where I look to feminist theorists of citizenship to develop the argument that ecofeminists would be better served by using the language of citizenship rather than the language of care in order to understand and theorize women's engagement in ecopolitics.

Of Questionable Virtue: Rethinking Care Ethics

Care has a very particular meaning in the ecofeminist literature to which I am responding. The best way to explain it is to draw a distinction between caring as a set of material practices (i.e., to take care of something or someone as a form of labour) and caring as a disposition (entailing particular values or ethics).[1] For many ecofeminists (e.g., Mies and Shiva 1993; Mies and Bennholdt-Thomsen 1999; Salleh 1997; Merchant 1996; Mellor 1992, 1997, 2000) the two are closely interrelated. Because it is women (as mothers)[2] who do the nurturing work that sustains human life, and that mediates the connection between humans and nature, women care about (assume a sense of compassion, responsibility, and connection towards) their environments, and this, in turn, leads them to take action to preserve and repair them. This relationship is to be celebrated, they argue, because caring for people and environments produces special insights into the interrelated processes of life – insights that are foreign to the individualistic and exploitative (read masculine) approach to these processes, which has led to environmental degradation. Men may *care about* their children and environments but may not be required socially – or may not be socialized – to do much work to *care for* them. This is the key gender difference. Maria Mies (in Mies and Shiva 1993, 304) suggests that most men probably do not care very much at all when she says that "women are more concerned about a survival subsistence perspective than are men, most of whom continue ... to put money and power above life." Therefore, for these ecofeminists, women are seen to hold the key to an ethical approach to socioecological as well as to social relationships that can solve the ecological crisis.

This way of joining everyday caring practices and caring values is variously described as "the subsistence perspective" (Mies and Bennholdt-Thomsen 1999), "the female principle" (Mies and Shiva 1993), and a "barefoot epistemology" (Salleh 1997, 2000). To illustrate further, I quote Salleh (1997, 161) at length:

> Women's relations to nature, and therefore to labour and to capital, is qualitatively different from men's in at least four ways. The first such difference involves experiences mediated by female body organs in the hard but sensuous interplay of birthing and suckling labours. The second set of differences are [sic] historically assigned caring and maintenance chores which serve to "bridge" men and nature. A third involves women's manual work in making goods as farmers, weavers, herbalists, potters. A fourth set of experiences involves creating symbolic representations of "feminine" relations to "nature" – in poetry, painting, philosophy, and everyday talk. *Through this constellation of labours, women are organically and discursively implicated in life-affirming activities, and they develop gender-specific knowledges grounded in that material base.* The result is that women across cultures have begun to express insights that are quite removed from most men's approaches to global crisis. (Emphasis mine)

Now I will admit that it makes sense for ecofeminists to avoid what is often identified as "masculinized" ethics and politics (i.e., the kind of thinking that may have led to the twin problems of ecological destruction and gender inequality) and to be drawn to some kind of feminized alternative. Like many feminist scholars, ecofeminists have sought to unearth the foundations of gender bias in Western philosophical traditions: the privileging of reason over emotion, objectivity over context-dependency, and justice over care – in short, the devaluation of the feelings and emotions associated with women, racialized people, nature, and the private sphere. Ecofeminists have been critical of liberalism, utilitarianism, and other political and philosophical traditions on the added grounds that they ignore human embodiment and human-nature interconnections. Ecofeminists categorically reject the assumption of an independent (male) subject that obfuscates the fragility of the body, its dependence on natural or biophysical processes, and its need for care. Ynestra King (1988, 19), for example, writes that the Western democratic tradition has "a political legacy that is founded on the repudiation of the organic, the female, the tribal, and the particular ties between people."

On this view it stands to reason that a key plank in the ecofeminist platform has been to make the invisible more visible and to envision a new perspective that revalues traits and experiences that support life on earth – traits and experiences that have thus far been left out of politics. Yet a leap is frequently made from recognition and validation to arguments for moral superiority. I have demonstrated that some ecofeminists (echoing feminist theorists such as Elshtain 1981; Noddings 1984; and Ruddick 1989) see women's experiences as nurturers or mothers as essential ingredients of an antidote to masculine thinking, and they see mothering as the foundation of an alternative politics of compassion that could improve the political sphere. As Anne Phillips (1993, 82) observes of such a position, women are seen to "bring to politics a kind of morality and civic virtue that can displace the selfish materialism that dominates today." Significantly, many ecofeminist arguments about care rest on epistemological grounds: the association of care with "women's ways of knowing" is highly relevant to building an alternative environmental ethics – "alternative" here meaning not only different from those now on offer but also superior.

For example, as I have noted, Merchant (1996) identifies the application of maternal and caring values to environmental problems as a form of "earthcare," a term she uses to describe the activities of women involved in toxic waste protests, the appropriate technology movement, and the fight to ban herbicides, pesticides, and nuclear technology. She advocates a "partnership ethic of earthcare" that draws on women's experiences of and historical connections to the environment and stands in marked opposition to the homocentric and egocentric ethics of dominant institutions.[3] The key to developing this ethic of earthcare, for Merchant, is to recognize and learn from women's experiences. I take this as evidence of a shift from ontology to epistemology in ecofeminist ethics, or from assertions about "women's nature" to assertions about what women know and, very often, what they *feel*:

Feminist biology, as proposed by Evelyn Fox Keller and practiced by Barbara McClintock, is based on a "feeling for nature" as a self-generating, complex, and resourceful process, not nature as a passive, simple, useful resource. The former set of assumptions also character-izes ecology, the scientific study of the earth's household, as pursued by Rachel Carson. Thus feminist science and ecology are not only philosophically compatible, they need each other. Moreover, they can be combined with an ethic of care, such as that proposed by Nel Noddings, that is *grounded in receptivity, relatedness, and responsiveness, rather than the abstract principles of rights and justice.* When these ideas and approaches are synthesized and applied to concrete situations, such as saving Australia's ancient forests, *an ecofeminist ethic of earthcare results.* (Merchant 1996, 206, emphases mine)

Although this approach to epistemological politics makes me uneasy, I be-lieve that it is in its rethinking of hegemonic understandings of ethico-politics and in its injection of hitherto "private" concerns into the political domain that ecofeminism has much to offer. As I discuss in Chapter 5, ecofeminist arguments about embodiment and the failure of masculinist environmentalisms to address the gendering of experience and responsibility in the domestic sphere are among ecofeminism's most valuable contributions (see especially Mellor 1997). They deserve greater analytic and theoretical attention in both ecofeminism and green political theory. However, there are important ques-tions to be raised about the implications of care metaphors and, specifically, care ethics for ecofeminist politics. The first is whether invoking an inevitably and/or intentionally *feminized* ethic of care is an advisable strategy for prob-lematizing ecopolitical and social relationships. Can it lead to a destabilization of gender codes? What are the risks in an approach that celebrates women's caring as a public virtue?

In response to these questions, and in order to show that caring is not an unqualified good, it is instructive to take note of a current in feminist philoso-phy that has combined arguments for valuing the capacity to care with argu-ments that problematize and politicize women's caring. Some feminist philosophers maintain that, for feminism, care ethics is a double-edged sword. While some believe that an ethics of care offers a way to assert a positive face for feminism (perhaps one more inspirational than a feminism that dwells upon women's exploitation under patriarchy), an uncritical emphasis on wom-en's care-related morality can also affirm harmful assumptions about gender and reify exclusionary notions about the nature of care and, indeed, of carers. Peta Bowden (1997, 18-19) explains the tension nicely: "Condemnation of caring runs the danger of silencing all those who recognize its ethical possibili-ties, and risks capitulating to dominant modes of ethics that characteristically exclude consideration of women's ethical lives. On the other hand, romantic idealization is also a danger."

Since the 1980s, when care ethics was in its heyday, questions have been asked about the validity and implications of care perspectives for feminism. There is resistance in feminist philosophy to the "strategy of reversal" (Squires 1999) that has been deployed by cultural feminists who choose to see "women's ways of knowing," "maternal thinking," or "feminine ethics" as superior to men's ways of knowing and masculine ethics, and as an ethic that can transform the world (Koehn 1998). Lorraine Code (1995, 111) points out, for example, that "it is by no means clear that a new monolith, drawn from hitherto devalued practices, can or should be erected in the place of one that is crumbling." An important lesson for ecofeminists here is that listening to and validating women's voices and those of other marginalized subjects is important, but it does not inevitably lead to epistemic privilege (Davion 1994). Not only is the idea that women may have greater access to "the truth" questionable on empirical grounds but it is also too risky a position to put forth within the context of a masculinist and misogynist culture that both creates and exploits women's capacity to care. Thinking about this point within the context of ecofeminist rhetoric, Code (1991, 274) writes:

> Women may indeed have the capacity to save the world, in consequence, perhaps, of their cultural-historical relegation to a domain "closer to nature" than men, whatever that means. Yet claims that such a capacity is uniquely, essentially theirs have consistently served as premises of arguments to show that women should be the moral guardians both of "humanity" and of nature. Such injunctions assign women responsibilities that are fundamentally oppressive, while excluding them from recognition as cognitive agents and creators of social meaning, precisely *because* of their alleged closeness to nature. An ecofeminism developed in this direction would be morally-politically unacceptable.

Questioning the morality of gender inequality that, in large part, is responsible for women's greater tendency to perform caring activities and to feel responsible for the welfare of others is an important project for feminist moral philosophers. It is significant that few of the ecofeminists to whom I have been referring explicitly challenge the feminization of care or acknowledge the negative consequences of women's sense of ethical responsibility for caring. I think they could learn from the arguments of feminists who have looked at caring through sceptical (as opposed to rosy) glasses (Card 1989; Koehn 1998). For example, an important criticism of care ethics emerges through a theoretical examination of why and how women care. Marilyn Friedman suggests that we recognize a "gender division of moral labour" that is largely responsible for the "moralization of gender" wherein specific, different moral commitments and behaviours are expected of men and women. She writes: "Our very conceptions of femininity and masculinity, female and male, incorporate norms about appropriate behaviour, characteristic virtues, and typical vices" (Friedman 1995, 64). These norms develop under conditions of sexual inequality and persist through stereotypes constructed through dominant institutions of mass culture. Even if the myth fails to live up to the "reality," our perceptions are filtered through these stereotypes: masculine thinking is believed to be abstract and concerned with justice, and feminine thinking is believed to be caring and selfless. Normative femininity is imposed on women through the disciplinary practices of the dominant culture, and this is disempowering for women so disciplined. Thus we may reasonably suspect that what appears as "care" (with all its qualities of selflessness and compassion) is often actually an unjust and "one-sided relational exploitation" (68). At any rate, we simply do not know what "feminine morality" would be under conditions of equity and freedom, and we should not confuse actions shaped under socially oppressive conditions for "natural" ones (Card 1989; see also Frye 1983).

Peta Bowden (1997, 9) contends that it is necessary for feminists to acknowledge negative aspects to caring as well as positive ones. She calls them dark sides and light sides of caring:

> The tendency to see the perspectives and concerns arising from maternal and other practices of caring simply in a positive light glosses the dark side of these practices: the frustrating, demeaning, and isolating dimensions of their routines. "Care" has a lengthy history in the (English-speaking) west as a burden, a bed of trouble, anxiety, suffering and pain; care ethicists ignore this history, and the dismal actuality of many contemporary practices of caring, at great risk.

Highlighting the relevance of this insight for ecofeminism, Chris Cuomo (1998, 129) writes: "put simply, caring can be damaging to the carer if she neglects other responsibilities, including those she has to herself, by caring for another."[4] Certainly self-sacrifice, exploitation, and loss of autonomy and leisure time are among the more negative aspects of women's caring. So is the inability to withhold care or to say no, which comes with an internalized duty to maintain relationships. It is important to look at why women tend to have little choice but to be caring.[5] Feminist critiques of violence against women often include the claim that women need to develop a greater sense of autonomy and separation. (Intimacy and abuse sometimes go hand in hand.) Such negative aspects of caring provide reasons to treat with scepticism any desire to focus solely on the lighter side of women's caring and life-affirming values. In recognition of this point, it is necessary to consider striking a balance between an ethic of care and an ethic of justice.[6]

Even when it is useful to value and affirm women's caring, we ought not to limit our interest in women's moral lives, or their moral possibilities, to care. Bowden (1997, 8) laments that "celebrations of caring reduce and simplify the range of women's moral possibilities to those displayed in practices of care." Ecofeminist texts are open to this very criticism when they fail to consider, or when they downplay, sources of women's concern for environmental well-being other than their maternal feelings of protection for their children. While it is important not to dismiss these feelings as invalid, there is value in exploring other forms of and motivations for environmental and community engagement that do not fall into a stereotypically or exclusively feminine orientation. Few of these, such as religious belief, academic training, scientific and philosophical curiosity, national and regional forms of identity, attachment to places or landscapes, and so on, have been given much play in ecofeminist scholarship.[7] Aside from care, have ecofeminists explored other emotions, such as anger, righteousness, and perhaps even selfishness, that are at play in many women's engagement with environmental disputes?[8] Is it all about care and cooperation? Or are more complex and multilayered interpretations possible?[9]

It seems that women's capacity for abstract and principled thought about moral issues and ethical decision making has been eclipsed by a focus on material practices and lived experiences that are presented as more "grounded" than theory can ever be. A focus on women acting on "survival" or "subsistence" imperatives erases moral choice and practices related to making principled decisions to act, or not to act, in particular ways. Many ecofeminists want to applaud "the view from below" (Mies and Bennholdt-Thomsen 1999): the moral insight that comes out of allegedly unmediated and embodied experiences of survival. There is a naturalistic presupposition in this celebration that plays into stereotypical representations of women's caring "as instinctual activities that require no special knowledge, no training, no education" (Code 1995, 107). This presupposition is especially apparent in ecofeminist literature, in which the claim is made, implicitly or explicitly, that grassroots women (especially peasant women) are more authentic knowers than feminist women and that their putatively *untheorized* knowledge is more valuable than feminist theory. Not only is this view unfair to women who may actually make a conscious political choice to care but it also denies the political significance of care.

Also problematic is an apparent lack of acknowledgment that many of the women whom ecofeminists claim exhibit a "subsistence perspective" or "barefoot epistemology" do so in conditions that are not of their own choosing.[10] It is unfair to romanticize values and knowledge that emerge from a subsistence way of life because the alternative picture (i.e., selfishness in an affluent lifestyle) is problematic. Perhaps it is worth questioning the assumptions being made about the way "lifestyle" determines human morality. For example, I find the assumptions being made in this statement highly problematic: "the Bangladeshi women teach us that the realisation of the subsistence perspective depends primarily not on money, education, status, and prestige but on control over means of subsistence: a cow, some chickens, children, land, also some independent money income" (Mies and Bennholdt-Thomsen 1999, 5).

The ecofeminist writers who celebrate women's ethic of earthcare often forget to look behind their observations (or, rather, their interpretations) of women's life-sustaining labour to understand its complexities, contexts, and conditions. I would suggest that ecofeminists who focus only on the positive aspects of this way of knowing/being (positive in that it helps others and perhaps bolsters the viability of fragile ecosystems even if the lives of the carers remain the same) are neglecting a feminist desire for social and political change towards equality. In so doing they give the appearance of giving up on the ideas that all those whose privilege serves to excuse them from caring activities might develop a greater capacity for caring and compassion and that care should be seen as central to any vision of a sustainable and equitable society.[11] Worse is the possibility that a change in the unequal gender relations that contribute to women's sense of moral responsibility for life would be incompatible with an ecofeminist alternative. As Victoria Davion (1994) has argued, and I agree, this position is inconsistent with feminist aims.

There are ecofeminist scholars, it is important to point out, who use this line of questioning and who are sceptical of an association between ecofeminism and an ethics of care. For example, Chris Cuomo, in her book *Feminism and Ecological Communities*, presents one of the most thorough interrogations to date of the ecofeminist adoption of the care ethic position. After a clearly articulated defence of ecofeminism against its anti-essentialist critics (similar in some ways to Sturgeon's), she concludes that "asserting that woman=mother, woman=feminine, mother=nature, feminine=caring is not a good idea theoretically and practically" (Cuomo 1998, 126). Karen J. Warren (1999) also raises doubts about the place of feminized notions of care in environmental ethics. Although she does not name recent ecofeminist arguments in her critique, she expresses her view that efforts "to capture the moral significance of care by defending a separate 'ethic of care,' one that is more basic than and in competition with traditional canonical ethics ... is ... the wrong way to proceed" (Warren 1999, 138).[12] To this I would add an argument, premised on the insight of Joan Tronto (1993, 89), that the espousal of an ethic of care has resulted in the "containment" of ecofeminist arguments: insofar as they attach themselves to women's specific practices and efforts to survive, they seem "irrelevant to the moral life of the powerful." I show how this is a problem in my discussion of ecological citizenship and green political theory in Chapter 5. I now turn to a second set of problems with the way care is invoked in ecofeminist literature.

From Carers to Activists: More to the Empowerment Story?

> Women become activists in part because their bodies, or the bodies of
> those with whom they have a caring relationship, are threatened by
> toxic or radioactive substances or when land or another species about
> which they care deeply is threatened with extinction. (Merchant 1996,
> xviii)

Ecofeminists have emphasized the specificity of women's identity as mothers
(or potential mothers) and the importance of including domestic concerns in
struggles for ecopolitical change. They have also provided a feminist reinter-
pretation of the traditional meaning of politics by showing that everyday practices in the private sphere can contribute as much to social change as can
action in the public domain, albeit in different ways. As Merchant (1996,
198) observes, for example, through their caring activities "women provide a
primary vehicle for transmitting social values to the next generation."[13] In
Chapter 3 I give several examples of the kind of grassroots activism that
ecofeminists have celebrated as evidence of women's heightened sense of responsibility for environmental quality (e.g., the Chipko, Love Canal, and
Greenbelt movements, the Mothers of East LA). A central plot line in
ecofeminist stories about women's involvement in grassroots activism is the
process through which hitherto apolitical women (often presented as ordinary
housewives) become "empowered" to act as political subjects when they learn
about an environmental threat to health, most often to their children's health.
Sandilands (1999a) notes that the discussion of women's politicization through
environmental struggles is one of the most important contributions of
ecofeminism to environmentalism. It serves to disrupt other green perspectives that ignore or misunderstand the role that so-called "private" concerns
play in ecopolitical struggles. Such stories also affirm a set of experiences and
an engagement in informal forms of politics that have been left out of the
dominant picture of the environmental movement.

Without denying that for some women the deployment of motherhood as a
political identity may feel empowering, I want to argue that there are pitfalls
inherent in ecofeminist narratives that celebrate a movement from carer to
activist. I consider two. The first is that there is scant mention, let alone critical analysis, of the difficulties that individual "housewife activists" may face
when they do choose to act in the political arena. In other words, the stories
are more romantic than realistic. The second is that many of these stories of
housewives becoming empowered as political subjects present an uncritical
affirmation of gendered knowledge rather than a process of consciousness-
raising that involves the self-reflexive creation of new political subjectivities
and new knowledges that disrupt gender constructs and gender relations. The
stories may not be very accurate either: there are examples in the literature

(e.g., Di Chiro 1998), and in my own empirical research (which I discuss in Chapters 7 and 8), to suggest that tensions and contradictions between gender codes (e.g., mothering) and political participation can lead to critical reflection (e.g., theorizing) and politicization among women activists. I shall discuss each of these points in turn.

The Political Economy of (Feminized and Privatized) Caring Work

Just as it is instructive to consider the shadow side of women's moral responsibility to care, so it is important to consider the problems that arise for women who perform caring work in societies that assume yet deny an exploitative gender division of necessary labour. In this context, I think an ecofeminist theory of women's environmental activism ought to foreground ways in which caregiving responsibilities and political engagement can, and often do, clash. There are stories that combine an acknowledgment of women's political contributions with insights into the costs they incur. Harriet Rosenberg (1995, 200) has found, for example, that women involved in local anti-toxics struggles report an increased level of tension and conflict in their families: "Preserving familist ideology, in theory, often results, in practice, in long absences from the home, unprepared meals, undone laundry, and kitchens turned into offices. When women become active publicly, their husbands may resent their new confidence and skills." Although Seager (1993) may inadvertently endorse the kind of ecomaternalist rhetoric that I find problematic, she seems well aware of the dilemmas it poses for women, not least because they are criticized for not living up to cultural expectations of what mothers ought to be like. They find themselves ridiculed as hysterical and naive by officials, harassed by men in their families for shirking domestic duties, and guilt-tripped by lonely children who expect more of their time. Several of the women I interviewed have experienced these conflicts. When Kenyan Green Belt movement leader Wangari Maathai (who is known as "Mama Miti," or the mother of trees, in her Kiswahili language) won the Nobel Peace Prize in 2004, journalists writing about her life as an activist made references to a comment by her ex-husband (from whom she was divorced in the 1980s) that she is "too educated, too strong, too successful, too stubborn, and too hard to control" (BBC News 2004).

What I make of this is that ecofeminist discussions of women's activism must not only recognize tensions between caring and politics but also engage in a critical political economic analysis of women's unpaid labour. Viewed in light of feminist critiques of the feminization of caring in capitalist societies, and in light of the current hegemony of new right ideology, it is dangerous for ecofeminists to uncritically celebrate women's roles as earthcarers. It is dangerous if it affirms rather than challenges the feminization and privatization of caring work. Feminist political economists, on the other hand, have tracked the changes in unpaid work over time and have analyzed the gender implications of a capitalist system that depends on the externalization[14] of reproductive labour (Folbre 1993). This tracking is done not to celebrate the fact that women do this work but, rather, to show how women's caring work is deeply implicated in dominant political and economic agendas. Scholars have argued that care and care-related practices are devalued in liberal-capitalist societies precisely because they are associated with femininity – that is, they are seen as women's work (e.g., McDowell 1992). Moreover, their theoretical interpretations of empirical data (such as those gathered in time budget studies) suggest that caring is a deeply gendered – that is, feminized – activity in Western/Northern (and probably many other) cultures and that the unequal division of unpaid care work between men and women has not changed dramatically in the past thirty years (Eichler 1997).

As feminist political economists have observed, not only is women's load of caring labour not being shared equally by men but it is also being progressively *intensified* by a right-wing privatization agenda that seeks to cut spending by downloading the work of caring to civil society and individual families (Brodie 1996a; Bakker 1994; Stinson 2005). Since the early 1980s, governments in the West have gradually privatized public services (in fields like health care) and have moved to contracting them out to private companies (Medjuck, O'Brien, and Tozer 1992; Giles and Arat-Koc 1994; Ehrenreich and Hochschild 2002; Stinson 2005). These changes are part of a quest for more efficient and cost-effective strategies that meet corporate and state concerns for competitiveness in the global economy. Feminists have argued that this strategy is also deeply gendered in that it relies on the cheap, even free, labour of women. As mentioned earlier, the most notable theme in the current feminist literature on the way care is implicated in processes of economic restructuring is that women are expected to act as the "shock-absorbers" of privatization (Brodie 1995, 19) by filling in for lost state-provided services with their own unpaid, caring labour in private households and through volunteer work in communities.

An important source of insight for an ecofeminist analysis of women's grassroots activism is the feminist critique of the concept of community care (e.g., Eichler 1997; Brodie 1996a; Bakker 1996b; Armstrong and Armstrong 1994). Examples of the shift to greater non-governmental "community" responsibility for caregiving include the deinstitutionalization of frail elderly people, mentally and physically disabled people, and people with chronic illnesses. Feminist economists, among others, have shown that the relegation of caring labour to the household or informal economy has resulted in a mutually reinforcing cycle of externalization and devaluation (Folbre 1993). Some feminists have argued that, rather than continuing to support volunteerism, women ought to demand payment for the work they do, including work without which the market could neither survive nor prosper.[15] Moreover, feminist research has shown that women who carry heavy loads of caring work tend to have little leisure time and high levels of stress (sometimes causing health problems) and that there are innumerable costs to individuals and communities stemming from an unfair and untenable division of caring labour (e.g., Doyal 1995). For many women, the load of unpaid caregiving work is expanding to the point of personal exhaustion and ill health, a situation that may actually result in keeping them from participating in politics or the workforce. There has been an increase in time spent on provisioning or consumption work (e.g., shopping) in industrial societies, wherein people are increasingly dependent on manufactured goods.[16] Women with low incomes (or who depend on welfare payments) who support families may need to devote even more time to provisioning work as help from public services diminishes (MacGregor 1997). With the rise of public campaigns for environmental awareness, those who manage households (the majority are still women) are expected to be more diligent in adopting time-consuming green practices like recycling and precycling. European feminist research has found that the work involved in living more sustainably in overdeveloped societies is being disproportionately performed by women (Littig 2001). (I discuss this point further in Chapter 5.) Aging populations in affluent countries, and the growing incidence of epidemics like HIV/AIDS in impoverished ones, mean that there are also more people who require care.

In this discussion must be included a critical analysis of the association of care and service work with women who are racialized, a situation that perpetuates a culture of white supremacy. In the context of globalization and neoliberal restructuring of the welfare state, the work of care is increasingly performed by foreign domestic workers hired by families that can afford to make their own child care arrangements rather than depend on the ever-decreasing supply of public services.[17] These women workers are not granted citizenship status and must abide by labour regulations that encroach on their private lives. They often cannot provide care for their own children, who may have been left behind in their countries of origin. Foreign domestic workers are increasingly commodified and are seen as a cheap "natural resource" for governments around the world; they have become a means of fostering private care arrangements in the affluent North (Ehrenreich and Hochschild 2002). They are also used as a means of acquiring foreign currency to help Southern debtor countries live up to the demands of structural adjustment policies imposed by the International Monetary Fund (Bakan and Stasiulus 1996). Among other things, this situation underscores the fact that "one woman's private sphere can become another woman's public" (Lister 1997, 123-24).[18]

Given the intensification of women's caring labour under present national and global economic conditions, it is unsatisfactory that so little ecofeminist research is aimed at showing the costs to women of maintaining a gender division of labour that ensures their growing burden of unpaid and under-valued work. How do women juggle their various caring roles, take on new kinds of caring responsibilities, and still manage to live fulfilling and meaning-ful lives? What are the ecological implications of this juggling act? I address these questions in Chapters 7 and 8, when I report the answers given by the thirty activist women I interviewed.

Ecofeminists have little to say about the role of public and collectivized services (or the welfare state) in the performance of socially necessary work. Perhaps the risks associated with care metaphors would be lessened if they were accompanied by arguments against the exploitation of unpaid caring labour as a privatized and feminized activity, and in favour of including meth-ods of fairly distributing necessary labour in any vision of a just and ecologi-cally sustainable society. It is interesting that several feminist political economists have applied the concept of "sustainability" to women's place in the capitalist economic system, arguing that women bear an *unsustainable* bur-den of responsibility for care work; for example, Nancy Folbre (1993, 254) asserts "the current organization of social reproduction is unfair, inefficient, and probably unsustainable." I would suggest that this line of argumentation vis-à-vis the gender division of labour is an important one – one that ought to accompany any discussion of women's environmental activism.

Motherhood, Feminism, and the Politicization of Gender Codes
A second significant limitation of ecofeminist "empowerment" stories is that they rarely consider, from a feminist perspective, the process through which women might move beyond the politics of survival to political resistance and transformation. Popular examples of grassroots women's narratives tend to give a very simplistic portrayal of women's empowerment as a process that rarely involves consciousness-raising or self-reflective political resistance to gender norms. It is entirely possible that the women who star in ecofeminist dramas are engaged in processes of political and personal transformation; how-ever, if they are, then this has not tended to be an important point in ecofeminist texts. It may be that in order to build a theory of "embodied materialism," the story needs to be that "women's political awareness is not merely reactive, but expresses qualities of personal synthesis, initiative, intuition and flexibility, *learned in caring labours*" (Salleh 1997, 175, emphasis mine). This does not sound like a process of political transformation to me but, rather, like an affir-mation of social expectations of what it means to be feminine or female, and a claim that political life is not a site for self-reflection.

My point may be illustrated by noting a distinction between Ariel Salleh's (1997) "ecofeminism as politics" and Lee Quinby's (1990, 1997) "ecofeminism as a politics of resistance": the former affirms the gendered status quo, while the latter opposes institutions of power at the same time as it persistently challenges its own assumptions. Should women not be encouraged to question the qualities, intuitions, and self-conceptions that they have learned in caring labours? Should they not learn new skills and knowledges in addition to drawing on the old? Should they not question the fact that they are expected to perform caring labour in the first place? Such questioning would involve a form of self-interrogation and socio-political analysis that has been central to feminism as a political movement and body of theory (Quinby 1997). But the place of consciousness-raising, the process whereby women look critically at their lives and question accepted norms, is necessarily diminished in ecofeminism if the assumption is that political and ecological awareness emerge intuitively (or "naturally") from women's social location. Why question a good and potentially planet-saving thing?

Related to this point, we should also ask why it is that some women believe there are few, if any, alternatives to appearing as mothers in political struggles, that their best chance to be heard and seen as legitimate in the public domain is "to play the mother card." Note that it is "Mothers against Drunk Driving" rather than "Citizens against Drunk Driving,"[19] "It's time for women to mother earth" rather than "It's time for citizens to take action to preserve our shared world." But of course we know the answer: motherhood is loaded with powerful cultural meanings that legitimate women's entry into politics in an apolitical and non-threatening way. "Motherhood issues" are not political issues. Everyone is expected to agree with them, or at least not publicly disagree with them (like "motherhood and apple pie," as the American saying goes). In drawing on these meanings, and perhaps on an unquestioned position of maternal authority, women may bypass politics. Lois Gibbs, a leader of the protests at Love Canal, has been quoted as saying, "We're insecure challenging the authority of trained experts, but we also have a title of authority, 'mother'" (quoted in Krauss 1997, 141). Thus we face a paradox. Seager (1993, 278) makes this important observation:

> For reasons both banal and deep, it "matters" what mothers say and do, and women can often bring attention to their cause if they speak as mothers. But a maternalism-based activism *that is not informed with a broader feminist analysis* can paint women into a corner – or, rather, keep women in the corner that society has cordoned off for them. It allows women to sneak onto the wings of the political stage without broadening the role for women in the script of the political play as a whole. It reinforces the notion that women's most useful and natural role is "bearing and caring," and that women's public activities are primarily appropriate only insofar as they remain rooted in this maternalism. (Emphasis mine)

Seager's characteristically feminist theoretical insight ought to inspire a critical interrogation of the difference between empowerment and politicization. While empowerment makes us think about the allocation and possession of power, politicization does something quite different. It brings us to the meaning of politics. Politics, as I understand it, is an end in itself, a performative activity that entails ongoing debate among equals in the public sphere. Following Hannah Arendt (1958), I believe that it is when people act politically and appear as citizens in public that they are allowed to express "who" they are, to realize their human distinctness. This public appearance, through speech and action, "does not cement the private self but disrupts it in the creation of something entirely new, something that cannot be grounded in or predicted by private life" (Sandilands 1999a, 160). As Mary Dietz (1985, 32-33) would say, then, the women in ecofeminist stories of grassroots activism may be empowered in some sense but they are not politicized if they do not act in the public domain as citizens rather than mothers: "Women who do not venture beyond the family or participate in practices beyond mothering cannot attain an adequate understanding of the way politics determines their own lives. Nor can they – as mothers or creatures of the family – help transform a politics that stands in conflict with maternal values. The only consciousness that can serve as a basis for this transformation ... is a distinctly political consciousness steeped in a commitment to democratic values, participatory citizenship, and egalitarianism."

If these women were to become politicized, then they would come to the realization that they are not only mothers "but [also] women who share a common political situation with other women, some of whom are mothers, some of whom are not. Accordingly the values that they must defend are not as much maternal ... [as] political" (e.g., freedom and equality) (Dietz 1985, 33-34). Moreover, in a patriarchal culture, acting as citizens rather than mothers or caregivers, women may be better able to "refuse who [they] are" than to "affirm who [they] are" (Foucault 1989, quoted in Ferguson 2000, 200). Ann Ferguson (2000, 200) links this argument to feminist consciousness-raising when she writes, "for women committed to reconstituting ourselves as feminists, this means that rather than first trying to revalue the feminine, we should resist the symbolic tyranny of the feminine over us by becoming 'gender traitors.'" In practice, this resistance may lead to demands for making debatable the kind of environmental and caring values upon which their activism is purported to stand. It may also give rise to demands for expanded notions of citizenship rather than acceptance of the role of overburdened voluntary public caregivers. It would certainly open up possibilities for public debate and challenges to traditional gender roles and responsibilities.[20]

Dietz (1985, 20) writes that "despite the best of sentiments, [maternalism] distorts the meaning of politics and political action by reinforcing a one-dimensional view of women as creatures of the family" – the very reason why women have been excluded from politics in history. Feminist political theorists have demonstrated that women's participation in the public domain is limited due to their responsibility for caring work and that this shows little sign of change in the last thirty years of feminist movement politics (e.g., Phillips 1993; Pateman 1992). Without problematizing women's voluntary, care-inspired engagement in environmental politics and arguing for the democratic renegotiation of the boundary between the public and the private spheres, ecofeminism will not contribute significantly to what historically has been one of the central goals of feminism. (How and why this point is ecologically significant becomes apparent in later chapters.) I suggest that, through the language of citizenship rather than through the language of care, a more useful ecofeminist conversation about women's ecopolitical engagements may occur.

The Promise of Citizenship

In *Finding Our Way: Rethinking Ecofeminist Politics*, Janet Biehl (1991) accuses American ecofeminists of rejecting the best aspects of traditional political theory – such as democracy, justice, and reason – and putting all their eggs in the basket of feminine virtue as the way out of the ecological crisis. She argues vigorously against using private life as a primary metaphor for ecofeminist politics, reasoning that "if women are to gain an understanding of their relationship with nonhuman nature that is liberatory, it certainly cannot be done by advancing a myth of the eternal feminine. Important as caring and nurturing undoubtedly are, humanity, it is to be hoped, has greater potentialities than caring and nurturing alone. What of such goals as consciousness, reason, and above all freedom?" (Biehl 1991, 25).

Taking issue with the desires of some ecofeminists to "extend the very concept of 'women's sphere' as home to embrace and absorb the community as a whole," Biehl (1991, 134) argues that ecofeminism has failed to offer a democratic vision of politics that can liberate women – and all people – from the more oppressive traditions of Western culture. She declares the need for a mutiny: self-respecting women active in the ecology movement should follow her lead and get off the rapidly sinking ecofeminist ship and swim towards a gruff but prophetic Murray Bookchin, awaiting them with open arms on the shores of universalist sanity. Biehl's analysis and portrayal of ecofeminist theory is, in my view, tainted by some unfair and unsubstantiated caricatures. But she makes important points about early ecofeminism's relationship to politics – points that contemporary ecofeminists ignore or dismiss at their peril. I think she was on to something that only a small handful of ecofeminists have since taken up: the importance of democratic politics and the language of citizenship (the liberatory traditions of Western thought) to the project of ecosocial change. Few ecofeminists, although there are important exceptions who have inspired my thinking,[21] have devoted sustained, critical attention to questions of democracy and citizenship, the role of the state, or the traditional feminist concept of consciousness-raising. It is unfortunate that these questions have been muted (or dismissed for being "liberal" and "Eurocentric") in a significant portion of ecofeminist scholarship, which tends to focus on survival, capitalism, and "women's wisdoms and skills" (Salleh 1996, 265-66).

In this final part of the chapter I argue that ecofeminist celebrations of care ethics, caring labour, and care as a form of civic virtue are problematic when considered alongside a feminist understanding of democratic politics and citizenship. In response to feminist political theories that rely on arguments for why the family and women's experience of mothering are superior models for politics, other feminist political theorists have asserted that maternal thinking does not necessarily promote the kind of democratic politics that feminism purports to foster (see, for example, Dietz 1985; Mouffe 1992b). There are too many dimensions of this argument to detail here; I carry on the discussion of feminist theories of citizenship in Chapter 5, in which I offer a critique of green politics and ecological citizenship. It is important to stress at this point that this is not a liberal feminist argument for embracing "masculinized" politics, as some critics may no doubt contend; rather, it is consistent with arguments of feminist political theorists aligned with radical democracy who ask feminists to be specifically political in a classical sense (e.g., Mouffe 1992b; Phillips 1993). These theorists argue that to embrace democracy and citizenship is to move feminism to a different terrain, one that is more general and potentially transformative for gender relations than the private sphere of the family. Even if ecofeminists have not shied away from politics, insofar as they have become preoccupied with what have been traditionally called private-sphere activities, identities, and feelings, a process of depoliticization (or apoliticization) is discernible. But this process is not irreversible: Sandilands (1999a) argues forcefully that ecofeminism has a democratic past and that there is the potential to reclaim democracy as a central theme in ecofeminist discourse today.

Two theorists whose arguments are useful in thinking about the relationships among and between citizenship, politics, and care are Mary Dietz and Joan Tronto. Dietz (1991, 250) argues that "feminism – at least in its academic guise – needs a calling back to politics." This comment signals her view that feminists have for too long been more concerned with making the claim that "the personal is political" (an argument that has helped catalyze and mobilize feminist struggles) than with understanding what politics means and how feminists could distinguish between private and political life. (Note that when Salleh sees "ecofeminism as politics" she does not find it necessary to define "politics": for her, it is a taken-for-granted concept.) And as Tronto argues, a myopic focus on the private sphere has contained feminism's political promise. She does not suggest that all references to care and motherhood should be expunged from feminist political theory but, rather, that care itself should be politicized: "care needs to be connected to a theory of justice and to be relentlessly democratic in its disposition" (Tronto 1993, 171). I suggest that this important insight is largely absent from a sizable proportion of ecofeminist engagements with politics.

As I have noted, Dietz is perhaps the most outspoken critic of those feminists who see a mothering or caring self as a model for a political subject. Starting from the position that politics is a very particular kind of activity, she echoes Hannah Arendt and other republican theorists in wanting to protect and preserve the public sphere as a space for debate on issues of collective concern. In contrast to the maternal feminist rejection of the public sphere as bereft of morality because of its separation from the private sphere and its creation by men, Dietz sees in the realm of politics a possibility of freedom, equity, and transformation. In the political sphere people claim common membership in a community where they can deliberate over concerns of others – others who are different from but equal to themselves – in order to reach a decision that seems fair and just (see also Phillips 1993).[22] Space is left open for dissent, and negotiations may be ongoing. For Aristotle, and the theorists who follow his approach, "the shorthand for this activity is citizenship" (Dietz 1985, 28).[23] Significantly, for feminists like Dietz the practices of democratic politics and citizenship offer the best way for feminism to embrace women's agency and diversity, to problematize the line between public and private spheres, and to politicize – as opposed to naturalizing – activities relegated to the private sphere (see also Lister 1997). Nancy Fraser (1997) affirms this position by noting the many examples of feminists making formerly private problems (e.g., domestic violence, sexual harassment, the gendered division of labour) into public concerns through sustained discursive contestation in the political arena.

Catriona Sandilands (1999a, 1999b, 2002) is perhaps the only ecofeminist theorist whose work engages an Arendtian understanding of politics. Important for her is the fact that Arendt sees politics as a *performing art* – not about creating a finished product but about the process itself. All people have the opportunity to perform on the political stage if they come to it in the role of "citizen," which, other than ensuring a rightful place in the conversation, is (or has the potential to be) empty of predetermined content. In other words, "citizen" is a common (i.e., universalizing) political identity that is more procedural and thus future-oriented than substantive and descriptive of existing norms. It creates a space for the expression and articulation of shifting and multiple identities. So in recommending that ecofeminism embrace "performative affinity" rather than strategic essentialism, I read Sandilands as agreeing with Dietz that the production of an open-ended and expressly political identity – like citizen – would be a better move for ecofeminism than the production of a narrow, pre-political and overdetermined identity like earthcarer or mother environmentalist. Remember that Sandilands' own desire to call ecofeminism back to radically democratic politics finds hope in replacing identity politics –

wherein a common identity of "woman," whether grounded in biology or experience or both is assumed – with a performative politics that subverts the very notion of a fixed political subject.[24] It is through political conversation among these partially and temporarily fixed and internally complex political subjects (i.e., citizens) that taken-for-granted assumptions may be challenged by means of open debate or acts of ironic parody. This proposal resonates strongly with Denise Riley's (1992, 187) anti-essentialist feminist defence of citizenship, in which she claims that, although there are risks in a notion of universal citizenship that masks real differences, "it also possesses the strength of its own idealism. Because of its claim to universality, such an ideal can form the basis for arguments for participation by everyone, as well as for entitlements and responsibilities for all ... Citizenship as a theory sets out a claim and an egalitarian promise."

And yet the work of caring in "the shadowy interior of the household" (Arendt 1958) still needs to be done (and living according to green values surely adds to the "to do" list). Avoidance of this fact has been a primary reason for feminist critiques of masculinist understandings of citizenship and a thorn in the side of feminist readers of Arendt. How do we value care at the same time that we resist its definition as a feminized and privatized pursuit? Whether to adopt an approach to political citizenship that downplays or emphasizes women's involvement in caring is a major debate among feminist theorists of citizenship (Lister 1997). Can we bring the inevitability of care into the realm of the political without affirming its gendered connotations?

In *Moral Boundaries: A Political Argument for an Ethic of Care* (1993) Joan Tronto's answer is to argue for the political significance of a *de-gendered* ethic of care. In addition to reminding feminists of the need to think differently about politics, which for Dietz entails broadening the focus beyond the realm of the particular, she asks feminists to think differently about care, to see it as a potent political concept. Following a persuasive critique of the feminization of care and the conflation of mothering and care, Tronto develops a position that interprets care more widely and places it in its full moral and political context: a political theory of care.[25] She does this because she believes that care should be seen as integral to any notion of a good society: a world "where the daily caring of people for each other is a valued premise of human existence" (Tronto 1993, x). It should not, therefore, be confined to the private sphere or, more important, to women (or mothers); rather, "the practice of care describes the qualities necessary for democratic citizens to live together well in a pluralistic society, and ... only in a just, pluralistic, democratic society can care flourish" (161-62; see also Bowden 1997). Viewing care as a political ideal in this way demands a reconsideration of the boundaries between private and public values and may contribute to an improvement in the way societies treat those who do the work of caring. Unlike the maternalists (e.g., Ruddick 1989), who say that everyone can and should *mother*, Tronto (1993, 167) argues that care can be practised by everyone and that care is a practice "that can inform the practices of democratic citizenship." In agreement with Nancy Fraser, Tronto argues that there ought to be more public deliberation over private needs and interests and that attentiveness to the needs of others ought to be part of the public values of a democratic society.

Deane Curtin (1991, 1999) has written about the politicization of care within the context of ecofeminist theory. His position is that ecofeminism ought to be expanded to include a "politicized ethic of caring for" (Curtin 1999, 142) that overcomes some of the dangers inherent in Gilligan-inspired care ethics. These dangers are that women's moral interests can be privatized, that women's capacity to care can be abused in societies where women are oppressed, and that caring can be too localized and parochial to have a political impact. Like Tronto, Curtin (1991) believes that only by politicizing care can members of a community address the question of how the work and responsibilities of caring are distributed, which is a question that goes to the heart of principles like justice and equity. He also sees this analysis as "part of a radical political agenda that allows for development of contexts in which caring for can be nonabusive," the goal being, ultimately, "to help undercut the public/private distinction" (Curtin 1999, 143). I have more to say about the politicization of care and its relevance to questions of ecological citizenship in Chapter 5.

So Tronto and Curtin wish to extend the notion of care beyond the private sphere as long as it is a politicized and de-gendered notion. To be sure, one can think of examples of caring practices that are public and political as well as some that are not strictly feminized even though they are still gendered.[26] Nevertheless, I tend to agree with those who see the care-politics connection as too closely and unavoidably associated with maternalism to be a good strategy for feminist politics. They see maternalist justifications of women's citizenship through arguments about care as fundamentally constraining of women's political agency and contrary to politics. Dietz (1985) argues, for example, that "maternal thinking" and the ethics of care are inappropriate as bases for political practice because they are inextricably linked to personal relationships rather than to the more abstract relations of citizenship.[27] Other critics warn that politics rooted in caring can easily become exclusionary and parochial, in that caregiving is extended only to particular, well-known others who are deemed worthy of care. Martha McMahon (1995), for example, notes that mothers may be more empathic and caring towards intimates, but the evidence suggests that this is not so with strangers. Kathleen B. Jones (1993) finds maternalism a "dangerous rhetoric" and so asks, "How far can we extend these moral categories, derived from intimate relations, into the arena of political discourse and public action?" (quoted in Squires 1999, 156). It may also be that the need to protect and care for a particular other (say, a child) can lead to actions that are harmful to generalized others. This possibility is extremely relevant to questions of ecological politics. For example, women earthcarers in one community could oppose a toxic waste incinerator out of fear for the health of their children and, at the same time, fail to "care" that their opposition might lead to its displacement onto another community (as tends to happen in NIMBY-type struggles).

While I like Tronto and Curtin's proposals for a politicized ethic of care, I think the scepticism of Dietz and Jones is well-founded, particularly in the case of ecofeminist discourse. Presenting significant obstacles to democratic conversation is the ecofeminist suggestion that women's caring work and life-sustaining values are so much better than the current ideologies, they ought to be taken from their particular locales and transformed into universal principles. This exaggerates differences between women and men and obfuscates differences among women. Casting maternal thinking as superior to other forms of thinking is incompatible with democracy because it eradicates the principle of equality upon which democracy rests: If the correct answer is known, then why deliberate any further? This problem is evident in ecofeminism when Mies (in Mies and Shiva 1993, 303) asserts that "a subsistence perspective is the only guarantee of the survival of all." I ask, Can she be certain that there are no others? Or that there can be a guarantee at all? Looking at similar claims by ecofeminists of the 1980s, Biehl (1991) wonders whether this desire to assert a universal "right answer" might represent a quasi-authoritarian tone in ecofeminism. Green political theorists with a passion for democracy have emphasized the importance of avoiding authoritarian approaches to solving the ecological crisis (e.g., Saward 1996; Dobson 1995; Torgerson 1999). I am in agreement with John Barry (1999, 218), who writes that "any ... notion of one 'true path' [to sustainability] is both dangerous and potentially undemocratic since it can function as a way to close debate and discussion." However, the kind of authoritarianism that Biehl and Barry oppose is not unheard of within the environmental movement at large. As David Harvey (1999, 128) correctly points out, there is a tendency to "hide behind respect for something deemed 'natural' and therefore 'authentic' in relations to the land ... [to] invoke notions of national identity, regionalism, authenticity and socio-ecological purity as badges of a certain kind of privilege." This assessment can be made of certain ecofeminist arguments as well.

Also undemocratic is the desire to foreclose debate by identifying a truth about the roots of women's political consciousness. In the interest of open debate and diversity in forms of counter-hegemonic political engagement, we should be suspicious when Salleh (1997, 170) claims that "the common denominator of women's struggles for survival in North and South is their holding work[28] and consciousness of enduring time." It is interesting that some ecofeminists want to privilege women's experiential knowledge as a solution to the ecological crisis without arguing for a public space wherein women as citizens can raise and demand deliberation on its merits. I argue that they contradict the meaning of politics by offering up a position without inviting open debate. Feminist politics (including, some would say, early ecofeminist politics) has made a point of asserting the need for greater inclusivity and a constant process of negotiation on a range of social and political questions. It remains something of a mystery what some contemporary ecofeminists see as the process through which their proposed solution to environmental problems might gain acceptance beyond those who seem to take it as self-evident. They say little about the role of public discourse. What makes my position categorically different from that of Shiva, Mies, Bennholdt-Thomsen, Salleh, and others is not only the fact that I am not willing to agree with them that the "subsistence perspective" should be privileged as *the* answer to all ecological problems but also the fact that I strenuously defend a need to open public space for its democratic consideration. In order to do this, I consider the development of feminist ecological citizenship – as an ongoing project – to be crucial.

In sum, I argue that, despite some of its strengths, a maternalist position has serious problems for ecofeminist discourse and political action. While ecofeminists contribute something important by revaluing the activities and ethics of caring for the environment and showing their relevance to ecopolitics, when they hold up care as a feminine ethic as something human beings should actively engage in, they give themselves little choice but to uncritically accept women's practices of care. They fail to consider the political potential of care as a moral orientation or how care as a set of practices might be organized socially. Ecofeminists who choose to highlight examples of women's earthcare as a moral orientation rooted in a set of practices are perpetuating some serious problems; for example, fostering the constructed identity of women-as-mothers/carers and supporting the idea that the "civic virtue" of women activists might be enough to bring about necessary ecopolitical change. Without a critique of the gendered division of labour and a call for the destabilization of care as a feminized and privatized activity, ecofeminists reaffirm a set of gender (and race and class) relations that have created and maintained women's oppression for centuries. Moreover, by reducing women's moral-political consciousness to material conditions and experiences, ecofeminists affirm the stereotype that women's most powerful or meaningful experiences are those connected to caregiving. The absence of a notion of consciousness-raising suggests an acceptance of women's knowledge as is, with no self-criticism or reflexivity needed. Such a stance accepts "what" women are, under current and entirely problematic conditions, while closing off a discussion of "who" women might become as citizens in a radically democratic, non-sexist, and ecological society.

Significantly, like strategic essentialism, the strategy of "uncritical reversal" (Plumwood 1993) is likely to backfire. In the realm of the political, appearing as mothers means all women are seen as mothers (or potential mothers) and so ecofeminism becomes synonymous with a set of concerns that are easily trivialized as apolitical "motherhood issues." Clearly, an awareness of how susceptible ecofeminist arguments are to being co-opted to support conservative aims should lead us to consider more carefully the implications of maternalist rhetoric. As I discuss further in Chapter 5, we should be concerned not only about the internal problems of ecofeminism but also about how ecofeminist rhetoric is likely to be perceived and received in the male-dominated context of environmental and left-wing politics. What are the implications of naturalizing women's caring within a green political agenda that envisions an expanded role for generic individuals as active citizens and as responsible stewards of the earth's scarce resources both at home and in the public domain? Few ecofeminists have considered the potentially negative consequences of maternalist politics for individual women in light of a thorough analysis of the larger context in which their discourse is likely to be read and heard. If they had, then perhaps more effort would have been given to finding a rhetorical strategy that makes effective arguments about ecological ethico-politics without essentializing women or feminizing care.

5 The Problems and Possibilities of Ecological Citizenship

Public life, obviously, was possible only after the much
more urgent needs were taken care of.

– *Hannah Arendt*, The Portable Hannah Arendt

While ecofeminists tend to avoid or dismiss citizenship as irretrievably patriarchal, many feminist political theorists have embraced it as an ideal that allows for the analysis of women's membership in political communities. Citizenship is also regarded as a promising strategy for challenging gender inequality while imagining a postessentialist form of solidarity among women. Yet feminists often leave gaping holes where ecological issues are concerned. Ecopolitical theorists, on the other hand, those theorists who make explicit links between nature and politics and question traditional presuppositions about human-nature relationships, are becoming intensely interested in what environmental or, less commonly, ecological citizenship[1] might entail in a reconceptualized green democracy. Few, however, have incorporated an analysis of gender into their visions. This omission is problematic because, to quote Greta Gaard (1998, 229), "insofar as democracy is concerned with relationships, with equality and power, feminism is a requisite component of any truly democratic theory."

Recognizing that there has been a lack of dialogue between them, the purpose of this chapter is to stage an encounter between feminist and green political theories of democracy and citizenship with a view to drawing lessons for an ecofeminist vision of politics. It is my position that there are good reasons for connecting ecofeminism and green citizenship discourse, not the least of which is that each stands to learn important lessons from the other. Following a brief overview of the relationship between ecofeminism and green political thought, I define and then deconstruct selected versions of green citizenship to reveal some of the problematic underlying assumptions. I provide a critique of some of the key elements of green citizenship discourse from a feminist perspective, appealing to insights from feminist political theories of citizenship and themes discussed in the preceding chapters. Far from proposing a simple rejection of masculinist ecopolitics and its defective conceptions of citizenship, however, I argue for the value of bringing together the best insights of an ecopolitics that reinvigorates citizenship, but that is largely blind to gender relations, with the best insights of an ecofeminist politics that is hypersensitive to the role of women in life-sustaining and caring work but that has little use for the concept of citizenship.

Ecofeminists and Green Men: Background to an (Imagined) Encounter
I begin by reflecting briefly on the relationship between ecofeminism and green political thought because this helps set up the critical analysis to follow. It is fair to say that ecofeminist ideas are rarely included in non-feminist discussions of ecopolitics, although some have made cameo appearances (e.g., in Dobson 1995; Barry 1999; Dickens 1996; Dean 2001). Most recent publications tend to ignore or treat very lightly ecofeminist contributions to green theory, relegating them to a discrete subsection or endnote, rarely integrating them into the thrust of the analysis. Although there are many ecofeminist theorists, whose work addresses key issues of environmental politics, the best known and most cited ecofeminists are, arguably, Vandana Shiva and Ariel Salleh. To the extent that ecofeminist ideas are taken up by green political theorists, they are often criticized or dismissed on unfair grounds, often due to the reduction of the complex whole of ecofeminist arguments to their most flamboyantly essentialist parts. In an early edition of *Capitalism, Nature, Socialism,* for example, ecosocialists Daniel Faber and James O'Connor (1989, 177) criticize ecofeminism on the grounds that it privileges body over mind, intuition over science and technology, and puts forth "organic theories emphasizing emotional ties to the community ('caring')." Although in his introduction to ecological thought Tim Hayward (1994) finds some value in socialist feminist analyses of relationships between production and reproduction, he mentions ecofeminism only as a theory that celebrates the primacy of reproduction in highly essentializing (and thus for him problematic) ways. Many ecopolitical theorists tend to reduce ecofeminism to a preoccupation with spirituality. Douglas Torgerson (1999, 27) is clearly not alone in thinking that ecofeminists in general believe that "change is to proceed from the level of spirit."[2] Interestingly, he identifies a concern with grassroots activism as one of two main tendencies in ecofeminism, the other being a "cultural tendency" associated with a feminist spiritual imagery (31).

Ecofeminists have not remained silent about this treatment at the hands of green political theorists, nor have they hesitated to comment on the fact that ecopolitics has been woefully gender blind. Most ecofeminist writers have observed that mainstream environmentalism displays sexist tendencies and overlooks specificities of gender. Of course, feminism has always had a contentious relationship with radical and left politics, often stemming from the failure of male-dominated perspectives and social movements to acknowledge feminist concerns (Segal 1987).[3] And just as radical feminism emerged out of the sexism and unequal gender relations within civil rights and student movement groups in the 1960s, one impetus for the birth of ecofeminist perspectives in the early 1970s was sexism within the green movement (recall the arguments of Françoise d'Eaubonne noted in Chapter 2). Joni Seager (1993) develops a thorough critique of what she calls "the greening of men's politics" in both the "ecology establishment" (mainstream environmental organizations like the Sierra Club where white men hold the top positions) and "the eco-fringe" (radical and direct action groups like Earth First! that make no effort to hide their "deep machismo"). A useful analysis of sexism in European green movements is found in Mary Mellor's *Breaking the Boundaries* (1992), in which she argues that, for much of their evolution, greens lacked a vision that integrated ecological sustainability and social equality, preferring to focus on capitalism and/or industrialism as the enemy. She also notes the problematic association of women with the so-called "population problem" that has led some environmentalists – especially deep ecologists – to come dangerously close to repudiating the principle of reproductive freedom. Similar findings are reported by Gaard (1998), who, after investigating gender relations in the US Green Party, contends that it lacks an understanding of feminism.

It may be fair to problematize, and to politicize, mainstream ecopolitical thought by looking at some of the key theorists who have made important marks on the developing field and considering how their visions and theories answer the question of how "we" should live. That they are predominantly white male academics and activists and living in advanced capitalist societies are not irrelevant facts in this discussion (hence my use of "green men" as a playful euphemism). Those who fit the citizen mould nicely are probably less well acquainted with the complexities of being and acting as a citizen than those who do not. However, given that I have questioned those ecofeminists who have relied on such observations to dismiss the theorizing of other ecofeminist scholars, I will not suggest that the analysis stop here, at the level of blaming patriarchy or academic men. Nor do I think the common response of ecofeminists – to compensate for the lack of gender analysis by celebrating women's ostensibly unique capacity for earthcare – is a very strategic one. I surmise that it is precisely this tendency to privilege caring and other values associated with the private sphere that has allowed ecofeminism to be relegated to the margins of green political theory.[4] Meeting an underemphasis on gendered locations with a response that overemphasizes gender specificities and ways of knowing seems a wrong move. Instead, I propose engaging in an open exchange between mainstream green political ideas about democracy and ecofeminist and feminist ideas about gender so that the respective strengths and weaknesses, and points of agreement and divergence, of each position may be considered.

For both sides there is much to gain from this kind of dialogue: new questions, new themes to explore within a different kind of conceptual framework, and constructive criticism of one's own approach. As it stands, while many ecofeminist scholars have documented the sexism of specific green men, and the gender blindness of many green campaigns and organizations, only a small number have critically investigated the implications of the new green discourses of democracy and citizenship to consider of what use they may be to ecofeminist projects. Perhaps this failure has occurred because few ecofeminists (save for a handful of notable exceptions, upon whom I draw in the second half of this chapter) have established their own self-consciously theoretical approach to politics. Engaging in dialogue with green political theorists may inspire movement in this direction. Moreover, it may lead to a different take on the central preoccupation of *Beyond Mothering Earth:* the place of care and motherhood in ecofeminist narratives. What does it mean to build an ecofeminist vision on gender-coded concepts like motherhood and care within the context of a social movement that envisions a sustainable society without acknowledging gender specificity or the need, ultimately, to equalize gender relations? What impact, if any, might this have on women as citizens, activists, and caregivers?

Sustainability, Democracy, and the Greening of Citizenship

There is a growing preoccupation in green political thought with the normative and practical implications of environmental sustainability. Some green political theorists disparage the concept of sustainability because, at best, it is an empty slogan that can be adapted to fit any cause (e.g., Worster 1995) and, at worst, it is a prescriptive "greenprint" that shuts down political debate. Within the current of literature in which I am interested, however, sustainability is an inherently political concept best defined provisionally through democratic public discourse. Because sustainability is a contestable concept, and because moving towards a "sustainable society" (or a less unsustainable one) will require such dramatic and sweeping changes in individual human behaviour and collective/institutional social practices, many ecopolitical theorists argue that it is necessary to involve people democratically in the process not only in order to promote justice and to create good policies but also to ensure the consent and ongoing active participation of all concerned (Gundersen 1995). As a consequence of these insights, a common theme among green political theorists is "a renewed democratic politics, an ecological democracy" (Dryzek 1997, 200). In studying this literature, I think a central question, following Drucila Cornell (1997), is: *What kind of subject would one have to be to fully participate as a member of an ecological and democratic society?* And what are the qualities, values, and commitments of such a subject?

Much of the green literature on citizenship stands firm on the point that the only political arrangement that will work in conditions of radical uncertainty – such as "the ecological crisis" – is a democratic one in which the voices of as many citizens as possible participate in public debate. This point may be seen as part of a renewed interest in civic republican meanings of citizenship and civil society among contemporary left thinkers, inspired by a conjuncture of (among other factors): economic globalization, the perceived weakening of the nation-state, the increase of international migration and transnational ecological destruction, and a need to reconstruct the left itself (Lister 1997; Van Gunsteren 1998; Clarke 1996).[5] Most ecopolitical scholars are critical of liberal democracy and the administrative state, seeing them as part of the root causes of the ecological crisis. They are dissatisfied with the disempowerment of citizens through representative government and the reduction of citizen participation to periodic voting (Torgerson 1999). They are also concerned about the apparent replacement of "the citizen" with the more self-interested "consumer" and "taxpayer" as the dominant political identities embraced by individual members of globalizing capitalist societies. These individualist approaches, which are encouraged by the new right, are part of a culture that supports unsustainable material accumulation rather than conservation, instant personal gratification rather than prudential social planning, and competition rather than cooperation. Alongside their enthusiasm for participatory models of democracy, then, many green political thinkers argue for a notion of citizenship that includes rights to a clean environment and, more important, a set of responsibilities: to protect the interests of future generations and nonhumans by actively participating in democratic political debate about sustainability and to engage in environmentally sound practices in daily life (e.g., Christoff 1996; Barry 1999; Newby 1996; Light 2002; Dobson 2003).

Green discourse on citizenship is still in its infancy. Although it has become a popular theme in environmental politics, it is thus far a relatively undertheorized and underdefined concept (Dean 2001). There are many different normative models of green democracy, ranging from direct democracy to representative liberal democracy and global democracy, but there are only a few explicit explications of what citizenship ought to be or become within a green democratic system. In the interests of brevity, the next section is limited to a discussion of authors who have directly addressed the concept of citizenship in their writings on ecological politics and/or democracy. I give an interpretation of three slightly different, but in some ways similar, kinds of discussion of environmental citizenship as part of the project of green political change towards something like a "sustainable society." All subscribe to some degree of civic republicanism (stressing political participation) and/or communitarianism (stressing moral responsibility to the common good) but differ in their emphases as well as on issues of scale (local, national, global, etc.). The first discussion is eco-communalist in its approach in that it emphasizes direct democracy in local communities combined with a notion of active, competent citizenship. The second calls for active and morally responsible citizens acting as *ecological stewards* and prefers to retain and transform the nation state as the institutional locus of decision making through the establishment of deliberative processes. The third discussion demonstrates a preference for cosmopolitan (or postcosmopolitan) values in a global civil society and the development of a conception of *earth citizen*. Although there are many similarities between the approaches and much compatibility between the individual arguments described herein, for the sake of clarity, I focus on the subtle differences.

Eco-Communalism: Citizenship in the Green Polis

A popular theme in the literature of sustainability is the quest for "sustainable communities": ways of living that encompass not only alternative economic relations but also particular social and political arrangements that would create more harmonious relations among human populations and between human beings and their natural environments. Andrew Dobson (1995) suggests that radical green approaches, in particular, tend to be drawn towards the anarchism end of the political spectrum, rejecting all forms of authoritarian control and embracing principles of face-to-face democracy, self-management, and egalitarianism. He identifies two commonalities: many radical ecologists are suspicious of the nation-state and many believe that socio-political arrangements should be guided by "environmental realities." Some scholars argue that these arrangements should be modelled after ecosystems like watersheds (e.g., Sale 1985). Within this tradition are the longest-standing approaches to green citizenship, which favour political decentralization and direct face-to-face democracy at the local or community level. David Pepper (1993) has called this approach, which includes bioregionalism and social ecology, "eco-communalism."

The best representation of the eco-communalist approach is found in the work of American social ecologist Murray Bookchin. His philosophy of social ecology is based on an analysis of the role of human hierarchy in the exploitation of the natural environment. It is premised on the belief that hierarchy among human beings predates, and was a precondition for, human domination and control of nature (see, for example, Bookchin 1989). Therefore, his view of a more sustainable (or ecological, as he calls it) society involves eradicating hierarchy and restoring egalitarian, cooperative communities. Bookchin advocates "human scale," self-sustaining, non-hierarchical eco-communities as the best and most ecological form of human society.[6] They are the best because, he says, they resemble "balanced, rationally guided ecosystems" and allow inhabitants to interact with their earthly surroundings and human and non-human neighbours in a meaningful way (Bookchin 1980, 99-110).

Bookchin (1982, 336) has written extensively on his vision of the ecological society, which entails the *re-empowerment* of people through "participation, involvement, and a sense of citizenship that stresses activity, not on the delegation of power and spectatorial politics" (see also Bookchin 1980, 1989, 1992). Libertarian municipalism is the proposed political operationalization of the vision, replacing the state with a confederation of autonomous municipalities and elected representatives who are responsible for the direct implementation of citizen decisions. This vision amounts to what he sees as a new political culture in which "words like 'politics' and 'citizenship' would be redefined by the rich meanings they acquired in the past and enlarged for the present" (Bookchin 1992, 61). In his writings on libertarian municipalism Bookchin refers often to the Greek notion of "polis" and displays a preference for classical democracy. He writes, for example, that:

> the municipality is the most immediate political arena of the individual, the world that is literally a doorstep beyond the privacy of the family and the intimacy of personal friendships. In that primary political arena ... the individual can be transformed from a mere person into an active citizen, from a private being into a public being. Given this crucial arena that literally renders the citizen a functional being who can participate directly in the future of society, we are dealing with a level of human interaction that is more basic (apart from the family itself) than any level that is expressed in representative forms of governance ... [It is] thus the most authentic arena of public life. (Bookchin 1992, 66)

Consistent with the Hellenic philosophical tradition, Bookchin (1982, 339) views citizenship as "the most important social role that the individual can take." He therefore advocates a diffusion of political power into the hands/ hearts of individual citizens in a *direct democracy* in which all citizens are free to participate in public debate, meaning they have an unimpaired opportunity to participate and can do so by choice. No one should be forced to participate, nor should issues be dumbed down for them, as this would degrade the very meaning of democracy. In addition, Bookchin believes that *autarkeia*, meaning "individual self-sufficiency graced by an all-roundedness of selfhood," should form the foundation of democracy (131). This point is used to justify why no state or bureaucracy is needed to represent the interests of the masses (although he does concede to the need for administration); citizens as free and autonomous individuals are competent (by nature) to decide collectively the direction of public affairs: "All mature individuals can be expected to manage social affairs directly – just as we expect them to manage their private affairs" (336). More recently, Bookchin's colleague Janet Biehl (1998) has argued that the virtues of citizenship are perhaps no longer inherent in human nature, particularly in a world that denies and erodes so much of what makes us human. As a response she has used another ancient Greek concept – *paideia* – to emphasize the process of cultivating the practices and ethical knowledge necessary for good citizenship. For her, following Bookchin, the arena for this type of education is the political realm itself.

Another expression of an eco-communalist approach to citizenship is provided by Deane Curtin (1999, 190), who, in outlining his ethic of "critical ecocommunitarianism," writes: "the best guarantee we have of preserving the wilderness of nature is through cultivating an informed and humble [local] citizenry that is genuinely committed to preservation." Arguing that the ecological crisis is "a crisis of citizenship," he sets out an approach to environmental ethics that roots moral knowledge in community and calls for people to "become native" to a place. Although his book *Chinnagounder's Challenge: A Question of Ecological Citizenship* gestures towards rather than spells out his conception of citizenship (a conception that seems to be more ethical than political), Curtin shares Bookchin's and other eco-communalists' belief that "true democracy" begins at the level of community. Here "community" is used in the spatial sense of a shared commons that can be fostered by individuals with "the right sort of character." Following bioregionalist Wendell Berry (1977), Curtin maintains that character should be cultivated in relation to place. By way of a brief explanation of how he conceives of citizenship, Curtin (1999, 179) states: "Care for and understanding of nature must come to function as an internal good, constitutive of what it means to be a citizen."

Green Citizenship as the Practice of Ecological Stewardship

A second category of literature on environmental citizenship shares a commitment to participatory democratic ideals, yet differs from the one just described in that it does not privilege communalist or localist solutions to ecological problems. This approach emphasizes instead the cultivation of the individual virtues of green citizenship (e.g., stewardship) and the establishment of deliberative democratic processes that can occur in all kinds of political spaces.[7] Irish political theorist John Barry and Peter Christoff may be discussed in this category, although they also appear to fit the third category because they each express interest in the global scale of both ecological problems and politics. I place them together here because a significant part of their visions of ecological democracy concerns the adoption of green virtue ethics or ecological consciousness by individual citizens.

A text that is representative of this stewardship approach is John Barry's *Rethinking Green Politics* (1999). In a chapter on green citizenship Barry seeks to develop an alternative conceptualization of green political theory that is more theoretical and less ideological than most others and more in keeping with what he believes are key green principles and values. Barry starts from a critique of what he calls "utopian ecopolitical visions," such as those advanced by social ecologists and bioregionalists.[8] For example, in his view, Bookchin is naive in thinking that people will emerge as naturally cooperative and earth-regarding if they are freed from the shackles of state and bureaucratic domination. Arguing that such "ideological accounts of 'ecologism' focus on describing the 'sustainable society' to the neglect, for example, of working out the implications of the principle of sustainability," Barry (1999, 5) suggests that "collective ecological management" based on a stewardship ethic is a better way to proceed. His vision is unapologetically founded on weakly anthropocentric (i.e., human-centred) ethics and involves transforming rather than abolishing representative democracy and the liberal democratic state.

In contrast to Bookchin, Barry thinks that representative rather than direct democracy is more suited to green concerns because it will allow for the representation of the previously excluded interests of non-citizens. He is not convinced that human beings will always do the right thing where nature is concerned: "there is no *a priori* disposition in favour of 'preservation' as opposed to 'development'" (Barry 1999, 224). Therefore, he believes that regulations, laws, normative principles, and procedural standards are needed to ensure that people take the interests of non-citizens (including non-humans and future generations) into account in environmental decision making. His support for institutional and structural change is supplemented by a belief in the need for cultural change: societies need to alter the way people think and what they prefer so that they may become responsible partners with the state in collective ecological management. Thus, *not more democracy but better democracy is needed,* and this, in large part, depends on better (i.e., more informed and virtuous) citizens.

Barry sees sustainability as a normative ethico-political principle that should guide deliberation and decision making in a green democracy. His understanding of ecological citizenship within such a political system is that it is the ethical core of collective ecological management – a core that extends beyond conventional understandings of rights and responsibilities and the necessary link to the nation-state. For him, the concept of green citizenship includes obligations that stretch beyond the boundaries of a community (spatially defined) and into the hitherto non-political – that is, private – realm. This is one of the ways in which ecological concerns fundamentally alter the traditional notion of citizenship as being specific to public life. Barry (1999, 231) explains:

> Citizenship, as viewed by green democratic theory, emphasizes the duty of citizens to take responsibility for their actions and choices – the obligation to "do one's bit" in the collective enterprise of achieving sustainability. There is thus a notion of "civic virtue" at the heart of this green conception of citizenship. A part of this notion of civic

virtue refers to consideration of the interests of others and an openness to debate and deliberation. This implies that the duties of being
a citizen go beyond the formal political realm, including, for example,
such activities as recycling waste, ecologically aware consumption and
energy conservation.

Significantly, Barry's ecological citizenship transcends public and private spheres
by being founded on a moral notion of "stewardship" that is to be embraced
by individuals. Barry sees green citizenship as at base a practice of ecological
stewardship, and so green citizens are, by his definition, active political agents
who have a sense of ethical responsibility for the well-being of the planet.
They approach the environment with a respectful "ethic of use," neither treating it self-interestedly nor treating human and ecosystem interests as one (as
an ecocentric position suggests). The stewardship position, which has roots in
and takes inspiration from small-scale family farming, "holds that care for the
environment cannot be independent of human interests" (1999, 7). As in
good farming, the ideal is a symbiotic social-environmental relationship in
which human needs are met through sustainable consumption and production over the long-term without unjustifiable exploitation of land and animals. Recognizing the fact of their dependence on nature, green citizens qua
ecological stewards are able to balance and sometimes sacrifice their own particular interests with the common and ecologically sustainable good.

How are the ethics of ecological stewardship to be fostered among citizens if
they are not so inclined "by nature" or by lived experience? The farming way
of life is no longer attractive or even available to the majority of people in
modern Western societies, as Barry admits. And appealing to individual interests will not be sufficient to inspire green behaviour or to justify environmental policy decisions. So, not unlike Biehl (1998), Barry asserts that citizenship
is itself a form of social learning: by participating in democratic forms of communication and action, citizens gain access to the opinions, interests, and
forms of knowledge held by others, and this learning better prepares them for
participation in debates about the "ethics of use" and the common good. Green
citizenship is thus a practice and a mode of acting and thinking (as opposed to
being strictly a political role or status) "within which ecologically beneficial
virtues such as self-reliance and self-restraint can be learnt and practised" (Barry
1999, 228). But participation and deliberative democracy will not be enough
and should not be seen as solutions to the environmental crisis. So, in keeping
with his provisional acceptance of the state, and his civic republican views,
Barry thinks that the virtues of green citizenship also need to be fostered
through the public education system and other government policies, such as
compulsory service in environmental projects (see also Barry 2006).

Peter Christoff (1996) also doubts that direct democracy and forms of face-
to-face community decision making are well suited to addressing issues of

international scale and transnational constituency, such as environmental destruction. He believes that decentralized direct democracy is a nice but unrealistic ideal within the current context of globalization. In addition to such processes taking too much time and being prone to inefficiency (as negotiations at global environmental summits have shown), the level of information required by participants to make good political judgments is too great due to the complexity of environmental problems. So instead he favours the development of global ecological citizenship through political action by the green movement to "pressure for more universalistic, inclusive constitutional guarantees of citizens' rights and for definitions of ecological responsibility which tie local and international levels together through the conduit of the nation-state's apparatus" (161). For Christoff, this development also depends on the "active transformation of private life through the creation of a 'green conscience'" (162) as well as on the revitalization of civil society. He notes that the green movement has by and large been successful in creating a public sphere wherein demands for environmental welfare have "increasingly [been] seen as an extension of existing civil, political and social rights" (160). However, the idea of a postnational ecological citizenship is, in his estimation, still more metaphorical than practical. In order to move in that direction, institutional foundations and structures must be built that enshrine ecological values in law, at the level of the nation-state and perhaps supranationally. He therefore advocates the development of an "ecologically guided democracy": a form of government that is ecological because it is driven by principles of sustainability and environmental rights and that is strongly democratic (in Barber's [1984] sense) because it legally and constitutionally guarantees the "rights, powers, and resources" for citizen participation in a range of deliberative processes (164).

Christoff (1996) adopts an approach to ecological citizenship that is compatible with Barry's in that it combines an emphasis on transforming the nation-state along with green values and a desire to instill in individual citizens a sense of moral responsibility for environmental sustainability. He uses the term ecological "trustee" rather than "steward" to describe his ecopolitical vision of citizenship, but the emphasis is very similar. Electing not to delve into liberal notions of rights, he asserts: "To become ecological rather than narrowly anthropocentric citizens, existing humans must assume responsibility for future humans and other species, and 'represent' their rights and potential choices according to the duties of environmental stewardship" (159).[9] Christoff's is "a notion of citizenship based on the praxis of individuals seeking to promote environmental concerns through their political engagements on the basis of 'ecological loyalties'" (ibid.). He goes on to advocate the "moral priority given to 'self-restraint'" and the "sense of active responsibility for representation and protection of environmental rights" in green political theory (162), stating that he accepts the importance of creating a "self-limiting culture of moderation and responsibility, producing individuals and corporate actors whose environmental awareness would morally and materially confine their actions to those producing ecologically sustainable outcomes" (166).

Earth Citizens in Global Civil Society

Several well-publicized environmental disasters have demonstrated that the "ecological crisis" is a transnational, or global, crisis (Yearley 1996).[10] At the same time, with the intensification of economic and cultural globalization, the ability of nation-states (much less local communities) to deal with ecological problems is called into question. Increasingly, there is interest in the idea of supranational forms of governance in civil society, as opposed (and sometimes in addition) to government by nation-states, as a way to adequately address the kinds of transboundary problems with which no local community or nation-state is equipped to cope on its own. Elmar Altvater (1999, 303) asserts, "Ecological sustainability needs participation, and globalization can be regulated only through the establishment of 'global governance.'"

The Earth Summits in Rio de Janeiro (1992), Kyoto (1997), and Johannesburg (2002) are examples of supranational forums that show that environmentalists are now *acting* globally in addition to *thinking* globally. Some green theorists have gone so far as to propose the establishment of a global environmental organization created within the UN (with powers similar to the World Trade Organization) and an international environmental court (Lipietz 1992; Postiglione 1994; Low and Gleeson 1998). Most, however, favour the empowerment of global citizens in social movements to the centralization of power on a global scale as the best avenue for pursuing a just and sustainable global society (e.g., Attfield 1999).[11] Richard Falk (1997) has famously called this "globalization from below." For a small number of green political theorists this kind of talk has inspired an interest in the concept of the earth citizen. John Urry (2000) names ecological citizenship first among his list of "new citizenships" that have become relevant to academic discussions in a rapidly globalizing context (also included are cosmopolitan citizenship, cultural citizenship, minority citizenship, and mobility citizenship).

This third approach to green citizenship takes a pragmatic stance towards the realities of globalization and a cosmopolitan stance towards environmental ethics and human rights. In an article entitled "The Cosmopolitan Manifesto," for example, German sociologist Ulrich Beck (1998) discusses the idea of world or global citizenship in a postnational world order: citizens with a cosmopolitan consciousness in a global, democratic civil society. Cosmopolitanism is a universalist ethical stance that stands in opposition to communitarianism (whose proponents believe that values are rooted in particular communal practices). It draws on the ancient political notion of world community, or *cosmopolis* (literally "city of the universe"), which can be traced back to fourth-century BC Greece and even earlier Eastern civilizations (Lister 1997).

It has become especially popular among western European social and eco-political theorists who have been responding to globalization and conditions of postmodernity, in part, as a response to concerns about the harmful impacts of traditionalism and fundamentalism in local communities. Because local communities may not consider the ethical needs of their neighbours, and because not all people are members of communities, cosmopolitans argue for universal moral responsibility, which moves people beyond their own particular interests and towards a more universalist notion of the common good. Environmental philosopher Robin Attfield (1999, 31) explains: "a sense of responsibility need not be confined to particular communities and their members, or to particular environments, much as local loyalties and a sense of place can nourish and renew a person's sense of responsibility. Besides, an increasing number of people, particularly those who trade or travel internationally or belong to international bodies (such as churches), are aware of being 'members of the global human community,' with its shared problems and possibilities."

Regarding this cosmopolitan approach, Bart van Steenbergen (1994) identifies two forms of global environmental citizenship: the "environmental manager" and the "earth citizen." The first is characterized as a managerial type who believes that the ecological crisis can be solved by implementing the right technical innovation and specialized policies within the existing socioeconomic system. He cites the approach taken in *Our Common Future* (World Commission on Environment 1987) as an example of global ecological management. Van Steenbergen is largely dismissive of this form of environmental citizenship because it sustains the status quo and fits too neatly with another kind of global (managerial) citizen: the global capitalist. The second type of global citizenship, which Van Steenbergen (1994, 151) claims is the *real* global ecological citizenship, is distinguished from environmental management by holding that "earth citizens" care for their environments (as opposed to wanting to control them) and extend equal rights to all living creatures, not just humans. He writes:

> Ecological citizenship emphasizes the importance of the planet as a breeding ground, as habitat and as life-world. In that sense we can call this type of citizen an *earth citizen,* aware of his or her organic process of birth and growth out of the earth as a living organism. The development of citizenship from the city via the nation-state and the region to the globe is here not just a matter of increase in scale. With the notion of the "earth citizen" a full circle is made. The citizen is back to his or her roots: the earth as Gaia, as one's habitat. (150)

Van Steenbergen goes on to argue, in effect, that earth citizens have a set of rights (e.g., to good air quality) and responsibilities (e.g., not to consume CFCs) that complement those stemming from the civil, political, and social citizenship of the Marshallian model (described below). Consistent with a cosmopolitan approach, he spends more time listing the moral responsibilities of the earth citizen than listing his or her rights.

John Urry (1998, 10) argues that environmental citizenship ought to be seen through the prism of "risks, rights, and duties." He explains that, because globalization has destabilized national societies – in modernity hitherto the locus of citizenship – through the emergence of "new global risks" (spread of diseases, cultural homogenization, financial crises, and so on), there is a need to define global rights and duties. These global rights and duties have particular connections to environmentalism: for example, "[the right] to be able to inhabit environments which are relatively free of risks to health and safety produced by both local and distant causes" and "[the duty] to engage in forms of behaviour with regard to culture, the environment and politics which are consistent with the various official and lay conceptions of sustainability which often contradict each other" (12-13). It is important to note similarities with the stewardship approach in that earth citizens not only bear rights but also a significant burden of personal responsibility for sustainability. In an early discussion of the topic, Fred Steward (such a fitting name) gives the following definition of the global citizen – or "citizenship of planet earth," as he calls it – which highlights the linkage of rights and obligations:

> Global citizenship expresses the right to a common human inheritance regardless of nation – the rainforests and coral reefs, as well as the earth's planetary resources of atmosphere, ocean, genetics. The concept also embodies an economic right to choice in terms of material consumption and lifestyle which should not simply be either constrained by poverty or facilitated by wealth. The concomitant obligations of citizenship [involves] an acceptance of the growing need for international and global regulation of industry and the environment, which itself entails a necessary foregoing of some elements of local and national sovereignty. *Individual citizens also owe a duty of care to the planet in terms of minimizing resource consumption and pollution.* (Steward 1991, 74-75, emphasis mine)

Finding this talk of "common humanity" inappropriate in the face of global inequalities and asymmetries, Dobson (2003) makes a case for a postcosmopolitan notion of ecological citizenship (I discuss some of the pitfalls of green cosmopolitanism in MacGregor [2004]). While in agreement with some aspects of cosmopolitan citizenship (namely, its non-territoriality and focus on virtue), he proposes an approach to ecological citizenship that rejects idealist, pre-political notions of world community and instead conceives of citizens acting in a community (or "ecological space")[12] that is "produced by the metabolistic and material relations of individual people with their environment" (106). The obligations of the ecological citizen are asymmetrical and non-reciprocal: the globalizers (i.e., those who occupy more than their fair share of ecological space) have a greater duty to care than the globalized (i.e., those whose labour and land have been and will be exploited). According to Dobson, "Only those who occupy ecological space in such a way as to compromise or foreclose the ability of others in present and future generations to pursue options important to them owe obligations of ecological citizenship" (120). For him, being a good ecological citizen entails taking responsibility both for one's causal role in environmental injustice and for ensuring a more just distribution of ecological space.

Significantly, Dobson draws on feminist theorists of citizenship to make the case for a blurring of the traditional boundaries between public and private, so that private acts (like recycling) count as acts of ecological citizenship. And he suggests that so-called "feminine virtues" (e.g., care and compassion) ought to inform a postcosmopolitan approach in addition to the traditional liberal ones (e.g., justice, autonomy, and courage). He devotes considerable space in his book *Citizenship and the Environment* to considering how (the admittedly debated) feminist ethics of care and qualities associated with women's roles as carers and mothers might inform his version of ecological citizenship (see also Dean 2001).[13] To my knowledge Dobson and Dean are unique among green thinkers in bringing these feminist debates about the ethics of care to the discussion of environmental citizenship. However, their treatment of care lacks a critical assessment of the kinds of cultural, social, and economic changes that will be needed if it is to be politicized, de-feminized, and de-privatized. Arguably, this criticism can be made of how "care" appears in the discourse of green citizenship more generally.

Although care and citizenship are conventionally regarded in political theory as opposites – one is private, intimate, and particular, the other public and impartial – it is interesting that, like many feminists, some green political thinkers are disrupting this dichotomy, albeit for different reasons and in different ways. We see it clearly in Curtin's (1999) eco-communitarianism as well as in various writings on green citizenship from both stewardship and cosmopolitan perspectives. It is often invoked as a concept relevant to both sustainability and citizenship; however, perhaps not surprisingly, it is often taken at face value and rarely problematized to the degree necessary from a feminist perspective. For example, Van Steenbergen (1994) names care as a fundamental value of the earth citizen, using it simply as the opposite of control. Attfield's (1999, 58) view is that humanity's role is "to conserve and care for [nature] as a trust," but he does not elaborate on what caring for nature might mean. Stewardship and trusteeship are commonly held up as metaphors for a "caring" human-nature relationship. Barry (1996, 118-19) argues, for instance, that sustainability is best seen as a coordinating social value, a political-ethical principle that "embodies a particular moral attitude to the future, expressing *how much we care for and are willing to make sacrifices for* our descendants and how, and to what degree, non-humans figure in this process" (emphasis mine). The language of "responsible stewardship" and "caring for nature" is particularly popular in public relations campaigns for corporate environmental citizenship. In each of these examples, caring is taken to be an unqualified good, a feeling that can easily be applied to human interactions with nature.

It is noteworthy that, unlike ecofeminist earthcare rhetoric, which is intimately connected to women's emotional, mothering, and provisioning work, some green theorists' treatment of stewardship as care for the land tends to borrow from stereotypically masculine (in the West at least) pursuits, such as religious study (the tradition of stewardship has long been central to the teachings of Judaism, Christianity, and Islam)[14] and yeoman agriculture (farming is an important exemplar for Barry, as explained above). While there are some arguments for feeling ethically responsible for the well-being of the ever-nebulous "future generations," there are very few examples of where a duty to care for the planet takes any instruction from the feelings of care exchanged by particular human subjects, such as parent and child. It is instructive to note that, unlike mothers, fathers are never given a privileged place in ecopolitical discussions. It does not seem relevant to include fathers in studies of environmental activism or attitudes. In their empirical study of "sustainability as a new public discourse" in the United Kingdom, for example, Macnaghten and Urry (1998) convened focus groups of mothers (along with other categories, such as unemployed men, Asian women, and working women) but did not have a focus group of fathers. No explanation is given for why they made this decision.

Although it is clear from this discussion that there is considerable overlap between green political theorists' treatment of citizenship as moral responsibility to "do one's bit" for the environment (in both public and private life) and ecofeminist approaches to the ethics of earthcare, I could find relatively few examples in which feminism or ecofeminism plays more than a minor role in the green literature on citizenship.[15] In all but a few cases the only time feminism or ecofeminism is mentioned is in relation to care ethics, giving the impression that this is the only contribution these rich bodies of theory might make to the conversation. Nor could I find any hints of reflexivity about whether (eco)feminists might object to or concur with the visions of citizenship or sustainable societies presented. So, then, how might feminists respond to the various arguments and assumptions in the discourse of ecological citizenship that I have just presented?

A Feminist Critique of Ecological Citizenship
Chantal Mouffe (1992a, 225) writes that "the way we define citizenship is intimately linked to the kind of society and political community we want."

While ecofeminist visions include notions of the good ecological society modelled on women's knowledges and practices of life-sustaining work, few ecofeminist scholars have engaged in explicit discussions of the socio-political arrangements that would promote sustainable societies, much less of citizenship. For many ecofeminists, the role of women in ecological struggles is an expression of women's gender-specific experience rather than of citizenship as a politically constructed identity. As I explain in Chapter 3, this raises questions about the kind of society ecofeminist theorists envision and about how, ultimately, it will be any better for women than the ones in which they now live. Green political theorists who take up the question of citizenship, on the other hand, generally work from a definition of citizenship that speaks volumes about their commitment to radical democracy at the same time as it reveals their assumptions about the organization of socially necessary work. They assume a gender neutral citizen and a gender neutral model of citizenship practice that masks the realities of gender (and other forms of) inequality while depending upon a division of labour that frees autonomous citizens to participate in the public domain.

Feminist theorists of citizenship have made it clear that citizenship is an important concept for feminism as a political project while simultaneously calling for a persistent critique of the masculinist biases and patriarchal dualisms that have undercut and shaped the concept for centuries. This immanent critique is central to the formulation of a feminist redefinition of citizenship that contributes to women's "liberation" and political agency (Lister 1997). Drawing on the work of feminist political theorists of citizenship, as well as a few ecofeminist theorists (namely, Plumwood 1995a, 1995b; Sandilands 1999a, 1999b), I develop in this section a critical assessment of some of the key areas of agreement and disagreement between feminist and green democratic approaches to citizenship. Although there are many interesting threads to pull out of the rich weave of green political approaches to citizenship, I focus on four themes that are particularly relevant to a feminist perspective on the gendered politics of care.

Sustainable Communities for Whom?

The first theme concerns the treatment of the concept of "community" in discourses of green citizenship. Like the greens discussed above, there are ecofeminists and many feminist theorists who place localism and direct democracy at the centre of their visions. Elizabeth Frazer and Nicola Lacey (1993) observe that widespread feminist attraction to community can be explained on a number of grounds, one of which is that the "community," or local neighbourhood, is the level of society at which feminists have had the greatest impact through their political activism (see also Lister 1997). Ecofeminists, as I have noted, are particularly interested in the experiences of so-called "grassroots women" who are engaged in struggles to improve or protect their local communities and environments. Imagining utopian communities wherein human beings live in a respectful relationship to nature has been an important theme in ecofeminist scholarship (e.g., Starhawk 1993). And ecofeminist ethics have much in common with communitarian and/or relational approaches to "self-in-community," especially in their critique of the disembodied subject, liberal individualism, and instrumental rationality (Cuomo 1998). In spite of this affinity, however, there are good reasons to be critical of the ways in which community is invoked in green citizenship discourse.

One reason is that the universalizing and homogenizing discourse of community and "the common good" in green political thought is implicitly patriarchal and often obfuscates unequal and oppressive power relations. Community, as a site for ecological citizenship, tends to be held up as the ultimate end without those doing so questioning its internal workings or the processes by which it is created and maintained (Sturgeon 1997; Gruen 1997; Donner 1997). There is well-established doubt among feminist scholars about the potential of small-scale, self-sufficient communities to be sexually egalitarian.[16] It is also unclear in communalist writings how cultural diversity would be fostered and protected in their ideal societies (it often seems that they are to be racially and linguistically homogenous and geographically specific), how traditions might be open to renegotiation by newcomers and minority groups, or how different proficiencies and capacities for political communication and participation among citizens would be accommodated (see Bickford 1996). It is for such reasons that many feminist political theorists are leery of the concept of "community" in communalist approaches (Frazer and Lacey 1993; Young 1990).

An uncritical celebration of community is also a weakness in social ecology and bioregionalism. Mary Mellor (1992) observes that Bookchin is more concerned with the balance of power among local communities than with the balance of power or work within them. In contemporary societies small rural communities can be extremely repressive or coercive places for women and other marginalized people (e.g., lesbians and gay men, people of colour, people living with disabilities) (Ackelsberg 1988). Patricia Allen and Carolyn Sachs (1993, 149) criticize green communalists for taking a rosy view of rural life when they hold up the stewardship practices of the family farm as a model of sustainable living: "The fact that family farms are based on historically inequitable relations between men and women is often not problematized." The anti-urban sentiment and romanticization of rural life on the part of bioregionalist writings is at odds with feminist assertions that urban life, with its accessible services and safety and anonymity in numbers, may be better for some women.

Feminist scholars have also noted that political philosophies rooted in romantic conceptions of community can be politically conservative (Frazer and Lacey 1993; Frazer 1999). Very often, communalist approaches incorporate an implicit lament for the loss of community as a cause of social problems while expressing disenchantment with modern life because it is increasingly fragmented and alienating. With their critiques of (post)modern and (post)industrial societies as anti-nature, it is fair to say that eco-communalists are no exception. Green communalist ideas such as Bookchin's (1992) tend to romanticize past notions of community, which were allegedly more nature-loving than today's notions. But this romanticization occurs without enough consideration of the fact that "traditional" (i.e., pre-industrial, colonial, etc.) communities were profoundly patriarchal and repressive for women and other non-elite groups. Mellor (1992) makes a similar criticism when she questions assumptions about the benign social and ecological nature of clan societies, noting that social ecologists and eco-anarchists have a partial and androcentric understanding of this history. Similarly, Margrit Eichler (1995, 19) asks that we not forget that "past times were certainly not good times for women" when envisioning sustainable societies. It is important for feminists to insist that invocations of community resist the regressive tendency to celebrate the past and, instead, consider new ways of understanding the concept of community – ways that stand against exclusivity and oppression.

Notions of citizenship that are founded on community can be both inclusionary and exclusionary, pointing to the Janus-faced nature of both concepts (i.e., citizenship and community). Eco-communitarians who call for a place-based ethic and conception of ecological citizenship are guilty of over-emphasizing the importance of place while underemphasizing the frequent diversity and conflict among inhabitants of places (especially true of Curtin 1999). While arguing for a human-nature connection grounded in place provides a welcome alternative to one grounded in "a linear, essentialized narrative self" (Code 2000, 73), their approach runs the risk of excluding many people from the status of ecological citizenship. Curtin (1999), for example, suggests that citizens establish their "character," or their identity as ecological citizens, in relation to the natural places where they live. Here it is important to note, as cosmopolitans have done, that in a globalizing capitalist economy not all people live in places long enough, or have the kind of lives that allow them, to establish a sense of (local) place. Some may live in places or "communities" that are not of their own choosing and in which they are denied membership status. To them, citizenship may have negative connotations as it can draw attention to their exclusion from the community (Lister 1997). This may be particularly true of women employed as domestic workers, who move from place to place to care for other people's homes and children. Are they to be left out of discussions of ecological citizenship? Or might there be reason to argue for a set of values and a notion of citizenship that are not tied to a specific place? Lister (1997) is one feminist theorist of citizenship who advocates a global conception of citizenship because it has the potential to be inclusive of a diverse range of experiences (e.g., those of refugees, guest workers, homeless people, and people whose lives are intimately connected to current forces of capitalist globalization, imperialism, and ecological change). Relatedly, she argues for a pluralist conception of community that is open to different inter- pretations and recognizes that there are many different sites for politics.

While few ecofeminists speak the language of citizenship, if asked many would likely point to the distinctive contributions women make in nurturing and protecting (i.e., caring for) communities as evidence of and/or justifica- tion for their status as ecological citizens. Recognizing the ways in which "com- munity" appears in ecopolitical discourse, I think this move should be avoided. Although I would not ignore women's community activism, a narrow approach that highlights only this aspect of women's political participation is a con- servative one: it serves to support rather than challenge the existing gendered division of labour in communities. Given my discussion of the gendered poli- tics of care (e.g., the shift to community care) in Chapter 4, I think it is fair to conclude that this approach is inconsistent with a specifically feminist politi- cal agenda; rather, what is needed is a stance that constantly interrogates power dynamics within and between communities and questions relationships be- tween individual autonomy and "community" as a political space or ideal. If women are to question their subordinate place in communities and the gender codes that sustain it, then a notion of citizenship that responds to conditions outside "everyday life" and community cultures is an important element of a transformative political movement. There is ample evidence to support the view that women's activism exists in and engages with a plurality of political and discursive spaces beyond community.

A Problematic Paradox: Doing More (Duty) with Less (Time)

Second, there is a problematic paradox in ecological citizenship discourse that, in my view, stems from the twin emphasis on lifestyle changes in the private sphere that promote both greater self-reliance and eco-friendliness and greater participation in the green public sphere.[17] Good environmental citizens are called upon to recycle, reuse, reduce, self-provide, and make green ethical consumer choices on the home front (i.e., buy things that are organic, non- genetically modified, cruelty free, locally made, fairly traded, minimally pack- aged, recyclable, and so on) while making a commitment to get involved in their community and with collective decision making in an increasing number of political spaces. Proponents of environmental citizenship assume that peo- ple will accept the inevitable increases in time and effort created by green lifestyle practices and will still have time for citizenly pursuits.[18] This reveals a lack of consideration for the politics of the private sphere, for the fact that these injunctions will result in an intensification of the activities that are al- ready divided unequally between men and women.

Green citizenship discourse privileges active participation as central to greening the public sphere for a variety of reasons. Bookchin (1992) believes that equality will automatically be enhanced if people can just participate more and differently. Barry (1999) celebrates various examples of deliberative democracy wherein well-informed and virtuous citizens play an active role in collective ecological management. In an ecological society, "with greater free time and a reduced need for constant employment, there would indeed be greater opportunity for enhanced discussion in a green public sphere," predicts Douglas Torgerson (1999, 153). As explained above, there are many green political theorists who model their visions of environmental democracy and citizenship after the Greek polis. It is curious that few green admirers of classical democracy point out the problematic premise upon which that system was established. It seems painfully predictable for me to note that, in Athens, citizens were freed for politics by the labour of foreigners, slaves, and women, who were not granted the status of citizen. (Salleh [1996, 271] seems to suggest that this history is a good enough reason to dismiss democratic citizenship as "really fraternal emancipation ... only ever gained at the cost of women tacitly absorbed in social provisioning"). Citizenship, understood as being about active participation in the public sphere, is by definition a practice that depends on "free time"; it is thus not designed for people with multiple roles and heavy loads of responsibility for productive and reproductive work. As feminist political theorists Carole Pateman (1988) and Anne Phillips (1991, 1993) have argued, modern theories of politics fail to take into account the sexual division of labour that not only sustains democracy but also makes it extremely difficult for women (and others with time scarcity) to participate as equal members of a political community. In fact, it is likely that "the more active the democratic engagement, the more likely it is to be carried by only a few" (Phillips 1993, 112). Viewing time as a resource for citizenship is integral to any feminist political theory that seeks to problematize the unfair division of labour that has constrained women from full participation as political citizens (Lister 1997).

Also central to feminist reconceptions of citizenship is an acknowledgment that, as embodied human beings, all citizens are inevitably dependent on others for care and nurturance, including, for ecofeminists, non-human others and the natural world. In her extensive critique of liberal democracy, ecofeminist philosopher Val Plumwood (1995b) argues that the liberal democratic conceptions of the self (and, by extension, the citizen) are flawed because, in embracing independence and self-determination, they are at odds with the kinds of dependency relationships necessary for ecological flourishing: relationships of kinship, mutuality, empathy, and care. (Note that these qualities are very different from the autonomy, self-determination, and rationality that traditionally have defined citizenship.) What she does not consider, however, is the extent to which post- and anti-liberal green visions differ from liberal ones in their assumptions about the self-reliance of individuals. On my reading, although many green theorists offer progressive revisions of democracy, when it comes to images of the self-reliant citizen they have one foot firmly planted on masculinist ground. Inspired in part by civic republicanism, the image of ecological citizens as simultaneously self-reliant and active is highly problematic from a feminist perspective.

One indication that the interdependency of human beings has been elided in green political theory is the fact that discussion of the private, domestic sphere is either non-existent or seriously skewed. As feminist ecological economists have pointed out, rarely do green theorists regard domestic provisioning work as productive and necessary to the functioning and sustainability of the economic system or society as a whole (e.g., Pietila 1997; Nelson 1997; Jochimsen and Knobloch 1997; McMahon 1997). Important for the present discussion is that the nature of household or family relationships is not considered relevant to democratic public debate, even though changing the practices and behaviour of individual citizens in the private sphere is becoming an important part of many visions of an ecological society. Moreover, when ecological citizenship is said to include a sense of personal responsibility for actions in the private sphere, the private sphere seems to be either synonymous with (unsustainable) consumption or a place in which people procreate (too much). Only in rare cases is it considered to be a space of productive and reproductive work, as feminists have been arguing since the 1970s. And in all cases self-discipline and self-reliance are ecological virtues.

Viewed through a feminist lens, the ability to ignore or dismiss the importance of the domestic sphere is part of a masculinist denial of dependency and bodily fragility that has roots in Western philosophical traditions. Feminist political theorist Nira Yuval-Davis (1997) argues that it is precisely this neglect of the private sphere that calls for its explicit inclusion in any discussion of citizenship. Green political theorists have recognized human dependency on natural processes and the fragile state of humankind in the face of ecological crisis (see Barry 2002). Most, however, neglect to acknowledge human dependency on the caring services performed by human beings and thus have failed to value the role played by domestic life in the search for ecological sustainability. Few, even among those who have recognized human interdependence at some level, have taken this a step further to look at its implications for human labour, at how necessary labour is distributed or at who is ultimately responsible for getting it done.

It may be that, left to their own devices, groups of people will find socially equitable ways to distribute necessary work among themselves. Marx seemed to think this would be so when he predicted that (to paraphrase) in the ideal communist society a person would be free to be a fisher in the morning, a farmer in the afternoon, and a social critic in the evening. This claim left feminist Mary O'Brien (1981) wondering, "Who will be minding the kids?" Bookchin the eco-anarchist is not much different from Marx the communist in his vision of the ideal ecological society. His libertarian municipalities are to be self-reliant and self-managing (how so, we never really learn) while decisions are to be made through a continuous and intensive process of face-to-face democracy in town hall meetings. This preference for time-consuming democratic processes and the assumption of unfettered ability to participate actively in the affairs of the polis flies in the face of feminist analyses of the unequal gendered division of necessary labour. As Phillips (1993, 111) writes: "We might ... expect male politicos to warm to a politics of continuous meetings and discussion and debate, all of them held conveniently outside the home and away from the noise of the children. But most women have been so grounded by responsibilities for children and parents and husbands and houses that they could well have settled for the less arduous democracy of casting the occasional vote."

Few green political theorists have addressed the question of how necessary labour – which is bound to be intensified if people are self-reliant and eco-efficient – will be distributed in a sustainable society. It has been well established that women do more unpaid household labour than men. Cross-national empirical research has found that women do significantly more environmentally oriented work in the household (e.g., recycling, precycling) than men (Hunter, Hatch, and Johnson 2004). Yet few green theorists call, as feminists have done, for the democratization of the household, which would allow for a more equitable distribution of this necessary work (e.g., Rowbotham 1986; Phillips 1991; Lister 1997; Plumwood 1995a). In fact, the question of how green practices in the private sphere are to be initiated, distributed, and sustained is seldom, if ever, asked. Barry (1999), for example, insists that the practice of ecological citizenship should transcend public and private but he makes no mention of the implications for women, racialized and working-class people, older people, or disabled people who live at the interstices of both spheres. Dobson (2003) also declares the private realm to be a site of citizenship because "all green actions in the home have a public impact" but does not consider the public or private impacts of an unjust distribution of these actions.[19] Green citizenship theorists may well take for granted that responsibility will be shared (and some probably would advocate this), but by failing to address this issue explicitly, they perpetuate the traditional view that it is not an appropriate matter for discussion in theories of politics.

At the same time, nearly all green theorists are silent about, unless they are critical of, establishing formal collective mechanisms for meeting social needs. Within green political theory there is both nostalgia for the self-reliant and self-managing community and ambivalence about the merits of a rights-granting nation-state. There is an apparent hostility towards the welfare state. Torgerson (1999, 8), for example, is typical of radical democrats when he blames liberal democratic welfare state policies for "bolster[ing] consumer demand and promot[ing] mass acquiescence" without mentioning that they also have provided the conditions (i.e., time) for many women and other marginalized groups to participate more fully in most aspects of society.[20] This oversight is consistent with a tradition in green theory of preferring mutual aid and individual responsibility for well-being over the administration of welfare by the state or market. I argue not only that this does not necessarily have to be an either-or choice but also that the green preference for self- and community reliance has not had the benefit of critical gender analysis. For example, when green political ecologist Alain Lipietz (1995) envisions an "end of work" scenario, in which people's work weeks are reduced to afford more time for leisurely pursuits and community and environmental service, he fails to recognize that "work" includes more than paid employment. Nor, rather tellingly, is there a discussion of the gendered distribution of leisure time: studies indicate that men use their time off to engage in personal hobbies and pleasures while women tend to use theirs to catch up on the housework. Bittman and Wajcman's (2000, 181-82) study of the quality of leisure time enjoyed by Australian men and women finds that men have more uninterrupted leisure time, whereas the majority of women's leisure time is "contaminated by combination with unpaid work." These gender differences in work and leisure time have been of crucial significance to feminist economists (e.g., Waring 1988; Folbre 1993) as well as feminist sociologists and theorists of citizenship (e.g., Schor 1997; Pateman 1992).

Although there are feminist critiques of the liberal welfare state for being paternalistic, racist, heterosexist, and alienating, it is also well established that the ability of some women to participate in the workforce and in public life has been facilitated by state provision of necessary services like health care and child care (Lister 1997). The model of social democracy in northwestern European (especially Scandinavian) countries is held up by many feminists as more "woman-friendly" than those systems that assume private responsibility for socially necessary work (Folbre 1993; Siim 1988).[21] Despite the weaknesses of welfare state approaches, many feminist theorists of citizenship have recognized the need for some socialization of socially necessary-yet-feminized work in order to offer women a promise of a better quality of life and a capacity to claim their place as equal citizens (e.g., Bowden 1997). Arguing for some forms of collectivization of necessary work may also be an alternative to accepting the various private solutions to privileged women's "time poverty," which sees them purchasing the labour of other women (who tend to be marginalized economically, politically, and socially) to supplement their own (see Ehrenreich and Hochschild 2002). While I have not seen the case made, I think it is worth investigating the extent to which collectivized approaches to necessary labour are less resource and waste intensive and therefore more ecologically viable than privatized approaches (see Littig 2001, Chapter 4, for a discussion of the ecological benefits of the collective use of things such as cars and domestic appliances).

I am not arguing against all private provisioning of care or other forms of socially necessary work. Nor am I suggesting that the establishment of organic, vegetarian, communal neighbourhood feeding centres offers a path to social and ecological sustainability. I accept that there may be an irreducibly private dimension to the production and reproduction of human life, such that collectivization and state-run service delivery can only ever be part of the answer to the provision of a society's needs. What I do want to stress, however, is that whenever and wherever the private or domestic sphere is implicated in strategies for social or ecological change, consideration must be given to the unequal and deeply gendered division of labour and responsibility, costs, and benefits. Taking for granted that duties will be shared and the necessary work will get done is tantamount to making "more work for mother" (Cowan 1983). Therefore, I suggest that, at the very least, public debate over who does what and under what conditions ought to be built into the very definition of ecological citizenship.

How is a woman to be a good ecological citizen when she has a heavy burden of caring labour with little help from intimates, neighbours, or the welfare state? This question is explored further in Chapter 7, where I report on my conversations with thirty women who are intimately acquainted with the answer. At this point, I argue that an ecofeminist perspective that aims to be transformative and disruptive of gender codes should insist that there are problems with a conception of citizenship that rests on a combination of active participation in the public sphere and greater responsibility for living green at home. How, ecofeminists must ask the green men, can one be an active green citizen and self-reliant and eco-friendly all at the same time? Who has time for all of this on top of the other demands of modern life, like jobs, child rearing, eldercare, household maintenance, food provision, and sleep? One recent study provides empirical evidence that their disproportionate load of caring responsibilities and environmentally friendly household practices are significant constraints on women's participation in public environmental activism (Tindall, Davies, and Maubouès 2003). Ecofeminists ought to respond carefully to these obvious contradictions. Surely celebrating women's capacity to care is an insufficient response that fails to challenge the gendered division of labour at the same time as it lets ecopolitical theorists off the hook with regard to addressing the deep contradictions and sexist assumptions in their visions of green citizenship.

A Dangerous Dovetail: Emphasizing Responsibilities over Rights
A third theme of interest to a feminist interrogation of green citizenship discourse is the disproportionate emphasis that is placed on individual "responsibility," "obligation," or "duty." A significant proportion of the literature on ecological citizenship tends to focus on citizens' moral duty to participate in

the kinds of activities that will help societies move towards sustainability (e.g., Smith 1998; Attfield 1999; Van Steenbergen 1994). As Dobson (2003) explains, the turn towards a Kantian-inspired cosmopolitan view that all citizens qua human beings have moral obligations to the human community has shaped recent conceptions of environmental citizenship (and its close relative global citizenship). While there is some discussion of the need for new environmental rights (e.g., to clean air and water, to participate in environmental decision making), green cosmopolitanism places greater emphasis on individual duty to care for nature, to engage in behaviour that allows life on the planet to flourish (e.g., Attfield 1999). Bart van Steenbergen (1994) notes that environmental citizenship is all about our obligations to the human community and to the natural world (see also Steward 1991). It is the acceptance of this responsibility by individuals that matters, along with the implementation of the kinds of behaviour that this acceptance demands. Moreover, many seem to argue that curbing liberal humanist rights and expanding ecological responsibilities are desirable goals. For example, Peter Christoff (1996, 159) writes: "To become ecological rather than narrowly anthropocentric citizens, existing humans must assume responsibility for future humans and other species, and 'represent' their rights and potential choices according to the duties of environmental stewardship."

It is important to examine the fact that some green political theorists place more emphasis on ethics (concerning rights and responsibility) than politics (concerning ongoing debate on such matters). For example, while sustainability is alleged to be an open-ended, ethico-political principle, the invocation of virtue ethics leads to prescriptive and moralistic language rather than constant debate and deliberation over its meaning. When citizenship is defined in terms of moral responsibility to the "common good," there is insufficient attention to a non-instrumental meaning of citizenship as membership in a political community, wherein the point is debate and negotiation and where fixing a set of duties or principles would amount to the death of politics.[22] Saward (1993) questions any vision of green democracy that rests on a set of principles, arguing that it is too easy to slide into authoritarianism when paired with apocalyptic talk of the environmental crisis.[23]

Feminist political theorists such as Mouffe (1993) and Seyla Benhabib (1992) argue that, in order to avoid this possibility, there should be a basic framework of political values, or "grammar of political conduct," to provide the foundations for citizen engagement (see also Lister 1997). Mouffe contends that this approach is more consistent with democratic pluralism than the notion of "the common good," which is found in the civic republican and communitarian traditions. Moreover, as I have noted, feminist critiques of communitarian ethics tend to focus on the ease with which virtues can become conservative (Frazer and Lacey 1993). The question of who decides the moral values of a political community or who sets out the list of ethical principles for good citizens to follow is of great concern to those (e.g., feminists) with a critical analysis of social inequality. I have argued that notions of maternal virtue are dangerous for ecofeminists because they can become naturalized and reified, thereby closing off political debate. It is just as important to resist overly moralistic approaches to sustainability if ecological citizenship is to develop as an inclusive political project.

What concerns me even more is that the notion of green citizenship as duty dovetails unintentionally with dominant political agendas that employ "duties discourse" (Lister 1997) in order to facilitate their campaigns to reduce state involvement in the public provision of social services. Since the 1980s the equation of citizenship with responsibility has become an escape route for governments as they move to dismantle the welfare state. In neoliberal discourse, citizenship is increasingly becoming conditional on the performance of duties (especially the duty to work) and is becoming synonymous with voluntary involvement in the community. The call for a rebalancing of rights and duties in order to meet sustainability goals (an instrumental approach to citizenship) seems dangerously similar to the stance of the so-called "modernizing left," which sees citizenly service as a way to meet its economic restructuring goals. For example, the current emphasis on citizenship in the United Kingdom is seen by some analysts as part of a reassertion of the connection between entitlements and obligations in the New Labour platform (Faulks 1999). It is often noted that the Blair government has been influenced by the writings of Amitai Etzioni, who argues that the major problem facing Western democracies is that too many social rights have made people passive and dependent on the state to administer their needs. This situation might be corrected if a sense of citizen responsibility with regard to making communities work (with minimal help from government) could be restored and strengthened (Etzioni 1995; Putnam 2000). Prime Minister Blair is on record as saying, soon after his first electoral victory, that at the heart of Britain's problems is an "undeveloped citizenship" and that the preferred way to change this is to nurture a sense of community wherein "the rights we enjoy reflect the duties we owe" (quoted in Benyon and Edwards 1997, 335). In other words, "no rights without responsibilities" (Anthony Giddens, sociologist and New Labour advisor, quoted in Dobson 2003, 44).

Significantly, it seems that citizenship has become a solution to the problem: it is regarded as a way to both enlist public participation in the management of national affairs and to relieve the duty of government to provide goods and services to the population. Relevant to the case at hand, some governments have appealed to citizens' sense of ecological duty by asking people to reduce, reuse, and recycle (the three Rs); to conserve water and electricity; and to use public transit instead of private automobiles. There are many examples of the use of stewardship as a concept in environmental policy and governance circles, and it is often held up as a way to increase public participation in ecological restoration projects and to establish the community-based administration of local services (Roseland 1998). In Canada, for example, the federal government has developed guidelines for environmental citizenship in *Canada's Green Plan*, published in 1990. These guidelines are put forth with an explicit recognition that the government cannot achieve its sustainability goals without the participation of the population. In fact, it is claimed that "self-regulation is better than government regulation, and that voluntary action is the most effective way to achieve enduring results" (Government of Canada 1990, quoted in Darier 1996, 595).

As part of this strategy, supporters of the concept of environmental citizenship place the onus on individuals, whether as citizens or consumers, to become more educated about environmental issues, to make the necessary changes in their own outlook and behaviour, and to take nature into account in both their personal and their collective decision making. Education is seen as a key tool for building the kind of society that will be able to transform human-nature relationships, and education reform has been held up as an important part of this rebuilding project. As of 2002, British children have citizenship as a compulsory subject in the national curriculum, and, while this does not specifically include "education for environmental citizenship," some effort has been made to integrate values relevant to "sustainable development." In Canada the federal ministry of the environment has developed materials for teaching environmental citizenship to children in a "virtual classroom," and it defines environmental citizenship as "caring for the Earth and caring for Canada."[24]

I think the underlying premises of education for sustainability programs are problematic. They make the Socratic assumption that "citizens fail to act only out of ignorance" (Cruikshank 1999, 16) and suggest that it is uneducated and irresponsible individuals, rather than unsustainable and unjust social and economic relationships, who are the root cause of the environmental crisis. Although there is promise in efforts to promote cultural change in this way, education for environmental citizenship can also become a way of disciplining the population to internalize a set of rules for behaviour – to become self-governing – thereby justifying minimal state intervention. Éric Darier (1996, 595) offers a useful Foucauldian critique of the state-designed and promoted notion of environmental citizenship as expressed in *Canada's Green Plan*, which he calls environmental governmentality, or "environmentality" (see also Luke 1997):

> Environmental governmentality requires the use of social engineering techniques to get the attention of the population to focus on specific environmental issues and to instil – in a non-openly coercive manner

– new environmental conducts ... If coercion is not the principal policy instrument, the only real alternative is to make the population adopt a set of new environmental values that would be the foundation of new widespread environmental ways of behaving. These new environmental values will be promoted by the establishment of an "environmental citizenship."

Darier does not address the gender (or class or race) dimensions of this process, but he makes it clear that the control of information by corporations and the state make it difficult for all citizens to develop the oppositional consciousness that could lead to meaningful acts of resistance to state power. From a Foucauldian perspective, the fact that citizenship is so easily co-optable (or dovetail-able) into state agendas makes it an undesirable ideal for guiding social-political or ecological movement.

While heeding the Foucauldian warning that "everything is dangerous" in this business, I am attempting to develop the kind of (eco)feminist perspective that accepts citizenship as a valuable ideal and practice at the same time that it seeks to bring its various blind spots into focus. For instance, one can agree that nurturing citizen responsibility for sustainability is important, providing that it is not done at the expense of taking steps towards structural and systemic change. I agree with those critics of green duties discourse who argue that the "privatization" of responsibility tends to take the onus off the larger problems (like corporate pollution) created by the costs and by-products of capitalist production (e.g., Luke 1997). Plumwood (1995b, 143) is correct in noting that this privatization "locates the major source of responsibility in the wrong places." The focus is on the end (i.e., citizens/consumers) rather than the mouth (i.e., producers/sellers) of the pipe of the waste stream. For example, household bottle and can recycling is encouraged so that governments can meet UN environmental targets, while it is business-as-usual for the beverage industry. Timothy Luke (1997) has called this "the ruse of recycling." One cannot help but see green citizenship in this case as an effective way of "greenwashing" neoliberal resistance to green regulation.

So what is the gender analysis here? Granted there are ecofeminists who see hope in women's greater sense of responsibility and their ability to instill green values in the next generation. Women will make endless trips to the bottle bank because they care, and want their kids to care, about the future of the planet. As I discuss above, however, I am interested in how appeals to citizens to be more ecologically responsible take on a gendered dimension, especially in domestic life. This point is very much related to an analysis of how women are socialized, or disciplined, to perform work that benefits others – "concrete" (i.e., those they know and love) as well as "generalized" (i.e., strangers and future generations) (Benhabib 1992). As feminist moral philosopher

Claudia Card (1989) notes, due to having been socialized within a patriarchal culture, women have a tendency to take on a greater burden of moral responsibility than men.

There may very well be a feminization of environmental duty taking place that only a few feminist theorists have acknowledged (Littig 2001). Sociologist Harriet Rosenberg (1995, 197) highlights the ways in which mothers can become targets of corporate and governmental campaigns to download environmental responsibility: "the individual mother is exhorted to accept personal responsibility for a crisis that she is said to be able to ameliorate through private practices within her household." Insofar as women are household consumers, they also become the intended audience for morally based prescriptions for greening the household (Sandilands 1993). Advertisers too know to whom they should target their ostensibly green products (e.g., unbleached cotton diapers, non-toxic and biodegradable cleaning supplies, organic and non-genetically modified food). Here the focus on individual choice confuses the meanings of citizen and consumer. Either way, when the future of their children (and of course their children's children) is used as the reason for being ecologically responsible, women are apt to feel guilty; their compulsory feminine altruism is thereby exploited for the common (and increasingly corporate) good.[25]

What happens when citizenship becomes all about individual responsibility, as though all citizens have an equal ability to accept it? For some, this raises questions of justice and the conditions under which citizenship may be meaningfully practised. And so we must return to the central issue of how and by whom socially necessary life-sustaining work is provided. Since T.H. Marshall's (1950) famous essay "Citizenship and Social Class," it has been held by many political theorists that the ability to perform one's duty as a citizen often depends on a set of enabling conditions (cf. Yuval-Davis 1997). Marshall recognizes that people need a minimum level of social and economic security (and the right to live the life of a civilized being according to the standards prevailing in the society) in order to participate equally in society, so he adds social citizenship to his two other dimensions of citizenship: the civil and the political.[26]

A focus on duty obscures this understanding of citizenship, which is important to feminist aims for gender justice, where rights in many ways facilitate the performance of duties. Arguably, a feminist conception of citizenship synthesizes the best aspects of the Marshallian liberal social rights tradition and the best aspects of the civic republican tradition of participatory democracy (especially the idea that – to paraphrase Hannah Arendt – appearance in public as a citizen allows us to discover "who" rather than "what" we are [see Bickford 1996]) (Mouffe 1992b). This "critical synthesis" (as Ruth Lister [1997] calls it) approach stems from an understanding of citizenship as both a practice that involves human agency and as a status whose attainment, with the political, civil, and social rights it entails, is important for protecting and advancing the interests of marginalized people. Lister (1997, 34) writes that "the case for understanding rights as constituting a mutually supportive web of the formal (civil and political) and the substantive (social and economic) has been made with reference to their status as a prerequisite for the realisation of human agency."

Besides overlooking or downplaying the question of social citizenship rights, many proponents of environmental citizenship fail to discuss human rights in any significant way, preferring instead to focus on duty and questions of whether rights might be extended to future generations or the non-human world. By contrast, in spite of their criticisms of liberalism and the limitations of masculine rights-talk, many feminists have accepted (albeit to varying degrees) an approach to citizenship that entails human rights and political entitlements that are enjoyed equally by every member of society regardless of their social, economic, or cultural status. They have argued (and fought) for the extension of rights to those to whom they have been denied and who have thereby been excluded from citizenship (e.g., slaves, children, migrant workers). They have also argued for new rights to protect disadvantaged groups from unjust treatment (Lister 1997). In particular, reproductive rights have been a central concern for feminists, and these are especially important in light of prevailing ideas about population control (including those held by some ecocentric greens).[27] I note in Chapter 2 that some ecofeminists have argued for reproductive rights so that women can choose when – and if – they will become mothers (Mills 1991). Civil rights that protect against systemic discrimination and hate speech, and that help foster social equity, are of great value to feminists and other movements for social justice. Rights that protect workers from exploitation and unsafe conditions are increasingly important in a global market that relies on the cheap labour of women (Bakan and Stasiulus 1996; Ehrenreich and Hochschild 2002).

These arguments about rights are central to most contemporary feminist discussions of citizenship. Feminists would be apt to agree that too many rights and not enough responsibilities may indeed be causes of the ecological crisis, providing that there is acknowledgment that this applies only to very specific social groups. For most people in the world the opposite is true. Human and social rights are under attack in most neoliberal capitalist places in the globalizing world, and communities, families, and the women who care for them have little choice but to shoulder the ever greater burdens of responsibility being created. Dobson (2003) makes a similar point about the fundamentally asymmetrical nature of globalization when he argues for a postcosmopolitan conception of ecological citizenship that does not assume a common human condition. Taking these points seriously, theorists who endorse the ideal of the responsible green citizen ought to acknowledge the importance of maintaining the workable balance between responsibilities and rights that is traditionally constitutive of citizenship, a balance that makes everyday practices of citizenship sustainable.

Ecofeminism and Global Citizenship

The final issue to be addressed in this chapter concerns the advocacy of global notions of citizenship by some green political theorists. It is fair to say that there is a degree of affinity between ecofeminism and cosmopolitan, or global, conceptions of green citizenship. There has been a rise in the number of international organizations and conferences dedicated to "women and the environment" in the 1990s.[28] In Chapter 2 I discuss the work of the Women's Environment and Development Organization (WEDO), a high-profile organization that seeks to influence environmental decision making by bringing women's perspective to the international policy arena. Women's Action Agenda 21 (WAA21), the outcome of women activists' participation in the World Women's Conference for a Healthy Planet in Miami in 1991 and, later, in the Earth Summit in Rio, similarly demonstrates an effort to bring women together across many boundaries (geographical, institutional, racial, class, etc.) to think and work at the global level (Sturgeon 1997). And, as Sandilands (1999a) notes, the wish to see ecofeminism as a global vision, rooted in the local grassroots struggles and knowledges of diverse women, is expressed in several recent ecofeminist publications (see, for example, Mies and Shiva 1993; Salleh 1997; Mies and Bennholdt-Thomsen 1999).

While I have noted my concern that these kinds of ecofeminist actions are often based on strategic essentialism, I also accept that it is in these efforts to develop a global perspective that a radical democratic promise in ecofeminism can be found, one that may actually run counter to the tendency towards essentialism and maternalism. Bringing diverse women together in democratic deliberation necessarily disrupts any fixed or simplistic understanding of women's identity while temporarily uniting them (in affinity) on a particular common interest. Sandilands (1999a, 147) writes that "the WAA21 document offers, despite its moments of strategic essentialism and problematic creation, a strong example of a universalizing politics that does not claim an embodied and stable alternative and thus leaves open multiple and useful spaces for future conversation." Although WAA21 does not employ the language of citizenship, Sandilands identifies a version of global citizenship in the WAA21 example that counts as the form of "performative affinity" she advocates (149). She asserts that, because the call to universalism is a future-oriented one based on the recognition of diversity, it necessarily demands a democratic process and a "space in which questions about the current shape of any identity may be asked," which, in turn, may result in the performative destabilization of existing identities (149). Relatedly, the "global cyborg citizen" subverts the central myths (both masculine and feminine) of Western discourses of citizenship and instead embraces the constructed, partial, and temporary nature of both identity and political coalition (Squires 1999, 188-89, referring to Haraway 1990).

If this idea were to be developed, it might look similar to the desire for "a politics of solidarity in difference" that several feminist theorists of citizenship have expressed (Lister 1997; Yeatman 1993; Benhabib 1992; Mouffe 1992a, 1992b). These theorists are clear in their support for the centrality of the concept of universal citizenship in any non-essentialist feminist political project for social justice. I have noted Lister's (1997) argument that a global notion of citizenship has the potential to be more inclusive than localized or communitarian ones. The argument also extends to the global level in a political defence of universal human rights (and of "women's rights as human rights," the internationalist feminist slogan made popular at the Beijing women's conference in 1995) and in the theoretical search for workable ways of balancing plurality and particularity (of culture, gender, race, ability, and so on) and universality. An example of this project is Benhabib's (1992, 153) "post-Enlightenment defence of universalism," which is an "interactive universalism [that] acknowledges the plurality of modes of being human, and differences among humans, without endorsing all these pluralities and differences as morally and politically valid." As an open, politically constructed, performative, and universal identity, citizenship may be the best context for the development of this approach.

Despite the promise of global citizenship for feminist and ecofeminist politics, however, there are two caveats that should be heeded, especially when ecofeminist ideas are placed alongside green political visions of ecological citizenship. The first concerns the dangers of an approach to green citizenship that expresses a cosmopolitan approach to ethics (e.g., Attfield 1999). Ecofeminists should be careful to differentiate their "solidarity in difference" approach to universalism from one that suggests the existence of a pre-political universal moral truth. This caveat comes out of the philosophical feminist position that questions the relative merits of universalist versus relativist approaches to ethics. In recognition of the ease with which universalist ideals can slide into Western and Eurocentric, androcentric, classist, and racist prescriptions, for example, Code (2000) recommends a "hermeneutic of suspicion" whenever the call to "think globally" is heard. She suggests, following Paul Feyerabend, that relativism can be "a weapon against intellectual tyranny" (69). Consequently, Code proposes a critical, mitigated relativist form of global thinking that is epistemologically responsible: put simply, it recognizes that knowledge is situated, contextual, and contestable, and that knowers should therefore engage in persistent self-criticism and dialogue with others.

While the methodological and epistemological implications of this approach cannot be explored here, an important point that I draw out of Code's analysis is that global citizenship should be about responsible and vigilant listening and not just about acting, thinking, and performing (see also Bickford 1996). This would leave space for the kind of epistemic humility that is needed to counter the risk of moral and cultural imperialism that often lurks beneath the surface of cosmopolitan approaches.

There is also a host of practical questions to be asked before placing too much faith in the potential of global civil society and global ecological citizenship to lead to a greater degree of social justice and equality. At the level of procedural justice, for example, the long-standing feminist critique of social movement politics is relevant to an optimistic green vision of global governance: how democratic are they? No matter at what level they operate, NGOs are often made up of unelected officials (Plumwood 1995b). Which NGOs and which activists get to participate on the global stage? Local grassroots organizations, often run by women, rarely have the capacity to engage in high-level international talks and summits. How are citizens' organizations run, who runs them, and whom do they serve? Who determines the dominant message or strategy? These questions are seldom asked, and the issue of internal dynamics of social movement groups is not raised by Beck (1992) and others who place great faith in citizens' movements and subpolitics to mount successful challenges to the reign of the technocratic elite. The assumption seems to be that corporate controlled liberal states are by nature undemocratic, while citizens' movements are naturally democratic. Ecofeminist and feminist experience has shown that this is not necessarily so. Thus attention to the "grammar of conduct" (as described by feminist political theorists) of global ecological citizenship should become an important part of the ecopolitical conversation.

Finally, while some environmental problems may be global and "democratic" in that they do not discriminate on the basis of nationality or class (as Ulrich Beck has famously argued about smog, ozone depletion, and nuclear radiation, but which is highly debatable), many others are local and undemocratic (e.g., toxic waste and water contamination). Plumwood (1995b) warns that assertions about the globalization of the ecological crisis may unfairly mask the distribution of ecological harms around the world as well as within nations, regions, and communities (see also Dobson 2003). Many environmental justice scholars and ecofeminists argue that, in addition to a division of environmental responsibility and labour, there is a gender, class, and racial division of environmental risks (e.g., Mies and Shiva 1993; Bullard 1994; Taylor 1997; Rocheleau, Thomas-Slayter, and Wangari 1996). Women, typically poor and/or racialized, tend to be the most involved in monitoring and responding to environmental degradation in local contexts (including in their own homes), while men tend to dominate in global campaigns for wildlife conservation and for the reduction of CFC emissions. Dorceta Taylor (1997) notes that women of colour make up the majority of activists in local struggles for environmental justice despite their unsustainable burden of paid and unpaid labour and cultural pressures to be responsible for family and neighbourhood welfare. Where do they reside in the discourse of global ecological citizenship? The feminist call for a sense of global citizenship that does not homogenize all experiences into one vision or analysis of the problem but, rather, allows for solidarity across local specificities, seems all the more urgent in light of such observations (see Ferguson 2000).

Conclusion

I conclude this chapter with a summary of the themes that have emerged in the encounter I have staged between ecopolitical visions of green citizenship and feminist citizenship theories. Not surprisingly, in each theme there are tensions that raise more questions than can be answered without further analysis and debate. These tensions and questions are central to the project of developing a feminist theory of ecological citizenship and so must be given critical attention here. I return to them again in the final chapter of the book.

That there are divergent opinions about the appropriate site for ecological citizenship clearly demonstrates that ecopolitical and ecofeminist scholars have differing sets of priorities. In taking stock of these differences, we run into the global-local tension that pervades ecopolitical discourse as well as feminist concerns about relationships between individual autonomy and community flourishing. Each group of green theorists gives good reasons for why the community, the nation-state, or global civil society is the best political locale in which to situate ideals and practices of ecological citizenship. Feminists in part support and in part reject or qualify many of these reasons. Communalist approaches to ecological citizenship, for instance, have the potential to create conditions of active, face-to-face participation among citizens and greater interaction with (and knowledge of?) immediate environments. But for feminists, communitarian approaches tread dangerously close to the line of authoritarianism (and patriarchal conservatism) when community notions and traditions are substituted for individual choice and the protection of minorities and dissidents through rights. Reified notions of "the community" in many green political approaches give rise to simplistic ideas about social relationships, thus masking inequalities and power relations among community members. There are also obvious problems with the nation-state from a feminist perspective, yet state policies that protect the rights of the vulnerable and promote the socialization of caring and necessary work through public, not purchased or privatized, services are important for women's citizenship. The potentially "woman-friendly" (Jones 1998) aspects of the nation-state are of minor concern to green political theorists. Barry and Christoff do not give them as reasons for their support of retaining and transforming the nation-state as a site for the development of ecological citizenship; rather, they place priority on creating better mechanisms through which virtuous citizens may participate in the green public sphere. As I have explained, feminists may see more promise in global and cosmopolitan forms of citizenship than they do in localized and communalist ones. It is clear that universalizing notions of citizenship and the existence of a global civil society wherein questions of sustainability can be deliberated upon democratically (e.g., electronically or through international meetings of NGOs) is attractive from a feminist perspective. Feminist citizenship theorists concur with cosmopolitans that a global citizenship has the potential to be more inclusive than territorially bounded notions of citizenship (Lister 1997). Yet there are pitfalls here, too, as noted earlier. Since I am arguing that both the status/practice of citizenship and the process of reconceptualizing citizenship through debate are central to a feminist vision, a global citizenship needs to include the democratically accountable and interactive practices that localist versions advocate, even if not necessarily "the local" in the reified sense used by theorists like Bookchin and Curtin. This might help avoid allowing the desire for global solidarity to mask environmental (and other) inequalities both locally and globally. Here I think Dobson's (2003) postcosmopolitan notion of ecological citizenship, which incorporates feminist and environmental justice concerns, has much to offer. A postcosmopolitan approach helps problematize the local-global dichotomy itself by considering the "nested" and interconnected nature of these sites within ecological space.

Second, there is insufficient consideration in green political theory of the kind of citizen relations that would promote a just ecological society, whereas relations among embodied, interdependent people are of central importance to feminists. Some feminists and ecofeminists wish to make this point by invoking the language of the family and intimacy (as described in Chapters 2 and 3), while the feminist theorists of citizenship upon whom I draw want to find a way of politicizing these relations and subjecting them to public debate. In contrast, while green political theorists are willing to acknowledge that individual human beings are dependent on nature for survival (thus the prudential responsibility to preserve it) – which is an important corrective to anthropocentric approaches to citizenship – they are generally less forthcoming with acknowledgments of the relations of dependence that are central to human well-being. In this way they preserve, or at least fail to challenge, the position of the powerful vis-à-vis those who do the caring and, as such, are unacceptable to feminists (Tronto 1993).

I am sympathetic to the hope that, in a different kind of society, collective processes of mutual aid would emerge and put an end to hierarchy and oppression. Many green theorists (especially those who embrace communalism

and anarchism) take such an optimistic view of the potential for human cooperation that they think it unnecessary to mention how and by whom necessary social and ecological labour will be performed. Including private-sphere
activities (like recycling and energy conservation) as examples of ecological
citizenship practice (as do Barry and Dobson) is a radical departure from
conventional theories of citizenship that consider household activities irrelevant to politics. This is a great improvement on past understandings. Feminists, too, would want to include such practices in their understanding of
citizenship because, like other forms of privatized and feminized caring, they
hitherto have been ignored. However, they would want to do so only as long
as there is sufficient attention to who is performing the work. There is too
much evidence to suggest that the gendered division of labour will persist
regardless of the adoption of new ecological values by citizens. Consequently,
even in spite of some of the dangers of state control, feminists may be more
inclined than the greens to argue for the preservation of social rights in a
democratized welfare state.

Feminist citizenship theorists would also note that, in contrast to greens,
who prefer change to flow from greater self-reliance or civil society, the nation-
state has the potential to be a useful means of redistributive justice that can
promote cultural change. As Peta Bowden (1997, 164) notes, Scandinavian
experiences show that welfare state policies have helped counteract the natu-
ralization and feminization of care: they "facilit[ate] the rethinking of public
values that connect the marginalization of women and their practices of care,
the injustices of gendered labour arrangements, and the irresponsibility of
most men with regard to our intrinsic vulnerabilities and interdependencies."[29]
With years of research and analysis of the gendered division of necessary and
caring labour (and its obvious imperviousness to change), feminists must be
sceptical of visions that neglect to mention the conditions – such as social and
economic rights – that make citizenship possible for a broad number of people. And they must continue to argue that, where the state does not provide
desirable substitutes for necessary labour in the private sphere, this labour
must be shared equally (i.e., by able-bodied men and women) as a matter of
justice.

Finally, there is an obvious tension between my feminist defence of citizenship (à la Dietz, Mouffe, and others) as a political practice that is not the same
thing as caring (see Chapter 4) and a feminist critique of citizenship approaches
that specify politics as something independent of the conditions that caring
labour make possible. It is important to highlight what my discussion in this
chapter has revealed about the tension between care and politics. In effect, it
has led to the same place as the discussion in Chapter 4: the question of how
to recognize the gendered specificity of caring practices and their importance
for politics and everyday life without accepting the naturalness of women's

caring, which renders it irrelevant to the concerns of citizenship. In Chapter 4 I argue that ecofeminists must come to grips with the possibility that simple revaluations of care will not lead to an improvement in women's lives, nor will they counteract the privatization and feminization of care that has led to the exploitation and marginalization of women as carers (a situation that has compromised their ability to act as citizens). It is problematic that few ecofeminists have taken their concern for sustainability beyond looking at women's mothering, household work, and informal grassroots activism to a consideration of citizenship and the public sphere of politics. Unless they do so they will be unable to make persuasive arguments for equity and fairness within a democratic and sustainable society – arguments that green theorists so obviously need to hear loudly and repeatedly. A green citizenship insulated from feminist analyses of the gendered politics of caring work and values is, and will remain, unsatisfactory.

I conclude with the inevitable question: What would a feminist ecological citizenship be? To provide a definition or list of necessary conditions would be contradictory to my discussion of democratic politics. The arguments made above do, however, suggest what it is not. Nevertheless, it is clear to me that putting the words "feminist" and "ecological" in front of the word "citizenship" draws attention to what has thus far been excluded from the discourse of citizenship. There is a need to value the specificity of citizenship as an intrinsically important practice at the same time that there is a need to recognize the foundational aspects of labour (provided by women and "nature") that allow this specificity to flourish. While there are several currents of political theory that do the former (i.e., civic republicans, radical democrats), feminists are alone in doing the latter – although only some feminists emphasize the need to de-gender and de-privatize the conditions that make citizenship possible. I am arguing that only a feminist ecological citizenship does both, and this makes it necessary for democratic political life and gender equity – two conditions without which sustainability will be impossible.

My aim in the first half of *Beyond Mothering Earth* is to argue that a critical feminist analysis of the gendered politics of care should be central to the development of democratic theories of ecofeminism and ecological citizenship. I now want to begin the second half by stepping out of this imagined theoretical conversation and into the face-to-face conversations I had with thirty women who, in their everyday lives, care for children and/or aging parents, work inside and outside their homes, are active in efforts to improve the quality of life in their communities, and try to maintain green household practices. In this sense, most of these women resemble what the green men would describe as ideal green citizens. They also qualify as examples of women involved in grassroots environmental struggles celebrated in ecofeminists texts. However, my conversations with them help disrupt rather than affirm such descriptions, and they raise important questions about the limits of the theoretical literature. Before presenting the findings of my research in Chapters 7 and 8, I provide in Chapter 6 an account of the research process and some of the methodological questions that are relevant to my interest in democratizing the theoretical politics of ecofeminism.

PART TWO

Conversations

This might be the secret

of the housewife theory of history: These women take the qualities that are supposed to render them irrelevant and use them defiantly as well as strategically. Starting with what they love, they cut straight through the quicksand of motives and purposes to point out that harm has been done and should be stopped. In some sense, they depoliticize politics, which is what makes them so politically potent.

– Rebecca Solnit, "The Housewife Theory of History"

There is talk of the emergence

of the "new citizen" (if there is such a thing). And the character of it is different because people are juggling all kinds of responsibilities. Now "citizens" aren't considered only to be the elites of society, whereas the Athenian citizen was. Still, the housewife citizen is at the bottom.

– from an interview with Nikola Patti

6 Conversations with Activist Women: Towards a Counter-Narrative

> Ecofeminism as a resistance politics has a great deal to tell us about the uses and abuses of theory as a power relation. It suggests that theory in the interrogative mode – as opposed to Theory in the prescriptive mode – asks difficult questions; that is, it asks questions that pose difficulties, even – perhaps especially – for one's own practices. In fact ... ecofeminism is most formidable in its opposition to power when it challenges its own assumptions.
>
> – *Lee Quinby,* Anti-Apocalypse: Exercises in Genealogical Criticism

As I discuss in Chapter 5, most green political theorists have failed to consider the so-called "realm of necessity" and the specificities of gender in their visions of ecological citizenship. At the same time, few contemporary ecofeminists have critically considered the political implications of their celebration of grassroots activism or of an approach to politics that is built on reified and romantic notions of care. In addition to engaging in dialogue with each other, both positions would benefit, it seems to me, from an exchange of ideas with people whose lives are implicated in their theorizing. In this chapter and the chapters to follow, my theoretical analysis of ecopolitical and ecofeminist scholarship is complemented by empirical research. I report on conversations I had with thirty women from the greater Toronto area, all of whom are actively involved in improving the local quality of life while they also have private caring responsibilities. Although these women are committed, in different ways, to environmental change, they do not call themselves "ecofeminists," so I make no effort to fit them into my narrative as examples of ecofeminist practice. But all of the women I interviewed are simultaneously caregivers (i.e., mothers, grandmothers, daughters) and activists, and they resemble the heroines of many ecofeminist texts. In that they are active participants in the management of their local environments and "do their bit" at home, they also represent what many ecopolitical scholars seem to have in mind when they write about ecological citizens.

Yet the story I tell, based on what the women told me in our conversations, is a *counter-narrative:* it differs from prevailing accounts of women's activism in ecofeminist scholarship by doing much more than simply celebrating their triumphs. I look at both sides of the public-private divide and ask difficult questions about the benefits and burdens of juggling caring responsibilities and active citizenship. Most significantly, I ask: "How does one live as an active ecological citizen while caring for others and running a household with the best of ecological intentions?" My research interprets the complex experiences of women activists who "struggle to juggle" (Frederickson 1995) and presents their own reflections about such notions as citizenship, responsibility, and social justice. I argue that their stories are significant to the development of both ecofeminist and ecopolitical theory because they help highlight relationships among gender, care, citizenship, and environmental change, about which both bodies of theory have made problematic assumptions and omissions. Moreover, by giving the women's thoughts and opinions a central place in my research, and by engaging with them as complex knowing subjects, I aim to model a more democratic approach to ecofeminist theorizing than that typically found in the literature.

In this chapter I discuss some of the methodological issues relevant to ecofeminist scholarship in general and to my research in particular. I begin by considering some of the problems in current ecofeminist research and then propose a methodological approach to researching women's activism that is consistent with my own theoretical commitments. I then provide a brief explanation of the social and political context within which the research took place. An account of participant selection and a description of the interview process are provided in the appendix.

Researching Women's Activism: Methodological Issues in Ecofeminism
In Chapter 3 I discuss how ecofeminists celebrate women's grassroots activism as prime examples of ecofeminism, partly in response to the problem of ethnocentrism in ecofeminism and partly to distance ecofeminism from overly theoretical and abstract academic discourse. I argue that it is probably the result of this move that women's participation in local environmental struggles, like those at Love Canal and Clayoquot Sound and in the Indian Chipko

movement, seem to have become the standard-bearers of ecofeminist practice. There is a growing body of literature by feminist and development scholars who, while expressing sympathy for the aims and concerns of ecofeminism, have been critical of the portraits of women's relationships to their environments that are painted in ecofeminist texts (e.g., Sturgeon 1999; Low and Tremayne 2001; Reed 2003). This criticism suggests a need to consider some of the weaknesses in contemporary ecofeminist research. The weak spots that are interesting to me involve how women's participation is represented and the limitations that appear to be placed on what (and who) counts as relevant in ecofeminist research.

Valuing women's hitherto invisible contributions to sustainability is a worthwhile project, but ecofeminist politics is weakened by one-dimensionally positive portrayals of these contributions and the women who make them – portrayals that are not always based on empirical research and seem conveniently to support academic and political positions. It is easy to begin a critical evaluation of ecofeminist claims with an obvious question: Are women *really* more caring towards the earth than men? Over the years, empirical research, such as quantitative opinion surveys, has yielded contradictory findings.[1] Even though studies have found gender differences in environmental attitudes and behaviours, it would be incorrect to suggest that all women in general care more and do more than all men (Littig 2001). Despite the evidence that some ecofeminists marshal to support their arguments that women care more than men, it is possible to find countervailing evidence to show that these are often highly selective accounts that entail many problematic assumptions, omissions, and projections. For instance, while they may engage in ecologically sound (perhaps "caring") practices, women are also often complicitous in environmental degradation. (And of course there are many men who are extremely caring and/or concerned about sustainability.) Downplaying or hiding this evidence only makes ecofeminists look dishonest and their research sloppy. In an essay entitled "Doing What Comes Naturally?" Cecile Jackson (1993, 1950) makes the important argument that "refusal to accept that women are agents of environmental degradation and the determined attempt to construct a positive image of women as custodians of, and carers for, the environment is to obscure and prevent a more useful analysis." It plays into a false assumption of women's altruism and natural propensity to care when in fact there are many complex – and not necessarily selfless – reasons for the work women do. Jackson continues: "collective action with regard to the environment has been 'naturalized' for women, but not for men, on the basis of implied altruism and with a failure to scrutinize the private interests of women adequately" (ibid.). Maureen Reed's (2000, 2003) research shows that women sometimes get involved in environmental politics for the purposes of saving jobs rather than trees. Hers is an important counter-narrative to the popular story of women's protest against clear-cutting the old-growth forests at Clayoquot Sound (e.g., Wine 1997).

Using interactive qualitative research methods, she interprets the experiences of the many "other women" involved in BC forest politics: those who actively support the forestry industry upon which their communities and livelihoods depend.

Finding some ecofeminist and WED accounts of women's activism and subsistence work problematic, Reed, Jackson, and others (e.g., Agarwal 1998a; Jewitt 2000) call for more field-based research that delves carefully into the complex and conflicting social, political, and cultural relationships that shape women's interaction with and knowledge of their local environments. More accurate representations would also include analyses of the problems that many women experience in trying to express or act on their knowledge in societies where women are discouraged from participating in the public sphere. An important reason for conducting more detailed research, beyond the scholarly desire to produce more reliable accounts, is that inaccurate representations may further perpetuate harmful myths about women. For example, as Jewitt (2000) observes, current ecofeminist and WED approaches that celebrate Indian women's roles as environmental managers may have inadvertently served to support development policies that use women as means to environmentalist ends, thereby intensifying their burden of work (see Littig [2001] for references to German research that makes a similar argument).

In addition to asking whether the facts support the claim that "women care more about the earth" than men, we may also ask: "What does ecofeminist activism look like?" Due to the apparent scarcity of empirical examples of *self-identified* ecofeminist practice, ecofeminist theorists have been looking to women's grassroots activism in the South, to the environmental justice movement in the North, or to indigenous women worldwide for evidence of ecofeminism. But many questions have been raised about the validity of their representations of these examples. Note, as the most obvious example, the difference between Vandana Shiva's (and other ecofeminists') portrayal of the Chipko movement as a women's movement, and Ramachandra Guha's (1990) social history of peasant protest in India. Guha denies that Chipko is in any way feminist and, in fact, characterizes it as conservative, as anti-change, and as predominantly led by men (the charismatic leader Sunderlal Bahuguna in particular). Comparing his research to that of ecofeminists, Guha (1990, 173) states: "Locating Chipko culturally and historically provides a long overdue corrective to the popular conception of Chipko, which is that of a romantic reunion of humans, especially women, with nature" (see also Kapoor 1993; Rangan 2000; Nagarajan 2001).[2] Bina Agarwal (1992, 1998b) has also taken issue with Shiva's examples of rural women's activism in India, arguing that Shiva inaccurately portrays "the feminine principle" as the central idea in Indian philosophy and fails to mention that it comes from Hinduism, which is just one of India's many religious traditions. George Nalunnakkal (2004, 57) criticizes Shiva's failure to mention the tribal and caste systems as being more relevant to women's lives than gender and for attaching an understanding of sustainability to Indian women that, because its central concepts come from elite forms of Hinduism, is "alien to the worldview of Dalits [untouchables] and tribals."

Agarwal (1992, 1998b), Sturgeon (1997, 1999), and Sandilands (1999a) each observe that some ecofeminist scholarship, especially that which attempts to be anti-racist and to promote global solidarity, unintentionally exploits Native North American and South Asian women when it holds them up as the "ultimate ecofeminists." Andy Smith (1997) and Greta Gaard (1998) argue that appropriating the struggles of working-class and marginalized women to support the development of a theoretical perspective is unethical and potentially racist. Gaard (1998, 13) writes:

> Naming the activism of others in a way that they have not effectively puts words in their mouths; contradicts, silences, or erases their activist speech; and colonizes or appropriates their labors for the use of others. The problem becomes obvious, finally, when one realizes that the naming and appropriation is taking place across the lines of races, class, or nationality: that is, the activism most likely to be named as exemplifying ecofeminism is the activism of women or communities of color ... or women of the third world ... and those most likely to engage in such naming tend to be white, middle-class academic women in industrialized nations.

It is troubling that these cases appear to represent all "Southern" or peasant women, giving the impression that all such women are naturally more caring about their environment than other women, because there is a risk of essentializing the very categories that, in the name of diversity and inclusivity, feminists turned to in the first place (Stone-Mediatore 2000).

This point leads to a discussion of the related problem of what and who counts as relevant in a discussion of ecofeminist theory and practice. Noting a preoccupation with women in the South, Dorceta Taylor (1997, 69) argues that "ecofeminists [seem] more aware of the struggles of women in developing countries than of the struggles of women of color close by." It seems to me that we know even less about the activism of white middle-class women in Northern/Western contexts than we do about economically marginalized and racialized women in the South, and there is a question of whether ecofeminist scholars should even want to know about them or the lives they lead (Reed 2000, 2003). This is despite a very useful analysis by Maria Mies (1986) – who has since written a great deal about ecofeminism – of the relationship between the oppression of women and environments in the colonized world and the exploitative process of *Hausfrauisierung* (housewifization) of elite women in Western cultures.[3] As Victoria Davion (1994, 19) observes, some ecofeminist scholarship omits important facts about "first world" women, not the least of which is that "industries supported by women playing out feminine roles are often responsible for gross environmental damage." While it may be true that women in the "minority world" (i.e., the affluent North and West) have received a disproportionate amount of attention in feminist scholarship, this is not the case in feminist scholarship on environmental issues. In this work, giving more attention to poor women and women in the South than to women in the North/West supports the misleading impression that the problem of global unsustainability lies with poor people, with people living in the South. This point has been made by environmental justice and postcolonial scholars from the majority world (e.g., Guha 1994). In light of debates over the potentially neoimperialist discourse of sustainable development (see Sachs 1993), I argue that scholars in the overdeveloped world ought to give as much or more attention to people's values and actions in our own societies as we give to those of people in less affluent societies who have a much smaller ecological footprint than we collectively do. Chris Cuomo (1998, 9) observes, "While there is a tendency in Western ecofeminist theory to describe the work of rural Third World women as paradigmatic ecofeminist activism, one sees little effort [in the literature] to develop specific models that examine the politics of 'first world' mega-consumption on ecofeminist grounds." This suggests that a central task of ecofeminist research, situated as it so often is in a Western/ Northern context, should be to investigate the lives and choices of economically privileged women. Rather than taking up this kind of project, however, there is a general avoidance of (and in some places an open hostility to talking seriously about) middle-class white women as well as the work of so-called bourgeois ecofeminists. This avoidance implies that only a particular kind of activism and resistance by women marginalized by class or racialized status are of interest to ecofeminists and that only poor women and women of colour can be authentic ecofeminists (Reed 2000).

As will become clear, my research with thirty women from diverse socioeconomic backgrounds who live and work in the largest urban region of Canada – a country that the United Nations repeatedly claims has one of highest qualities of life in the world (ranked fourth, behind Norway, Sweden, and Australia, in 2004) – disrupts this exclusionary and selective focus. Although I do not claim that the women I interviewed are ecofeminists, or that their work in some way demonstrates ecofeminism-in-action, by including them in this study I am broadening the scope of women who are relevant to ecofeminist research, politics, and theorizing. I am making the point that the experiences and ideas of urban-dwelling women in the overdeveloped world are as interesting and as informative to ecofeminist thought as those of "peasant" women in developing countries.

I now want to respond to these criticisms with a discussion of two methodological issues that I think ecofeminist scholars need to consider more carefully:

(1) the approaches feminist researchers take (or ought to take) in interpreting the "lived experiences" of the women they study and (2) relationships between researchers and activists.

Interpreting Women's "Lived Experience"

A methodological issue that is of great significance to ecofeminist research on women's activism is the interpretation and presentation of "lived experience." As noted earlier, some ecofeminists view women's experiences as a fundamental source of knowledge about the human-nature relationship and as an inspiration for activism. Greta Gaard (1998, 29-31) includes "the path of lived experiences" as part of the geography of ecofeminism; even though they are different for every person, lived experiences "are just as strong as the streams of feminist theory that have shaped the intellectual and philosophical aspects of ecofeminism."[4] Other ecofeminists make much of the role of mothering experiences and women's experiences of environmentally related physical health problems with regard to women gaining a sense of environmental concern. A central goal of ecofeminist scholarship of late has been to foreground women's experiences as an alternative to established (read theoretical, masculine, Eurocentric) ways of knowing.

As I discuss in Chapter 3, ecofeminist texts in which particular experiences of grassroots activists are highlighted provide an important corrective to the absence of women in masculinist ecopolitics. Feminists have for many decades argued that theories that ignore or discount women and the ways in which their experiences are different from men's are inadequate. But what does it mean to give "experience" a privileged place in ecofeminist thought, and is it wise, on the whole, to do so? In thinking about this question, I take instruction from Jean Grimshaw's (1986) philosophical interrogation of the relationships between experience, reality, and theory, in which she raises questions about how feminists have typically viewed women's experience. Grimshaw (1986, 84) is critical of those feminists who assume, rather naively in her view, that there is a fundamental disjuncture between male and female "realities," that "female experience simply needs 'naming,' and that it is always 'valid' – a final court of appeal – and that experience should be contrasted not just with particular theories but with the notion of theory in general." Code (1995, 115) is also wary of the tendency of some feminists to take women's experiences as uncontestable truth. In fact she warns of "the risk [of] replacing the old tyranny of an expertise deaf to experience with a new tyranny of experience hermetically sealed against criticism and interpretation." She argues for a more tentative and provisional approach to things like "reality" and "experience" – one that does justice to the complex nature of female experience and the many ways it intersects with male experience while at the same time contributing to the development of theories (not just "realities") that allow us to analyze and conceptualize oppression, exploitation, and domination on a grand scale.

There are problems associated with taking women's experience as an unmediated line into the truth: we may fail to see that these experiences are always already filtered through and situated in specific contexts, ideas, and context-dependent and ever-fluid interpretations, as are those of the theorist (Scott 1992). Furthermore, will studying women's "lived experiences" lead us to superior analyses? Not necessarily. Women's experiences in one small corner of the world will not help us address all of the interrelated factors that contribute to the complicated, global problems of gender inequality or environmental degradation. Grimshaw (1986, 102) writes that "the activities of things such as multinational corporations are usually extremely remote from everyday experience, yet they have profound effects on women's lives. And these effects do not depend for their existence on the recognition accorded to them." It is questionable whether "lived experiences" will provide sufficient insight into macropolitical problems or global ecological developments like climate change. In my view, it simply does not follow that because women have experiences of caring for children or tending the earth they therefore know how to solve the global ecological crisis. The problem of environmental unsustainability is best considered in conjunction with other kinds of knowledges besides the everyday experience of women, and those knowledges include scientific, spatial, economic, and policy analyses. And in many cases, knowledge goes hand in hand with uncertainty and ambivalence.

From a slightly different angle, one could argue that women ought to move beyond everyday lived experience to other sources of knowledge that help them question their own experiences.[5] Grimshaw (1986) invokes the work of Italian Marxist philosopher Antonio Gramsci to remind us that "experience" is made up in part of the internalized values that sustain hegemonic ideologies. Women, for example, see themselves partially through the eyes of men. It may well be in the interests of the powerful that women go no further than their own experiential knowledge. (This is certainly the case in cultures in which girls and women are denied access to formal education.) In the areas of environmental politics, a reading of the work of scholars who have been influenced by the power/knowledge theories of Foucault (1977, 1984) would be instructive for ecofeminists who wish to see women's experience as an unmediated path to understanding the realities of environmental destruction.[6] Their work suggests that we be more sceptical of our own understandings of "reality"; resistance depends on it.

As feminist methodologists argue, there is a need to strike a delicate balance between a desire to present the hitherto invisible experiences of women as valid and a desire to construct valid feminist theories about the place/production of women in heterosexist, patriarchal, capitalist, and white supremacist societies. In my view, there is a need to employ research methods whereby ecofeminists can listen to the voices of non-academic women engaged in local campaigns,

to ask for their interpretations while retaining the option of respectfully offering their own arguments and alternative interpretations. To treat women's
experiences otherwise is extremely patronizing. Taking this notion seriously,
Jackson (1993, 1953) presents what I think is a very important suggestion to
ecofeminists: that instead of taking women's experiences as "truth," they need
to rely on standard techniques of social research such as "scepticism, 'triangulation,' ... secondary sources, and objective [quantitative?] indicators." In this
way, they may be able to represent the women with whom they conduct research in a more honest way: to co-theorize rather than reify their experiences,
and avoid the temptation to draw firm conclusions that help to support their
theoretical aims. Code (1991, 291) summarizes this approach succinctly when
she writes: "a theorist cannot always take experience at face value if she wants
to construct an emancipatory analysis of its sources and structural location.
Hence feminist inquirers have at once to resist treating experience as an invio-
lable, unconditional datum and to resist claiming a position of theoretical
expertise that exempts them from the need to understand." Like Code, I think
there may be other kinds of stories to tell and different, even better, ways of
telling them. Moreover, "the rejection of the idea that experience simply speaks
for itself should not be taken to deny the importance of listening" (Grimshaw
1986, 102).

On Activist-Academic Relationships

As I have discussed and illustrated in preceding chapters, there is a tendency
in ecofeminist texts to construct what I think is a strange and troubling relationship between academic researchers and the activist or grassroots, non-
academic women about whom they write. Alongside a desire to learn from
and construct theory out of the everyday lived experiences of activist women,
research and theorizing done by feminist academics is sometimes portrayed in
a trivializing light in the ecofeminist literature. For example, Mies and
Bennholdt-Thomsen (1999) assert that the work of the theorists who would
question their subsistence perspective or their characterization of women's
knowledge is "not authentic" (209) but, rather, mere "intellectual acrobatics"
(188) that is out of touch and unconcerned with real life problems. Ariel
Salleh (1997, 106) takes many opportunities in her book to position the life-
affirming practices of thousands of grassroots women activists as superior to
and "deeper" than the abstract theorizing of postmodern feminism, which she
says is "quietistic bourgeois idealism by default [whose] scholasticism pacifies
an emerging generation of women." Similarly, Mary Mellor (1997) argues
that ecofeminism is about concern for women's lives and experiences, for human embodiment and embeddedness in "real" nature, and so is incompatible
with postmodern feminist theorizing (see also Littig 2001).[7] She also laments
(perhaps rightly) the fact that privileged Western academics get to publish

their ideas and analyses of the movements that interest them, when they will probably never know what it is really like to struggle to meet their most basic needs under conditions of environmental and economic crisis. Environmental justice writers add a new dimension to this critique by sometimes drawing a distinction between ecofeminists as a group of privileged white theorists (by their definition) and socially marginalized women activists who work to improve the quality of life in their communities (e.g., Di Chiro 1998).

Certainly it is important to be critical and self-reflexive about one's social location as a researcher; to write authoritatively about struggles to survive in conditions of economic and ecological crises without acknowledging that one lives in relative luxury would be dishonest. But are the suspicion of Western/Northern feminist academics and the embracing of grassroots women as more "authentic" knowers the only alternatives? The portrayal by some ecofeminists of women activists as more involved in acting/surviving than in thinking/theorizing is questionable, but so is the rather one-dimensional portrayal of "academics." There are serious flaws in the representation of postmodern feminism (which is the label given to those who criticize essentialism or make anti-essentialist arguments about women and nature) as apolitical and incompatible with materialist analyses of capitalism. As a reading of theorists such as Donna Haraway (1991a, 1996) and J.-K. Gibson-Graham (1996) shows, postmodern feminism draws on materialist feminist analyses and is concerned with the material conditions of women's lives, just as materialist feminist scholarship draws upon the theoretical insights of postmodernism (among other "posts" like postcolonialism and post-Marxism). These are complex and interconnected discourses (Hennessy 1993). Granted they have different approaches and focuses, and debates over essentialism and realism are heated, but reducing social constructionist theorists' work to "a few hours' work at a word processor" (Mies and Bennholdt-Thomsen 1999, 200) is an unfair rhetorical move.

We must be aware of the power imbalances that inevitably pertain between privileged academic researchers and the activists about whom they write, particularly if the latter are socially marginalized. It is important to point out, however, that these power imbalances cannot be corrected by celebrating grassroots women and criticizing women who write theory or conduct research for a living. It does not *necessarily* follow that women who live in affluent cultures and work in "first world" universities have a limited capacity to understand or develop valuable insights into the problems faced by people in other situations and parts of the world. As I explain above, I think that there are dangers in the argument that anyone has authority to speak on an issue by virtue of personal experience. Moreover, those ecofeminist academics who want to distance themselves from postmodern feminist scholarship and identify with "grassroots women" are unable to change the fact that there will frequently be more at stake in the research for the researcher than there is for the participant, no matter how collaborative or "empowering" the relationship between them might be. As Linda McDowell (1999, 236) has observed, many feminist methods that purport to establish non-hierarchical relationships, "share" experience, and contribute to empowerment are over-optimistic: "It is increasingly recognized that relations of power, and even exploitation, are not insignificant just because we are all women." Referring back to Gaard, it is important to be vigilant against using examples of activism uncritically to support one's own ecofeminist positions, or presenting women as ecofeminists without allowing them to challenge one's interpretations through conversation.[8]

How, then, should one proceed as a researcher given these concerns? We may first make a commitment to destabilizing the strict separation of theorizing and activism by, for example, embracing the arguments of some feminists that feminist theory can be a form of activism (McClure 1992). Similarly we could note, *pace* Salleh, that activism is always based in theory, even if sometimes unarticulated theory, and that activists are always also social theorists who make sense of the world and their own actions by drawing on abstract concepts of power, justice, and resistance. To me it seems accurate to view women activists as complex people who engage with the world in a variety of ways. Lee Quinby's (1997, 157) "activist/theorizer" is a term I find highly useful to describe women activists "speaking for themselves on their own terrains, discerning power's specific effects on them and conducting skirmishes against its operations."

Moreover, perhaps we can consider another way of looking at the activist-academic dualism and imagine a more cooperative relationship based on mutual respect and constructive open-ended dialogue. This would mean accepting each for what they are able to contribute at particular moments and recognizing that academics do have things to offer.[9] Considering just such an issue, feminist philosopher Lorraine Code (1991, 289) writes:

> It would be politically irresponsible to argue that the oppressed just need to get on as best they can, for they are no concern of ours. But neither is it legitimate for the privileged simply to renounce their privilege in a guilt-ridden repudiation of hierarchy per se ... unilateral renunciations and accusations would serve only to produce a stand-off in which each actor in the piece could present her position as fixed and argue abjectly and aggressively from it. Women who have the insight and power that epistemic privilege [stemming from being a member of the academy] confers need to acknowledge its value, so that they can draw on it to devise strategies for subverting oppressive structures. Analogously, women who do not have that (interim) power need to devise strategies of empowerment and resistance that do not "merely reflect the situation and values of the theorizer." By finding

ways of engaging in dialogue across the boundaries of their illusorily coherent positions, women can produce a collectively informed empowerment that neither group would realize alone.

If we take Code's suggestion to heart, then perhaps there are ways to foster more mutually beneficial exchanges between ecofeminist academics and women activists, while recognizing the (in some ways) *necessarily* different goals of each (e.g., getting published to support a career, raising funds to support a specific community project, and so on). Ecofeminist academics are in a position to lend information and support – in short, to use their privilege in positive ways – to help the struggles of non-academic women. At the same time, they need to be open about the fact that certain practices are required for them to retain their privilege as an academic. Vandana Shiva is an appropriate example of an elite academic (a theoretical particle physicist, no less) who has used her status to assist the efforts of activists and farmers the world over in very important ways.[10]

On my reading, most feminist researchers hold a methodological commitment to conducting research and presenting scholarship that supports and contributes to activist struggles (Naples 1997a, 1997b; see also Mies 1983; Cook and Fonow 1986; Lather 1991). This commitment can include chronicling the history of particular organizations, collecting the stories and artefacts that come out of activist struggles (analyzing and respectfully criticizing them), gathering data that can be used in an organization's advocacy work, and "getting the word out" (i.e., publishing results in accessible places) so that activists may learn from each other's experiences. It also entails using research findings and, by extension, the researcher's power as academic to inform government task forces or to pressure policy makers to address women's concerns. To this might be added that research can be (and has been) used to challenge the assumptions of scholars in other academic fields or activists in other social movements. An important consideration in publishing community research is ensuring that research findings are not misappropriated and used for sexist, anti-feminist, classist, racist, or other oppressive aims. I see this "making the research public" aspect as an indication that research can be not only a form of activism but also a practice of citizenship: by publishing her views, a scholar is engaging in political discourse in a public arena; she is appearing in public and can be held accountable for her positions. If we follow the political philosophy of Arendt, then this is what citizenship is all about.

Conversations with Activist Women

My empirical research began with two interrelated questions that emerged from an analysis of the ecofeminist and ecopolitical literature: First, what is life like for women who combine the work of caring in the private sphere with that of active civic participation on issues of environmental quality? Second, what is the relationship between the prescriptions and portraits found in ecofeminist and ecopolitical literature and the perceptions of the women who come close to emulating them?

Feminist sociological research in North American contexts over the past several decades has yielded pictures of women's experience with juggling multiple roles. Much of this work looks at the so-called "second shift" (Hochschild and Machung 1989), the dual role played by women who are employed in the labour market while performing the typical load of domestic provisioning and caregiving work at home. Most research suggests that employed women with caregiving responsibilities have a double day of labour, and have longer work weeks[11] and less sleep and leisure time than men (Hochschild and Machung 1989; McMahon 1995; Eichler 1997; Arai 2000; Bittman and Wajcman 2000). As volunteers, women do approximately two-thirds of community care or companionship work and three-quarters of community food service work (Armstrong and Armstrong 1994).[12] Thus some North American feminists have referred to women's "triple role" to describe the combination of paid employment, unpaid housework, and community management that many women undertake.[13] With a double and sometimes triple workload, weekends and holidays mean something entirely different for many women than they do for most men. For example, Canadian sociologists Pat Armstrong and Hugh Armstrong (1994, 92-93) report in their comprehensive study, entitled *The Double Ghetto*, that "on the weekend women do more than men, and their tasks and time are less flexible than those of men. Not only do women put in a full day's work during the week; they also work on holidays and weekends. The load is particularly heavy for women who have paid employment and for those who parent alone."

For lone-parent households, such family-related time comparisons by gender are obviously inappropriate. Studies have shown that the majority of lone-parent households are led by women (Eichler 1997), yet there is a surprising lack of data on the division of labour within sole-support women-headed families (especially in low-income and racialized households [see Orleck 1997]). One speculation is that the absence of a second adult (e.g., a spouse or partner) in a household may decrease the amount of work required (Negrey 1993; McMahon 1995). However, other research suggests that, because over half of these families live in poverty, the burden of making ends meet, and thus the amount of work, is greater (Eichler 1997; MacGregor 1997). In fact, for all household types income is an important variable: being poor may mean that a greater number of hours needs to be devoted to caring labour and particularly to provisioning work. This variability raises questions about the relationship between consumption and work. For example, does the time required to care for a household increase as the ability to consume commodities decreases? In what circumstances do people "buy time" in the form of services (e.g., cleaning women, dry cleaners) and labour-saving convenience products (e.g., ready meals)? These are important questions for the sustainability agenda, and ones that ecofeminists need to address in response to the claims of some greens who envision a sustainable society characterized by *less work and less consumption*.

Feminist analyses of women's double and triple role within a variety of cultural and economic contexts are important in highlighting the persistently unfair and unsustainable gender division of labour in capitalist society. My research contributes more and different things to that discussion. First, it investigates the implications for women of adding a fourth role – that of earthcaring – to their already busy lives. Second, as I discuss in Chapters 7 and 8, it considers these implications in light of a theoretical understanding not just of the division of labour but also of active citizenship, particularly as it relates to green visions of an ecological and radical democratic society. In this sense it fills a gap in the existing ecopolitical literature and responds to the challenge of feminist political theorists to democratize and politicize the conditions of the private sphere. It also looks at negative implications for women who, in many cases, go against dominant cultural conventions of "feminine" behaviour to become political activists.

There are few precedents for this particular kind of research on women activists. Most feminist case studies of women's activism focus more heavily on the public, community-focused nature of activist work than on the implications of activist work for their everyday lives in the private sphere.[14] (I give examples of the ecofeminist and environmental justice research that highlights the contributions women make to their communities and environments in Chapter 3). Moreover, few social movement theorists consider the implications for activist movements of a persistent gendered division of labour at home. One important exception is sociologist Randy Stoecker (1992), whose research on social movement organizing asks "who takes out the garbage?" The answer to this question yields insight into the impacts of the gendered and classed structure of social reproduction on the activities and strategies of social movements. He explains that there are significant implications for the success of social movements "when the movement's constituency lacks the time and money to meet their social reproduction needs" (240). He found that women, in particular, tend to experience tension between caring for a home and organizing community projects and that this tension makes it difficult for them to sustain participation. He concludes that encouraging women's involvement in social movements may "require providing social reproduction services as part of the movement's activities" (243).

One example of feminist research that focuses on the individual life stories of women involved in community activism is Anne Witte Garland's (1998) *Women Activists: Challenging the Abuse of Power*. Lee Quinby (1997, 157) cites it as an example of a text that provides a "politically astute and emotionally moving" testament to the micropolitics of feminist resistance. The book consists of the narratives of eight American and British women and is based on long interviews with them and shorter interviews with colleagues and family members. Although the stories do not dwell on the everyday struggles of women who attempt to combine a number of (frequently conflicting) roles and responsibilities, a common theme is that, through their activist experiences, women gain insight into political systems and a better understanding of power, becoming "empowered" in the process. Celene Krauss' (1993) research on women's anti-toxics activism has found a similar process of empowerment among women whose entry into politics has been inspired by local quality-of-life concerns. Her studies, and those of Dorceta Taylor (1997) and Giovanna Di Chiro (1998), are helpful in documenting the high rates of participation of marginalized women (working-class women and women of colour in the United States) in the growing environmental justice movement. As I noted earlier, these studies do not include the contributions of middle-class and professional women, thereby creating an impression that only certain kinds of women are concerned with the quality of life in their communities.[15] And while I find their narratives interesting and useful, I am left wondering whether different kinds of questions might produce different interpretations – not least of which would be one that recognizes that, for activist women, empowerment comes at a price.

The Process and the Participants

Inspired by these examples of feminist research and activism, and in order to gain insight into the experiences of women in my own social and political milieu, from September 1999 to July 2000, I conducted empirical research into the views of a socially diverse group of Toronto-area women who were juggling caring work, community work, green household practices, and, for most, paid employment. I interviewed thirty women in total, from a wide range of local organizations working on different kinds of quality-of-life issues. I conducted guided interviews (or what I prefer to think of as conversations) in which I asked for the women's personal stories rather than for the accounts of their organizations' goals or projects. My focus was on the women activists as people with complex lives rather than as representatives of a particular organization. An account of how I selected women to interview, a description of the interview process, and my approach to interpreting the data is provided in the appendix.

Based on the data collected from a background questionnaire sent to each woman prior to the interview, I can report that my participant group consists of sixteen "white" Anglo-Canadian women, five Jewish women, and nine women of colour (including two African women, two Caribbean women, two Latin American women, one Indian woman, and two bi-racial women). This is not representative of the diversity of cultural groups that live in the greater

Toronto area; people from well over eighty ethnocultural groups live in To-ronto. Nine of the women were relatively recent immigrants. With respect to socioeconomic status, thirteen described themselves as working class (includ-ing six who said they live in poverty) and seventeen described themselves as middle class (which includes both "lower" and "upper" middle class). At the time of our meeting, the women ranged in age from thirty to sixty-eight years of age. All had been involved in activist work for a prolonged period of time, ranging from a minimum of three years for one woman to "all my adult life" for ten women. All but three of the women reported being involved in more than one organization or project at a time, and several said they were involved in more than four each. The amount of time the women said they spent on their unpaid activist work each week ranged from two to forty, with an average of about fifteen, hours per week. Twenty-one women had paid employment (of these, eleven worked part time or less than thirty hours per week, by Statistics Canada's [2000] definition), six were self-employed, six had contract or tem-porary employment, and four had more than one job. Nine women did not have a paid job (of these, four were not in the paid labour force by choice [as full-time mothers], two were looking for paid employment, one was on dis-ability leave, one was a graduate student, and one was receiving social assist-ance). All but two of the thirty women had a university or college education.

The background questionnaire also asked about the nature of the women's caring responsibilities. All of the women have caring responsibilities; all are mothers. Of the thirty women interviewed, the majority (twenty) were living with a husband and one or more children (average number of children was three). One woman reported being in a same-sex partnership and was living with her children from a previous marriage. Nine of the women were living independently (a.k.a. "single mothers"), and, of these, eight were raising chil-dren, two with the help of their mother who was living with them. Children ranged in age from infant (under one year old) to adult (i.e., in their thirties; most of these adult children were living at home because they are disabled and so remain dependents). Four women had parents living with them, three had disabled adults living with them, seven had unrelated household members living with them (i.e., friends of their children or lodgers), and one was living with her husband and child in a communal home with four other adults. Only one of the thirty women was not then living with her children; she was living with an elderly friend who required as much, if not more, care than a child.

Because I am interested in how women manage to juggle their various car-ing responsibilities, I asked questions aimed at gauging the women's level of satisfaction with the distribution of these activities/responsibilities within their households. Their responses to the questionnaire are reported, along with what they said in the interviews, in Chapter 7. I also wanted to know to what extent they attempted to "live green" and, if they did, how the work involved was distributed in their households. I also asked the following:

Which of the following environmentally friendly practices do you normally exercise in your household? (check all that apply)

____ recycling
____ buying foods in bulk
____ composting
____ growing your own food
____ buying organic foods
____ preserving your own foods
____ cleaning without chemicals
____ precycling
____ conserving energy
____ substituting homemade goods for commercially produced goods
____ others (please specify):

This checklist provided specific examples of what I (and many greens) mean when referring to the ideal of living more sustainably in everyday life. I based this list on readings of the academic green literature and popular eco-lifestyle guides like *Get a Life! How to Make a Good Buck, Dance around the Dinosaurs and Save the World While You're at It* (Roberts and Brandum 1995). Including the list meant that I did not have to spend time explaining "green household practices" in the interviews and that the women had already had a chance to think about the extent to which they lived up to the goal of living green prior to our discussions. I report on the women's responses in Chapter 8.

In presenting the findings of the interviews in Chapters 7 and 8, I have used a large number of direct quotations and in many cases (especially in Chapter 8) I have used the women's real names with permission so that they are given credit for their own ideas and experiences. Although there are some risks to non-anonymity, such as attracting negative attention to the women's organizations or violating the privacy of their colleagues, friends, and family members, I believe that treating the women as anonymous subjects would diminish their role in the research and contradict one of the study's goals: to recognize the personal rewards and critical insights that women gain as a result of their activist work. Precedents for using the real names of women activists in feminist research of this kind include Naples (1998), Garland (1988), and Kaplan (1997), although none of these researchers explains the choice to do so. All of the women have agreed (and have given written permission) to be identified by their real names; those who have asked not to be named have been given pseudonyms (indicated by an asterisk) and the communities where they live have not been identified. As a precautionary measure, in cases in which their comments are very personal or could cause discomfort for the women or their families, I have not identified the speaker by name (instead, I say, "one woman said"). This decision was made when I discovered that a few women wanted to change some of their more revealing comments after reviewing their transcripts. Comments about involvement in activism and theorizing about politics and public life are generally attributed to the women who made them. I believe that attributing comments about domestic life to particular women is less important than giving them credit for their public contributions and for their ideas about the substantive themes under investigation.

With regard to the use of direct quotations, space considerations dictate that I cannot provide the answers given by each woman for each question, so a few representative answers have been chosen for presentation. In selecting quotes to include I have used my own judgment about which are most relevant and interesting to the themes discussed in this book.

Setting the Stage: Toronto in the Late 1990s and Early 2000

My study is located in and around Toronto, a city with surrounding suburban areas that has a population totalling approximately five million people, located on the north shore of Lake Ontario. Toronto is the largest metropolitan centre in Canada and in 1998 was amalgamated into a "mega-city": the six municipalities that once made up the Greater Toronto Region are now part of the City of Toronto, and have one centralized local government.[16] It is also the most prosperous urban region in Canada, considered to be the centre of the nation's economy. There is a wide and growing gap between income groups: Toronto is home to the most affluent as well as to the most impoverished people in the country. The homeless population of the city reportedly exceeds 20,000. There are many affluent and economically depressed neighbourhoods within the region, both in inner-city Toronto and in surrounding suburbs. Some areas are extremely affluent (e.g., Forest Hill, Rosedale) while other neighbourhoods, such as Junction Triangle, Jane-Finch, Parkdale, Regent Park, and St. Jamestown, are known for having the worst living conditions in the city. The popular perception is that they have high crime rates and so people who live there (a high percentage of whom are new immigrants and/or nonwhite) carry a negative social stigma. Six of the thirty women I interviewed live and/or work in these neighbourhoods, and of these six, four have been engaged in work that explicitly aims to improve the reputation of these places and their residents in the media and in the eyes of the rest of the city.

Toronto is one of the most culturally diverse cities in the world, home to immigrants from over eighty countries. More than one-third of all immigrants to Canada settle in the Toronto area, creating a high demand for support services to help them integrate into Canadian society. With waves of immigration, often the result of conflict in other parts of the world, come different kinds of needs and concerns: for example, in the past few years there have been influxes of refugees from war-ravaged places such as Kosovo, Sierra Leone, Rwanda, and Somalia. Six of the women I interviewed are immigrants to Canada from developing countries and, of them, five – Jamila Aman (originally from

Somalia), Ruth Lara (Peru), Alejandra Galvez (Chile), Murphy Browne (Guyana), and Wangari Muriuki (Kenya) – have been active in immigrant support work.[17] Demographic trends also indicate a growing elderly population resulting in increasing demands for health care and residential support services. Five of the women with whom I spoke were at the time living with an aging parent or friend for whom they were providing care in their own homes.

Throughout the 1980s, 1990s, and into the 2000s, the reality of a growing population, combined with pro-development policies, have led to urban sprawl, which is placing tremendous strain on the public infrastructure as well as on the natural environment. Local governments are struggling to cope with the need to provide housing and jobs and socioeconomic support to the unemployed as well as to provide basic services such as public transportation, waste disposal, and water and sewage treatment. Air quality is fast approaching a crisis situation as a car-dependent population with a need for heat in winter months consumes ever-higher quantities of nuclear and fossil fuel energy.[18] Environmental organizations in Toronto, like the Toronto Environmental Alliance (TEA), have named air quality as one of their top priorities for political action. Asthma rates continue to grow at alarming rates; smog is said to kill more than 1,800 people in Ontario each year. Programs to reduce car use are popular, including increasing the use of public transit and other modes of transportation (like bicycles). Another major issue for environmental groups is waste management. Canadians produce more garbage per capita than the people of any other country (RCFTW 1992). In an effort to curb the growing quantities of garbage produced by a large population, the local government charges tipping fees to industries and provides household curbside recycling programs (called the blue box), but the amount of waste-reduction efforts in Toronto pales in comparison to those in other cities in Canada (e.g., Halifax and Edmonton). At the time of my research, an acrimonious debate was taking place in the aftermath of a plan by local government to close the city's largest landfill site and transport the city's garbage to an abandoned mine near Kirkland Lake in northern Ontario (Walkom 2000). Other pressing local environmental issues include preserving important wetlands (the Don River Valley and the Oak Ridges Moraine), banning residential and parkland pesticide use, and cleaning up lead and chemical contaminated soils left over from Toronto's industrial past and that threaten the health of inner-city residents.

The pressure on local governments to address these and other social and environmental problems has been intensified in recent years with the election of the Progressive Conservative Party, led by Premier Mike Harris, to the provincial government. After its election in 1995 (the year I moved to Toronto), the Harris (and later briefly the Eves) government implemented a number of policies that have affected the operation of local government as well as the quality of life for residents of the Toronto region.[19] Like other governments around the world, the Ontario government adopted a host of neoliberal economic policies and socially conservative social policies that, together, form a new right agenda (Teeple 1995). As part of this agenda, the provincial government cut funding to many of its ministries and social programs and downloaded the responsibility for a variety of public services to the local level. A provincial workfare program has been instituted, to be administered by local governments (one of the women I interviewed has taken part in a "workfare" program). In an effort to reduce the unwieldy burden of responsibility of the local government, many of these services, particularly care and support services, have in turn been contracted out to private companies or downloaded to the volunteer sector and to private individuals in families. One of the women I interviewed who has a disabled adult daughter living at home has experienced an intensification of her twenty-four-hour caregiving responsibilities because of the cuts to social services.

The Tory government attempted to justify these policies, at times, through pushing a socially conservative vision of community self-reliance and the duty of the family to take care of its own. As explained in Chapter 4, feminist political economists and policy researchers have explained the overall effects of new right economic policies on women and argued that policies such as Harris' take for granted that households (and the women who do unpaid caring labour in households) will be able to absorb the costs of restructuring and a diminished state role in the provision of basic services to citizens. In Ontario, while there are no explicit policies for forcing women to "take up the slack," there is evidence to suggest that this is what is happening. From helping reduce the impacts of cuts to education through home-school committees to taking care of disabled or ailing family members at home, women all over Canada are shouldering a greater burden of unpaid work than men (Statistics Canada 2000).

It goes without saying (or it should, after over three decades of feminist scholarship) that in Canada, and most other countries around the world, women continue to perform the majority of caring work in households. Statistics Canada (2000), whose census in 1996 included unpaid housework for the first time, reports that women spent an average of 2.8 hours a day at paid work and 4.4 hours at unpaid work, whereas men spent an average of 4.5 hours at paid work and 2.7 hours at unpaid work. (Unpaid work was defined in the Census by three categories of activity: housework/home maintenance, child care, and care/assistance to seniors.) In coping with this division of labour, Canadian women have relied on the kind of welfare state social policies that were designed to allow them greater access to the paid labour market. It was (and still is) a mission of the Canadian women's movement to fight for and recommend necessary social programs to benefit women. Feminist activists enjoyed a good measure of success on this front until the 1990s, when the welfare state was rapidly eroded by right-wing governments (Brodie 1995). Recognizing this, feminist researchers have documented the impacts of cuts to all aspects of social welfare on women as recipients or clients of state-funded services (Cohen 1995; NAC 1995) and as unpaid caregivers in the private sphere.[20] On the former issues, the erosion of social programs has resulted in increased rates of poverty and a decreased quality of life among women and their children. Single mothers have been hurt by cuts to social assistance and family allowance payments like the Canadian Social Assistance Plan (CSAP). Nine of the women I interviewed are raising or have raised children without a partner. In Canada, the partial de-indexing of the Old Age Pension program has further impoverished elderly women whose paid employment histories (and lack thereof) leave them economically disadvantaged relative to men. Cuts to subsidized child care services have increased costs for employed women with children and prohibited the acquisition of paid work for some. Sixteen of the women I interviewed have children living at home who were then under twelve (and thus legally required child care). Cuts to health care programs have reduced the quality of women's health care, moving it in the direction of treatment rather than prevention (Armstrong 1996). As the majority of residents of subsidized housing, long-term care facilities, and emergency shelters, women also have been severely affected by cuts to social housing (Cohen 1995; Novac 1995).

Since 1995 labour unions and other social movement groups in Ontario have become more active in opposing the right-wing social policies of the provincial government. There have been several strikes by teachers, transit workers, and other public service employees who have all been affected by regressive policy changes. Several of the women I interviewed – namely, Joanne Green, Maureen Noonan, and Kathleen Wynne – have been active in supporting teachers and in protesting the government's new education policies, which affect the quality of their children's education. There have been a number of major anti-government rallies in recent years.[21] As the government moved to crack down on the poor, for example, by making pan-handling and "squeegying" illegal, anti-poverty groups staged sit-downs in local parks and engaged in violent clashes with the police. Anti-poverty organizations like the Ontario Coalition against Poverty (OCAP) and Low Income Families Together (LIFT) have worked to help people survive the cuts while taking every opportunity to express their outrage at the injustice of the government's treatment of the poor. Josephine Grey (interviewed for my study), a founder and social justice coordinator with LIFT, has gone to the United Nations to expose the plight of Canada's poor to the international community. Food bank use is increasing in many communities (by 1.4 percent per year nationally, according to the Canadian Association of Food Banks [2000]): two of the women I interviewed, Karen Marcelle and Joanne Green, have been active in running food banks in their neighbourhoods. Members of African- and Caribbean-Canadian communities have been mobilized to fight back against racially motivated police harassment and the racism of civic officials like Toronto's former mayor, Mel Lastman.[22] Murphy Browne, one of the women I interviewed, has become a leader in the movement against racism and police violence in Toronto (Di Matteo 2000).

Moving back, finally, to the topic of environmental politics in Ontario, it must be noted that the Harris government revoked many environmental regulations and cut funding to the Ministry of the Environment by approximately 40 percent. These changes have resulted in a reduced ministry capacity to monitor environmentally risky activities, and local governments and private citizens remain on their own in taking responsibility for the quality of their environments. Several environmental disasters have occurred in Ontario since 1995 (e.g., the Plastimet fire in Hamilton, the E. coli water contamination in Walkerton), some would say as a direct result of the weakening of environmental regulations.[23] There is a large number of groups and organizations in Toronto dedicated to either resisting environmental deregulation or pressing for environmental regulation and clean up or, of course, doing both at once. Many of the women who took part in my study have been actively involved in the local environmental issues described above. Sixteen of the women I interviewed have been involved in anti-pesticides organizations. Others have been involved in lead remediation in Riverdale, safe sewage and waste management, and green community programs like the walking school bus and community gardening. Much of this work has been done with little or no funding from government sources, and the majority of women run their activist groups out of their homes. As will become evident in Chapters 7 and 8, these facts make the intersection of private caring, active citizenship in the public domain, and the values of "living green" all the more challenging.

7 The Private, the Public, and the Planet: Juggling Care and Activism in Daily Life

It's time to take responsibility and to take action. Environmental citizens must become better informed and get involved. How? By learning more about the environment and taking actions that show we care about planet Earth – our air, land, water, wildlife, fisheries and forests. Individuals, communities, organisations and governments must think about the environmental rights and responsibilities we all have as residents of planet Earth. We all have to become part of the solution – in our schools, in our communities, at work and in our own backyards. Individual efforts taken together can be powerful forces for environmental change. In fact they can make all the difference in the world!

> – *Environment Canada,* What Is Environmental Citizenship?

In the summer of 1997, Ann Gallagher's engagement with environmentalism went from participating in household recycling and green consumerism to becoming one of the leaders of Community Action North End (CANE) virtually overnight. That was the night a plastics factory caught fire and forced the evacuation of her family from their home in a working-class neighbourhood in the north end of Hamilton, Ontario. As she recalls it, it was a traumatic experience that changed the way she looks at the quality of life and politics in her city. She has worked since then to demand the cleanup of the site and to get compensation for the community through a class-action lawsuit.

> When we first came back to our home after leaving, I cried and cried because it's almost like you feel like you're poisoning your kids. And you can cry about it or you can get really pissed off. When one of the guys from Public Health said something like, "See? It's not all that bad," I said, "You know what? Get this through your head: I'm sitting here through sheer politeness because I want to get this job done. Don't think for one moment that I don't hate your guts and that I do not blame you for what you did to my kids" ... It was very frightening. You can't live someplace where you are no longer comfortable. A lot of my neighbours don't mind it: this is where they were raised. I've had people from other parts of Hamilton say to me, "How can you live there?" and I always look at them and go, "You think that it's just this area? You think that all of that crap in the Northeast End isn't blowing all over the city? You are kidding yourself." I've discovered that although there are lots of beautiful parks and green spaces in Hamilton, they are all severely contaminated and cannot be built on. And people have no idea.

As Karey Shinn became aware of the cancer and asthma rates in her neighbourhood in the Beaches area of Toronto, home to the largest sewage treatment plant in the country, she grew concerned about health implications for her own family:

> So many people in the neighbourhood were sick. I literally knew mothers who had their vans kitted out like emergency vehicles with respirators and everything else for their kids. Everybody seemed to be coming down with something. I had never lived anywhere that so many people had cancer. The day I sold my house the real estate agent's daughter, who was all of fourteen, died of leukemia. It was really nuts ... When I started this my daughter was two and that was over ten years ago ... So the years I had left with them at home, I didn't want them living there. So I moved. The more I found out about how badly this was affecting the community, the more I didn't like it. I read all the reports.

In the late 1980s she, along with six other women, founded the Safe Sewage Committee (SSC), a group that in 2001 had a membership of eighty (and a mailing list of 2,000). It has been lobbying for changes in the way the city thinks about and handles its sewage. Working on a minimal budget, the group does research and tries to educate decision makers about environmentally sound sewage treatment technologies. It is calling on the city to use sludge as fertilizer on farmland rather than incinerate it, treat it with chemicals, or dump it into Lake Ontario. The SSC has been so visible in the community that Karey Shinn and two other group members have been nicknamed the "sewage sisters" by local residents.

At first sight, the stories told to me by Karey Shinn and Ann Gallagher sound similar to the classic tales of grassroots women's activism in contemporary writings on ecofeminist politics and women in the environmental justice movement that I describe in Chapter 2. But upon closer inspection, these stories, like those of the twenty-eight other women I interviewed, are more complex and multidimensional. While it is possible to celebrate many of the women I interviewed as examples of "activist mothers" or "grassroots warriors" whose experiences affirm a unique connection between gender and environmental concern, I shall instead highlight the diversity of their experiences and the tensions and contradictions they face when juggling public activism and private caregiving. What I heard them tell me is that finding time and resources for participating in community and environmental activist work while attending to the myriad roles and responsibilities of mothering is no easy feat. In fact, they told me that motherhood can both enable and constrain their political activism.

In this chapter I discuss some of the resonances and dissonances between my research and similar investigations of women's grassroots quality-of-life activism in developed countries.[1] My interpretations of what the thirty women told me about their everyday lives as mothers and activists add depth and texture to the portraits of women activists often found in ecofeminist writing. I present these interpretations here in a way that resists drawing general conclusions that can be applied to all women everywhere who are community or environmental justice activists. Other studies of this kind tend to slip subtly from findings about a small group of women activists to making statements about women activists in general (see, for example, Krauss 1993; Kaplan 1997). I, on the other hand, make transparent the fact that I am drawing on conversations with thirty specific women activists at a particular time and that these conversations (and my own reading of their significance) ought not to be considered representative of the vast complexity of their "lived experience."

The analysis in this chapter is organized into four parts. In the first part, I present what the women said were their reasons for getting involved in activism; here the question of whether motherhood is a principal motivation is considered. The second and third parts highlight what the women described as the implications of the "struggle to juggle" activism and care in their everyday lives. Finally, the fourth section lists some of the rewards the women said they gained from their activist work, such as personal satisfaction, increased self-esteem, and heightened political awareness.

"Mother Activists": Complicating the Profile

> The identity and experience of being a "mother," and the outrage at
> watching local corporations and government officials exhibiting total
> disregard for the lives of their children, have significantly motivated
> many women to become politically active. (Di Chiro 1998, 119)

As I explain in Chapter 3, "re/sisters" in the South and "housewife activists" in
the North are two paradigmatic examples of women's activism upon which
contemporary discourses of ecofeminist politics draw. The typical profile of a
woman activist in the environmental justice movement in the United States is
of a working-class white woman or woman of colour (mostly African or Latin
American) who begins as an apolitical housewife and is transformed into a
grassroots community activist when the health and welfare of her children is
threatened. My conversations with the Toronto-area activists in my study support my suspicion that this characterization of women's involvement in local
quality-of-life struggles ought to be questioned. I was able to problematize, or
at least to complicate, the profile by including women from a variety of class
and cultural locations and by asking them to reflect on the relationship between their motherhood and their engagement in activist work.[2] In doing so, I
found that the women I interviewed draw upon a combination of personal
resources to sustain their activism, including spiritual, cultural, political, and
intellectual traditions, in addition to maternal ones. This finding serves to
challenge the claim of many scholars that women activists frame their grassroots political engagement primarily in terms of "traditions of motherhood
and family" (Krauss 1993, 249).

I spent some time at the beginning of our conversations talking to each
woman about how she came to be involved in community activist or volunteer
work[3] and what motivates her to work on her chosen issues.[4] About half of the
thirty women reported that concern for their children's welfare was indeed an
important source of motivation for their activism. These women said that
feeling responsible, as mothers, for their children's health now and in the future led to (what I would call) their "politicization" on issues of environmental quality and social justice. Responding to a generalized sense of angst about
the quality of the environment, these women said that working to ensure their
children a safe and secure future is part of "being a good mother." For instance, when I asked Karen Buck of Citizens for a Safe Environment (CSE)
"What motivated you to get involved when you did?" she replied:

> Reading about environmental degradation in newspapers and
> books, hearing it documented on radio, and seeing it on television
> raised within me a concern for my daughter and the future world
> she would have to live in. It was a gloomy future of uncertain

greenhouse gas effects, air and water pollution, overpopulation, and food scarcity. I believed this would definitely happen within her lifetime or perhaps even within my lifetime. Along with the story of doom and gloom there was also the story of hope. The environmental degradation that I was hearing about was reversible if action was taken now ... so I made a decision to become involved, to act locally, and to believe that my actions could and would make a difference for her and her generation.

Marcie Goldman said that getting involved in anti-pesticides activism "initially stemmed from wanting to be a good mother because I felt that in taking care of my children I had to provide a safe environment for them and that this extended beyond my own home." It is interesting that, like her, most of the women involved in anti-pesticides campaigns reported that it was out of concern for the health of their children that they started getting active. For Karen Woudstra, finding out that her children's school playground had been sprayed with Par-3 (a herbicide) made her take action on a long-standing concern for environmental issues. Soon after, she founded the York Region Environmental Alliance (YREA) to lobby for tougher regulation of residential pesticide use. According to several other women, the experience of seeing pesticide warning signs on their neighbours' lawns or smelling chemical fumes while strolling with a young child was the "click moment" that motivated them to ask questions and seek answers about the health effects of pesticides. As Cheryl Shour of the Organic Landscape Alliance (OLA) explained:

> Pesticides was just one of those moments. I was home with kids and got caught in the drift of a spray. I was walking with one of my babies and we got caught. I don't know if I was conscious or not conscious about environmental issues before that. I didn't ever spray or do things like that, but that's mostly because I was too cheap ... I was in between jobs, I had a business job before that and then I was at home and it was very hard making that adjustment. So I picked up a phone and I called Pollution Probe and asked them to send me some information on pesticides. I knew nothing about it and I could not believe it. I was mortified that that's what those little signs meant. That's how it started.

Even when women named it as an impetus for political engagement in quality-of-life issues, maternal responsibility or concern meant different things to different women. As a result, I think it is inaccurate to point to an "ideology of motherhood" (Krauss 1997) to explain the activism of the thirty women I interviewed. These women come from diverse class and cultural backgrounds. While some of them come from backgrounds that may seem to accept dominant

North American (white, middle-class, heterosexual) notions of motherhood, others (especially those raised in non-Western cultures) have been accustomed to quite different familial ideas and practices. Some are sole-support mothers who are family leaders. Others have experienced parenthood as a joint (or equal) venture between themselves and their partners. Some women said that protecting their children from environmental threats is part of their maternal duty, while others spoke of a sense of responsibility to children in general because focusing strictly on the welfare of their own children risks parochialism (more on this last point in Chapter 8). Some women were social and/or environmental justice activists for many years before they became mothers. Noting these and other differences in the women's understandings of motherhood is important not only if we wish to avoid reifying their experiences as mothers but also to let us acknowledge women's roles in actively constructing, interpreting, and practising their own motherhood.

The responses of some women suggest that we ought to look at the relationship between maternal concern and political activism as one of negotiation and mutual influence that changes over time rather than as women's instinct. Compare this suggestion to a statement used to describe the Mothers of East LA: "If one of her children's safety is jeopardized, the mother turns into a lioness" (Gutierrez in Di Chiro 1998, 119). In contrast, Jackie Kennedy, chair of the North Toronto Green Community (NTGC), told me that her involvement in environmental work was inspired by what her daughter was learning at school. A few other women explained that they became involved in environmentalism by volunteering to run environment clubs at their children's schools. These women suggested that the best way to change adults' attitudes towards the environment is to educate their children. While learning about environmental issues from one's children is different from acting out of instinctive maternal concern for one's children, it may be the case that public campaigns for environmental education are effectively playing on mothers' concerns for their children's health. This analysis is informed by the concept of "environmentality" (Darier 1996): the Foucauldian argument that the state deploys various institutional techniques (e.g., through environmental education) to discipline citizens to accept responsibility for environmental sustainability. Some women may feel that their children (armed with the latest school-sponsored scoop on living green) pressure them – for better or worse – to live up to eco-friendly standards or that their children "police" their household behaviour. Anti-pesticide activist Terri Mittelmann told me that her children play an important role in holding her to her professed environmental values:

> My kids motivate me, like when I'm tired out of my skull because I went to bed at 2:30 AM and I throw something away and the kids say, "Can't that go in the blue box?" Try explaining the grey areas!

> Kids see the world in black and white. They really see it and can
> help you along. In other words, they can really be a thorn in your
> side when you'd like to be a terribly inconsistent person but just
> espouse consistency.

As I note in Chapter 5, some ecofeminists have questioned state efforts to
privatize environmental responsibility through education programs largely
targeted at children (Sandilands 1993). They argue that such "environmentality" has a gender dimension that should be recognized.

It is significant that even when they named their concern for their children
as an important source of inspiration, the women I interviewed also named
other reasons for getting involved in activism and other kinds of resources
upon which they draw. One could highlight motherhood alone but that would
only be part of the picture. The women named a number of other resources
for their activism that help "decentre" motherhood. First, several women made
connections between their environmental and social justice concerns and their
cultural and/or religious beliefs.[5] When I asked in our interview: "When you
think back to when you first started to do volunteer work, where do you
think you got the motivation and the drive to do the work?" Jamila Aman
responded: "I think it has do to with my culture and my religion, even though
a lot of people might disagree, in my religion they say that you have to give
back. And as a Muslim, you give 10 percent of your savings and income every
year to the poor; you take care of your neighbours. I came from that kind of
background."

Three of the women have been active in the Religious Society of Friends
(Quakers), a tradition that espouses principles of non-violence, simplicity, and
stewardship of the earth's resources. Three other women spoke about the influence of their Jewish faith on their involvement in environmental campaigns.
For example, Julie Starr, founder of the Vaughan Environment Action Committee (VREA), said: "It is written that this world is a gift and we can destroy
it or take care of it; we have a choice ... for me it's all connected because I am
a soul in a body and every action must be responsible."

Another apparent connection between cultural practice and activist work
can be found in the responses of some of the immigrant women I interviewed.
A few said that their experiences as new immigrants to Canada motivated
them to help other immigrants settle into their new environments with more
comfort than they had experienced themselves. These women also said that
activist work is an important way to maintain ties to their communities and
countries of origin. These aspects of activist work are important to recognize
in an era of growing global migration, and this is particularly relevant in cities
like Toronto, with diverse immigrant populations. Ruth Lara and Alejandra
Galvez both explained that their activism was imported: they were youth activists in their home countries and upon immigrating felt it necessary to help

those left behind. Several women explained that they were raised to believe that activism was an important way to contribute to their community; whether they had children or not, it would be just something they needed to do. One woman could not explain the origins of her environmental concern, stating that she had "just always been interested" in the environment. Others either had parents who were activists or got involved in activist communities at an early age. For example, community activist Li-Lien Gibbens attributes her activism to being raised by parents who are active in the microfinance movement in developing countries. She does activist work partly to stay connected to her Chinese culture and partly to develop skills in development work. Significantly, there appear to be cultural dimensions to this notion of "upbringing," as a number of the women who talked about their upbringing made specific reference to their culture or way of life "back home." Wangari Muriuki, Murphy Browne, Jamila Aman, Karen Marcelle, Ruth Lara, and Alejandra Galvez each noted that it is part of their culture to be community-oriented and that "community" includes what they mean by "environment."[6]

Another reason for getting involved in activist work mentioned by several women, particularly women who are less affluent and/or socially marginalized, is that becoming engaged in community organizations is a way of coping with their own personal hardship and isolation. For women living in poverty or in abusive relationships, "survival" was identified as a source of motivation (although perhaps not in the same sense as it is by ecofeminists who attribute it to women activists in developing countries). These women said that their activism was initially aimed at establishing better community support systems. Three of the women said that their experience of raising children by themselves while living in poverty made it necessary for them to connect with groups that work to change an unjust system. Josephine Grey co-founded LIFT because of this kind of experience:

> What got me started was essentially supporting a family on my own
> and having a lot of struggles and needing help and not being able
> to get it appropriately or when I did it came with such a price. When
> I had to turn to social assistance I found it a really extraordinary
> experience. Just also the experience of being a mother without a
> community or extended family. And from my knowledge of anthro-
> pology and history, I knew how wrong that was and so I wanted
> things to be better. Also because I made a commitment when [my
> children] were born that I would do whatever I could in my power
> to make the world better for them, otherwise I couldn't justify
> having them. I was in crisis for lack of resources and the difficulty
> in getting them really pissed me off. So I just wanted to work on
> the causes of the things that made life difficult, and I started realiz-
> ing that a lot of other women had the same kind of experiences.

It is worth noting that, for some women, including those who are relatively privileged, getting involved in activist work can be an important escape or diversion from their everyday lives as mothers and homemakers. In our conversations, several women told me that community work has helped them expand their lives beyond the narrowly defined role of mother. For example, one woman said: "Actually, when I think back to the period I liked the least, it was when I was home with two kids and I had quit work and I didn't have anything. That was the worst for me. I was bored and I didn't have a focus. That was terrible. This is much better even though it's crazier." Nikola Patti, who is involved in several different community campaigns aimed at addressing environmental quality in Hamilton, told me:

> I was at the point in my personal development where I'd been
> home with a baby for a couple of years, I hadn't been using my
> brain, and I desperately wanted to get involved with something ...
> I remember being in my kitchen thinking, "please please, send me
> a way to meet people and something to do because I can't just
> do this baby thing. I don't want to not to do it, but I need some
> balance." And sure enough two days later somebody knocked on
> the door with a petition.

This points to aspects of mothering and care that are rarely acknowledged in ecofeminist narratives. It may resonate with Lesley Doyal's (1995, 37) discussion of the "occupational hazards" of being a housewife: "Both clinical experience and community research have shown that many women staying at home experience intense frustration, which is usually expressed in feelings of emptiness, sadness, and worthlessness."

While some women described a combination of maternal concern and other motivating factors such as these, there were several women who, although they are mothers, did not emphasize connections between their motherhood and their involvement in activism. This was especially true of the (mainly but not exclusively middle-class) women whose professional lives and educational backgrounds inspire their work in the community. Several of the women see their activist work more as an extension of their professional commitments than of their responsibilities as mothers. Ruth Morris, for example, spent her whole career as a social worker and academic doing activist work for peace and social justice (she was the executive director of a non-profit organization called Promoting Economic Action and Community Health [PEACH] in the Jane-Finch neighbourhood).[7] For her, it was difficult to distinguish between her paid position and her community activism. The same thing can probably be said for Nita Chaudhuri, Jamila Aman, Ruth Lara, Murphy Browne, Karen Woudstra, Wangari Muriuki, Helen Melbourne, Kathleen Wynne, and Li-Lien Gibbens, who are each engaged in professions and/or educational pursuits that are intimately connected to (perhaps inseparable from) unpaid community work. Kathleen Wynne, for example, is a conflict resolution consultant with a master's of education degree who founded Parents Education Network and was a leader of Citizens for Local Democracy (C4LD). She said, "To a large extent my activist life is my work." For such women it is not evident that a singular line can be drawn from their identity as mothers to their activist commitments.

Finally, it should be noted that a small number of women expressed ambivalence towards the idea that there are causal links between their motherhood and their activism. Jane Smith*, a woman who works on a wide variety of environmental health issues, said:

> Before [my daughter was born] I used to spend most of my time doing work at the social level and the structural level, thinking this is where you make change, but since I've had a daughter I've had to re-shift it to make sure that the household level is equally radical. Because I have someone living and breathing right with me who I love. But I'm not a mother-activist, I'm a combination of a number of things and I always have been and I just keep adding things on as my experiences grow.

Perhaps the strongest expression of ambivalence about the connection between activism and motherhood came from one woman who said that she wants to be seen as a professional and advocate and not as an "activist mother." She said, "I wanted to be seen as a professional. And the activists ... were moms who were quite emotional and very smart, but their approach was such that it was like 'screaming mothers.' I needed to have another way."

The many sources of inspiration and resources for activism named by the thirty women I interviewed leads me to question the standard story that places motherhood firmly and unproblematically at the centre of grassroots activist narratives. Even when maternal concern was named as a motivation for activism, it was rarely the only one and it took on different meanings in articulation with other motivations. I suggest that looking at the diverse motivations of a group of women activists yields a much more accurate (if more complex) picture of women's engagements with environmental and social justice activism than the one now provided in much of the contemporary ecofeminist literature.

Juggling Act: Activism and Care in Everyday Life

> [SM: What's it like for you to juggle all of these different commitments?]
> What's it like? It drives me crazy! It stresses me out! If I was a person with better boundaries, which I guess I kind of am now,

it would be easier because I could say, "I'm only going to do this much." But it's never been that easy to say no.

[SM: Do you ever feel that there's just too much to do?]

There is too much to do! Yes. And my way of coping with it all in the past was to just be superwoman and just find the hours to do it all. But since becoming a parent it's just not possible, especially with sleep deprivation, and having to do paid work from time to time.

An important interpretation that emerges from my conversations is that being an activist who is also a mother can be a far more complex and conflict-ridden combination than one might conclude after reading more celebratory accounts. Moreover, from examples of the difficulties involved in juggling household and caring responsibilities and active participation in the public domain, it is possible to shed light on the weaknesses of gender-blind green approaches to citizenship. My aim is not to construct a narrative that casts the women activists as martyrs to the environmental cause, nor to tell a horror story that would dissuade women from engaging in activist work; rather, I simply wish to show that there are many implications for women's lives that come with the struggle to juggle activist work with the already heavy load of domestic work that women do in everyday life (Frederickson 1995). As I note in Chapter 5, research conducted by Tindall, Davies, and Mauboues (2003) finds that having to juggle a double day of work is a significant constraint on women's participation in environmental activism. Most of the women I interviewed are managing to cope with their double burden – or I probably would not have been able to interview them – but some cope better than others. Ability to cope often depends on class/income, household/family makeup, access to support networks and services, and time available for different commitments. There are aspects of each of these women's unique stories that are thus far unacknowledged in those ecofeminist narratives that focus on the community-directed nature of women's engagement with environmental and other quality-of-life issues (e.g., Salleh 1997; Taylor 1997; Di Chiro 1992, 1998).

As I explain in Chapters 4 and 6, one impetus for my research is an interest in exploring the hidden costs of women's activism. For this reason, I asked the women what impacts their involvement in unpaid work in the community has on their everyday life at home and vice versa. While there are many interesting facets to their answers, I focus on those common themes that have particular relevance for my inquiry.

Time Scarcity

There are ecopolitical theorists who contend that it is a sign of a liberated society that people have access to leisure time in which to pursue "individual development, self-expression, and realization of potential" (Lipietz 1992, 85).

Some have written of "the right to be lazy" (Darier 1998), while others envision a postindustrial, postconsumerist civilization founded on the reduction of working time and the (allegedly related) growth of leisure time (Gorz 1993). And if, as Arendt (1958) contends, citizenship is a project of self-realization, then it should be practised for its own sake – which requires time. But the gender implications of these ideas become obvious when one listens to women who, even though their paid working hours are few (or even non-existent), make a practice of denying themselves time for leisure.[8] The most common theme in my conversations with women about the effects of juggling is that activism comes at a price, and that price is time. Well over half of the women said that "lack of time" is a significant cost of their activist work and that they subsidize their activism by depriving themselves of time for themselves. This claim is not out of line with a Statistics Canada (2000, 111) finding that in 1998 at least one in three married mothers aged twenty-five to forty-four who are employed full time are severely "time-stressed."[9] Consistent also with feminist research on women's double and triple day, most women – even those without a spouse or a full-time job – said they lack personal leisure time (Frederickson 1995; Schor 1997; Bittman and Wacjman 2000). Many of the women I interviewed have school-aged children and, thus, can be expected to have the highest burden of unpaid work among all categories of parents (Frederickson 1995).

It is paradoxical that, for many "activist mothers," one of the costs of activism is having less time to spend with the children for whose welfare they are working. Brú-Bistuer (1996) heard this complaint from the Spanish women activists she interviewed. As I discovered, for some women this situation results in feelings of regret and sometimes guilt, clearly demonstrating the tensions between private and public caring. Vasta Gibbons, a sole-support mother of a disabled adult daughter, who (among other things) coordinates the Healthy Homes program in her neighbourhood, said:

> The biggest costs? Well, giving up my time to do things for other people is sometimes not convenient ... Being woken up at 6:00 AM on Sunday morning and being told, "Vasta, there's bugs running around all over my house, what do I do?" Time I guess. Just taking the time I would have for myself or my daughter, to take that time and give it to somebody else, that is probably the biggest cost.

Several women told me that their efforts to make time for activist work has led them to give up the social time they would normally spend with friends. This means that they rarely take a break from their "causes" to engage in leisurely activities or to spend time in ways that are non-instrumental (i.e., play for play's sake). As one woman explained:

My social life is pretty well non-existent. Well, I shouldn't say that, my non-environmental, normal, going-out-for-dinner kind of thing – oh, I would love to go out for dinner and have someone else cook for me, it's the best thing in the world! But we don't socialize except for in and around [my activist] stuff. So for example ... the Toronto Environmental Alliance has the Ecobunk Awards and that's my big outing. I haven't gone out in over two months. Part of me says maybe I should take a break or go see a movie. But the one night I do go out will be to go to Ecobunk. But I feel better with that because I'm having trouble socializing with my friends who don't quite get it. Like I said before, it's very hard to separate.

A few women mentioned the loss of friends due to lack of time for socializing. Perhaps they deprive themselves of important support networks in order to juggle their commitments:

Well one of the things is that if you're really, really active, you have to get it through to your closest friends and relatives that there are times when they don't take precedence. That's the really difficult juggling act: how do you keep people from feeling totally left out of your life and yet still do what you need to do? It's tricky and it's a constant kind of battle.

Even though most of the women in my study identified the lack of time for themselves as being problematic, many also discussed their difficulty in saying no. Learning how to say no and how to protect their time is something that most women mentioned as important to being able to cope with multiple roles and responsibilities. Some reported that guilt about saying no and thus letting people down, or fear that stepping away from a project will result in its demise, keeps them from taking time off for leisure. For example:

I think what keeps me going is that I don't want to disappoint people, sometimes I know a lot of people are relying on me ... I'm not in a position to back off or give up.

I cannot just stay home because if I stay home then the viewpoint of African people will not be expressed [at meetings]. A lot of times when I go to meetings I am the only black person there and sometimes I'm the only person of colour there and I think it's a good thing I did come. Because if I did not come it would look like we are not interested in this topic. So I need to be there.

It is valuable to recognize the gender specificity of this inability to say no. Socialized to be caring, women tend to think that they should sacrifice their own time for the sake of others' well-being (I discuss this in Chapter 4 as one of the negative aspects of women's caring). As Wangari Muriuki told me, it is difficult for women to let people down and thus risk being perceived as uncaring:

> Time-management was the biggest issue because I didn't know how to say no. I couldn't say no. People would call me at whatever hour and I would be there and I would join whatever cause that was happening without ever recouping [anything] for myself. I have found ways since ...
> [SM: Your daughter has been an impetus for that?]
> Yes.
> [SM: So you can say no for her, but you can't say no for you?]
> Isn't that always the case? I think it was before the pregnancy that I learned to say no. But it's one thing to say no and it's another thing to say no and not carry that guilt. A healthy no is difficult for women. It's an extremely difficult thing for women in my culture. I watch my mother now and see just how difficult it is for her to say no and how difficult she finds it for me to say no. We don't say no. We carry the burden and it doesn't matter if it breaks our backs.

What's Private, What's Public? On Lacking Boundaries

As some of these comments suggest, lack of guilt-free time for themselves seems for many women to be related to the inability to maintain a boundary between their various responsibilities and between "home" and "work." Whereas some researchers have focused on the "spilling" of domestic-sphere values and activities into the public domain (Brú-Bistuer 1996, 120),[10] several women expressed concerns about their ability to negotiate the conflation of their public and private lives. I note in Chapter 4 that the ideological separation of domestic and economic spheres is a key reason for the feminization and devaluation of caring work. I would add here the argument of feminist urbanists that the gendered public-private dichotomy is not only ideological but also spatial (MacGregor 1995). Feminist urban geographers have explored how the design of cities and suburbs has segregated the concerns of women, yet their findings are seldom appreciated by citizenship theorists (Jones 1998).

For women who "work at home" – as homemakers, activists, or as self-employed consultants and entrepreneurs (or some combination thereof) – maintaining boundaries can be difficult. There is sometimes the problem of how family members adjust to home as workplace or kitchen as office. One woman

– who juggles activism, paid part-time freelance work, and raising three teenaged children – told me, for example, that she finds it a challenge to get her family to understand that she "works at home":

> [SM: Is it difficult to use your home for so many different activities and have to draw lines between them all?]
> Yes, there is that. And even though this is my home and that's my office, everybody goes in there. And I have to say, "Don't touch my stuff" and "Look, you're making a mess and I can't find papers." So I don't have a place that's totally mine. And then sometimes when I'm doing work and the kids come from school I get resentful, or not resentful, but I feel like they're not going to leave me alone to do my work and I can't stop. So my space gets invaded. And yeah, it has so many roles ... and my kids don't think I work either. Other mothers go out to work, so they work, so I therefore don't work and am more able to take on things. And I'll look at them and say, "But I do work, just because it's [not] out of the house, I do, I spend hours and hours working." But they don't see it because I don't go out to an office ... When I say I work out of the house I think people think I clean it or something.

This point resonates with sociologist Harriet Rosenberg's (1995, 199) discussion of "housewife activists" who base their work in the private sphere and thereby open themselves up to all the "contradictions of maternalist ideology". Another woman remarked:

> Sometimes there's that preoccupation because I can't leave the work at the office, the work intrudes into my kitchen. And it takes time to shift gear and be attentive to [my family], so they might perceive that as a sacrifice that I've had to make.

Although there were women who said that working at home helps them juggle their multiple roles,[11] for some the lack of boundaries between home and work life can be suffocating and isolating. Doyal (1995, 39) reports that "lack of boundaries" and lack of "physical and mental space" is a particular problem for mothers, contributing to the high stress levels they experience in their lives. Their difficulties may be exacerbated when they choose to take on an extra load of commitments as activists. Some of the women in my study said that it is often difficult to take a break from their activist commitments and concerns: where does one go to get away from the home office? This question is important in light of the suggestion by green theorists that home-working is a potential solution to urban sprawl and unsustainable car-oriented

transportation practices (e.g., Paehlke 1994). Some urban sustainability advocates see great hope in new technologies (e.g., electronic cottages, telecommut-
ing) that allow people to combine home and work life more easily. But for women,
the notion of "working at home" is unavoidably imbued with gender ideologies that make it difficult to negotiate this scenario as easily as most men.[12]

In addition to the gendered politics of private space, the lack of public space
for political or community association can be problematic for women activists. American urban theorist Michael Sorkin (1992) has commented extensively on the privatization of space in cities that has resulted in the
disappearance of public spaces *(agora)* once thought central to democracy and
citizenship.[13] The women who base their activist work in their homes reported
that this situation causes problems for their family life and for their own sense
of boundaries. Interestingly, comments about having physical spaces for activism came up several times. A few women wished that they had an office or
meeting place. Some commented that doing activist work out of their homes
can take up too much physical space and thereby disrupt the family environment. Several women who run organizations and campaigns use their homes
as "command central" and so get phone calls at all hours of the day and have
to store vast numbers of documents and other materials in their home. Hamilton community activist Burke Austin told me that her bedroom is being
taken over by boxes of documents:

> [SM: You have a big stack of clippings there. Are you keeping a
> scrapbook?]
> Yeah. Except I've lost a lot, things get so scattered. But my office
> kind of takes up half my bedroom with documents and binders and
> computers.
> [SM: Do you wish you had an office somewhere else to go to?]
> I do.
> [SM: This is probably command central for the whole
> organization.]
> Pretty much.
> [SM: How does that feel for you?]
> It's pretty cramped and it's getting more cramped all the time
> with all the different issues coming up. And we are kind of hoping,
> we're working on a community centre because that's something our
> community is lacking at the moment. And if we could get an office
> in there that would be great.

These interpretations raise questions about how some feminists tend to
regard the public-private dichotomy. Donna Haraway (1991a), for example,
suggests that with technological change in a postindustrial society, it is now
misleading to draw a distinction between public and private, workplace and

home. She suggests that recognizing "a profusion of spaces and identities and the permeability of boundaries in the personal body and the body politic" is preferable to the conventional feminist approach to "separate spheres" because it is a more accurate description of power (212). While I agree with her, it is interesting that some of the women activists I interviewed seemed unhappy with the blurred and very permeable boundary between their public and private lives. This finding may suggest that, just like the women who turned to activism as an escape from their domestic roles, some women may not appreciate the constant interrelationship between the public and the private: they may wish for a degree of separation and autonomy.

Caring Responsibilities Make Activist Participation Difficult
When green political theorists speak of active participation in the affairs of the polis, they seldom ask: "Who will be minding the kids?" For activists who are mothers and/or have responsibility for the care of children or dependent adults, it is often difficult to operate in a society that relegates children to the private sphere on the assumption that they will be cared for there by parents (generally mothers, grandmothers, and so on). As a few feminist researchers have recognized, this presents a paradox in that motherhood and caring responsibilities become both resources for and constraints upon women's activism (e.g., Seager 1993; Rosenberg 1995; Tindall, Davies, and Mauboués 2003). I argue that this paradox is something that ought to be addressed rather than obscured or avoided both in ecological citizenship discourse and in ecofeminist discussions of women's grassroots activism.

Not surprisingly, most of the women named their care responsibilities as a particularly significant challenge in their daily efforts to juggle. Finding someone to care for their children while they are at meetings or having to miss meetings when their care responsibilities are too great seem to be the most common challenges. As one woman explained: "Well, first of all there's the unexpected things that make it more difficult to participate. Like for instance if you have to [do something] for your kids or go deal with [the housing authority] or whatever and whether you like it or not you'll have to miss a meeting if they're sick and you have to stay home. Things like that can throw you off in terms of the continuity of your participation."

Many women reported that they have no choice but to take their children to meetings. Involving children may not only affect women's ability to participate as equal members in public proceedings, but it may also challenge cultural expectations that children be relegated to the private sphere. A few said that by involving their children in activist work they are acting as role models and teaching their children important lessons. Perhaps by being taken to meetings by busy mothers with no other child care options, children not only become exposed to political issues and forms of engagement but are also exposed to what it means to be a citizen.[14] Is it possible that in the process of participating alongside their mothers, children's understanding of their mother's "proper role" in the household is challenged? Marcie Goldman alluded to this possibility when she said: "I like my kids ... to look at me and see that part of me is an activist and that's part of being a good mother."

Those women for whom child care is not a (reported) obstacle have older children who do not need much supervision, although most of these said it was difficult when their children were younger. Many have partners and/or paid child care arrangements to take over the responsibility when they themselves are unavailable (most women implied that it is their job to organize the child care). But for several others, lack of child care services or help with child care at home are significant obstacles to participation. Six of the women I interviewed are raising their children without a partner living in their home. For so-called "single mothers," it is understandably difficult to juggle a double or triple load of work (paid and unpaid) while taking care of children and maintaining a household.[15] Of course most women with young children are constantly searching for child care arrangements that would allow them to take part in their activist commitments. They rely either on friends and family for help with child care or they find more formal paid care arrangements.

> Child care is a very important factor. I happen to be one of the lucky ones that in the daytime I have a paid child care. In the evenings when I need to go to my meetings, me and my husband juggle. I don't make appointments until I talk to my husband and I know that my child is covered because that's my priority. The community is also very important but my main priority is my daughter because I am the only one who can care for my daughter. There could be other people in the community, but I take it upon myself to be the advocate for the community, and that's my priority, so I make sure that my daughter is well taken care of. Either my sisters are taking care of her or my husband is taking care of her and then I can do what I need to do. That's a lot of planning and scheduling. I juggle my schedule all the time.

Very often, these women are themselves the ones providing care (paid and unpaid) for others in addition to looking after their own children. Nikola Patti runs a child care centre in her home and finds it difficult to get child care support herself. Vasta Gibbons and Laura Jones take care of their grandchildren on a regular basis, and Karen Woudstra takes care of her younger siblings after school. And consistent with reports about the "sandwich generation" several of the women I interviewed provide daily care for their aging parents.[16] All of this care work must be juggled with their other responsibilities – paid work, activist work – and this makes for constant time management challenges. I discuss below how the women manage to cope (when they do cope) with the level of stress in their lives.

The lack of affordable and reliable child and eldercare and care programs for people with disabilities is a significant problem for women with a heavy load of caring responsibilities who also choose to do activist work.[17] For Vasta Gibbons the cuts to publicly provided care programs (part of the Harris government's privatization agenda) have been devastating. She now has only a few small windows of opportunity in which to focus on activities that do not involve her daughter, leisure and home maintenance included. This lack of support has led to great personal hardship, and at times she has no alternative but to withdraw from her activist commitments. As I have argued, new right governments seem to assume that families can take up the slack when public services are cut, but the negative consequences of this assumption for individual women are seldom recognized (Brodie 1996a). This point underpins my position that celebrating women's capacity to care without limits is risky and that resistance to privatization of caring by the state should be central to an ecofeminist political agenda.

Tensions in Family Relationships

While most of the women said they get various forms of support from their families for their activist work (discussed further below), at the same time most report that their activism can create tension and sometimes conflict. For many women this means a constant process of negotiation and, for a few, the tension has made it difficult to juggle multiple roles. This finding is congruent with the observations made by some feminist researchers, which indicate that women activists commonly face the disapproval and resentment of family members when they are believed to be deviating from their expected gender roles (Hamilton 1990; Krauss 1997; Kaplan 1997). Kaplan (1997, 41) writes, for example, that "not only do women, accustomed to polite dealings with those in authority, learn to confront those who call them 'hysterical housewives,' but they must also face their husbands and children, who accuse them of withdrawing affection and attention while pursuing political goals." The problems experienced by women at Love Canal were so great that they published a list of tips for activists on handling family tension (Zeff, Love, and Stults 1989). Caring for people at home and looking after communities as political activists are not always compatible, especially in societies in which women are expected to place more value on the former than on the latter.

Several of the women I interviewed reported that their children have, at some point, responded negatively to the amount of time their mothers spend doing activist work, especially if they are also engaged in paid work that takes them away from home during the day. As I have noted, this situation appears to cause tension at home: resentment in children and feelings of guilt among mothers. Here are two comments that illustrate this point:

> [SM: How does your daughter feel about you doing a lot of extra work?]
> At times she gets pissed off. She doesn't see how it's helping her and really I guess it's mainly mostly helping the church but she didn't see it. All she sees is mommy typing up the address lists and the duty roster. All she sees is mommy sitting at a PC and going to meetings where when I'm at meetings she goes to the daycare. I think she'd rather I was at home spending time with her.

> Sometimes there was a lot of tension. Sometimes I could only see my kids for half an hour in a day and sometimes I didn't see them for three days. There was tension and I felt distanced, especially from my daughter, sometimes my relationship with my husband wasn't good because I was so involved. And at that time I didn't really think about it and just felt this is my right, I am a woman and I have to do all that I want to do. Now, looking back, I realize that it was a lot. My husband had a lot of patience, and the kids also, but they were growing up and they would say, "Mommy, we don't want to you to study anymore, can you quit?"

Some women said that children can sometimes feel resentful that their mothers impose their values on them at home, particularly concerning their consumer choices.[18] It can be difficult to explain one's values and political commitments to a young child. Jane Smith* explained, for example, that it has been challenging to explain to her three-year-old daughter why she does not eat the same kind of food as other children. (Jane does her best to avoid overpackaged and overprocessed foods.) Children may also grow frustrated with having to participate in green household practices (forever being reminded to recycle) or get tired of hearing about "the issues." For example, an anti-pesticide activist said:

> Sometimes I think my kids are sick of it. They'll probably work for Chemlawn when they grow up. One of my daughters had to do a biography [project in school] so I took her to the library and they had one on Rachel Carson at her age level. So I said, "Here, read this one on Rachel Carson," and she said – she's nine – she said, "Who's that?" And I said, "She was the woman who sort of started the anti-pesticide movement." And she said, "No, no more pesticides!" There was no way she was going to touch that book.

Some of the women reported that their activist commitments sometimes cause tensions between themselves and their partners and/or other adults living in their homes (e.g., parents). These tensions seem to be caused by clashes in expectations about what the women ought to be doing with their time or how much time they ought to spend at home. Even in households that are purportedly influenced by feminist or egalitarian values, elements of "traditional" gender ideologies can emerge to cause conflict. One woman told me that, although her husband is supportive of her work, he also "doesn't feel that I'm doing my household duty and [feels] that I'm not there for my kids," which has at times caused tensions in their marriage: "At the beginning of this job I worked so many nights that it was a stress on my marriage. A lot of stress on my family relationships because you're not there. It costs in child care, when you start to have children; it's very difficult and you can't do the nights that you did before. And right now because I am going to school, my daughter is saying, 'Mommy you work too much.'"

Other women said that their partners sometimes feel resentful that the women's extra commitments outside of the house mean more domestic work for them. Their comments resonate with those studies that have looked at the impacts of women's activism on spousal relationships: they highlight the ways in which gender ideologies are challenged in the process of women's politicization (Kaplan 1997; Krauss 1997; Brú-Bistuer 1996).[19] One of the women was very forthcoming with her thoughts on this issue, admitting that her problems had to be worked out with professional counselling:

> I had a problem with my husband that's not so bad anymore
> because he sees me going back to school and there's a light at the
> end of the tunnel. But as I mentioned before, there was a resent-
> ment on his part that, I was doing all these volunteer things and
> other household chores would just slip and he would end up taking
> up the slack for that, and he would be resentful because he'd work
> hard all day as the main breadwinner and then he didn't have a
> chance to do the volunteer things that he'd like to do, because he
> had to pick up after my volunteer stuff. So that was a problem for a
> while; it's not so much anymore because I'm at school and there is
> a direction to this volunteerism. Because, as I said before, I will use
> my university education to do this environmental stuff and actually
> get paid for it. So that pressure is off. It was not nice for a long
> time because I couldn't not do this.

For most of the women I interviewed, tensions at home were minor and manageable with some reorganization and negotiation, but for others, activist participation has had more severe consequences for their family life. Two women

told me about the extent of their husbands' (now ex-husbands for both) negative reactions to their involvement in activism. Interestingly, both stories involve the women's exposure to public scrutiny in the media. Women in Krauss'
(1997) study had similar experiences: the women who emerged as visible community leaders experienced the greatest level of conflict with family members,
particularly their male partners. One of the women explained that her husband used her high-profile involvement in an activist organization against her
in their divorce proceedings. Another woman's ex-husband would react so vio-
lently to her activist work that she often had to hide it from him. Hiding her
work from her husband became more difficult once she began acting as a
spokesperson for anti-poverty organizations:

> I had the limitation that my partner didn't approve of what I was
> doing. I had to be very careful of him when I did it and try not to
> get caught. That was a little weird. As I became more and more of
> a spokesperson going to government agencies, I had the bizarre
> experience of dressing up and wearing makeup and trying to throw
> them off a little bit because they'd be expecting a single mom with
> messy hair and spit up on her sweat pants. I wanted them to have
> to figure out who was the token. So I would do that: rush off to the
> meeting and then rush home and change all my clothes and pretend
> I'd never been anywhere. And try to clean up enough and get dinner
> ready. That was a bit of a nightmare.

Although she did not report marital problems per se, one woman's involvement in environmental activism cost her husband his job at a local factory
and thus caused financial hardship for the whole family. She was reluctant to
tell this story while her husband was in the room and so waited until he left
for work:

> One thing that really got us into trouble, I'll share this with you,
> about my activism ... [my husband] worked for a company [name
> omitted] and they are a company that fell as fast as they rose. And
> two years ago he was working for them and they bought the
> company and changed everybody around and they put him on this
> team of people that were stripping down tin-lead cables – the
> cables were coated with lead – which was a totally unsafe thing to
> do. They were another of the big, strong conglomerates that felt
> that they could get away with anything. So every month he had to
> have his blood tested. And every month he had his blood tested,
> the lead level in his blood kept going up and up. And I was getting
> worried and felt that I was going to have to do something about
> this. So I called the Ministry of the Environment and the Labour

Board and they went down to the site and issued five orders where they were totally out of compliance. There was lead dust in the air and no filters. So instead of complying with the orders, they laid everybody off, and they knew it was me because nobody else would have done it. So [my husband] was permanently laid off, but they found jobs for just about everybody else. So that threw the whole household into turmoil because he was the main provider and I did everything else. He just started working three weeks ago at this [new] full-time job. So now it's another adjustment for us ... which is good though, because his self-esteem was just about washed away.

[SM: Did you feel guilty about blowing the whistle?]

Yes and no. Even some of his fellow workers called me and thanked me because they were worried about their health. And I kind of had to juggle it where, "Okay, I've been married to this guy for twenty-seven years, so do I watch him maybe get lead poisoning, which affects the brain and the nervous system, or do I do something?" So that's where we got into trouble for sure ... We had to choose health over finances.

The fact that women experience both support and conflict in families is an important reminder that women's work as activists should not be seen in isolation from life in the private sphere; they should not be treated as disembodied, autonomous selves (like the traditional liberal male citizen) who act only in the public domain but, rather, as situated selves-in-relationship who are shaped by different allegiances, obligations, traditions, and values. Moreover, it is important to consider not only that their actions are informed by their experiences as mothers and caregivers (to differing degrees) but that they can also be constrained by them as well (see Reed 2003).

Burnout: Compromising Personal Health and Well-Being

I think for me, as an advocate, I would not encourage women to jeopardize their health because if they are not healthy then it is not good for the community. The most important thing is that women should take care of themselves first, which is difficult to do. (Jamila Aman)

It would be false to say that the juggling acts being performed by the women I interviewed, and the kinds of implications it has for their personal lives, are unique to women activists. Even if they do not take part in activist work, millions of women (and men) are overextended and feeling the effects of burnout on their health and well-being (Schor 1997). Popular women's culture in

North America is particularly preoccupied with women trying to "do it all," finding methods of coping with hectic lives. One need only tune into the Oprah Winfrey show to hear stories about women (especially mothers) caring too much for those around them and too little for themselves. While I am not interested in pop psychology, I did ask the women whether they have ever compromised their own quality of life in their efforts to juggle their many commitments. In other words, I asked them whether they had ever experienced burnout.

The majority of the women reported that they have experienced burnout due to their involvement in activist work. The most common cause they gave was stress, which included mental, physical, and financial stress. Many of the women told burnout stories that highlighted the emotional exhaustion – including frustration and anger – that comes with engaging in activities that are controversial and that often meet with little or no success. Especially when they are fighting to change the immediate conditions of their lives, such as cleaning up a contaminated site in their backyard or trying to stop an expressway from being built through their neighbourhood, there is an understandable level of anxiety. Some others, who have dedicated their professional and personal lives to making changes in "the system," said they feel "devastated" when they see the erosion of public services at the hands of the Harris government in Ontario. Many said that frustration makes them tired and ready to give up; a few described their burnout as minor "mental breakdowns." Here are two examples of the comments I heard:

> I can see that I would be in a much better frame of mind if I had enough sleep. And if you're not always in an antagonizing situation, so many issues are so confrontational. Some meetings you go to and are just brow-beaten the whole night or ignored by people and then you go home and wonder, what's the point of anything I do?

> When I have burnout, I become frustrated and completely disoriented to the point that I can't function. I can't stick with one task because I lose my train of thought. I become very sick. And that's also because you're overstimulated, there's just too much happening. And a lot of people burn out that way. It's just too much stimulation because you're doing too much, juggling too many responsibilities.

The comments of these and other women suggest that self-neglect and lack of sleep can lead to physical exhaustion and health problems that then interfere with the ability to juggle caring and activist work. Several women reported that a common strategy for coping with time scarcity was staying up late, thus depriving themselves of time for sleep.

> Oh yeah, time saving? Number one: I keep late hours.
> [SM: But that's not time saving, that's fitting everything in by depriving yourself of rest.]
> Sure, this is my time saving: don't sleep as much!
> [SM: Don't you ever get tired?]
> I'm tired all the time. Since I had my last child, I keep on falling asleep at the kitchen table at night. Then I wake up and go off to bed.

It sounds to me as if the women spend little time taking care of themselves, while they take care of many others – a finding that appears to affirm what some feminists have said about the negative aspects of women's caring (e.g., Bowden 1997). As I discuss in Chapter 4, many feminists are critical of a "normative femininity" (Bartky 1990) that equates caring with self-sacrifice, that disciplines women to neglect their own needs and interests. One woman said:

> I guess it has an effect in that there is a tug of war between the needs of other people and needs of the outer world and then the interior needs of who you are, and I find it easier to care for other people than to care for myself. So I've had to learn how to care for myself because my body said enough and it kind of shut me down. Over the past two years I've practically lost the use of my arms at various points in time. It's going to obviously be an ongoing issue of simply not having the strength and having frozen shoulder and tendonitis and all the rest of it. There's obviously a penalty in there for stretching myself too far.

These comments also bring to mind Doyal's (1995, 48) question: "Who cares for the carers?" (see also Kittay 1999). In asking this, she points to a situation, common to women around the world, in which women who do caring work burn out because they do not receive enough support from the state (I explain the "reprivatization of care" and the erosion of welfare state policies in previous chapters). Nor can they count on consistent support from spouses or children, given the persistence of the gendered division and feminization of caring labour. Several women noted that their tendency not to care for themselves as much as they care for others may be responsible for their burnout and consequent need to cut back on activist work. For example, one woman has had to reduce her level of involvement in recent years. She believes that her health problems have been exacerbated by burnout:

[SM: I'm just wondering about the connection between your busy life and your health.]

I think that it's very connected and I think it's more connected to the devotion to work than to any individual cause. I'm trying now to figure out a way to be involved in things without ignoring my own body because I think that I was raised to ignore my own body, that other people were far more important. And I'm finding it difficult now to have to slow things down because I enjoy it. It isn't that I do it out of a sense that I need to suffer, I actually enjoy being involved in things.

[SM: But you said you have to cut down now so that you can take care of yourself.]

Yeah, and then when I think I've learned to take care of my own self then I want to be involved again. I need to find a more balanced way of doing it. I'm still involved in things, but they're smaller.

The decision to stop or drastically cut back on their involvement in extra-household activities seems to be more common for women living in poverty and women without adult partners. One woman said she has been stretched to the point of physical and emotional exhaustion:

I've had to cut down a lot. Like at the beginning, when I first started I was gung-ho – go go go all the time. I was so busy I didn't even have time for my daughter. So I was dragging her with me wherever I went so I could do what I had to do and it got to the point where I was depressed and stressed out. And I had to say, "That's it, I can't do anything right now. I don't want to do anything, I don't care about anybody, just leave me alone. Take my daughter for a couple of weeks; the community can go to hell. Leave me alone!"

It is important to acknowledge, therefore, that for many women (and for a variety of reasons) a high level of political activism is unsustainable. Women's experiences as activists may be so intense and exhausting that when they win their battle – and probably more often when they realize the battle may never be won – they retreat from political participation and go back to the way things were before.[20] Kaplan (1997) observes that while some of the women involved at Love Canal (like Lois Gibbs) went on to found the Citizens Clearinghouse for Hazardous Waste, others (like the less-known Barbara Quimby) have dropped out of environmental activism and the public eye altogether.

(Re)organizing at Home, Challenging Gender Expectations

> When these women assume leadership positions in the community
> and demand changes in family expectations and responsibilities as
> they "leave the house and enter the trenches," they break down tradi-
> tional notions of gender, race, and class and construct new empow-
> ered identities. (Di Chiro 1998, 123)

In spite of the fact that their involvement in activism sometimes creates tension at home and personal struggles with burnout, it is important to note that
activism also provides opportunities for women to reinterpret their role as
mothers and to reorganize their households towards a more egalitarian division of labour. Most of the women I interviewed reported that they receive
support from their family members for the activist work they do; several women
commented that they would not be able to do activist work if they were not
supported at home. This support includes moral support and sympathy for
the issues as well as, in some cases, financial support (e.g., family income used
to support campaigns; partner's income makes it possible for the woman to do
paid work part time or not at all so that she can do activist work full time).
Perhaps more significantly, the limitations of traditional gender roles are highlighted when the women realize that they cannot "do it all." Many women
said that they have created household environments that are (more or less)
cooperative and therefore allow them to integrate their activist work into their
already busy schedules. Some women said that their families have always been
egalitarian, even before they chose to take on a heavy load of activist work.
When asked, most of the women claimed to be very or somewhat satisfied
with the distribution of household work at home.

Krauss (1997) suggests that women's experiences as household organizers
serve as a resource for organizing politically. This is certainly the case for the
women I interviewed, all of whom must devise elaborate schedules and carefully organize their hectic home lives for maximum efficiency. The most important form of support the women reported is that family members share the
household work so that their load of responsibility is lessened, freeing up time
for activist commitments.[21] For those women who have partners or other adults
living with them, this most often means taking care of children when there are
evening meetings to attend. Li-Lien Gibbens is the only woman among the
thirty interviewees who lives in a communal house with her husband, daughter, and four other adults. She told me that this arrangement makes juggling
her various commitments much more comfortable than if she lived in a "traditional nuclear" household. Like Li-Lien Gibbens, several women noted that
their partners do an equal amount of household work, which contradicts statistical reports that women still do more hours of housework per week than men

(Frederickson 1995; Statistics Canada 2000). These women commented on their exceptional household arrangements, for example:[22]

> I would have to say that I'm pretty fortunate in that ... well, my husband wasn't quite as adamant as I was about certain things, but since the whole food allergy thing and the asthma, we've become so much more aware. [Our son's] food needs have really changed the way we eat, the way we buy, the way we think about food, and now I think I can say [my husband] is on board. And I'm fortunate that I can rely on him to do some of the household upkeep. He works outside of the house, I work in the house and consider that my work is raising the children and I consider that my activist work is connected with that and so what's outside of both our jobs is keeping up with the housework, doing groceries, taking out the garbage. And so I don't take it upon myself to do all of it and he certainly doesn't take it upon himself to do all of it, either. He understands that that has to be balanced between the two of us and respects that what I do is work rather than sitting around all day and playing or whatever. Probably the balance on that has changed and not just on my part, on his part, too, but I've said I can't do it all.

Some of the women commented that, in order to fit their activist work into their lives, they have given their children more responsibility at home than they might have done otherwise. For example, some said that their children help support their work by taking on more household chores, such as cooking meals and grocery shopping. A few commented that it was particularly good that their sons were learning to be more responsible for household work, perhaps upsetting traditional gender roles in the process. Although Frederickson (1995) reports that there is a gendered division of unpaid work among youth in Canada (see also Eichler 1997), some of the women reported that they try to give their sons greater responsibility for household work.[23] Perhaps this finding suggests that "more work for the boys" may be a benefit, rather than a cost, of women's struggle to juggle activist work and caring labour:

> My sons fend for themselves. And I think that's a good thing because I think we're becoming a society where guys aren't going to be served as well as they were in the past decades. So with all that change going on, I think it's a good thing.

A significant number of the women indicated in the background questionnaires I gave them prior to their interview (see appendix) that their activist work interferes with their household responsibilities (i.e., when the assumption is that the responsibilities are theirs) "constantly" or "sometimes." In addition to reorganizing family relationships and household responsibilities, the women interviewed said that they employ a number of different strategies for coping with their household maintenance responsibilities, for which they have less time when they are most active. It is not surprising that one of the most troublesome issues is finding time to keep up with everyday tasks like shopping, cooking, and house cleaning. What I did not expect was that several women commented on the links between their polluted local environments and the standards they apply to household maintenance. For example, the women who live in the Hamilton area said that increased awareness of the implications of toxic dust in their homes in recent years has led them to vacuum and dust more frequently than usual. A few women have children with food allergies and environmental illnesses, so meeting their needs for specialty products and services demands more time. This finding appears to support Beck's (1995, 52) argument that ecological risks, "even when they remain impossible to calculate, involve greatly increased labour for housewives and mothers." He writes (in a rare display of gender awareness) that: "In order to fulfill their own expectations, [mothers] must now privately clear away the socially created hazards that break in on all sides. Furthermore, the failure of institutions that permit and normalize the poisons threatens to turn into the personal guilt of the mother" (ibid.).

Some women noted that along with some of their coping strategies come a variety of tensions and contradictions, not only regarding gender roles but also with respect to social and environmental values. One coping strategy that is somewhat contentious is that just under half of the women I interviewed hire domestic workers (or cleaning women) to help them cope with their household responsibilities.[24]

> [SM: What kinds of strategies do you use to be able to juggle all these things? Do you have any time-saving strategies?]
>
> Well, first of all, I have part-time help, which, now that I'm working, has a new importance in my life. Having some sort of cleaning help plays a role. And now that I have two days and I'm working three afternoons – my mother today is watching my daughter – things are very, very tight. I see why people who can't afford to have, or people who don't have, support – you can pay for support, you can have family support, friends, community, there's all sorts of ways of having support – but I see that that's absolutely crucial in being involved with anything beyond survival. Having some sort of support network. Not necessarily paid, but that is one way. It's just central.

I note this here because, for me, it is important to grapple with the contradiction that some women are able to subsidize their active participation in the community with the work of women domestic workers who may or may not be granted citizenship. Feminist critiques of the way Athenian democracy was facilitated by the invisible labour of non-citizens (i.e., slaves and women) come immediately to mind (e.g., Phillips 1991, 1993). Recognizing that it felt uncomfortable to address this contradiction directly, I asked the women in a follow-up question to interpret the finding that many women activists employ other women to clean their homes. Their answers revealed, not unexpectedly, that the employment of other women to perform what is typically regarded as one's own household duties is a difficult issue for many women. When asked, some felt it was an acceptable coping strategy as long as they pay a fair wage, while others said they feel guilty about "contracting out" their cleaning work. I include some of their reflections on this issue in the notes to this chapter. It would have been interesting to have had a debate, but we did not, so I am unable to give an interpretation of their various positions.[25]

> Time saving: what else do we do? ... I do have help cleaning the
> house. That's a bit of a concession.
> [SM: Why do you say that?]
> Because I feel guilty. I feel guilty about everything!

The women who do not employ paid domestic help reported using other kinds of strategies. Besides establishing a cooperative household, for example, many women have rejected (or at least reconsidered) standards of housekeeping that they have been socialized as women to accept.[26] By rethinking these conventions, they may be reflecting critically on the feminization of housework and perhaps passing along a different set of gender expectations to their children:

> There's a lot of pressure on women to be great housekeepers and
> everything and I kind of dismissed that a long time ago. Let's be
> realistic here: I think I have more valuable things to do, like
> actually talk with my children. I could spend three hours cleaning
> their room for them or I could actually communicate with them
> and let them clean their own room. So I'm not all that hyper about
> it, as you can see. I don't have the energy anymore for it, frankly.

> I will never drop dead from using too many chemicals in my house
> because I don't clean it very often ... I guess I'm lucky that I don't
> have a husband or children who will ridicule me for not cleaning or
> be on my case in some other way for doing things like that. I think
> that some women take an awful lot of pride in how clean their house

is and then they get very neurotic about not being able to do that. I'm not that kind of person ... I'm not neurotic about things being really tidy, but if you're like that I don't know how involved you'd be at the level I'm at in the environment[al movement].

"Why Do You Do It?" On the Personal Rewards of Activism

As I discuss in Chapter 4, typical stories of women's environmental justice activism tend to present a trajectory that starts with an apolitical housewife and ends with a politically astute and empowered activist. I was curious to find out how the women in my study would compare: Do they speak of their own "empowerment" as an outcome of their activism? Have they had major victories that make it all worthwhile? It is important to address these questions because, although I have found it valuable to highlight some of the costs of juggling activism and caring responsibilities, I do not want to leave a false impression that the women regret their choice to do so. After hearing about some of the costs and obstacles to doing activist work, I asked, "What keeps you doing it when it gets difficult, when it would be easier to walk away? What's in it for you?" Just one woman felt that it was difficult to identify any rewards at all. She said:

> I would say that there's no reward. Nothing. We've learned an awful lot about engineering and we've learned more than some of the engineers know and yet we have no way to present credentials. And we've had to shame some of these engineers into reading new books and learning about new technologies, and I think part of it is they say, "Well, the housewives know what this is, so we'd better learn." So it's not really a good experience for us because, although they think we know this stuff, at the end of the day when we write our letters we still are competing with people who've got degrees and who are earning $75,000 a year from the city, and quite frankly we're doing their work for them. We're being totally exploited for the information we have. I do find that is really disappointing.

Most of the other twenty-nine women had many positive things to say about the rewards of activism. They stressed that activist work is an important part of their lives and that they would not want to live without it. Unlike in many other stories of women's activism, however, their sense of accomplishment was mostly found in small rewards rather than in big victories. What makes many of the women in my study different from the typical profile of a grassroots woman activist is that there is no singular purpose to their efforts and no end in sight: they continue to struggle – often to the point of exhaustion and burnout – for a number of different improvements in the environments in which they live. Very few of the women have experienced the kind of urgent life and death struggles reported at Love Canal (although Hamilton activists Ann Gallagher and Burke Austin may be two exceptions); rather, most are working on small policy changes or on improving specific aspects of their communities that may take years to realize. Although these may not make for dramatic tales of eco-heroism, they probably reflect more accurately the experiences of the majority of activists who work to improve the quality of life in their communities.

When asked what the biggest rewards of activism are, about half of the women responded along the lines that doing what they do is satisfying and meaningful to them in various ways. Similarly, Brú-Bistuer (1996) found that the women in her case studies most often named "feeling useful to the community" as their biggest reward. Community activism, it seems, simply makes some women "feel good." For example:

> I guess I feel good about doing things for other people and have been able to put aside my more personal needs.

> I think my reward for taking care of the community is that you feel good when somebody does come to you with a question. Like, "I've got some maggots or bugs in my garbage outside, what should I do?" ... Or when somebody stops me on the street and says, "Oh, you've done a wonderful job. The information you gave me really helped me, my daughters asthma's a lot better, she's not as sick anymore." That sort of stuff. It feels like they recognize me. They look up to me. That's my reward.

For many women, rewards are found in the expression of deeply held values and commitments. As I have mentioned, the impetus for these commitments may come from spiritual beliefs, but they may also stem from a general sense of one's purpose in life. Whether that includes maternal duty or some other sense of duty depends on the woman:

> It fulfills my philosophy, I guess. I don't know, there are these sayings, I don't know who wrote them, but like, "Life's an adventure, dare it; life's a mystery, solve it." And it's true. I'm not a religious person, I'm an atheist and don't believe that there is an afterlife and I believe that we're only here for x number of years. And if you want change, you're the one who's going to have to do it. I guess it's morals and beliefs.

> It comes to the individual and now more to the spiritual aspects. Back home the spiritual part was cut out, you don't talk about it. You are a political being so you don't talk about spirituality. With

the collective there wasn't time to talk about spirituality too because we were focusing on the political. After that, all of us in the collective have started the discussion of how to think about our spirituality and how to take care of ourselves.

Several women said that their activist engagements are "learning experiences"; that being an activist has given them the opportunity to learn more about "the issues" and to develop new kinds of skills and a better understanding of how political processes work. This finding resonates with Brú-Bistuer's (1996) study, wherein the majority of women reported that their activism has led to heightened awareness of environmental issues and problems. When I asked her what she had learned through all this, an anti-pesticide activist replied:

> Tons. I was never involved in local politics whatsoever. I was involved in some activist work in other areas but I didn't have an understanding, and I still don't – it's a learning process all the time. Now we know a certain amount and wonder how we ever got anything accomplished when we first started, we were so ignorant. Like we just went in there and just did it. And when you have that naiveté, shall we call it (rather than ignorance), you just go in full blast and you don't care because you don't know that there's a protocol and an expected and established way of doing things. We just went in there and boom boom boom ... There's no going back now – I look at people who were like me and ... I see them as totally unaware. They'll say, "No, if you call it doesn't make a difference," and I know it makes a massive difference because I've seen it happen. So now it's hard to put myself back into the position of not knowing, but I know there's still a lot that I don't know. But I have seen that grassroots activism can have tremendous impact.

A few women have managed to turn activist involvements into positions or projects for which they are rewarded financially. Several women wished they could be paid for the activist work they do. Most women, however, mentioned that a significant reward they derive from being involved in activist work is simply making connections within the community and meeting new, like-minded people. So even though some may lose support networks because they lack time for socializing, others may gain new support networks through their community work. Susan Anthony, for example, said: "I feel more connected to the community and more informed about what's going on. And the more informed you are the more you want to become involved." A small number of women spoke of establishing mentoring relationships with other women activists who help them learn the skills and gain the confidence needed to be

effective in public meetings. Some said that, through their activism, they over-
came the feelings associated with staying at home to care for children and
found ways to utilize old skills and to develop new ones. Their comments
echo the finding of Brown and Ferguson (1997, 252) that women activists
typically mentor each other in the process of developing into political actors:

> It's been wonderful, lately more so because of coming together with
> these women. That was a long time coming. And meeting people
> that are like-minded is always wonderful and it's energizing and
> gives you a lot of hope ... because I did stay at home for a long time
> and didn't talk to real adults and I'd hear myself talk when I'd go
> to these things and I'd say, "I know a lot; all this research and
> reading didn't just disappear, I do know."

> I came here five years ago, I didn't know anybody, I had a wee baby,
> and a non-school-age child, and I was somewhat isolated. My own
> personal life was so isolated that I was going a little stir-crazy. And
> also I didn't have any way to get to know the city – and I wasn't
> too fond of it actually. And just in the last two weeks I've been
> talking to all these amazingly feisty people all over the city from
> community groups and a lot of them are women who have poured
> their heart into their communities and into this city. And who have
> really fought battles and who have been around the block more
> than a few times. I was really genuinely moved.

Finally, although none of the women used the word "empowerment" to
describe the impacts of activist work on their lives, several did talk about how
they have personally and politically developed. Brú-Bistuer (1996, 115) writes
that, for the women she interviewed, activism has "begun an important process of personal empowerment ... through their increased range of activities,
self-assertion, and voice within the community." Like the women in that study,
the women I interviewed identified greater self-confidence as a positive outcome of their participation. For example, two women said that their activism
has helped them to establish a better sense of self-esteem:

> I was really extremely shy – it's hard to believe that now – but [a
> woman who was also active as a leader in the lead contamination
> issue] was trying desperately to get me to take over and do more
> things, so she'd sit beside me at meetings and tell me, "Go ahead,"
> and I'd be, like, "No, no, I don't want to say anything." But she'd
> encourage me and so she was a wonderful mentor in that way. [She]
> was a huge factor in getting me involved and in me becoming more
> verbal. I'd always been involved but I'd always been more of a

background person. And then eventually you know the history and so you have to be more out front ... I think I have more confidence in myself now – but it is very important to pass those skills on and to try and encourage people.

I've certainly gained a lot of knowledge. It's pushed me to connect to people and I find myself talking to people that I have such great respect for and admiration for what they are doing. And I feel so honoured to be a part of that group. So that personally is a really nice thing. I feel valued and I've gained more respect for myself and I feel valuable in terms of what I'm doing.... not that I didn't have any self-esteem before but ... I've become more educated on the topic which is also a nice thing. I feel intelligent and knowledgeable.

Another woman explained that she has cultivated a political analysis of her own place in the community. She said, "I have become a better human being with a better political understanding."

In the end, I am left wondering whether it would be appropriate for me to suggest – as some ecofeminists have done (e.g., Krauss 1997; Seager 1993) – that the women I interviewed have been "empowered" through their involvement in quality-of-life activism. The process may have only begun for some, while for others the activism about which they spoke is the result of a lifetime of political engagement. Whether their accounts of satisfaction, spiritual fulfillment, learning, and self-development discussed herein should be considered evidence of "empowerment" will remain an open question. Patti Lather (1991) cautions against reducing the concept of empowerment to such individualistic qualities. She suggests instead (following Gramsci) that empowerment ought to mean "analyzing ideas about the causes of powerlessness, recognizing systemic oppressive forces, and acting both individually and collectively to change the conditions of our lives" (Lather 1991, 4). Taking this definition seriously, in Chapter 8 I present the women's politically informed theorizing of their experiences as activists, along with their critical analyses of some of the central themes with which I have been grappling in this book.

8 Activist Women Theorize the Green Political

I certainly don't think that women are great heroes in
knowing implicitly how to do all this. Perhaps we're curious
and want to understand things and that's our gift, which is
what allows us to then go about doing it. But I don't think
it's because we're born with some innate gift that we're
able to let it all flow. It hasn't felt easy or "natural" to me.

– from an interview with Jane Smith*

In an essay entitled "Making a Big Stink: Women's Work, Women's Relationships, and Toxic Waste Activism," Brown and Ferguson (1997, 242) write that
"women activists have a different approach to experience and knowledge."
Different from whom, they never specify. By making this claim, however, the
authors imply that there is something special about the lives of grassroots
activist women that (1) we can identify and that (2) might make studying
them as a group a particularly valuable ecopolitical project. Many representations of women's local quality-of-life activism are filtered through the lenses of
"women's ways of knowing" (as in Brown and Ferguson 1997) or "standpoint
epistemology" (as in Krauss 1993), often found in feminist research. These
approaches tend to focus on women's "experientially based knowledge and
expertise" and rest on the belief that "the subjective truths that arise from
women's experience and struggles [are] 'a significant indicator of reality'"
(Krauss 1993, 250 quoting Harding 1987, 7).[1] As I have noted, such research
on women activists often constructs their activism as a natural extension of
their experiences as women and as caregivers. Historian Joan Scott (1992, 25)
would argue, critically, that researchers who talk about experience in this way
"take as self-evident the identities of those whose experience is being docu-

mented and thus naturalize their difference." Following Scott, it is my position that, in order to avoid reifying the identities of women activists and naturalizing their "experience," it is best to regard their accounts as *interpretations of their own experiences* – interpretations that are political in nature and that are informed by a variety of knowledge sources. Through this lens, the women activists I interviewed do not look like "subjects" with "experience" to be filtered, interpreted, and represented by me; they are, to use Lee Quinby's (1997) term, "activist/theorizers," and I want to discuss them as such.[2] Consistent with my interest in democratic citizenship, moreover, I do not see the women I interviewed as fixed subjects whose interpretations of their experiences are static and transparent but, rather, as women living complex identities, whose analyses may be provisional and prone to change over time.

As I explain in Chapter 7, I aim to disrupt and complicate a particular profile of women engaged in quality-of-life activism that is constructed in the ecofeminist and feminist texts to which I am responding (e.g., Salleh 1997; Merchant 1996; Kaplan 1997; Brown and Ferguson 1997; Seager 1996; Brú-Bistuer 1996). In this chapter I enlist the assistance of the women I interviewed to demonstrate the importance of women's gendered perspectives in broadening conventional meanings of activism and citizenship in male-dominated green political theorizing. To do so, I present and engage with some of the interpretations and analyses of the themes that were offered by the thirty women I interviewed. Where appropriate, I make links between their reflections and arguments made in the relevant literature.

Politicizing Women's Activism
A significant part of each of my interviews was dedicated to discussion of the politics of activism. The conversations typically began with me asking the women to tell me about their activist work: What are the issues they are working on, how do they judge success, and what are the obstacles to achieving their particular goals? I followed up by asking how they feel their "social locations" (e.g., class, race/ethnicity, gender) help or hinder their ability to be heard in the local political arena. In this section, I highlight five areas of analysis that emerged from this part of the interviews. They are: the meaning of "activism," socioeconomic obstacles to civic participation, self-presentation and the housewife label, disillusionment with government, and critiques of/ engagements with scientific and expert knowledges.

Rethinking "Activism"
Interestingly, some of the women were ambivalent about the term "activist." This finding and the fact that they evinced different understandings of the term suggest a need to reflect on the meaning of activism itself. Some conversations lead me to rethink my uncritical use of the label "activist."[3] According to the *Oxford English Dictionary* (1990) an activist is "one who follows a policy

of vigorous action in a cause." But, as feminists have pointed out, conventional meanings of activism in political theory tend to exclude the kinds of actions and strategies most commonly used by women working to advance a "cause" (Ackelsberg 1988; Lister 1997; Reed 2003). Moreover, despite the growing popularity of grassroots protest activities in some areas of political thought and practice, mainstream political scholars and policy makers continue to trivialize and dismiss as "special interest groups" the community-based and single-issue struggles of informal groups. Focusing on traditionally masculine forms of "vigorous" political protest like labour activism, they also exclude from the conceptualization of politics those issues that can be confined to the private or domestic sphere (Bookman and Morgen 1988; Staeheli 1996; Jones 1998). Some of the green political scholarship I review in Chapter 5 confirms this view. Temma Kaplan (1997, 6) observes that because women participants in grassroots movements "are attempting to accomplish necessary tasks, to provide services rather than to build power bases," their activism "and the gains they make hardly seem politically significant" to many studies of politics. The term "municipal housekeeping," used to describe the activities of women's groups in the progressive era, can be considered an example of the trivialization of women's citizenship practices (Bowden 1997, 209n20).

The women I interviewed disrupted the conventional meaning of activism in a number of ways. While most of them accepted for themselves the label of "activist" (unqualified by me), others were less comfortable with it. Some agreed to participate in this study, in which they would be identified as activists, but later sought to problematize this identification. For example, a few said they prefer the terms "advocate" and "volunteer" over "activist" because their work aims to improve small things rather than radically challenge the political system. Naples (1998) writes that women may be reluctant to consider their actions "political" activism at all; rather, they prefer to see them as a form of apolitical "civic" or "community work." Some of the women with whom I spoke expressed ambivalence about the connotations and stereotypes associated with the term "activist." Of those who said they shy away from the term, most were middle-class women who suggested that they will be taken more seriously in the civic arena if they avoid the term, thinking perhaps that it is more strategic to present oneself in less assertive ways. For example, one woman said that while she thinks what she does is activism, she tends to avoid using the word publicly:

> I actually have mixed feelings about the term "activism" and so
> many people I talk to say, "I don't really think of myself as an
> activist" and I guess that's my first reaction, my emotional reaction.
> Because it's so fringe and that kind of bothers me ... I look at
> myself as an environmental educator. (Cheryl Shour)

A few women are uncomfortable with the term "activist" because they somehow do not "measure up" – in that they do not possess the stereotypical traits of environmental activists. For example, Sari Merson said:

> I'm a very reluctant activist. That's not how I tend to define it because I'm not very assertive. So I don't think it's activism that I'm doing, I think I'm just trying to live ... This is the only way I think I can live; once you start having a conscience about it you can't not do it. There's that saying: not doing anything is worse than being an offender, or something like that.

Some women wanted to downplay the significance of their work by explaining that they are "just being responsible," rather than being activists. Such statements resonate with Naples' (1991) explanation that grassroots activist women often do not regard their work as political activism, instead seeing it as "just what needed to be done." Similarly, Kaplan (1997, 23) says that it was important to Love Canal activists to present themselves as "traditional mothers trying to do their jobs" rather than placard-wielding radicals. After describing various aspects of her work with the Campaign for Pesticide Reduction, Marcie Goldman added the following qualification:

> Not that I'm an activist. I have strong beliefs that I take action on. I think that's a very important role model for your children to see. It's just being responsible.

The women discussed various strategies they use for addressing their chosen causes, which may or not be considered "activist" by conventional standards. Many of them are involved in small "grassroots" groups that try to lobby governments and the public (most often neighbours) to change their actions and priorities. Their affiliations range from province-wide networks that involve cooperation among many diverse environmental groups (e.g., Campaign for Pesticide Reduction) to small groups of parents concerned with conditions at their neighbourhood schools. The strategies the women listed include: organizing petitions and public awareness campaigns; running an Earth Day poster competition; presenting deputations at City Hall; writing letters to councillors and newspaper editors; sitting on municipal, tenants, and home-school committees; doing research; and organizing and participating in strikes, demonstrations, and lawsuits. Some women are active in organizations and projects aimed at helping people who are disadvantaged by government systems (e.g., social service and immigration systems) and advocating policy changes on their behalf. These women have established and/or run food banks, women's centres, housing co-ops, and shelters; advocated for the rights of immigrant women; and assisted victims of racial harassment in schools and by the police.

Activism is typically associated with activities in the public domain. Yet the association of activism and publicity (and the concomitant depoliticization of the private sphere) is challenged when women choose to regard household issues as political issues and thereby make their homes a focus of their activist engagement. Their homes are both the base for their public activism (i.e., "command central") and a place where political action and conversation takes place. An exchange I had with Jane Smith* helps illustrate this point:

> [SM: You were saying ... that a lot of your activist work gets done in your own home. Those types of choices – consumer choices and parenting choices – are a form of activism?]
>
> I didn't always think like that, I thought that consumer change at the household level was somehow less political or less important than doing it at the macro-level. Mind you, I don't think that one can come without the other. But at certain times in our lives we have to follow the open spaces we have and to start from where we are at, not from where an external person tells us we should be at ... I make political choices all the time. At the household level, it used to be seen as the three Rs but as you start learning more, [you ask] how do you live without buying PVC plastics? What furniture should I buy for my house or what carpet? ... [Or you] talk about the possibility of solar panels or alternative technologies. Those are things I'm interested in and try to bring more and more into my household level. And I get lots of comments from other people ' about making my house a scent-free zone and about perfumes. Yeah, it can be a courageous thing to make your household a political [space] when often you just want to make it invisible and just do it at an organizational level ... It takes courage to show your politics at the household level when you have people walking in and out of your household who may not share your perspective.

This comment offers a counterpoint to those green political theorists who present the household as only a place of consumption at the same time as restricting their discussions of politics to the *formal* public sphere. As I note in Chapter 7, most of the women indicated in their background questionnaires that they regard green household practices as "very important." Their activism thus transcends the public-private divide as they attempt to live consistently with their political commitments. While this finding may appear congruent with green political theorists' call for citizens to "do their bit" at home in addition to taking an active role in local politics, the women presented some interesting challenges to this position. They offered important analyses of the relative ability of women and other marginalized people to engage in effective activist work. In the process of talking about their activist work, I found the women eager to explain the things that frustrate them as activists as well as the systemic and structural obstacles that make it more difficult to achieve success. Most acknowledged that some people are more able to be activists than others.

Socioeconomic and Cultural Obstacles to Citizen Activism

In Chapter 7 I discuss how caring responsibilities complicate, and often interfere with, the women's ability to participate in activist work. The women I interviewed also analyzed how their social location and situation as citizen activists influence their ability to participate in their communities. First, with regard to their role as volunteer (i.e., unpaid) activists, a significant number of the women – more affluent women included – said that "lack of support" is an obstacle to doing their political work. For most this means lack of financial and organizational support for their groups and campaigns. Li-Lien Gibbens, Jackie Kennedy, Kathleen Wynne, Julie Starr, Karey Shinn, and Josephine Grey are each trying to run organizations on limited or no budgets. Even though their work often amounts to a full-time job, they receive no pay and minimal (if any) official recognition (through funding) from the government. This lack of support dramatically restricts what they are able to do and accomplish.[4] Karen Buck and Karey Shinn each told me, and this may be true of others who describe themselves as middle class, that they have used their family's money to support the organizations with which they are involved. When I asked Karey Shinn to describe the most significant obstacle she faces as an activist, she replied, "I think money is the biggest obstacle. And I think the government knows that and that's one of the reasons why they've cut back on funding us."

This comment resonates with feminist analyses of neoliberal economic restructuring and the concomitant downloading of public services to volunteers in communities (see Chapter 4). A few of the women had strong criticisms of the economic marginalization and exploitation of unpaid activist and volunteer work. For example, echoing what many feminist political economists have said, Jackie Kennedy commented:

> I think there needs to be a balance: volunteering is a good thing to do and we should do it at younger ages so that we do help other people who are less fortunate. But I don't think we should use it as an excuse like this government is, to do all of the good work. You know, "Well those people can go to the church for help, they will fix it up." That's not going to work; there has to be a balance and an organization like the North Toronto Green Community should be paid something – whether it's from the government or whatever, because the work that we're doing is important.

Non-profit and volunteer organizations run by women may be disproportionately disadvantaged economically because the work they do is assumed to
be a natural extension of what they already do as caregivers. Calling this situation "re-privatization," Janine Brodie (1996a, 1996b) argues that shifting more
responsibility onto women's groups at the same time that funding is reduced
is part of a new right attempt to redefine and perhaps limit practices of citizenship. On the other hand, when women's participation is encouraged, even
invited, it can lead to the exploitation of their volunteer time as a way of lend-
ing credibility to public processes. As Burke Austin observed, the processes
involved in local community planning in Hamilton benefit a range of people
(most of whom are white men) who make good money being professional
planners, lawyers, politicians, academics, and health policy consultants. Yet
they increasingly rely on the time and labour of citizen volunteers (many of
whom are women) to monitor the health of their own communities and to fill
the seats at the public consultations needed to validate their progressive-
sounding plans (MacGregor 2000). This situation brings to mind Sherry
Arnstein's (1969, 216) argument that "participation without redistribution of
power is an empty and frustrating process for the powerless." She suggests
that a distinction be drawn between participation that leads to citizen control
and the kind of participation that can be co-opted and manipulated to support the desires of the power elite. It is this kind of critical analysis, it seems to
me, and those based in women's interpretations of the way local politics work,
that are needed in discussions of the merits of women's active participation in
quality-of-life struggles.

Many of the women I interviewed offered their interpretations of relationships between their class locations and their ability to engage in activism. For
example, several women noted that their middle-class status facilitates their
activist work and acknowledged that activist work can be a luxury that is not
an equal option for everyone. Marcie Goldman, for example, recognized that
the women she works with in anti-pesticides organizations are "not poor." She
said, "It helps if you can afford to do it," and "my social class, race, and gender
make it easier to do activist and volunteer work." In contrast, Laura Jones
suggested that there are both pros and cons to being a relatively privileged
white middle-class woman activist. She made the following comment:

> As a white, middle-aged, middle-class woman, I find I blend in and
> am not taken very seriously by people in power. I am not consid-
> ered a threat. So I am able to, almost invisibly, continue to work on
> one issue after another, providing information to my community.

It comes as no surprise that several women commented that their working-
class status can be a significant obstacle to activist work. One woman named
"being poor" and not having a car as the two biggest obstacles. Women with

relatively modest incomes and women living in poverty report that it is sometimes difficult to justify devoting time to unpaid community work when they
are not able to make ends meet. I have already discussed the impact of lack of
access to child care on women's activism. In addition to not having the resources to engage in active participation, living in poverty makes for a stress-
ful life that is not conducive to community engagement. Even though they
have at times considered themselves part of the "middle class," both Helen
Melbourne and Karey Shinn said they had to cut back or stop their activist
involvements altogether when household finances were stretched too thin to
support them.[5]

A few women identified another kind of class- and race-related discrimination that can act as an obstacle to effective activism: "neighbourhoodism," a
concept I learned of from Ruth Morris, who, as a member of the Coalition
against Neighbourhoodism, was active in working against the negative stereo-
typing of the Jane-Finch community in Toronto. Although she does not use
the term, sociologist Celene Krauss (1993) heard a similar analysis from African American environmental justice activists she interviewed. She quotes one
woman as saying "I'm here to tell the story that all people in the projects are
not lazy and dumb!" (256). In my study, both Ann Gallagher and Burke Austin
suggested that the stereotypes about people who live in the north end of Hamilton, a low-income and working-class neighbourhood, may be an obstacle to
their being taken seriously by city officials. What follows is Burke Austin's
response to my question:

> [SM: When I was talking to Ann Gallagher this morning, she
> said that she gets really frustrated by the way the North End gets
> stereotyped and by the belief that people don't know any better or
> because they are working class they aren't treated with the same
> respect by politicians in public meetings.]
> Yes. That's an obstacle all the time. I really don't find that an
> obstacle because I know that sooner or later I'm going to be able to
> catch these guys, or whoever, with the information that they can't
> really refute. And all of a sudden there's a little bit more respect.
> It's funny because, I'm pretty well known now, but a few years ago
> I'd walk into a meeting and it was just, like, "Well, here comes the
> homemaker" and here too, living in the Northeast End, we're
> categorized.

Related to Austin's assessment, it is noteworthy that many of the women
(both working-class and middle-class) said that social attitudes and stereotypes,
especially on the part of public officials, can hinder or impede their ability to
do effective activist work. Feminist political theorist Iris Marion Young (1990,
59) writes that, for the disadvantaged in particular, "their appearance in the

world has a peculiar paradoxical quality; they are at once made invisible yet marked out by stereotypes" (see also Bickford 1996). Being white and middle class might make it easier for some women to blend into established organizations and be taken more seriously than working-class women of colour when they act in the political domain. However, for other women, being invisible and/or having their identities reduced to stereotypes hinders the possibility of being listened to as citizens.[6] Two of the women said that racism plays a significant part in the way they are treated as activists. For example, Murphy Browne said: "As a woman of African descent, I am hindered in my activist work and volunteer work. I find that I have to prove myself repeatedly. I have been assaulted and called racist names by police in my role as activist."

Self-Presentation and the Housewife Label

"Politically speaking," writes Bickford (1996, 101), "it matters quite a lot how others regard us ... how we are perceived affects how we can appear in public." Several of the women commented that gender stereotypes, and particularly stereotypes about "housewives," influence how they are perceived by local officials and community members. As a result, it seems to me, they have developed an analysis of the effects of sexism on their ability to participate in political processes. Their comments suggest a particular stance towards their self-presentation in public. For example, Karen Woudstra said: "When it comes to public speaking you've got to be a citizen before a mother because – it's a very sad statement to make but – 'You're a mother, who cares?' You know? But 'Oh, you're the founder of the York Region Environmental Alliance?': that has a bit more perceived power behind it." Her comment seems to echo the argument of feminist theorists, which maintains that when women appear in public they are seen as women or mothers first and as citizens or activists second. As Ann Snitow (1989, 40) observes, "In a cruel irony that is one mark of women's oppression, when women speak *as women* they run a special risk of not being heard because the female voice is by our culture's definition that-voice-you-can-ignore."

It is interesting that some women expressed frustration with the fact that being identified as "housewives" is a convenient way for people in power to dismiss them or to distort the meaning of their participation. For example, Ann Gallagher recalled: "I had basically people patting me on the head and saying 'there there, go home and take care of your kids. We are looking out for you.'" This comment highlights an important point made by many of the women I interviewed: when they speak as women, and particularly as mothers, women activists risk being (and often are) ignored or dismissed by people in power. Here are two other comments:

> [The term "housewife activist"] kind of implies that, "Oh, you're at
> home with the kids and have nothing better to do," so you'll just

go out and do this – your cause of the week or something. Yeah, I don't like that either because there is a negative implication there, whereas it's just activism at its finest. And yet being a mother at home isn't negative either. It's a positive thing. I mean if you can actually make that choice, and have someone – male or female – at home, then more power to you. It shouldn't be negative but we're still living in this brotherhood society where the men are still in control and all they have do to do is say, "Oh, well, it's just these housewives who have nothing better to do" and it's believed because it comes from a male source. (Karen Woudstra)

The other thing I've found going to [City] Council is there's an assumption that ... all activists are hippies – and you go down to Council and do a deputation and it's obvious that you're literate and you say things that an educated person would say, but they still assume that you're a middle-class housewife. (Karey Shinn)

From what the women told me, it seems they do not even have to speak or present themselves intentionally as women or mothers: just appearing in public and being a woman is enough to engender sexist assumptions that serve to make one's concerns less valid and less likely to be heard. Terri Mittelmann commented:

I'm sorry to say it, but I believe that it's unavoidable that being a female is not an advantage, and I'm very careful when I go about how I dress and how I present myself and I'm pretty good at doing it. Some of our best coverage is when we've had men representing us ... the initial public perception when you carry a title and you're male, those are definitely two advantages. Can I say we haven't made progress without that? No. But we're coordinating something and there is no question that there is an advantage to putting a certain type of personality or gender in to speak to certain people at certain times.

Joni Seager (1996, 279) also recognizes this problem: "when women walk out of their homes to protest ... their gender and sex identity goes with them – in a way that is not true for male activists." But several studies of women's anti-toxics activism claim that women who have been labelled "hysterical house-wives" respond by turning the label around to suit their purposes, either by deploying it ironically or in defiance of popular assumptions (e.g., Krauss 1997; Brown and Ferguson 1997; Kaplan 1997).[7] The most common example is Lois Gibbs' famous admission that she was "hysterical and proud of it" (quoted in Brown and Ferguson 1997, 255).

Ann Gallagher expressed resistance to being stereotyped in this way with the following comment:

> When you meet someone for the first time they have this pre-conceived notion that you're just some dense housewife from the North End. However, the opinion changes very quickly. I've had people say to me, "How do you know this?" And I think, "Why are you surprised that I know this? I'm not the only one who knows this, lots of women do. And you know what? Your preconceived notions make *you* look like an idiot, not me!"

In contrast to findings from other studies, I did not hear any of the women I interviewed accept the hysterical housewife stereotype for their own purposes; instead, several women commented that they want to resist sexist (my term, not theirs) attitudes of public officials about their work as women activists because they might interfere with what may be accomplished for their campaigns. This claim does not deny that some women have deployed their housewife identity politically (with or without success), but there are other women who do not find this a good strategic move. Cheryl Shour, for one, said that she tries to avoid drawing attention to gender

> because in some of our experiences, they respond and say you're a bunch of hysterical housewives. So if we use that model, then we're just reinforcing their idea that it's "a girl thing" as opposed to a human thing. I have a real problem with that.

Comments about how social location and identities affect the ability of women to participate actively and be received as citizens in the formal political arena are important in light of the green literature on ecological citizenship. While active participation is a worthy goal, support for it must be tempered by an understanding of the impacts of social inequality on political engagement. The women I interviewed have developed critical analyses of the pitfalls of using feminine and maternal identities in the public arena, which allow me to problematize celebrations of housewife activism found in the ecofeminist literature. At the same time, some women's ideas reflect back on feminist theories of citizenship to suggest that, because claiming an identity as citizen (or "activist") can be difficult for women under existing socio-political conditions, there may be greater meaning and inspiration in politicizing their maternal roles. It is not a simple either/or proposition.

Disillusionment with Government
Di Chiro (1998, 108) observes that anti-toxics activists tend to move from an

unquestioning acceptance of authority to mistrust of their local governmental officials; that they are "usually utterly shocked to learn that their public officials and other experts can be so indifferent to the health and well-being of their neighborhoods" (see also Newman 2001). I heard similar stories from the women activists I interviewed, although with varying degrees of shock and disillusionment. There were many accounts of frustration that turned into analyses of how officials with government ministries and public health departments try to deny the existence of problems that are readily apparent to lay observers, including to the women themselves. For instance, one woman said:

> The fact is that every one of us [in this area] is on an inhaler. Every one of us. And another particular concern ... is the effects on reproductive health. Every woman that I know who lives here has suffered miscarriages above and beyond the norm. I suffered two and I have no familial history of it and it wasn't early: they were at sixteen weeks. And so many women in this area that I've talked to, all my friends – every one of my girlfriends who I walk my kids to school with – have gone through it. The level of asthma is so high. We've questioned public health and asked if they are keeping stats and they said, "Oh, we don't keep stats." I've gone to meetings and said, "What the hell do you people do? Don't call yourself Public Health because you're not working for the public. You don't keep stats because you don't want to know."

From accounts such as this, it is possible to identify two stages in a process of politicization: first comes an awareness of environmental problems, second comes the development of a political position in response to government (and industry) indifference (such a process is also observed by Krauss [1983]). This suggests a relationship between knowledge and position that is reflexive rather than given or "natural." Some of the women explained the importance of vigilant scepticism when dealing with politicians and government officials, and several of the women spoke of a loss of faith in the government and in the political system in general. Krauss (1997) claims that women's belief that government will take care of them is thrown into question through their activism: the more they engage with the system, the more they realize that the reality does not live up to the ideal. As Cheryl Shour commented:

> The government should represent people's interests and nothing could be more important than our right to clean food, air, and water, and social justice. However, government appears to be rather the pawn of big business and has no will to further the environmental and social causes.

Another comment resonates with Lauren Berlant's (1997) theory of "infantile citizenship," which argues that adult citizens in the United States are taught to regard the state – to trust and depend on it – as if it were a parent whose job it is to look after them.[8] Describing her disillusionment as a process of "growing up," Nikola Patti said:

> When I first jumped in, I was completely immersed in coordinating and research and the biggest shock was finding myself in my late thirties believing that, in this case, the Ministry of the Environment looked after my best interests. What an eye opener! To find out that that's not entirely the role of government agencies. In the space of a few weeks I grew up and entered the adult world for the first time.

Some women said that their disillusionment with government has fuelled their commitment to improving the quality of life and of political processes in their communities: they use their transformed understandings to guide their activist projects. Nikola Patti went on to say that, although she has come to regard the government differently, she has not lost hope: she is more committed to and engaged with the ideals of government and democracy now than ever before:

> Particularly now, in this climate of "the global village," governments are beginning to abdicate their responsibility to the people and to the environment. We must hold our governments accountable with much more resolve than we have. Government is there to serve the people. We must insist on this. In order to protect democracy we need to appreciate it and we need to practice it, collectively.

Similarly, several women have translated their disillusionment into taking on the role of public "watchdog" who monitors the words and deeds of politicians. This strategy is viewed as a way of keeping politicians accountable, catching them when they act in dishonest ways. Perhaps they theorize this as a way to make the system better:

> I think changes for the better are possible. Because they don't really expect citizens to read and when we dig up the documents, how can they dispute them? We've got the testing and the results. So instead of saying there's nothing wrong, it comes to the point where they are going to have to do something because we caught them. (Burke Austin)

But some women offered a different kind of critique of government. Resonating with Krauss' (1993) finding that African American women do not become disillusioned because they have never trusted the government in the first place (due to experiences of systemic racism), many of the working-class and women of colour I interviewed were not as optimistic as were those who believed that "the system" can be improved as a result of the hard work and persistence of activists. Some women expressed a lack of interest in direct engagement and cooperation with government. Vasta Gibbons, for example, was thoroughly pessimistic about government in general and the Harris government in particular:

> I feel there is no real relationship between government and the people. Some government has made some good changes, but it's not because you or I asked for it. It's because they have to do a little something every once in a while to make it look like they are working for the people and to get re-elected. (Vasta Gibbons)

Her words do not, like those of the white working-class women described by Krauss (1993, 254), "reflect a strong belief in the existing political system." As a woman living in poverty who has little access to the institutions of power and whose life is constantly affected by the dismantling of social welfare, she is understandably cynical.

Citizen Science and Working with Experts

Some ecofeminists and researchers who study women's environmental justice activism highlight incidences of women questioning conventional science and developing their own more "reliable" forms of expertise on environmental problems. For example, Brown and Ferguson (1997) refer to "housewife data" and "housewife studies" and Seager (1996) writes of women using their "gut feelings" and "expertise grounded in daily experience" to assist them in working for environmental change (see also Kaplan 1997; Newman 2001). Invoking maternalist philosopher Sara Ruddick, Krauss (1993, 253) writes of women activists calling upon their "everyday practice of mothering" and forming informal networks with other women to develop "oppositional knowledge" that helps them "resist the dominant knowledge of experts." In contrast, Di Chiro (1998, 128) makes the likely more accurate point that women activists call on a variety of knowledges – "experiential," learned, technical – in order to challenge scientific experts and their research: "Women activists in environmental justice organizations possess not only 'experiential knowledge' of the effects of toxins in the environments and bodies but also extensive understanding and ability to apply scientifically generated knowledge of ecosystem dynamics, chemical production processes, and the specific uses of a variety of industrial technologies."

Perhaps Di Chiro is acknowledging that a focus on "gut feelings" can obscure the ways women engage with and evaluate a range of different sources of knowledge about the issues on which they are working. A theme that emerges from the interviews concerns the women's reflections upon dominant practices and expressions of scientific expertise. Since several ecofeminist and environmental justice texts (such as those mentioned earlier) hold up women's experiential knowledge as categorically different from scientific knowledge, it is important to examine how different ways of knowing clash, overlap, and intermingle. A blending of knowledges was an important aspect of the way the women I interviewed approach their activism.

Since the burden of proof tends to fall on activists who challenge authority, it is not surprising that many of the women place value on having a technical analysis of the particular problem their campaigns address. "I know more about carbon dioxide than I ever wanted to know," said Burke Austin. Karen Woudstra commented, "I do a lot of scientific reading. My husband is very logical and scientific – very Spock-ish – and I guess I have him to thank because otherwise I might have been coming from a more emotional base versus a scientific or logical base." While few have engaged in the kind of popular epidemiology (or citizen science) described in much of the women and environments and environmental justice literature, the women I interviewed did have political analyses of the use and abuse of science and scientific expertise. A few spoke of their experience with doing the kind of research that challenges mainstream (i.e., "official") scientific knowledge, especially as it is conducted and reported to the public. One woman suggests a strategy for resistance in the face of government-sponsored scientific expertise aimed at managing a public relations problem with the example of people in her community refusing to participate in a study that seemed illegitimate:

> [SM: Do you think that because Public Health is not keeping track of these things, there are other people you could rely on or even collect data yourselves?]
>
> We have tried. We got money for a health study and initially it was our money but we were being pushed by Public Health, which became a huge fight ... I went to a meeting and they brought in a facilitator ... to explain to us what is going on, and it's, like, "Okay, we're not idiots." So we're sitting in this meeting and the woman with the PhD got very agitated because I was questioning her data ... And then the facilitator drew a picture on the blackboard to explain it to me ... And he said, "You're not looking," and I said, "You know what? I don't have to look because this is bullshit. And you will never do this study because you have already predetermined

the outcome. And you must be pretty stupid yourself if you think that we don't see that. And if you go ahead and do the study without us, we will go to every household in the [neighbourhood] and tell them not to cooperate with you. We will blacklist you." So they had to cancel it.

As this comment also suggests, women activists or volunteers are less likely to receive credit as experts, even though they have important insights and analyses to offer. Some told of participating in public deliberations where they received no recognition or credit for their input, yet their ideas were taken up and represented as the ideas of (mostly male) professionals or politicians. According to Josephine Grey, working-class women and women of colour are even less likely to be credited with making valuable contributions than white middle-class women.

Many women told me about their quest for and exposure to scientific and technical knowledge as an important part of their work as activists. They demonstrated a sophisticated understanding of statistics and of how research is conducted in a politically charged climate. For example, Karey Shinn's organization has been active in evaluating the data collection methods used by the Toronto Department of Health:

> The statistics don't really tell you who is sick. Even with all that, there is still twice as much asthma in the East End as there is in the West End ... and yet they will still do nothing ... We want to know why it is that the Ontario Medical Association can put out a directive that states categorically and definitively that 18,000 people in Ontario are being basically killed by exposure to air pollutants and yet our Department of Health can't even come to a study that would draw any remote conclusions to affect planning initiatives. You know? Is it smart to put a highway through here or should we put another incinerator in this community? I don't know where this is going these days because it seems to be so useless. We are at the point where we will not accept just this version of the Environmental Defence Fund's score card approach and we want some survey data as well, we want monitors. I mean, it's just hopeless the way they collect data and what they don't do. I can just see that there is an incredible vulnerability on the part of any community with a proposal that comes, because there is just no way you can defend yourself. Dead bodies is all you've got.

And, in addition to developing a critical stance towards the politics of scientific expertise, some have formed alliances with "experts,"[9] having found that their limited experience and technical knowledge is simply not sufficient to sustain a credible activist campaign. Some expressed a desire to take courses in environmental studies and a few have followed through on this desire.[10] Others spoke of the need to form partnerships with what Beck (1999) might call "counter-experts" within the scientific community in order to lend greater credibility to their efforts.[11] Karey Shinn's organization worked with Rosalie Bertell (an internationally known epidemiologist, writer, and president of the International Institute of Concern for Pubic Health) when they carried out a qualitative health study in South Riverdale. Karen Buck spoke of the key role that a chemistry professor at St. Lawrence University in New York State has played in helping Citizens for a Safe Environment (CSE) make its case, in public forums, against incineration. She commented that the support of academics is an important strategy for bolstering the work of activists:[12]

> I firmly believe that the research done at universities and colleges has an important role to play in supporting activism. CSE takes the position that when we say no, we do the "research" and present the alternatives. We have sometimes found that alternatives put forward by ourselves as activists can easily be dismissed at the political decision-making level when we go without the help of an expert with credentials ... This has raised the question for me: "Do I need to go back to university for an environmental, law or medical degree?" The answer is no. It is the volunteer activist who raises the issue, proposes the alternative and needs the unpaid expert to come forward to present his or her peer-reviewed research in support of the alternative. This is the credibility that is indispensable to the activist cause.

Contrary to the suggestions in some ecofeminist narratives – that women listen to their bodies and "lived experiences" first in order to discover environmental problems – it is clear to me from listening to the comments of the women I interviewed that many knowledge sources are important in their efforts. This finding and many of the findings discussed in this section are instructive in developing a more complicated, more politicized view of women's activism than that found in present-day ecofeminist texts. It is interesting that the women appear to regard the acquisition of scientific or technical knowledge, so that they may credibly debate and discuss it with others in public, as part of their practice of citizenship.

On Citizenship, Motherhood, and "Doing One's Bit"
As I have noted, demonstrating the links between maternal concern and women's engagement in grassroots political activism is an important aspect of many ecofeminist and environmental justice narratives. "Ordinary women" who get

involved with local quality-of-life struggles out of concern for their children's welfare are transformed in the process into "sophisticated political organizers and citizens" (Kaplan 1997, 21). At the same time, green political theorists incorporate privatized responsibility for ecologically sustainable behaviour into their notions of ecological citizenship. But few if any theorists have put the question to those activist/theorizers who model such behaviour in their everyday lives. Because the women I interviewed are juggling mothering, caregiving, and active participation in grassroots politics, they occupy an interesting vantage point from which they reflected upon and interpreted some of the key themes I have found in the literature.

On Relationships between Motherhood and Citizenship

> The transformation of what it means to be a homemaker in Love Canal over the three years of the community's struggles shows the way citizenship can sometimes grow out of conscious motherhood. (Kaplan 1997, 40)

I asked the women to reflect on whether they consider their activist work a part of their role as a mother, as a citizen, neither, or both, and to say how they make sense of the relationship between the two: Are they related or entirely different practices and identities? And in either case, how? Their interpretations of the connection between motherhood and citizenship are quite diverse.[13] Some women seemed to be more comfortable thinking about their activism as an extension of their maternal role rather than as part of being a citizen. This is not to say that they reject citizenship (although "citizen" does not resonate as an identity for some women) but, rather, that their motherhood provides a more salient rationale for their political engagement than does citizenship. Their comments on this question were consistent with several women's claims about their underlying motivations for activism (see Chapter 7). For example, Marcie Goldman said:

> It initially stemmed from wanting to be a good mother because I felt that in taking care of my children I had to provide a safe environment for them and that this extended beyond my own home. So a citizen, yes, but first and foremost is the maternal thing.

This finding may point to how maternalism is embedded in the way some (especially white middle-class) women are socialized – *to the extent that they are socialized* – to think about citizenship (Voet 1998).[14] Their comments demonstrate a strong sense that the common element that joins the two identities/practices is care and concern for others. For example, Ann Gallagher said that her understanding of citizenship means taking care of or protecting her community in the face of both environmental risks and political incompetence. She explained it this way:

> It's a caretaker role. The opportunity is there for the (primarily male) civil servants – particularly within the Ministry of the Environment – to do what's right, but if they don't then the caretakers are going to come in and kick their asses until they do. And I have said to people, "I will punish you like a child – you do your job and do it properly because I'm watching you." And it is being a caretaker.

Her comment sounds like a twenty-first century version of a "civic maternalist" describing her desire to clean up politics and urban environments in the progressive era (Birch 1983). Perhaps, like other women activists described in the ecomaternalist literature, Ann Gallagher and some of the other women I interviewed have a more politicized ideology of motherhood (see Krauss 1997, 148) than that entrenched in the dominant culture, and one that entails a public and activist component. It is noteworthy that a majority of the women claimed to see their activism as part of their role both as mothers and citizens; they did not want to separate the two aspects of their identities.

When asked for their personal definition of citizenship, the overwhelming response of those women who placed importance on the term was that citizenship is synonymous with "responsibility."[15] Jamila Aman, for example, said: "Every time there is something to be done I feel as though it is my duty to go out and do it." This finding is significant in light of my discussion in Chapter 4 of the discourse of responsibility and duty in ecopolitical and right-wing meanings of citizenship. The answers given by many of the women suggest that they have a strong sense of responsibility for the welfare of others both generalized (i.e., their communities, inhabitants of the planet) and concrete (i.e., their children). Further research is needed to make comparisons with how responsible men feel for others and how men define citizenship, but feminist theorizing about "gender and moral luck" (Card 1989) provides one set of explanations for why women may have a greater sense of responsibility than do men. As mentioned earlier, some feminists argue that women are socialized (or *disciplined*, in Foucauldian terminology) to accept responsibility for the welfare of others as part of being feminine (e.g., Bartky 1990; Mendus 1998; Friedman 1995; Card 1989). The socially conditioned, gendered sense of responsibility for community found in the women in my study may stem not only from environmental discourse but also from what Kaplan (1997, 6-7) calls "female consciousness": "women in many societies and historical periods learn from youth that they will be responsible as mothers for providing food, clothing, housing, and health care for their families. When toxic pollution or expulsion from their homes threatens their communities, certain women will take action according to female consciousness, confronting authorities to preserve life. Far from being a biological trait, female consciousness develops from cultural experiences of helping families and communities survive."

Activism that is rooted in a sense of caring responsibility may contribute to a sense of political empowerment and perhaps even to a reinvigorated sense of citizenship. I still wonder, however, whether this perspective disrupts the gendered associations of women and caring – although for women who take great pride in their activist caretaking, this question may not be an important one. They may not be as concerned as I am about the dangers of equating "good mothering" with "good citizenship."

A few women said that they see their activist work as more related to their sense of citizenship than their maternal identity. For instance, Joanne Green told me that she thinks her sense of citizenship came first; the fact that she is a mother might almost be secondary. She said that she does her activist work "definitely as a citizen. I think if I hadn't been a mother I would have done other kinds of volunteer work. Being a mother, I chose to do what was closest at hand." Interestingly, some women reflected critically on the limits of motherhood as a broad enough vantage point from which to view environmental and social justice issues. In fact, Cheryl Shour's answer resembles the feminist citizenship theorists' critiques of maternalism that I discuss in Chapter 4, particularly those that highlight the inadequacy of basing political action in private sentiments like care for one's children (Biehl 1991; Dietz 1985). She said:

> I would say that I do my work mostly from a citizen's point of view, not to say that the health and well-being of my kids aren't foremost. But the problem with just focusing on your kids is that it's a very provincial attitude.

Like Cheryl Shour, some women were critical of the relationship between women's responsibility for caring for their children and for citizenship. Although they believe that citizenship ought to mean "taking responsibility," a few argued that generalized responsibility is preferable to private caring. For example:

> Private caring is something where Adolf Hitler could be kind to his mistress and his dog. The meanest people, usually but not always ... can be caring. Everybody wants to be caring towards their inner circle. What is missing in getting to a more advanced state of a caring world is respecting the out-group and valuing diversity.
> (Ruth Morris)

I don't know because I do know women who don't care and don't do things. And they're hard workers and good mothers and every-thing, but they won't find time in their lives to do anything about the environment ... They'll see that they have to take care of their family and it's totally apart from taking care of the environment. So I don't know how you teach people that by taking care of the environment you are also taking care of the world. (Sari Merson)

Karen Marcelle's analysis was that perhaps women's caring for their chil-dren is less praise-worthy than their ability to extend care to generic others:

Maybe there is a little bit of connection, because you're caring for your child, but you're supposed to. And remember, some people have kids and they don't even care for them. You're supposed to. [We] grow up and learn as girls that we'll get married and have kids and take care of our kids and our spouse. So I figure that if you do that, you learn to care for your family and if you care for your family and care for strangers, that's really super. You don't have to care for the strangers. So if you do, then that makes you a doubly good person.

Her comment brings to mind what feminist sociologist Martha McMahon (1995) has noted: mothers may be more caring towards intimates but the evidence suggests that they are not always so with strangers. As I note in Chapter 4, feminist theorists of citizenship who take a civic republican ap-proach argue that relations among citizens are better modelled on the being-together of strangers and friends than on care among intimates (i.e., mothers and children) (Dietz 1985). Perhaps the tension some women noted between feelings of responsibility for their own children and for the community or world at large suggests that these women's analyses of citizenship cannot be reduced to feminine consciousness alone.

A small number of the women expressed discomfort with the notion of citizenship for different reasons, and most of these were immigrant women and women of colour. It appears that the experience of being an immigrant, where one has had to apply for and earn one's citizenship status, might affect the ease with which a person adopts the ideology of citizenship (i.e., they may see it as exclusionary). Alejandra Galvez, for example, said that she does not see herself working as a citizen but as "a political and social activist." It may also be the case that some women understand citizenship only as it is con-nected to and granted by the nation-state.[16] Laura Jones, who immigrated to Canada from the United States and is a Quaker, said that she finds citizenship to be a problematic concept:

> People see citizenship as being a loyalty to their country and you
> can see how loyalty to your country, taken to its absolute extreme,
> can end up in war. So when people talk about duty and obligation,
> I tend to overreact to them. I tend to use words like "community"
> or "caring" ... that mean the same thing.

Relatedly, some women expressed discomfort with having their citizenship
tied to a country or nation. Josephine Grey explained that, as a woman of
mixed race, she feels as though she does not belong to any country and that
her concept of citizenship is informed by a critique of its role in social exclusion. In light of my reading of global and cosmopolitan citizenship, it is interesting that several women preferred to think of themselves as "citizens of the
world."[17] According to Susan Anthony:

> I'm not really a patriot, so that's where I have difficulty with the
> concept. Are we talking citizenship in a country? I'd prefer to be
> just a citizen of the human race and that's where some of the
> ecofeminist stuff comes in as well. I think it's the reproductive
> responsibilities of the female that make that kind of citizenship.
> Responsibility for human beings and also the knowledge of human
> needs – not just the needs of particular people.

Ecological Citizenship and Green Household Practices

As I explain in Chapter 5, responsibility is an important aspect of ecological
citizenship: simply put, good green citizens take part in the affairs of the polis
while making ecologically responsible choices at home. Feminist environmental research suggests that this responsibility is shouldered primarily by women
(Littig 2001). When asked, all but one of the women said that green practices,
such as recycling and composting, are either very or somewhat important in
their households.[18] Responses to the background questionnaire and to interview questions indicate the following: twenty-eight recycle (the two who do
not live in social housing); nineteen compost (those who do not said they
have no space or have given it up for lack of time or cooperation from family);
four women are "master composters," having taken a government-run course;
eighteen buy organic food (those who do not said it is too expensive); twenty
clean without chemicals (one who does not said it is too expensive and time-
consuming); twelve precycle (few understood what this means); twenty sub-
stitute homemade for store-bought items (those who do not said they do not
have enough time or cannot due to disability); twenty-three conserve energy;
sixteen buy foodstuffs in bulk (those who do not said it was due to no space or
having an allergy or disability); ten grow some of their own food (three do not
trust the soil, others have no space for a garden); ten preserve some of their

own food (others said they have no time). Other practices that were mentioned include: buying non-GM foods, awareness/avoidance of electromagnetic fields, not driving a car, not using pesticides (five women), practising water conservation, using non-toxic pest control, and buying second-hand things, especially clothes (six women mentioned doing this). However, none referred to these actions as an expression or practice of citizenship.

Our conversations included a discussion of who takes responsibility for living green at home and whether the women see it as another layer of work to add to their already substantial list of domestic duties. Several themes emerged. First, most of the women said that they are the ones who initiate and maintain green practices at home while significantly fewer said that the work of living green is shared more or less equally among family members. Although they did not necessarily complain, about half felt that they do not get as much cooperation from family members as they would like; some expressed frustration at the need to constantly manage their families' participation in green household practices.

Second, in a discussion that brought out expressions of guilt from some of the women, about two-thirds of them said they are unsatisfied with the success rate of their efforts to live sustainably: a common response can be paraphrased as "although we try, we could always do more!" The conversations tended to become confessional at that point.[19] Not surprisingly, several women said that time scarcity leads to tensions between, and trade-offs among, their environmental values and their consumer choices (this is similar to their comments on hiring cleaning women). I admitted that, in the process of doing my research, I made good use of microwave dinners and overpackaged take-away food in order to save time. Like me, some women said they use prepackaged foods and other convenience items when life gets too hectic; some said that they drive their cars too much. This too may cause feelings of guilt, demonstrating that environmentalism is highly disciplinary (i.e., causing people to police their own behaviour to ensure that it complies with particular normative rules) as Darier (1996) and Sandilands (1993) have explained.

> Because we're busy we tend to use some of the things that are not environmentally friendly to make our life a little easier and more comfortable.

> I order in food and I do feel badly when I do because there is so much packaging and plastic.

In line with what the feminist research has indicated, a few of the women said that their green household practices create more work and take more time than ecologically unfriendly practices. However, even more women said that living green is not difficult and that they had very few complaints about adding another layer of things to be responsible for at home. In fact, a few challenged my assumption that trying to "do one's bit" for the environment at home intensifies women's burden of domestic labour:

> The amount of time that some people I know spend shopping and buying things that they don't need or things that match ... these are things I've never particularly cared about. So in a way I have a whole lot more time. We have more time because we're not obsessive about pretension ... Of course I can't [invite] just anybody into my house as a result! (Laura Jones)

> I think it's a myth that living in your household in a sustainable fashion takes a lot of time. In actual fact this whole issue of time and convenience is something that we've been sold by manufacturers who want us to buy their products. (Jackie Kennedy)

For many of the women, green practices have become a part of daily routine. They seem not to mind the extra layer of responsibilities if it is seen as an extension of their activism. When I asked "Doesn't that add another layer of things to be responsible for?" Helen Melbourne said:

> Only if you haven't patterned yourself into it. You see, I think I've patterned myself into the recycling since my kids were very small. I got into the habit of recycling way back before there were any municipal projects for it. I'm a packrat and so I don't throw things out, I tend to pass them along. Even my activism brings me into the job of finding homes for things and finding ways for people to trade things. It is part of my activism – I hadn't thought of that – and it's what we call stewarding the earth's resources and it helps other people. Why should something go in the garbage if it's reusable?

However, when I asked them to reflect on the concept of ecological citizenship, there were women who claimed that green household practices do indeed add a layer of work and expense to their lives. I described to the women what some environmental political theorists and policy makers say about environmental citizenship – namely, that it is in large part about "doing one's bit" in the political domain and accepting responsibility for private duties like recycling and energy conservation – and asked them to comment. Not unexpectedly, many of them agreed that citizens ought to take responsibility for their actions vis-à-vis the environment. What I find interesting, however, is that my description of the theory prompted some women to reflect critically upon the underlying assumptions and expectations of being a good green citizen. Several women wondered whether the green concept of citizenship was "realistic." They suggested that it may overlook the fact that "real people" with busy lives may find it difficult to live up to such high standards. An exchange with Terri Mittelmann offers a direct challenge to theorists who fail to consider the exigencies of everyday life:

> [SM: It is possible that the environmental principles for living sustainably have been thought up by people who perhaps are not in the position to have to do it all.]
> They've been thought about by people ... living in an ivory tower [rather than by people who are] living life with kids who · have to be taken for physiotherapy, and [with] an aging parent, whose house is accumulating dirt, whose kids have homework or who are getting into big fights with their friends, who have a car pool that's falling apart, who have to get ready to teach or go to work. Life is a dynamic process!

Some women said that, given that it is often frustrating that they are the ones to take care of the green household practices, with insufficient help from family members, the idea of spreading the duty around is a good one, even though it may not happen in practice. For others, my explanation of ecological citizenship prompted a discussion of the obstacles to living green. In keeping with their commentary on the difficulties involved in trying to live consistently with one's green values, several women said that the green vision of citizenship for sustainability would be difficult for them to live up to.

Further, with regard to the ideal of incorporating environmentally friendly activities into their practice of citizenship, several of the women activists wondered how they could be expected to accomplish this in light of some significant obstacles, such as lack of time, space, and money. Their analyses raise the point that, if the visions discussed in Chapter 5 are to be extended to a broader population, it is important to address the conditions of ecological citizenship. For instance, some women wondered how they could be expected to be eco-friendly when they live in inner-city neighbourhoods that do not have recycling programs (as is the case for Karen Marcelle and Vasta Gibbons, who live in public housing) and/or sufficient space for a composter. In areas like Hamilton, where the soil is contaminated, it is unsafe to eat homegrown produce from a backyard garden.[20] A couple of women said that physical constraints inhibit their green practices: they have disabilities that render impossible a number of labour-intensive activities. Some women also commented that green consumer choices can be significantly more expensive than non-green choices and so are out of the question for lower-income people. For example, several felt that although they would like to give their families organic food it is too expensive to make this a habit. Many of the middle-class women reported that they buy organics, but the working-class women either cannot afford them at all or purchase organics only once in a while. In a follow-up question I asked, "What would make 'living green' a real option for the majority of people?" Here are some examples of their answers:

> Accessibility and price. (Vasta Gibbons)

> Having access to blue boxes for everyone. Living in an apartment, it takes a bit of extra effort to live green. (Murphy Browne)

> A value of a simplified lifestyle, wanting less, a pride in a moderate lifestyle in a wider community less oriented to excess. (Laura Jones)

> It's all a matter of perception. If you shop "green," reducing money spent on excess packaging and cleaning products, the money you save will pay for organic food, et cetera. Time is not an issue when you get it in your routine. Our family is extremely green and we seem to have more time than others. (Jackie Kennedy)

> Society and our government have to make it less of an option and more of a standard practice. Instead of coming up with more packages and useless niceties, we should be developing easier and more convenient methods of "living green" that are accessible to everyone! (Sari Merson)

In addition to these comments, there were some interesting critiques of recycling and precycling[21] from a few of the immigrant women I interviewed. While they did not, in principle, object to the practices, they pointed out that there is an obvious cultural specificity to the kinds of things I have been call-ing "green household practices." It was as if using such a specialized phrase should not be necessary to describe activities that are just common sense:

> Where I came from [Eritrea], my mother never threw away any cans, she kept them and we recycled. With clothes, we never threw away clothes partly because she was giving birth every year, but the other part was the environment, you don't dump on the environ-ment. And the spiritual part, it's a sin – to me, dumping this and that into the garbage is a sin. So they have to find a way of reusing it in a different way. (Jamila Aman)

> Many women in Peru are very into the work of the environment even though they don't say it. They save everything. They recycle

there, and it's not because they are conscious, it is because they need it. My sister saves the paper from tea-bag wrappers and uses them for her shopping lists. They separate everything in their garbage and it is recycled inside the kitchen – this is for the dog, this is for the person down the street who keeps chickens. And there are no piles of garbage like here. (Ruth Lara)

And sometimes you find that back in China some of these practices were just normal. Because things are less developed there – like they don't use as many plastic bags or they've always ridden a bicycle for example, so they might just do some of these things normally – and mostly out of economic reasons. (Li-Lien Gibbens)

Some women's critical responses to my explanation of green citizenship resonate with ecofeminist critiques of environmental privatization. Sandilands (1993), for example, expresses concern that an emphasis on green household practices like recycling and green consumerism effectively downloads ecological duty to those most involved in domestic labour (i.e., women). Echoing this critique, Alejandra Galvez said that, because it focuses on the responsibility of individual citizens, the green ideal lacks a broader analysis of structural issues that contribute to environmental problems. Her comment also echoes Luke's (1997) analysis of the "ruse of recycling" in that she suggests that public and private green acts may not "naturally" go together. She said:

I took a course in my undergrad in political science on the discourse of the environment and I did a paper on the discourse of environmentalism in Toronto – you know, the blue box. And at the time I was doing it it was a really hot topic and people were thinking that they were doing so much by recycling. And I was just disgusted! Feeling like they were good citizens by doing their part ... But for me that was such a way to take people's attention from the big issues ... it takes attention away from the big issues of who is polluting and who's benefiting and why are we just being content with a garden or a blue box when we should be lobbying governments to stop the transnationals and corporations from polluting our environment? That's the big thing, right?

Finally, for Jane Smith* and Wangari Muriuki, my definition of ecological citizenship inspired the kind of gender analysis and politicization of sustainability discourse that I have been trying to develop. I include their comments here to illustrate the resistance of women activists to the gendering of environmental responsibility.

I guess the problem with the way it's framed is that it makes it sound like, "You down there, [you] have to do this and we know what you need to do." So it feels very paternalistic. And I don't think that that's necessarily the way to inspire people, especially women who have been paternalized for centuries. We don't need any more of it. Again, my problem is that it's someone from outside telling you how to change inside. Do I think at a pragmatic level that we have responsibilities? Sure we do, for our choices, absolutely. At a mental level, it can seem reasonable enough. At a spiritual or emotional level it seems a bit weak.
(Jane Smith*)

As people working in environmental justice, we've really got to put the burden back where it belongs. It does not belong on the backs of women. And for us, right now living in downtown Toronto, to tell a woman like myself who owns this meagre home to go green 100 percent, I can't. I can't even get green energy to come into my home. I've been trying for months now to switch to natural gas, but [there's] a whole thing that is involved. So I think we need to bring back the burden and place it where it belongs. And that whole big burden really does belong with the people who have the power. And people who have the education and the knowledge, and people who have the opportunity to carry that information – people like you who are at university and doing the research – really need to be instrumental in taking the burden off the women, because really and truly, the women have enough to carry.
(Wangari Muriuki)

Theorizing the Gendered Politics of Care

In this final section of Chapter 8 I provide space for the women's theorizing of what I have identified as the gendered nature of quality-of-life activism. In response to my questions about the apparent feminization of environmental concern and participation, the women gave interpretations that at times closely mirror, and at other times indicate resistance to, those in some of the feminist and ecofeminist literature to which I have been referring. Their responses demonstrate that women's thinking about the politics of quality-of-life activism is influenced by and reflective of both dominant ideologies and oppositional discourses of resistance to gender codes and identities.

Many ecofeminist and environmental justice discussions of grassroots activism claim that women make up the majority of activists in local environmental struggles. My first line of questioning about this issue, then, was whether the women have noticed an unequal level of participation of men and women in quality-of-life issues. Most of the women I asked said that women make up the majority of members in their organizations and projects. Only a small number said that their groups include an equal number of men and women. That all of these were either working-class and/or women of colour makes an important point about how gender, race, and class intersect to produce activist commitments and communities. In fact, Dorceta Taylor (1997) notes that it is common for women and men of colour to work together on issues of social and environmental justice because they share an analysis of racism. Murphy Browne, Alejandra Galvez, and Josephine Grey made comments that seem to support this view. Josephine Grey, for example, agreed that more women than men tend to get involved in the community because they feel more responsible than the latter, but she was reluctant to make generalizations about all men: "I think there's a lot of men who do it too and I think we're at great risk when we forget that ... I know a lot of really exceptional men and I should say that 85 percent of them are black. They have already had to deal with being excluded so they have a different way of approaching the world." She went on to admit: "I never had any gender loyalty: a good person is a good person."[22]

I asked the women activists to interpret the fact that women tend to dominate the groups in which they are involved and, relatedly, I asked, where are the men? Not surprisingly, their answers tended to focus on why women are so interested in environmental and quality-of-life issues, and their analyses seemed to stem from a range of knowledge sources: personal experiences, philosophical and spiritual beliefs, and popular and/or academic literature. A common response was what might be called an essentialist explanation that assumes something like a "female consciousness." Consistent with a strong sense of maternal responsibility that some women expressed themselves, and perhaps with a measure of pride in women's capacity for care, they suggested that maternal identity is a source both of women's knowledge and responsibility for community well-being. For example:

> It's the nurturing instinct in women I guess ... Women can handle more stress than men, they can handle stress at home, stress at work, and then go and do volunteer work. But men cannot handle that ... like I see my husband, he's an activist in the social work field, but he draws a line and says, "I have done enough." But for me it's never enough ... For women it's never enough. It's like parenting. You give to your children and no matter how much love you give, you still feel that's not enough. A lot of women say, "I am a bad mother, I have not done enough," and they never give credit to themselves. I think it's instinct. (Jamila Aman)

Some women's answers relied on an understanding of gender role socialization and "tradition." Echoing many ecofeminists who offer sociological essentialist explanations, they seemed to regard the gendered division of quality-of-life activism as a traditional part of Western (and in some cases non-Western) societies:

> Women, by and large, are the people who are most interested in the quality of life. They've been most connected to their communities, to their schools, and to their children. It's not that men can't be connected, it's that traditionally they haven't been. There are more now [who are connected] than there used to be. (Helen Melbourne)

> When you have rocked a baby through the night and dealt with colic and a child crying from kindergarten because some other kids teased him, you learn about what caring is about and that this world is about healing not hurting. (Ruth Morris)

While these women made strong connections between gender roles and identities and public caring, other women seemed to think that opportunity has more to do with it. Nikola Patti, for example, theorized that there is perhaps a combination of gender role socialization and opportunity (i.e., time):

> It makes perfect sense to me that men more often than not are the ones who are out of the house working and being financially responsible for the family. A lot of women either have part-time jobs or are at home. But there are women who have full-time jobs, kids, and do a lot of volunteer work, and I don't know how they do it. So I don't condemn men for not being involved for a number of reasons, that's one of them. But, also, I hate to fall into stereotypes, but stereotypes exist for a reason, and women work cooperatively well together. It's second nature for women: in all kinds of societies women share resources, whether it's water from a well or baby-sitting your friend's kids across the street. So activist work is communal work, it's not sitting in your office making decisions about whether your company is going to sink or swim.

A few other women also suggested that perhaps women get involved because they have more time to devote to activist work. For example, Karen Woudstra said:

> There are a lot of reasons: for one, some of the women are housewives so they have time – in all fairness to men, and I guess like a lot of issues, and I'm speaking about men here, unless it hits home they don't want to become involved, unless it hits home for some

reason. Whereas with women, we're at home or have been at home and perhaps have had more time to read or see specials on TV on all the issues and so they know more. And a lot of them are affected environmentally health-wise and a lot of us are fighting for the sake of kids. I love kids and the spraying is just incomprehensible to me. So it's the maternal thing and that women are more knowledgeable because they've had more time to read, whereas men who work a ten- or twelve-hour day just want to come home and don't want to be bothered with trivial matters, unless it hits home. That's my theory.

The suggestion of women having more time for activist work than men is interesting in light of my discussion of time scarcity in Chapter 7. It may be the case that women who have part-time or no paid employment have greater flexibility in how to spend their time than men and women with full-time jobs. However, from a feminist perspective it is important to challenge the idea that "free time" means time not spent in paid employment, since many women rarely have time free from the responsibility to provide care for others. It has always seemed paradoxical to me that women with a heavy load of caring and work responsibilities, and thus a small amount of "free time," appear to do so much unpaid activist work. Perhaps the women I interviewed would agree that it is not that women have more time to spare but, rather, that women and men make different choices about how to use their time.

To evoke thoughts on how ecofeminists portray women's caring and its significance for sustainability, at the end of the interviews (when there was time) I asked some of the women to read and reflect on the following excerpt from an essay by Ariel Salleh (1994, 121): "Ordinary women, a global majority, already model sustainability in their cycle of reproductive labors. The labor of Finnish housewives ... or of Indian women farmers, [demonstrates] this. Here, in practice, are ways of meeting community needs with low disruption to the environment and minimum reliance on a dehumanizing cash economy. Honoring the 'gift' of nature, such women labour with an independence, dignity, and grace that people looking for sustainable models can learn from."

I found the women's reactions to this statement interesting. Several women appreciated the spirit of the excerpt and agreed with Salleh's suggestion that women deserve more credit than they now receive for the valuable work they do. For example:

The fact that women deal with kids and have to labour on the home front as well as in other places: I think that does model a healthier way of being, the sharing of that load. If more people were in touch with what people like to eat, for instance, or how to take little kids to the bathroom, [the world] would be a healthier place. (Kathleen Wynne)

I like the words "independence," "dignity," and "grace." The word "sustainable" is an important word in my vocabulary these days because I see things becoming less and less sustainable. And that's very frightening to me: I want to leave things for my children, I want them to enjoy all the basic things in life. And independence, dignity, and grace are certainly the qualities that I wish for my children. (Susan Anthony)

In contrast, some women expressed ambivalence about the quotation; especially those who had been concerned about playing into gender stereotypes. Some wondered whether Salleh was overemphasizing the uniqueness of women's work as a model for sustainability. For example:

Sustainable? I don't know, I mean it's been going on for hundreds of years and here we are in 2000 and women are still doing it. I think maybe what we need to do is to look at these models – the women – and somehow use what makes it work for them and somehow incorporate that into a system ... Maybe we should take these gifts that these women have that make them work – and somehow incorporate that into systems that are already in place, like government, business, to incorporate those philosophies into those practices. But a lot of it is just common sense, it's not any more special that I'm doing it. (Marcie Goldman)

It sounds romantic and it sounds nice, but there's something wrong with it. It strikes me as too romantic. "Honouring the gift of nature?" Although I realize that people can see a sustainable model within this framework, it's not sustainable in terms of society and what about in terms of gender issues? I don't know, it's hard ... I think I will need more time to think about it because of the gender issue. (Alejandra Galvez)

I have more of a problem with that, although I admit that women are way better at it and they're more intuitive. And I guess it's true that we have this built in; the whole process of how we live and give birth is sort of built-in sustainability. But I guess the part that bothers me is that I try to be gender neutral. Do we have any greater stake because we bear children? I don't think so. I don't know. I just read this book on ecosystems and think they are naturally sustainable, so we should all be, both male and female, responsible. (Cheryl Shour)

Many of the women I interviewed offered a critical analysis of the gendered division of labour, and particularly of the devaluation of women's caring work. Although only a few used the word "feminist" to describe their views, I think some of their responses demonstrate a feminist consciousness that includes a political analysis of the exploitation of women's unpaid work.[23] Kaplan (1997) distinguishes feminist from female consciousness by arguing that "feminist" stems from a critical analysis of patriarchy and sexism and a political desire to improve the status of women in society. Such an approach was apparent in a small number of the women's comments. Ruth Lara, for example, said:

> Maria Mies says that if you counted the work of women and you then had to pay for it, the economy will collapse. It's not only the fact that in this society you are valued because of the pay: if it's not paid, it's not valued. We are not in a society where the exchange will work, where if I go and cook your dinner for you, you will come and do my shoes. No, if you do my shoes I will pay you and if you do my cooking I will pay you. And in this case, we don't get paid for cooking or cleaning or child care. And society benefits for all of that.[24]

And Wangari Muriuki said:

> I look at people in this country working with the elderly who are now devalued because they don't have a nine-to-five job where they get taxed every week. I see them as in a similar category as mothers and similar to people who don't count because the dollar is not part of whatever they're doing. It's diminishing. I think that mothers particularly need to be – and it's not the money thing, it's just that the work needs to be – respected, valued, and appreciated in one manner or another. It is work. They are the society builders and if people, particularly young men, grow up thinking that their mothers just sit at home and cook and clean, then they grow up with these ideas, and when they get into positions of power they carry that with them. As women, we need to really work hard at bringing that concept home.

My preliminary review of the interview transcripts left me uncertain about what the women *really* thought about the fact that the activist and volunteer work they do is disproportionately performed by women. It was puzzling that many seemed to regard it as "natural" but at the same time expressed ambivalence about Salleh's portrayal. Perhaps there is a more subtle difference between the women's and Salleh's understandings of gender roles than I had initially expected. While there was a critique of men's lack of involvement in "unglamorous" or "trivial" quality-of-life issues, few women said they resented women's seeming to do more than men (i.e., that men do not seem to do their fair share), and most said that they had never thought about the issue of fairness. In an effort to make sense of these apparent contradictions, I sent out a follow-up question and asked for their comments. The question read: "I will argue ... that it is unfair and probably unsustainable that women do more volunteer environmental and social justice work than men. Some women interviewed disagreed with this argument. How do you feel about this?" I now present some of the responses I received, particularly those that illustrate how the women sought to challenge my position:

> I disagree. Women do a great job on environmental and social justice issues from a different perspective. Women are better suited in many instances to lead this work because of their "care-giver" mentality. (Ann Gallagher)

> This has not been my experience but I'll be looking forward to hearing the whole argument. However, in my mind I separate environmental work from social justice. Then I can see more women involved in the environment here in Canada, while social justice has both genders involved. (Alejandra Galvez)

> I do agree with this statement; however, I also feel that women are this planet's only chance for survival. I am not sure how to reconcile this dilemma. There is no power or financial clout with environmental or social justice work, the two elements are needed to make enduring change. (Cheryl Shour)

> I agree with you. "Unfair" seems like a weak word; however, I am not sure the word "unfair" really expresses women's feelings on this. (Jane Smith*)

> I feel more women do volunteer work than men. I don't feel that it's unfair, it just is. (Vasta Gibbons)

Asking the women to respond to this follow-up question illuminates important tensions in my effort to combine the analyses given by activist women with my own theorizing of the gendered politics of care. First, there is an obvious tension between their private experiences and their public expressions of gender identity. On one hand, many women find meaning and fulfillment (philosophical, spiritual, and so on) in their care-inspired or maternally motivated activist work. Though their caring and activist work may periodically conflict, quality-of-life activism provides these women with a means to express care for their children and a more generalized sense of responsibility for their communities. On the other hand, the women expressed ambivalence about their own socialized tendencies to care too much and to neglect the quality of their own lives (i.e., their personal health and well-being) in the process. And they understand what happens in public when they appear as mothers: gender codes and stereotypes get in the way of their practice of citizenship. For many, the response is to ignore these obstacles and go about their work rather than try to resist or overthrow the existing social order. Others took steps to actively resist their labelling as mothers and housewives, suggesting that women's private identities do not always translate unproblematically into public ones. In other words, it is possible for women to choose a public identity (i.e., as citizen) different from their private ones. The question remains: How and under what circumstances is this choice likely to be made?

While I stand by my commitment to avoid appropriating women's activist experiences to support my own argument, it is nevertheless interesting, in light of this tension, to speculate about the extent to which the women's voices speak to my feminist theorizing about private identity and public appearance, about essentialist and anti-essentialist thinking. A difficult question emerges regarding how, if at all, the actions of the women interviewed measure up to my understanding of feminism. There are two possible ways to approach this question. One could say that, whether or not they realize it, what the women in my study are doing is politicizing motherhood, performing in ways that disrupt cultural ideals (held by ecofeminists and non-ecofeminists alike) about women's gender-related roles. This could be considered a feminist gesture because by acting in the public domain they resist the notion that women's/ mothers' proper place is in the private sphere and that their concerns are merely parochial (i.e., "motherhood issues"). Even though many gave potentially essentialist explanations for why women are more involved in quality-of-life activism than men, they nevertheless practise a gender politics that disrupts essentialist constructs. As Lee Quinby (1994, 44-45) points out, "it is possible to find instances of essentialist politics with little or no evidence of [reflexive and persistent] critique but which nevertheless have resisted hegemonic power." On the other hand, although they have politicized mothering, it is questionable whether they have politicized care or done anything to break the connection between mothering, care, and women's citizenship (i.e., between private identities and public appearance). My sense is that they have not. Many accept a gendered sense of responsibility for the welfare of their children and their environments rather than argue for making this responsibility part of what it means to be a citizen, although some did suggest that this goal is an important one to pursue in the long run.

A second tension arises concerning my position as a feminist researcher: I want to value the work and opinions of activist women at the same time that I want to problematize the fact that they are expected to do so much. It is a tension that cannot be resolved here. Noting it, however, along with the points of disagreement among the women activists and between the activists and me, provides an example of a different kind of activist-academic relationship – one that is part of the development of an ecofeminist project that is more compatible with feminist citizenship than is currently presented in much of the literature.

Conclusion

> We live in both/and worlds full of paradox and uncertainty where close
> inspection turns unities into multiplicities, clarities into ambiguities,
> univocal simplicities into polyvocal complexities ... Upon close inspec-
> tion, "women" become fragmented, multiple, and contradictory both
> across groups and within individuals. (Lather 1991, xvi)

As Lather suggests, through my "close inspection" of the lives of women activists I have developed a counter-narrative that at times supports and at times disrupts a unified and univocal portrait that is all too common in recent ecofeminist texts. An important criticism I am making in this book is that ecofeminist narratives that move from academia to the grassroots to find stories to support the ideals of ecofeminism may be dangerously flawed. I argue that a more internally consistent (and democratic) discourse has to resist reducing the motivations of women activists to a reified picture of maternal responsibility. My narrative, therefore, does not tell the stories of other women but, rather, draws from their ideas and accounts to construct a story that complements and challenges – in effect *vivifies* – my theoretical interrogations in the first half of this book. Significantly, by creating space for their provisional interpretations of their experiences, what has come out is that the women in my study rely on numerous diverse resources for political action that both include and extend beyond their sense of maternal concern. I have also shown that they draw upon a range of knowledges and expertise in order to do their work and that they are themselves at times ambivalent about (if not resistant to) the way they are perceived as women/mothers in the public domain. Although "care" remains central to their identities and practices of citizenship, some women have challenged gender norms by becoming political activists, and some have reinterpreted and renegotiated their private roles and responsibilities in the process of finding time to participate actively in quality-of-life campaigns. Together, these findings lead to the conclusion that the profile of the "housewife activist" serves to depoliticize precisely what the women in my study are politicizing. This conclusion does not prove the feminist citizenship theorists (or me) right, but it adds complexity and depth to the stories now on offer.

My conversations with activist women have also helped me respond to and resist the assumptions of ecopolitical theorists of citizenship that people will be able to "do it all." Most important, I make visible many of the hitherto hidden costs to women who struggle to juggle a variety of public roles and private responsibilities. The accounts of the women I interviewed demonstrate that there are limits to what individuals can take on and that, without sufficient support from families, communities, and governments, women who try to do it all often neglect their own quality of life. Although the women derive a variety of rewards from their efforts, this situation is both counter-productive and unsustainable in the long run. And it runs counter to feminist goals for equalizing (if not undermining) the gendered division of labour and facilitating women's equal participation as citizens in a democratic society. So while I want to value and celebrate the accomplishments of women activists – and their expressions of care for their children, communities, and environments – I also want to avoid the trap of playing into dominant as well as left-green visions that take women's caring work for granted. I argue, therefore, that conceptions of ecological citizenship that avoid the exigencies of everyday life, and the gendered division of the labour that sustains daily life, are irretrievably defective. The picture of feminist ecological citizenship that I draw from this research, therefore, entails giving greater attention to the conditions necessary for active citizen participation: child care and eldercare, a more egalitarian division of labour at home, participatory processes that respect the time scarcity of people who juggle multiple roles, and public – as opposed to privatized and feminized – responsibility for human welfare and the quest for environmental sustainability. As I argue in my concluding chapter, working towards the universal availability of these conditions ought to be part of the project of feminist ecological citizenship.

9 No Motherhood Issue: The Project of Feminist Ecological Citizenship

> Whereas the problem for women's liberation was once how to assert personal issues as political, the problem has now reversed to one where feminists need to argue that the political does not reduce to the personal. As I have argued ... "conflicts of global and apocalyptic proportions are tackled as matters of the heart." And this is not the analysis women need if we are to win our battles.
>
> – *Lynne Segal,* Is the Future Female?

In calling for ecofeminists to move "beyond mothering earth," my aim in this book is to propose a strategy that does not rely on maternalism for speaking about women as actors in environmental movements. Although women may make meaningful connections between their mothering roles and their engagement in ecopolitical and grassroots activism, ecofeminists who translate these connections into narratives that reify their "lived experiences" and reduce them to care tread perilously close to undermining the democratic potential of ecofeminist politics. In response to those who may take this point as an unwelcome and perhaps unsisterly criticism, I argue that recognizing that maternalist strategies are dangerous opens up new and hopefully more fruitful conversations. When "the feminine principle" is asserted as the solution to ecological problems there is little left to talk about. But, as Foucault (1984, 343) points out, "if everything is dangerous, then we will always have something to do."

In keeping with this argument, it is not my intention here to offer a definition of feminist ecological citizenship but, rather, to propose it as a project that entails ongoing thought, practice, and debate. It is therefore important to end the present discussion by highlighting what I think are the central goals of the project and by saying something about how it might be informed by questions asked, and provisionally answered, in the two parts of this book. Looking at how the two stories I tell converge and diverge is useful to this search for greater clarity. When the theoretical narrative I present in Part One is juxtaposed with the empirical narrative I offer in Part Two, some interesting contradictions are revealed, and they present difficult challenges to my project of feminist ecological citizenship. Specifically, the women activists' accounts speak back to the theory in ways that shed light on the plausibility of my ideals. Perhaps it is unavoidable that when "abstract theorizing" and "real life" collide, the insights that emerge from the latter always sound more sensible (and perhaps less hopeful) than the former. This observation makes empirical research both necessary to the development of theoretical ideas and frustrating for the desire to arrive at pat conclusions. I chose to include the first-hand accounts and interpretations of women activists in my research because of a dissatisfaction with the absence of "the empirical" in the writings of green theorists of citizenship and the over-reliance on women's experiences (as incontestable truth) in ecofeminist scholarship. While my effort to synthesize theory and practice makes for a much messier narrative than the ones now on offer, it is my hope that it will also provide a much more useful one.

There are five interconnected points of tension and contradiction within and between the two halves of this book that I want to elaborate and reflect upon in this concluding chapter. Expressed as questions, these tensions are:

1 What is the balance between feminist and ecological political goals?
2 Should the aim be an instrumental or performative approach to politics?
3 Should it be a local and particular or a global and universal sense of citizenship?
4 Should there be public or private means of redistributing care?
5 Should feminists demand that men change or ... is the future female?

It would be easy to "resolve" each of these tensions by simply embracing both sides of the dualisms and claiming that it is not "either/or" but "both-and," and in many cases my discussion of them suggests we do just that. While this may be a less satisfactory approach than choosing sides, I think there is much to be gained in the process of exploring the relationships between options in a way that brings together theoretical positions and empirical research. Taken together, then, my answers to these questions constitute a mapping of, rather than a recipe for, the project of feminist ecological citizenship. It is my hope that this map suggests possible directions for new ecofeminist explorations and the inspiration to keep on moving.

The Project of Feminist Ecological Citizenship

In contrast to Sturgeon (1997, 5), who suggests that "ecofeminism ... is required to solve the mystery of how to create an anti-essentialist coalition politics while deploying a strategic politics of identity," my argument is that a better way to build an anti-essentialist movement is to eschew identity politics (along with its essentialist constructs) and make citizenship the local struggle that animates and articulates an internally complex ecofeminist agenda. In opposition also to those feminists who contend that citizenship is too tainted by its masculinist and elitist past to be of use to a feminist agenda, I am in agreement with Lister (1997, 195), who writes that citizenship "provides an invaluable strategic theoretical concept for the analysis of women's subordination and a potentially powerful weapon in the struggle against it." I have supported this position by demonstrating that the language of citizenship offers a way to develop ecofeminist positions that are both *feminist* and *democratic* because it provides a space for the public performance of the multiple and shifting identities that women simultaneously hold. By focusing on citizenship as appearance in the public sphere, the emphasis can be placed more on "actions and their consequences than on the nature or characteristics of the [actor]" (Robbins 1993, xvii). It therefore allows for women's expression of (or resistance to) *who* they are rather than *what* they are in patriarchal-capitalist-racist-(hetero)sexist societies.

Citizenship discourse also has the potential to politicize women's environmental concerns, to assert that they are not mere "motherhood issues" but deeply political ones that should become relevant to all citizens regardless of their private identities if a sustainable, democratic, and egalitarian society is to be possible. Significantly, the notion of feminist ecological citizenship, as I envision it, offers a direct challenge to left-green conceptions of citizenship. I have shown that insofar as they are blind to the specificities of gender, most ecopolitical theorists make proposals for recasting citizenship that will not contribute to gender equality. For example, without an analysis of the gendered division of necessary labour, green notions of self-reliance, sustainable community, and "doing one's bit" at home and in the public domain threaten to intensify women's already unsustainable burden of responsibility for care. Placed alongside a new right agenda that shifts from public to private the responsibility for health care and child care and the protection and cleanup of the environment (among other welfare state goods), the ecological citizenship discourse of the new greening left seems a betrayal of the women who are purportedly part of a movement for a different and better kind of society.

The accounts offered by the women I interviewed help illustrate that, in addition to providing inspiration for activism, caring responsibilities can also interfere with the practice of citizenship. This is not surprising, since – as feminists have been pointing out for decades – the public practice of citizenship has been kept separate from private life, even though private acts are a precondition for citizenship. The women in my study find that, without the support of such services as child care and eldercare, it is difficult to juggle their caring for people and households and participation in local quality-of-life campaigns. As right-wing governments in Ontario (and in many other jurisdictions) have downloaded increasing amounts of unpaid caring activities to the private sphere, citizenship has been made conditional, redefined in terms of participation in paid work and tax-paying. Poor and marginalized women face myriad obstacles to citizen participation that make their engagement in local politics all the more remarkable. A paradox of these women's lives is that they continue to work to improve the quality of life in their communities at the same time that they jeopardize their own health and well-being. Rather than ask "who cares for the carers?" celebratory narratives of women's earthcare sweep this paradox under the carpet. As I argue in the first part of this book, such narratives are *inaccurate* insofar as they overlook women's diverse interpretations of their own roles as activists and mothers; they are also *non-strategic* because they do very little to change the structures that produce and support gender inequality and continue to leave the gender blindness of green men unchallenged.

I suggest that a feminist approach to ecological citizenship call into question the public-private divide that is taken for granted in both green political theories and in ecofeminist narratives that celebrate care. The very fact of its redrawing by those on the left and the right shows that the boundary between public and private spheres is not fixed but, rather, is a social and political construction that is fluid and changeable. What makes feminist ecological citizenship distinct from other approaches is that it refuses the privatization and feminization of care and calls for public debate and action on how foundational acts of labour (e.g., care) can be reorganized to allow for women's equal participation as citizens. Care is thereby *politicized* as a necessary part of citizenship. While green politics questions the boundary between public and private in terms of the obligations and duties of citizens, there is scant recognition that what takes place in the private sphere is much more than consumption and reproduction. Ecopolitical thinkers must begin to see care not only as an ethic or virtue that can inform citizenship but also as a set of time-consuming practices that make citizenship possible. They need to take this feminist analysis seriously so that a counter-hegemonic coalition of greens and ecofeminists can be established. I suggest that joining with the green men in this kind of conversation about citizenship is more strategic for ecofeminism than continuing to assert from the margins women's moral-experiential superiority on matters ecological.

Bringing care and ecopolitics together in a critical synthesis is thus central to the concept of feminist ecological citizenship as I would develop it. The dilemma remains, however, of how to revalue and politicize care at the same time as challenging its association with women. Feminists have been grappling with this dilemma for centuries, and I do not presume to solve it here. But I have noted a tension between two feminist political positions on care that I find useful to explore: one (i.e., Dietz's [1985]) that wants to break the connection between care (associated with intimacy and maternity) and politics altogether and one (i.e., Tronto's [1993]) that wants to recast care as a political ethic that is essential to both justice and democracy. In agreement with Tronto (1993), I have problematized the tendency of some theorists (both ethics of care proponents and their radical democratic critics) to conflate mothering and caring. It is important to make a distinction between them, to say that people can care without being mothers and that caring can be generalized in a way that mothering cannot. This argument is important because, as my conversations with women activists make especially clear, there are things about care that are worth keeping and making part of politics (Plumwood 1995a). But it is also necessary to acknowledge that, although it is important to argue for a degendering of care, doing so will not change the association of the two (i.e., care and women) in the popular discourse and, as such, there will always be risks for feminists in adopting the discourse of care. So I think both insights are important to incorporate into feminist ecological citizenship praxis. Concretely, to politicize care is to show its value as both a practice and an ethic in addressing issues of social and environmental justice and to note the similarities between the exploitation of women's caring work and "natural" processes in the capitalist economy and as preconditions for democratic politics. Through the generic identity of "citizen," women are seen in theory as agents who can politicize cultural notions of femininity and maternity and disrupt the ways they are implicated in social, economic, and political structures. In practice, this might mean that feminist ecological citizens can demand public recognition of care as a political ideal for which society must be collectively responsible and, recognizing that the association of women/mothers and care is dangerous, refuse to be the only ones responsible for putting it into practice.

Tension 1: Balancing Feminist and Ecological Political Goals

I have been arguing that citizenship is important for ecofeminism because it is an alternative to maternalism that (re)places emphasis on feminist political goals of equality and democracy. But how does citizenship address the eco-political goal of redefining human-nature relationships in a more "sustainable" way? And how, exactly, do feminism and ecology work together in my project of feminist ecological citizenship?

I began the discussion by noting the growing interest among ecopolitical thinkers in the links between sustainability and citizenship. Against some greens who would dismiss a focus on citizenship as anthropocentric, the ecopolitical theorists to whom I refer in Chapter 5 argue that, in conditions of uncertainty, the best way to deal with decisions about how to sustain human life into the future is through the expansion of democracy so that the interests of "nature" can be taken into account (even perhaps represented). Although there is a range of approaches to ecological citizenship, they share a common element: by recasting the ethico-political boundaries between public and private, human and non-human, and present and future generations, ecological citizenship aims to redress the neglect of nature by changing the attitudes and behaviours of institutions and individual citizens. Most ecopolitical thinkers see this as a revolution in the study of politics and society itself: ecological politics creates a space for recognizing the limitations and blind spots of most other social-theoretical movements, feminism included. Indeed, the feminist theorists of citizenship upon whom I have drawn tend not to mention the environment, much less consider how the rights and obligations of women citizens might change in response to environmental problems (e.g., Dietz 1985; Mouffe 1992a, 1992b; Phillips 1991, Voet 1998).[1] At the same time, as I explain in part two of Chapter 5, ecological politics cannot be counted on to address feminists' concerns about gendered power relations or their goals for gender equality. Thus the case is made for a union of feminism and ecology in ecofeminism. But what is the link between ecofeminism and citizenship?

Val Plumwood (1995b, 155) captures in one sentence the basic link between feminist and ecological politics: "The demarcation of the household and the economy as private removes from political contest and democratic responsibility the major areas of material need satisfaction, production and consumption, and ecological impact." It is a unique analytical insight of ecofeminism that it is this very (hierarchical) dualism of public and private that underpins the devaluation of nature and women. The link to citizenship lies in Plumwood's endorsement of the virtue of "political contest" and "democratic responsibility": it is through the action of citizens that questions about the private-public split may become subjects of political debate. By demanding the valuation of hitherto invisible and externalized services (performed by non-citizens, colonized peoples, women, animals), moreover, ecofeminist politics presents a fundamental challenge to liberalism's denial of the inevitable interdependence of human beings. To the extent that scraps of the liberal gender blindfold exist in ecopolitical approaches to citizenship, ecofeminism offers the insight that the gendered politics of care must be addressed if the concept of ecological citizenship is to be effective.

My research with women activists complicates this picture in (at least) two ways. For one, it helps us recognize where the feminist concern for gender equality and ecological concerns can, and often do, clash. In postindustrial societies like Canada, people make trade-offs between their different commitments every day. The women in my study noted clashes between their green and social justice values and their responsibilities to family and paid work. A woman activist may be committed to green household practices, advocate green values in her community work, and then resort to wasteful consumer practices in order to save time. She may drive her minivan to anti-smog meetings, dropping her daughters off at hockey practice, stopping to see her elderly parents, and picking up groceries for the family along the way. While I am not suggesting that green theorists explicitly demand complete consistency in eco-logical living, I do contend that they have not asked questions about who does the work or what kind of subject the ideal ecological citizen would have to be. Feminist ecological citizenship, by contrast, recognizes the importance of eco-logical principles but speaks up to say it is not fair that women should do it all, that overburdened women will not be able to live green without incurring significant personal costs. Instead, what is needed is the extension of demo-cratic and feminist principles into ecologically important aspects of daily life, especially in the private sphere of the household.

The women activists' approach to "environmental" quality-of-life issues also complicates the neat distinction between "the environment" and "the social" that is often found in ecopolitical and ecofeminist scholarship. For example, few women talked about "nature" in the reified sense used in ecopolitical dis-cussions. And in contrast to the rhetoric of ecofeminism, none spoke of "car-ing for nature"; the women's caring practices and feelings were largely limited to care for people. This observation would no doubt trouble deep ecologists and others who want to move away from anthropocentrism. It was also inter-esting that the women's definition of "environment" was varied: some accept a conventional definition and do work to improve the quality of the "natural" environment (water, soil, air), while others do not distinguish the quality of natural from the quality of social and economic "environment." For the latter, not unlike those in the environmental justice movement, economic security and access to public services like education and housing were included in their list of environmental concerns. Listening to accounts of women from diverse social and cultural backgrounds helps support the development of a feminist ecological citizenship that leaves the concept of "environment" as open-ended as the subjects it surrounds. Perhaps this blurring of boundaries will help dif-fuse "environment" into conversations about "quality of life" and thus allow us to resist casting environmentalism as a separate (white, middle-class, and so on) interest group. As Plumwood (1995b, 160) argues: "the health of na-ture is not just another set of interests but the condition for any sustainable democratic practice." If ecofeminist politics is about a redrawing of these boundaries and politicizing what has hitherto been regarded as private, then the language of citizenship, rather than the language of care, is a better language for communicating this message.

Tension 2: Instrumental or Performative Politics?
There is a contradiction in my narrative between instrumentalist and non-instrumentalist views of politics. I have suggested that citizenship can contrib-ute to the realization of feminist and ecological goals. Yet in Chapter 4 I argue in favour of civic republican and feminist notions of performative politics

and citizenship as a form of self-expression important for its own sake. In Chapter 5 I ask how it is that I can simultaneously embrace the specificity of citizen politics as something other than care, while criticizing greens who imagine a society in which citizens are free to participate without mentioning how their daily need for care will be met. Many of the women I interviewed are not doing their activist work in order to learn more about politics or about themselves (even though these may be welcome results) but, rather, are responding to particular concerns about the welfare of their children and their immediate living conditions. Some said (to paraphrase): "I'm not doing this for the hell of it, I'm doing it to protect my children." Others feel forced into their activism by a crisis and some will likely step out of the activist arena once their goals have been achieved. Perhaps this contradiction is inevitable: by their very nature, social movements like feminism and environmentalism, even small-scale citizens' groups, engage in politics as a means to achieving a desirable end rather than as an end in itself.

Just as engaging in feminist research may be something of a luxury open only to paid researchers and full-time students, it is important to ask who gets to "do politics" as anything other than an instrumental goal. One of the most significant contributions of feminist theories of citizenship is the point that time is a necessary resource for the practice of citizenship, whose distribution is in large part determined by the gendered division of labour. Lister (1997, 201) writes that "citizenship politics is ... in part a politics of time." As I discuss below, feminists have made recommendations for social policies that serve to free up more time for women by taking over some of the necessary work of caring. In agreement with some green theorists, I think an important aspect of any vision of a sustainable society should be increased time for non-productive and non-consumptive pursuits such as leisure, education, and civic participation. But is having time for citizenship enough to compel people to engage actively in its practice? While I am resigned to the idea that citizen participation will always be in some measure instrumental, I also believe that feminist ecological citizenship should be more than a means to achieving a particular end. Following civic republicans like Dietz (1985, 1998), feminists must not focus on material conditions necessary for citizenship to the exclusion of the specific value of citizenship as active participation in public life. Part of the project, therefore, is a discussion of how a democratic public culture may be cultivated so that politics is not just about formal mechanisms for achieving particular ends but also about a way of interacting in the public sphere. Though the women in my study entered activist struggles with the aim of solving particular problems, they also said that they learned a lot about politics and developed greater political and self-awareness in the process. Perhaps it is useful to come back to the concept of *paideia*, what Janet Biehl (1998, 89), following the Greeks, calls the "intentional cultivation of the civic and ethical qualities necessary for citizenship." Writes Biehl: "The school for citizenship and the character structure that sustains it is the political realm itself. Citizenship is created in the course of democratic political participation, amid a plenitude of discussion and interaction that engender[s] knowledge, training, experience, and reason. In the very process of decision-making, the citizen develops both as an individual and as a political being, for citizens are the result of their own political activity" (ibid.).

If citizenship is about self-expression and discovery and a commitment to developing a political ethic in a public sphere, then the project of feminist ecological citizenship must address the question of how these aspects might be cultivated. Although Plumwood (1995b, 154-55) writes of the "possibility of a public ethic" and the need to develop a "public morality able to express care and responsibility for nature" and fairness to future generations, she neglects to consider the means through which these goals might be achieved. It is important to be clear about how this public ethic should be fostered because, as Foucauldian critics of environmentality point out, current efforts to spread green and citizenly values have generally been disciplinary (e.g., Luke 1997; Darier 1996). Feminists note that, given the gendered division of responsibility, women so disciplined are likely to accept green practices as part of the private duty of citizens, thus taking the onus off the state. Most of the women in my study have done just that, and several have taken on the task of teaching green duties to the next generation. This is yet another reason to argue against the rooting of public ethics in private values like care and to find different metaphors that do not implicate women quite so obviously.

Tension 3: Local-Particular or Global-Universal Citizenship?

By recasting citizenship as a distinct political activity valuable in its own right, one cannot avoid the question about what is the most appropriate site for citizenship: is it in community, a nation-state, the planet, or some nebulously inclusive, perhaps virtual, public sphere? Or perhaps it is more useful theoretically to eschew either-or dichotomies in favour of a more complex and "nested" picture of social, political, and ecological space(s). In any case, given that citizenship has been about membership and exclusion, any feminist attempt to reclaim and recreate citizenship must be founded on a principled stance in favour of inclusivity. Some feminists seek inclusion into an exclusionary definition of citizenship by deploying a strategy of reversal (i.e., rehabilitating masculine citizenship with feminine and maternal values), but they generally leave its territoriality – its connections to particular places – unquestioned. Against this approach, I am in agreement with feminist theorists who consider the concept of universal citizenship to be central to a non-essentialist feminist political project for social justice.

As I explain in Chapter 5, although I am cautious about some aspects of cosmopolitan thinking, I think that a cosmopolitan approach to ecological citizenship, with its emphasis on universal rights, responsibilities, and risks, is more in line with a feminist desire for a politicized and generalized ethics of care than eco-communitarian or individualist approaches to green virtue. A postcosmopolitan approach, as suggested by Dobson (2003), is even more compatible because it allows us to envision a global civil society that transcends the particular concerns of private life, the local community, and the nation-state (thereby holding the possibility for inclusivity and "solidarity in difference") while also addressing issues of international social and environmental injustice (e.g., the global asymmetries produced by the North's economic exploitation and pollution of the South's natural resources). A postcosmopolitan approach to citizenship offers an alternative to the view that powerless people in specific places (i.e., countries in the South) are to blame for the purportedly interrelated problems of environmental degradation and global insecurity because they are exhausting scarce resources to sustain unchecked population growth (see, for example, Kaplan 1994; Homer-Dixon 1999) – a view that may be used to justify the violation of their human rights. It instead turns the blame back on the powerful and persuades us that with affluence and power come the *responsibility* for global unsustainability and, by extension, the obligation to work – ideally as an ecological citizen – towards a just and sustainable society. I would argue that postcosmopolitan citizenship values are vitally necessary in light of the global impacts of terrorism and US neoimperialism. These are issues about which ecofeminists (should) have much to say (e.g., Sturgeon 2001; Shiva 2004); the language of postcosmopolitan citizenship provides an effective way to communicate ecofeminist arguments.

As I have also suggested, quoting Sandilands (1999a), the "performative affinity" of global citizens who interact with a plurality of actors and issues on a world stage has the potential to destabilize reified notions of identity. It is important to note that this potential is not inevitably realized, however: WEDO, for example, is at once part of global civil society and uses maternalist language to communicate its agenda. The feminist approach to citizenship that I favour, because of its principled stance against exclusion, also embraces a notion of global citizenship so that it includes all those who are noncitizens in current conceptions of place-based citizenship (e.g., refugees, temporary guest workers, nannies, etc.). In sum, my vision of feminist ecological citizenship provisionally entails a commitment to inclusivity, the protection of universal human rights, a view of environmental problems as globally complex and interrelated (yet asymmetrically caused and experienced), and the development of a public democratic culture that entails multiple public spheres not tied to place or territory. To quote Jones (1993), it is a "citizenship without walls." Alluding to something similar but with regard to nature, Plumwood (1995b) calls for an "unbounded community" so that non-human and future generations may also be included as an important part of ecological democracy.

There is a tension, however, between my interest in a citizenship that is universal in scope and transcendent of local and national (and perhaps temporal and species) boundaries and the women activists' rootedness in their own communities and their particular interests as mothers and carers. As I discuss in Chapter 3, recent feminist scholarship on women's grassroots activism suggests that women are more likely to direct their political participation towards their local communities and the local state than to the nation-state or global civil society. Most of the women activists I interviewed are part of small, single-issue groups and do not venture much further than their own neighbourhoods or the meeting rooms at City Hall. For them, the local as a site for the expression of citizenship makes more sense as it is at the local level that they can get things done (thus echoing green political theorists such as Bookchin 1989 and Light 2002). Like "grassroots" environmental justice activists who define the environment as the place where they "live, work, and play," the women in my study derive meaning and satisfaction from improving the quality of life in their own locality, not from working to save a distant rain forest or from some abstract concept of Gaia. As communitarian political theorist Michael Walzer (1983, 225) points out, people are "most likely to be knowledgeable and concerned, active and effective when they deal with issues close to home, in their neighbourhoods." Vasta Gibbons certainly echoes this sentiment when she says that "most of the women that I work with have the same feeling as I have: they want to improve their community." Her comment is not surprising since, global anti-globalization movements notwithstanding, there is little in contemporary political culture that fosters an understanding of politics that is not tied to the local community. Indeed, the women in my study are a long way from resembling global feminist eco-citizens. So on one hand my notion of feminist ecological citizenship is challenged by the observation that grassroots, place-based activism appears to be more "realistic" and meaningful than a citizenship without walls. On the other hand, however, I think feminist ecological citizenship offers an important challenge to "grassroots" activism to, in principle, become more expansive and inclusive in its scope.

Coming back to concerns raised in Chapters 3 and 5, what is to stop grassroots campaigns (even those run by women) from becoming parochial and exclusionary? As Catriona Sandilands (2002, 123) points out, "it remains important to distinguish acts of community defence and empowerment from the acts of political reflection and imagination that cultivate a common world. They may coexist, but they are not the same." I would argue that what distinguishes Not In Anybody's Back Yard (NIABY) movements (to protect the quality of life everywhere, now and in the future) from NIMBY struggles (to protect one's own child's health) is a cosmopolitan consciousness that transcends local and private interests. A truly public, truly global, political sphere is a long way from being created. This recognition provides an important reality check on globalist discourse yet holds out the ideals of global citizenship and public culture. Thus, it is also an important alternative to an ecofeminist perspective that is preoccupied with the private identities, material practices, and parochial concerns of a select group of women (worthy subjects though they may be).

It seems clear that feminist ecological citizenship cannot escape or resolve the interconnected tensions between global and local, universal and particular. What it can do, however, is follow Lister's (1997) recommendation of a critical synthetic approach to feminist citizenship. I agree with Lister that there needs to be a critical synthesis of the local and the global into a *multi-layered notion of citizenship* that encompasses many different yet nested sites for the practice of citizenship (perhaps including some aspects of the private sphere, but I remain ambivalent about this idea) (see also Yuval-Davis 2000). As I note in Chapter 7, this notion also includes the need for public spaces for the practice of citizenship, such as town halls and community centres, perhaps even in cyberspace. There should also be a critical synthesis of a universal human rights approach that transcends local tradition – so that inclusivity is fostered and protected in a complex, multicultural, and unsustainable world – and communitarian traditions that envision the responsibility of citizens to participate in their local political communities. With this in mind, my project could include developing a language of feminist ecological citizenship, with a "grammar of political conduct" as a foundation for citizen engagement, that can transform the local issues about which women activists are concerned into global ethico-political issues while still recognizing the centrality of the local and the private in many women's everyday lives. A tall order – here I open it up to debate and further theorizing.

Tension 4: Public or Private Means of Redistributing Care?

My second and third points about performative and universal citizenship must be tempered by the argument that people cannot be expected to engage in politics for its own sake unless sufficient conditions for citizenship practice are in place. This observation suggests that there is an unresolved tension in my discussion between civic republican and liberal notions of citizenship. Civic republican and communitarian theorists of citizenship believe it is "natural" for human beings to join together in pursuit of the common good, while liberals are concerned about the equal rights of citizens (which includes a just distribution of basic needs) to pursue their own individual notion of the good. As I explain in Chapter 5, that there are strengths and weaknesses of each approach suggests that some kind of "third way" is needed. Here it becomes important to incorporate a modified version of Chantal Mouffe's (1992a) radical democracy into my project of feminist ecological citizenship. In proposing a radical democratic synthesis, Mouffe's concern is to (1) embrace a republican vision of citizenship as a common political identity that centres on active participation in the public sphere while (2) rejecting the imposition of a notion of a substantive common good on the liberal grounds that this interferes with individual liberty. I accept this as an important project and would modify it by adding to the second action a rejection of the assumption, on feminist grounds, that citizens will naturally cooperate in their pursuit of the common good. Feminists know all too well that the gendered division of labour will not disappear in putatively communalist social arrangements. Given that basic needs will always have to be met (and the work of meeting them will not be replaced by robots or clones anytime soon), it is central to a feminist vision of an egalitarian society that care be organized socially and institutionally rather than privately and voluntarily.

An interesting defence of Hannah Arendt's decision to rule the "social question" out of the bounds of political debate is that she took it as a given (rather than as a matter of opinion) that the state would provide such necessities as adequate housing (Torgerson 1999). But here in the early twenty-first century, amid a new right drive to dismantle public services, it seems we can no longer depend on the state to supply the social conditions that allow people to participate in public life as citizens. Instead, women's unpaid caring and provisioning work is being exploited as if it were a natural and inexhaustible resource. The accounts of the women I interviewed affirm the arguments of feminist political economists that women's burden of labour is being intensified by the implementation of a neoliberal economic agenda. However, these women said very little about universalizing care or the need to win back some of the losses to the welfare state dictated by neoliberal policies (i.e., in Ontario, the Conservative government's Common Sense Revolution). Most try to juggle their various commitments on their own by making informal care arrangements, devising elaborate time management strategies, and doing less than they feel is expected of them, while sometimes incurring the resentment of their families, feeling guilty, and burning out in the process. While some women have succeeded in forging egalitarian household arrangements and/or finding state-provided child care, many of the affluent women find privatized solutions like cleaning women and nannies in order to help them combine their activist work, paid work, and household responsibilities. I am uncomfortable with these private ways of responding to the lack of public services, although I do not want to criticize individual women for doing the best they can under the circumstances. In my view, privatized solutions are problematic because they can only work for economically privileged women and because they have the potential to perpetuate exploitative colonial, racist, and sexist relations in society (see Ehrenreich and Hochschild 2002). Meanwhile, trying to "do it all" unfairly burdens women and takes the onus off societies to take collective responsibility for their own reproduction.

A key task in my project of feminist ecological citizenship, then, is to join green political arguments about public ecological ethics (that are in many ways connected to communitarianism) to feminist arguments about social citizenship rights (that have a history in liberalism and social democracy). Feminists have proposed a range of ways to destabilize the public/private divide and to redistribute the division of care so that more women have more time to participate. Marxist feminists, for example, have envisioned the "withering away" of the family (as an instrument for passing on private property) once its functions are socialized by the state. I suspect few people would find this an attractive proposition, and, as I note in Chapter 5, I am not suggesting the replacement of all private caring with state or institutional care.[2] In less extreme terms, like feminist proponents of social democracy, I see the provision of welfare state-type policies as necessary in order to overcome some of the historical, gender-related obstacles to women's participation as citizens and therefore as an obvious, although not uncontroversial, part of this project (e.g., Savarsy 1992). Many care-friendly social policies have been proposed by feminist theorists of citizenship, such as extended paid maternity and paternity leaves; universal provision of services like health care, child care, and eldercare; and a guaranteed annual income that supports carers who do not participate in paid employment (Lister 1997).

At the same time, feminist critiques of the welfare state remain important (e.g., that it can replace private with public patriarchy and interfere in areas of life that should be kept private such as sexuality and reproductive choice), as does the call for greater democratization of institutions and popular planning for social need (Wainwright 1994). While I disagree with Plumwood's (1995a) fear that moving towards state-provided care would be bad for women because it would erase the sphere in which most women define their identity (and expand the sphere in which most men define theirs), I support her interest in reviving utopian socialist and feminist ideas for collectivizing care in a way that blurs and transcends the public-private distinction. Some of these ideas include collective kitchens and nurseries and designs for communal living (e.g., Hayden 1981; Spain 1995). Danish and Dutch co-housing arrangements, in which men and women agree to participate equally in the running and maintenance of a large communal household as a formal condition of residency, have also been held up as good ideas for redistributing necessary labour.[3] As I note in Chapter 7, activist Li-Lien Gibbens lives in a communal house and reports that her load of domestic labour is much lighter than it would be in a "traditional" nuclear family living arrangement.

These proposals address the need to create a just balance between time for citizenship and time for care so that women do not have to choose between these two very important pursuits. Because feminist ecological citizenship is also about rethinking human exploitation of the environment, it is interesting to consider how a *care-friendly politics of time* might have advantages from the perspective of sustainability. The project could benefit from innovative work by feminist and green economists who might attempt to quantify the connection between the devaluation of women's time and the exploitation of natural resources in the private sphere. They might calculate a kind of "socio-ecological footprint" for the household that includes measures of both human labour time and natural throughput. This would show, for example, that, unlike the post-industrial workplace in the information age, the typical Western/Northern household still relies on *labour-using* rather than *labour-saving* technologies (Schor 1997).[4] Some of these technologies, like washing machines, are also very energy-, water-, and waste-intensive (see Shove 2003). This is not to call for a return to the washbasin and mangle, as some greens have done. (For instance, on a recent television series on the BBC called *No Waste Like Home* – during which the host gives tips on how to make homes more eco-efficient – a woman with four young children was forced to give up her washing machine and do her eleven weekly loads of laundry by hand. Typical of most green lifestyle advice, the earth wins at the expense of a mother's undervalued time.) Rather, it is important to think about why such tasks have been privatized in the first place, and how the barriers to collectivization might be overcome so that everyday living can become both environmentally and socially efficient. One place to start is to reconsider the shape of modern cities, as feminist urbanists have done. They argue, for instance, that North American cities have been designed so that each single family home in the sprawling suburbs "needs" to be equipped with its very own set of consumer durables (ten houses on the block = ten lawnmowers, ten tumble-dryers, and so on), which are time-consuming to clean and wasteful of land and other resources (for an excellent history of this social phenomenon, see Hayden 1984). Modern cities are designed to separate living from working, so people often have no choice but to use fossil-fuel-guzzling vehicles to get to work, to do their shopping, to take the children to schools, and to engage in their various recreational and citizenly pursuits (see MacGregor 1995). If unpaid working time and natural resources were valued more highly, then it would be incomprehensible to design such places and things.

Juliet Schor (1997) sees hope in the idea that the creation of a care-friendly society in which all people have the time and the inclination to engage in caring activities might also have ecological implications if it could slow down the treadmill of "work and spend" in the affluent North. Although there are important social policies that could assist in this change, Schor specifically recommends the democratization of the workplace as a key strategy in bringing about an ecologically sustainable and egalitarian society (something that Plumwood [1995a] has also recommended). Echoing left-greens such as Lipietz (1995) and Rifkin (1995), Schor suggests that instead of rewarding workers with higher pay, which they then spend in ways that will make up for their alienating work (what Herbert Marcuse [1966] calls "compensatory consumption"), they would be given more time with which to pursue other postmaterialist and socially valuable activities such as further education, civic participation, and spending time with children. This would be an excellent strategy provided that the gender division of labour is taken into account. Ideally, from a feminist perspective at least, both men and women would take part in postmaterial and care-related pursuits with equal enthusiasm. It is important always to recall the socialist feminist argument that "because it is the labour of ensuring human subsistence, the production time of domestic labour can never be reduced, it can only be shared or redistributed" (Luxton 1987, 172). As I argue in Chapter 5, finding ecologically friendly *and socially equitable* answers to the question of how to share or redistribute it is central to my project of feminist ecological citizenship.

Tension 5: Can Men Change or Is the Future Female?

All of these proposals sound good on paper and may even be real options for facilitating women's equal civic participation, but there is no avoiding one crucial question: how to get men to equally participate in caring labour, to take equal responsibility for caring for and about other people and their environments. This is an endpoint to which feminist discussions about changing the gendered division of labour seem inevitably to lead. Feminist research shows that, even when policies and programs are implemented that give men and women more time to devote to necessary, unpaid labour, women in general still end up doing more of it than men in general (of course we all know exceptions).[5] Australian sociologists Bittman and Wacjman (2000, 174) note that even in "gender-equity-conscious Sweden" women's share of unpaid work is 70 percent. They have also found, in their multinational quantitative study of the quality of leisure time by gender, that "fathers of children below the age of two years enjoy, on average, almost three times more hours of adult leisure time [meaning time not spent with children] than the mothers of these children." This prompts them to comment that "the uneven distribution of this scarce resource is truly striking" (183). Schor observes that even though men may be doing a greater share of household work today than they did in the 1960s and 1970s, they tend to take on the more rewarding and enjoyable tasks, like playing with children. "Women," meanwhile, "are still cleaning toilets" (Schor 1997, 45).

As I note in Chapter 8, many of the women I interviewed gave what I would call maternalist explanations for the high rates of women's participation in quality-of-life activism. Echoing prominent ecofeminists, they said that women, because they perform the work of mothering, just *care more*. Several were reluctant to problematize women's sense of responsibility, suggesting that women were the planet's best hope for survival. One woman said: "I see women as

'guiding lights' of the world. I feel women are capable to make the changes."
Not surprisingly, when I asked the women activists "where are the men?" in
their organizations, they gave a range of responses that demonstrate potentially essentialist assumptions about the typical behaviour and concerns of
men. They noted men's lack of interest in unglamorous issues (e.g., chemical-
free house cleaning, lice infestations at school, and food banks in the community) that are perceived to be women's concerns, women's work. Some suggested
that men are more individualistic and would rather make the mess (ecological
and otherwise) than clean up after it.[6] "Women traditionally have been the
ones who fix the things that men do wrong ... As soon as you let men make the
decisions, you know someone is going to have to clean up the mess," observed
Jackie Kennedy. Significantly, several women made connections between men's
lack of involvement in local quality-of-life campaigns and their lack of responsibility for caring for children:

> Men are not as connected to the concept of their children's future
> world. It seems like men are more black and white about it and it
> doesn't pain them in the way that it pains women. I can't speak
> for men; I can only speak from my personal observations of men ...
> Personally I know there is a connection between my feelings about
> my children and my family and my role in the world. (Terri
> Mittelmann)

> I hope that the boundaries between men and women are gradually
> changing to the point where all people feel more responsible. I've
> certainly tried to raise my sons to have that sense of responsibility
> ... It's been a sadness that it's been only women and it's been a
> sadness that men haven't had that joy of being around children.
> Whole generations of men only saw their children in passing as
> they did their duty and went off to work. (Laura Jones)

Also concerned about men's lack of participation in caring activities,
maternalist feminists see "shared parenting" as a solution to myriad social
problems in our male-dominated world (e.g., violence, greed, and ecological
destruction) and thus propose it as a long-range strategic priority for feminism (e.g., Ruddick 1989). In much the same vein, the Women's Action Agenda
21 holds that "men should participate in child care" as part of its code of
environmental ethics (quoted in Merchant 1996, 219). In summarizing the
main features of the subsistence perspective, Maria Mies (1993, 321) says
that men "must give up their involvement in destructive commodity production for the sake of accumulation and begin to share women's work for the
preservation of life. In practical terms, this means they have to share unpaid

subsistence work: in the household, with children, with the old and sick, in ecological work to heal the earth."

Is the aim to make men take on the work of women (i.e., mothering) so that they act and think more like women? If so, then the added bonus, of course, might be that women will have to do less. Some of the women in my study follow this logic and have tried to make their sons take more responsibility for cooking, cleaning, and taking care of their younger siblings. I commend these women on their efforts to redefine the gender codes at home, but I remain sceptical of privatized and psychologistic responses like "shared parenting" that aim to change attitudes of men one man at a time rather than destabilize the structural power relations between the sexes. Although many claim to have egalitarian households in which their male partners share the caring work, it sounds as though (consistent with available empirical data) the women continue to shoulder the bulk of the responsibility. In an age when intentional childlessness, lone parenting, and non-nuclear and non-heterosexual family forms are commonplace, "shared parenting" seems an anachronistic, even conservative, solution. Perhaps more significantly, it does nothing to challenge the ideology that caring is a largely private responsibility. As Segal (1987, 159) argues, "it does not, in itself, promote the crucial struggle for *public commitment* to and improved state resources for caring for all dependent people, many of whom do not have couples to care for them. The relation between private and public caring still needs much more thought and discussion" (emphasis mine). Still more thought and discussion are needed, nearly twenty years after Segal's call.

And so we return to the small matter of how to affect sweeping cultural and structural change that can answer Joan Tronto's (1993) call for a political ethic of care. Perhaps the creation of a care-friendly and democratic public culture along the lines that I have suggested would contribute to a destabilization and redefinition of gender codes. A key part of the project of feminist ecological citizenship is to call for the democratization of the household so that household and caring tasks are divided fairly between men and women. As Plumwood (1995b, 157) points out, "a better integration of democracy with everyday life can provide some of the necessary conditions for a public political morality." The other side of the coin is that caring work needs to be supported institutionally – by the state and by the market and in the workplace, as I have described thus far. But I also think that another key part of the project should be principled feminist resistance to gender codes through the language and practice of citizenship. The project may thus involve the renewal of feminist consciousness-raising that inspires women to "refuse who they are" and claim the political identity of "citizen." As citizens, women activists in volunteer organizations might refuse being exploited and demand recognition through state support either through direct funding or tax breaks.

As citizens, when the tasks are being divided among members of a social movement organization, women might challenge gendered assumptions about appropriate tasks for men and women. As citizens, women might resist social expectations that they should "naturally" be able to take on ever-expanding loads of care at home and in the community. I have great sympathy for women activists who have said, "I cannot do it all" and have rearranged their lives accordingly, often challenging gender codes and politicizing motherhood in the process. Ecofeminists who celebrate women as eco-superheroes are perpetuating a myth. The many burnt-out women activists in my study will no doubt attest to this claim.

And what about the men who write about ecological citizenship? Mouffe's (1992b) idea that citizenship can be an articulating principle for many social movements never deals with what feminists know through decades of social movement experience: even when the ideals of liberty, equality, and solidarity (formerly known as fraternity) are held in common, the masculinism of men persists. Segal's (1987) analysis, on the other hand, leads her to conclude that a coalition of feminists and left men, while necessary, will not work as long as the latter remain stuck in their patriarchal ways. She then argues that feminists should engage politically "with" and "against" men in left-wing social movements, that they should be neither their "foes nor loving friends." The same might be said about the pervasive (subtle and often denied) masculinism of many of the men who are the intellectual leaders of the green movement. Some have taken ecofeminist and feminist ideas on board (e.g., Barry 1999; Dobson 2003), and it would be counter-productive not to give credit where it is due. But fruitful conversations between the green men and ecofeminist theorists, in which the exchanges are balanced, rigorous, and open, have thus far been lacking. As a strategy for addressing this problem, I propose that part of the project of feminist ecological citizenship should be to engage with masculinist green scholars – in journals, at conferences, and so on – in order to learn from their insights into citizenship, democracy, and politics and to draw public attention to their blind spots and omissions where gender relations are concerned. For example, when, say, an ecosocialist presents a paper at a conference that looks at the benefits of reduced working time for people and the planet but neglects to explore its implications for the gendered division of labour, the feminist ecological citizen should ask: "Why do you feel intellectually justified in leaving these questions out?"[7] The way to challenge the fact that care is "irrelevant to the moral life of the powerful" (Tronto 1993, 89) is not to claim it as women's special gift but, rather, to assert it as a political ideal that no democratic and sustainable society can do without. If we accept Mouffe's (1992a, 225) suggestion that "the way we define citizenship is intimately linked to the kind of society and political community we want," then gender-blind green men must be called to account for why an analysis of (much less a calling for an end to) masculinist privilege has thus far been absent in their definitions.

Coda: Towards a New Theoretical Politics for Ecofeminism

These tensions and contradictions are made apparent through an encounter I have staged between theories and practices that until now have been casual acquaintances at best. Inviting an encounter between an expression of ecofeminist ideas about women activists and women activists themselves is something that, to my knowledge, no other ecofeminist scholar has done. In so doing, I have created a space for debate that will contribute to the project of feminist ecological citizenship in important and, I hope, unpredictable ways. Each of the women I interviewed has ambivalences as well as certainties, questions as well as answers; several said they have been challenged to think differently about some of the issues I presented for discussion, while others have helped challenge some of my assumptions. Interestingly, when I asked the women I interviewed to read and respond to Salleh's (1994) claims about housewives and "ordinary women" modelling sustainability through their everyday caring practices, signs of resistance were obvious (see Chapter 8). There is something about Salleh's characterization that did not sit right with some of these women. Some said her portrayal of the kind of work they do is too simplistic; others suggested that environmental issues are too important to be represented as "a girl thing." I suggest that their discomfort stems from feminist consciousness, but I make this suggestion cautiously because I did not directly ask them this question.

By allowing "who" they are to speak in this book, moreover, I demonstrate a methodological approach that is different from the one in those ecofeminist narratives that focus on "what" women activists are. Far from claiming them to be "grassroots warriors" or "housewife activists," I present the thirty women I interviewed as activist/theorizers with complex identities and politically astute analyses of the obstacles to civic participation, the uses and abuses of scientific expertise and government policies, and the feminization of quality-of-life struggles in their communities (among other issues). By presenting their comments and analyses in this way I demonstrate the fallibility of the acting-thinking and activist-academic dichotomies that I discuss in Chapters 3 and 6 while making space in my narrative for women's theoretical agency. This is a form of theoretical politics that has thus far not found its way into ecofeminist discourse. Not only does my research demonstrate a different relationship between the roles of "academic researcher" and "research participant" but it is also consistent with my approach to citizenship. I argue that women activists should be engaged with and listened to (even disagreed with) rather than spoken for, and, even more important, that they should have the choice to appear and be heard in public and by academics in ways that they themselves determine rather than being hidden behind a mask of fixed identities and stereotypes. I also hold that theorizing is a practice of feminist ecological citizenship when it resists and undermines patriarchal gender codes and dominant ideologies about human-nature connections.

In "A Cyborg Manifesto," an (in)famous essay in which she rails against totalizing feminine identities, Donna Haraway (1991b, 181) writes that, although both are "bound in the spiral dance," she would "rather be a cyborg than a goddess." I would be remiss if I did not end this discussion by disclosing that an inspiration behind the feminist political analysis that I have presented has similarly personal roots: in public appearance, and on matters of ecopolitical debate, I would rather appear as a citizen than as a mother. It is my hope, therefore, that this counter-narrative, in which I have questioned assumptions about women's maternal connections to their environments, will be read as my own act of feminist ecological citizenship and that the ensuing debate will be a carefully political one.

Appendix: Research Process and Methods

> If we are to accept that there is no unity, centre or
> actuality to discover for women, what is feminist research
> about?
>
> — *J.-K. Gibson-Graham, "Stuffed If I Know!"*

> Is feminist research still possible? Indeed is a feminist
> politics still necessary if we have deconstructed the
> category "Woman"?
>
> — *Linda McDowell*, Gender, Identity, and Place

I begin this account of my research process and methods with these two quotations because they help explain my commitment to approaching feminist questions from what many will call a "postmodern" feminist perspective. Both quotations are by scholars whose work has been instructive to me because they incorporate postmodern insights into feminist theorizing about "women" and gender relations while continuing to do explicitly political research. They approach research in a way that does not take "lived experience" as a path to the truth but, rather, takes both material and non-material (i.e., discursive) conditions to be relevant subjects of interpretation. Their research treats women as potential co-theorizers rather than representative subjects, and endeavours to "eschew easy, ahistorical answers ... to consider gender in all its contingency" (di Leonardo 1998, 268). Unlike those (eco)feminists who reject postmodern approaches as depoliticizing and even frivolous in a time of socio-ecological crisis, I believe postmodern feminist research has been shown as more humble, democratic, and politically generative than that which presents women's knowledge and experience as necessary ingredients of an alternative vision for planetary survival.

As I have explained, my feminist approach rejects reductionism and embraces uncertainty and openness as vital to democratic debate. It also puts the desire for more accurate narratives about the complexity and diversity of women's thought and action ahead of a strategic desire for sisterhood and solidarity. I think feminism is up to the challenge of being a viable political-academic movement even when the very thing at its core is in question. The same can be said, it seems to me, about environmentalism. We may not know the truth about "nature" and we may not trust the science that purports to measure "nature," but we can still analyze it, debate it, and do research that contributes to struggles to preserve it. Likewise, refusing to cling to a unified notion of "woman" does not mean a denial of the existence of women or the problems they experience because of poverty, (hetero)sexism, racism, and so on. It simply means that we must be committed to asking more questions about more women and to being provisional in our analyses.

In writing *Beyond Mothering Earth,* in which I criticize the reductionistic tendencies within ecofeminism and employ some of the analytic tools of postmodern feminism, I am aware that I will be met with counter-criticism from those whose work I have questioned. When I read a statement such as this one by Maria Mies and Veronika Bennholdt-Thomsen (1999, 199), I am tempted to come to my own anticipated self-defence: "Postmodern feminists' criticism of 'essentialism,' for example of ecofeminism, has its roots in [a] denial of our own origins as 'of woman born,' of real mothers and the symbolic order of mothers and of the female body. For women this denial is self-destructive."

However, as I have explained, it is not the aim of this book to pour fuel on the debates that have been burning for too long between feminists, ecofeminists, and feminist environmentalists of various different descriptions. Nor am I interested in engaging in the kind of self-disclosure that has been found in feminist research since the "reflexive turn" (McDowell 1999) (for instance, I am not going to talk about my mother or about the fact that I am not a mother). The aim of this work is to point to a way out of the current impasse, a way that moves beyond the implication that "women" know things because they are "women" or are uniquely skilled at caring for people and the planet because of their exploited and oppressed situations as "women." One way I have suggested we do this is by embracing the discourses and practices of citizenship – specifically the project of feminist ecological citizenship. Another way is to do more careful empirical research with (yes, real live) women, using the insights from postmodern feminist methodology that I discuss in Chapter 6. I offer what I hope may be an example of ecofeminist research that is consistent with its theoretical and political commitments. Here, I provide a detailed account of how I went about conducting this research.

Participant Selection and Background Information

Early in the research process I developed a list of criteria for selecting women to interview. I wanted to talk to women who were unpaid caregivers (i.e., responsible for the care of dependent children or other relatives at home) as well as actively involved in local environmental justice projects or organizations. I hoped that there would be diversity among the thirty women selected, and I kept this in mind when choosing which potential participants to contact. It was important that the women's activist work was unpaid and defined by them as time-consuming. I decided to interview a total of thirty women because that number seemed small enough to be manageable, given my resource and time constraints, and large enough to allow for a diverse array of social, political, and economic variables. My constraints were that I was conducting the research alone, I needed to finish my degree within a respectable time, and that I had minimal funding (in 1999-2000 I had a scholarship from York University to cover both my research and subsistence costs; the award stipulated that I could not take on paid employment). Thirty participants would appear to be more than adequate according to McCracken (1988), who recommends eight as a suitable number of participants in a long interview situation. I am confident that this number has provided me with sufficient material from which to draw some important conclusions (although not *generalizable* conclusions, as I explain below).

I located participants using purposive sampling; that is, I used key informants and the snowball technique. Purposive, as opposed to random, sampling is based on the notion that in order to gain the most insight into a particular question one needs to select a sample that can provide the most appropriate information (Lincoln and Guba 1988). Key informants (i.e., people in environmental and social service organizations as well as from universities, whom I thought would have good community connections) were contacted by phone or e-mail and asked to recommend women who fit my selection criteria. Most of these informants were well-known and respected local professionals and activists whose endorsement lent credibility to my work. Their endorsement thus helped open the door to a trusting relationship with potential research participants. In some cases I asked the women who agreed to participate to recommend other women who might fit my selection criteria, and the list grew (i.e., "snowballed") from there.

I initially cast my net widely in an effort to find women from a diversity of organizations and communities. Prospective participants were contacted first by phone or e-mail, at which point I explained my goals and rationale for the research and attempted to assess their suitability and availability for the study. I presented myself as a researcher interested in hearing about the experiences of women who have a large load of unpaid work, with the goal of making the value of this work more visible. I explained that I was most interested in listening to the kinds of personal rewards and costs that are involved in juggling activist and caring work. Presenting myself as a sympathetic and respectful listener, I used the telephone conversation to begin establishing a friendly rapport. I then sent them a letter that described my research project in greater detail and formally invited them to participate in an interview. If they said yes, then we arranged an interview time and place that was suitable to them.

In order to find women from a wide range of social and cultural backgrounds, I shifted my framing from environmental activism to "quality-of-life" activism – a phrase that implies a broader understanding of environment and is consistent with the literature on environmental justice discussed in Chapter 3. It was difficult to find women of colour using my original definition of "environmental activist": someone who works actively in civil society to address issues relating to or stemming from the degradation or contamination of the natural environment. From what the women told me later, I suspect that it is less common for women of colour to characterize their work as being about "environment" than it is for white women because it has not become a part of the discourses of non-white and immigrant communities in Toronto. In my conversation with public health researcher and advocate Nita Chaudhuri, I asked why she thought it was that I had a hard time finding environmental activists who are women of colour. She suggested that it had something to do with my choice of terminology:

> [Those other than white middle-class people] don't use "environment" as a defining issue, they probably use jobs and community. The smaller communities have their own internal support networks. Regent Park is like that; their issues aren't defined as environment. And the women who originally start working on environment don't consider themselves environmentalists, they do it because of health ... so they work from the same premise, it just happens that it's the environment that's being affected. It's like a catch-all phrase ... environment can be the social environment or it can be the physical environment.

In addition to this important insight, it is a fact that (at the time of my research at least) there are very few organizations that use the term "environmental justice" in Toronto (the exception is the Multi-Racial Network for Environmental Justice [MNEJ]). The environmental justice movement has apparently has not caught on in Canada to the same extent that it has in the United States. So the kinds of organizations that are included in my expanded "quality-of-life" definition are community-based food security projects; neighbourhood cleanup and park restoration projects; urban safety initiatives; and anti-toxics and environmental health campaigns in homes or schools. The majority of the women interviewed said that "quality-of-life" activism was an accurate way to describe the work they do.

Once I opened my sampling criteria, I was able to find a more internally diverse group of women. In order to be able to accurately describe their social locations as "diverse," prior to the interview I sent each of them a background questionnaire that asked them to describe (by answering both open- and closed-ended questions) their ethno-cultural background, socioeconomic class, educational and occupational experience, and household makeup. These details are reported in Chapter 6. The background questionnaire was a very effective way to prepare myself and the participants for the recorded interviews. I was able to come to the conversation already having a sense of the women's lives, concerns, and commitments, and they had an opportunity to reflect on their own situations and why they might be of interest to me as a researcher. Two added benefits were that during the interview I could clarify and refer back to what they had said in the questionnaire and that we could launch straight into the interviews with open-ended substantive questions rather than having to begin with demographic and other closed-ended quantitative questions.

The Semi-Structured Conversations

The conversations were guided by an interview schedule developed out of the theoretical questions that emerged from my literature reviews as well as from some of my own assumptions and queries. I decided against unstructured interviews in favour of semi-structured ones because I had a clear sense of the issues I wanted to discuss with the women. I also favoured the semi-structured format because, while the interviews were guided by a list of questions to be raised, it allowed for flexibility: neither the exact wording nor the order in which they were asked remained constant (Merriam 1988). In this way I could respond to the situation at hand, to the flow of each individual conversation.

The interview schedule consisted of three sets of questions touching on three main themes. The first set consisted of questions about the women's community work: what were the projects and issues they were working on, what were their motivations for getting involved, and what were their goals. The second set of questions was designed to get at the implications of juggling activism and mothering/caregiving for their own personal and familial lives. I asked the women a general question – "what is it like for you to juggle all these different commitments?" – and then let them tell their stories, prompting them if necessary to tell me about how their families react to their work and the kinds of coping strategies they employ. I then asked them to tell me the key rewards and the most notable costs associated with juggling their community work, paid work (in many cases, but not all), and caregiving work. The third set focused on more abstract issues, such as how the women define citizenship and how they think their unpaid work is regarded in the wider society. I asked questions such as "what does citizenship mean to you?" and "do you see your activist work as part of being a mother or a citizen, neither or both?"

In most cases I sent each woman a copy of the interview questions that I would use to guide our conversations prior to our meeting. This gave them a chance to reflect on what they might say in advance. I conducted interviews from September 1999 to July 2000. Before beginning the conversations I asked each woman to sign a consent form giving me permission to use their words and names (see explanation below) in publications based on the research. I asked permission to tape-record the interview and said I would begin to wrap up the conversation after two hours. With a few exceptions, the interviews were held in participants' homes, typically over cookies and tea at their kitchen table. They quickly became the kind of conversation that I often have with friends: exchanging strategies for coping with a hectic life, commiserating on how guilty we feel when we fail to live up to our publicly expressed ecological values by buying overpackaged convenience goods or driving a car. And when the fact that I do not have children came up, some women gave advice and bits of wisdom about what motherhood is like and how it changes one's life. Conversing in this way created a very friendly atmosphere and a trusting relationship between us. All thirty women seemed to appreciate the purpose of my research, and many told me "it is nice to be asked" about the work they do and how it affects their lives. I suspect, from our conversations, that women in activist leadership positions tend to feel responsible for how others are managing with heavy workloads but rarely take the time to consider the toll it takes on themselves. Several said they were eager to hear what other women said about their activism and how they cope at home.

The conversations were audio-taped and notes were taken to record non-verbal and contextual/spatial information. Where appropriate, I asked the participants for newspaper articles and other written material that helped describe their activist work. In many cases, I had the opportunity to meet members of the women's families, most often children who were home during the day. By conducting the interviews in the women's homes, I was able to get a good sense of their daily lives and to experience first-hand how hectic they are: there were in many cases frequent interruptions by children, pets, and constantly ringing telephones. In trying to schedule a meeting time, I also recognized how little time these women have to spare, so I tried to be as flexible with them as possible (e.g., by agreeing to meet on weekends or late in the evening).

I transcribed the interview tapes verbatim myself, using a transcribing machine. I included "ums" and "ahs" and did not attempt to edit their words for clarity or grammatical correctness. Some months after our conversations I sent the transcripts back to each participant for review. In an accompanying letter, I asked them to read their transcript carefully and then edit, clarify, change, or add to it anything they felt necessary so that it best reflected their thoughts as well as how they would want them to appear in print. I also included some specific follow-up questions for each participant where answers were missing. In addition, I gave each participant a preliminary summary of the findings (i.e., the main themes in the interviews) and asked them to reflect on these themes based on specific questions. My questions were chosen in part to re-flect some of the issues with which I anticipated having difficulty. These were questions that I did not explore face to face, such as "what does it mean that many women activists employ other women to clean their homes" and "how does your particular social and economic location (race, class, age, and so on) affect your ability to do activist work?" Since I felt uncertain about how to handle these questions – that is, I was concerned that my interpretation might offend some participants – I wanted to put them to the women first. I felt it was better to welcome disagreement and make room for differences of opinion between me and the participants in the data than to present them unilaterally. Draft copies of Chapters 7 and 8 were sent to each participant in July 2001.

These follow-up contacts were designed to ensure that the data were as accurate and as representative of the participants' views as possible. Asking participants to review the transcripts and chapters is one of the key means of ensuring the internal validity of the findings in qualitative interview research (Lincoln and Guba 1988). With respect to my relationship with the partici-pants, I hoped that it would maximize their satisfaction with the way I pre-sented their thoughts. It gave the participants a degree of control over the data, a safeguard against misinterpretation, and a relatively active role in the research. I received follow-up responses from fifteen (50 percent) of the par-ticipants, which I take as a sign that they felt engaged in the research and interested in its progress. I recorded the changes and new responses in their files and then proceeded with my interpretation of the data. Unfortunately, the conversation-by-correspondence stopped there and I did not follow up on the women's follow-up answers. For this reason I have not delved into those interesting but tangential issues about which there is controversy. I have insuf-ficient information to analyze or interpret them and, further, I do not want to make interpretations without checking them with the women I interviewed. The most obvious example of an issue that has been raised but not analyzed is the employment of other women to provide domestic and caring services. If I could return for an additional round of questions and conversations, I would include that issue in addition to more searching questions about the participa-tion of men in private and public caring work.

Interpretation and Analysis

My method of interpreting the themes that emerged from the interview tran-scripts can best be described as qualitative content analysis. My approach was informed by Kirby and McKenna's (1989) method in their book *Experience, Research, Social Change: Methods from the Margins*, wherein they make sense of data through a reflexive process that includes assessment of the words of the participants as knowing subjects, and critical reflection of the social context. They write: "Giving priority to intersubjectivity and critical reflection on the social context throughout the analysis ensures that we are able to hear and affirm the words and experiences of the research participants and at the same time be able to critically reflect on the structures that influence the actuality of their lives" (Kirby and McKenna 1989, 130). This resonates with the hermeneutical approach that is popular among feminist researchers in the social sciences. For example, in *Community Research as Empowerment: Feminist Links and Postmodern Interruptions*, Ristock and Pennell note the influence of Clifford Geertz's approach to hermeneutics, wherein the "aim is 'to turn from trying to explain social phenomena by weaving them into grand textures of cause and effect to trying to explain them by placing them in local frames of reference" (quoted in Ristock and Pennell 1996, 90). In making my interpretations, however, I looked for links to, and resonance and dissonance with, the theoretical literature and other related empirical studies in addition to studying the local context. I also asked participants for their interpretations of the findings, and I left it to them to decide what "interpretive method" was right for them.

As I explain in Chapter 6, I have used a large number of direct quotes and in many cases I have used the women's real names (with their permission) in order to give them credit for their own ideas and experiences. The idea that I could break with the academic convention of "anonymizing" research participants originally came up in conversation with Margrit Eichler (an expert in feminist research methodologies); my decision to adopt this approach was made after more conversations about its risks and benefits with my other research advisors. Although there are some risks to non-anonymity, such as those of attracting negative attention to the women's organizations or violating the privacy of their colleagues and family members, I am convinced that treating the women as anonymous subjects would diminish their role in the research and contradict one of the study's goals: to recognize the personal rewards and critical insights that women gain as a result of their activist work. Precedents for using the real names of women activists in feminist research of this kind include Naples (1998), Garland (1988), and Kaplan (1997), although none of these researchers explains their choice to do so. After I explained my reasoning and gave the women a choice to be named or anonymized, all of the women agreed to be identified by their real names. As a precautionary measure, however, in cases in which their comments are very personal or they could cause discomfort for the women or their families, I have not identified them by name. Comments about involvement in activism and theorizings about politics and public life are generally attributed to the women who made them. I sent letters to the women (to their last known address) in summer

2005 to let them know about the forthcoming book. One woman wrote back and asked to be anonymized in this book.

Internal Validity and Limitations of the Research

Because there is much debate about how to evaluate the quality of qualitative research, I briefly explain my approach to assessing the validity of this investigation. Some methodologists contend that because qualitative research is based on ideas about knowledge and truth very different from those of positivist or scientific research it should not be judged on the conventional grounds of generalizability and replicability (Lather 1991). As Sharan Merriam (1988, 166) argues, "if *understanding* is the primary rationale for the investigation, the criteria for trusting the study are going to be different than if discovery of a law or testing a hypothesis is the study's objective." Because my research is based on conversations I had with thirty different women at a particular time and in a particular context, it could not possibly be replicated. Asking these same women the same questions could yield different answers in the future: their lives are in flux, they change from day to day, as does the context in which they are lived. That social research findings should be able to be replicated is a positivist assumption to which I and many feminist researchers in the social sciences and humanities do not subscribe. Generalization from a single study like mine is neither possible nor desirable. It must be seen as a unique and very particular snapshot: an interpretation that only partially represents the "realities" I observed and the stories I was told. Assessment of applicability of the findings of this investigation to the wider social and cultural context should be left up to readers who wish to interpret them based on their own experiences and expectations. They may do so with a full understanding of how the results were obtained and the philosophical assumptions that informed my research process.

With qualitative research, a case can be made for rejecting the notions of replicability and generalizability in favour of an assessment of the study's "internal validity" or coherence (Merriam 1988). According to the qualitative methodology literature upon which I have relied, there are six basic strategies that researchers can use to ensure internal validity. They are: triangulation (using three kinds of research methods), member checks, repeated contact or observation, peer examination, participatory modes of research, and revealing researcher bias. I have involved all of these strategies in my investigation.

While my findings can be considered internally valid and quite dependable, some limitations should be noted, and these are related to the specificity of my research design. One obvious limitation of my research is that I specifically asked women who are now coping to some extent with their juggling act, leaving out all those who have not been able to cope at all (i.e., who do not have time to take on activist work in their communities). All of the women I interviewed are able to juggle various roles, in one way or another, because they have the financial means to be able to meet their household needs (with varying degrees of comfort) and still have the time and energy to take on volunteer projects. Many of the women are middle class and have partners who contribute to the family income and to the work of raising children and managing the household. Several women have the economic means to be able to work part time or to be stay-at-home moms and/or to be able to hire a cleaning woman or a babysitter to ease their burden of domestic labour. I also suspect that the working-class women with whom I spoke are exceptional cases. I recognize that a significant percentage of women living in poverty, perhaps as sole-support mothers, are unable to contemplate taking on more unpaid labour. I have not gained access to their stories. For example, I did not ask those who work as cleaning women or "domestics" for the activists I interviewed about their interest or ability to do community activist work, and I did not ask them what citizenship means to them.

I specifically asked *women* to talk about the experience of juggling, leaving out men who also juggle the same complement of responsibilities. I have no doubt that such men exist. As a feminist, however, the decision to study women is a consciously political one. I also decided to focus on women because I am responding primarily to the discourse of ecofeminism. In order to be able to comment on ecofeminist celebrations of women's particular knowledge of and labour for sustainability, it felt right to restrict my focus to women. This is not to say that a comparative study of men and women's experiences would not be extremely important; such research is sorely lacking in the ecofeminist and ecopolitical literature in general.

Finally, a limitation of my research comes from my own social location: the fact that I am white and middle class, and, at the time, was a doctoral student limited the range of communities and women's activist projects to which I could gain access. Despite repeated attempts to find women from new immigrant and refugee communities, I was unable to make connections. For example, I approached a group called the Environmental Centre for New Canadians at least five times to no avail. Obviously, language (or, rather, my unilingualism) is a barrier: all of the women I interviewed speak English fluently, even those for whom English is not their first language. But I also recognize that, in order to be willing to participate in a research project, people not only have to have time to spare but they also have to feel comfortable enough to answer the questions of a total stranger. Many women from new immigrant communities may not trust a person like me and/or feel reluctant about being interviewed by such a person. Meanwhile, the women who did agree to participate had enough understanding of and sympathy for the research project that they were perhaps predisposed to answer my questions in a particular way (a form of self-selection). In addition, by asking the questions I asked, I may have unwittingly encouraged them to link their answers to environmental issues in particular when they might not normally have done so. Such is the nature of social research. Having provided a transparent account of my research process, however, I trust readers to assess for themselves the validity and usefulness of my interpretations for their own particular projects.

Notes

Chapter 1: Introduction

1 Seager (2003, 949) argues that it is time for ecofeminism to move past the question of whether or not women are closer to nature because it is "counterproductive to the larger enterprise of putting and keeping environmentalism on the feminist agenda and feminism on the environmental agenda." I agree with her. My aim in *Beyond Mothering Earth* is not to fuel the nasty debates between ecofeminists but, rather, to offer a more productive way to engage in them: to call ecofeminism back to a notion of politics wherein the discourse and practices of citizenship are central.

2 A few words about the complexities involved in my choice of terminology: I have chosen to use the term "feminist ecological" citizenship rather than "ecofeminist" citizenship because I want to keep the two concepts in explicit tension (in that order) and to disrupt rather than simply add to ecofeminist discussions. I am sticking with ecological feminism (ecofeminism) for Noël Sturgeon's (1997) persuasive reasons, which include the important point that changing it to "feminist environmentalism," as has been advocated by Seager (2003), Alaimo (2000), and Agarwal (2001), not only risks disconnecting it from its activist roots but also fails to resolve underlying problems. In conjunction with this choice, then, "ecological citizenship" is a more appropriate term than "environmental citizenship," which is perhaps the more commonly used term in the ecopolitical literature. I have also taken ecological citizenship to be more compatible with my feminist analysis, following Andrew Dobson's definitions, first of "ecologism" as having a more radical potential than environmentalism (Dobson 1995) and, second, of ecological citizenship as being more fundamentally challenging to (and potentially transformative of) the traditional concept of citizenship than the more liberal, rights-focused conception of environmental citizenship (Dobson 2003). Dobson also puts feelings like care and compassion for the non-human world and future generations at the centre of his notion of ecological citizenship.

3 Segal's (1987, 6-7) only reference to ecofeminism appears early in *Is the Future Female?* where she characterizes it as "a new wave" in feminism that "suggests that women must and will liberate the earth because they live more in harmony with 'nature.'"

4 The World Commission on Environment and Development's (1987, 43) definition of sustainability in *Our Common Future* is "development which meets the needs of the present without compromising the ability of future generations to meet their own needs." It is interesting to compare this definition to Segal's (1987) central political question.

5 The new right agenda is generally understood to combine neoliberal economic policies that support minimal state intervention in the market and neoconservative social policies that provide an ideological rationale for the free market. In Canada, this definition can be confusing because there is the Liberal Party that has traditionally been economically and socially centrist and the Progressive Conservative Party that has tended to be more right-wing on both fronts. However, both parties have moved towards favouring neoliberal economic policies that are in keeping with trends in the global economy. For a useful discussion and overview, see Teeple (1995).

6 There is also a body of work that looks at the gender and race implications of changes in immigration policy and citizenship requirements. For example, Bakan and Stasiulis (1996)

discuss the denial of citizenship rights to foreign domestic workers, a disproportionate number of whom are women of colour. This is a different analysis from that dealing with the demise of social citizenship. I discuss this point again in Chapter 4.

7 Differences between Canadian and American approaches to ecofeminist and ecopolitical issues are interesting to consider, but to my knowledge they have not yet been analyzed. In Chapter 2 I offer some provisional comments on possible differences between them.

Chapter 2: The Roots and Rhetoric of Ecomaternalism

1 For thorough overviews of the development and categories of ecofeminism, I recommend the first chapter of Greta Gaard's (1998) *Ecological Politics,* Chapters 1 and 2 in Mary Mellor's (1997) *Feminism and Ecology,* and Chapter 1 in Catriona Sandilands' (1999a) *The Good-Natured Feminist* as useful descriptions of the roots and branches of ecofeminism. In her *Ecofeminist Natures,* Noël Sturgeon (1997) provides a comprehensive history of American ecofeminism. Joni Seager (2003) has written a more recent historical account of the evolution of ecofeminism and of what she calls "feminist environmentalism," which she insists is a much broader term, in the United States. I shall not address her ecofeminism-feminist environmentalism distinction here, although it does come up again briefly in Chapter 3 in conjunction with Indian economist Bina Agarwal's desire (which is similar to Seager's) to distance herself from ecofeminism. See also Chapter 1, note 2.

2 American scholarship is dominant in this field. I have tried as much as possible to include research from Canada, Britain, Australia, Aotearoa/New Zealand, India, and other countries where the material is accessible to an English-only speaker. For a comprehensive overview of feminist perspectives on the environment that includes many European references (from English and non-English-speaking scholars), see Littig (2001).

3 In Chapter 6 I discuss my discomfort with giving "lived experience" a special place in this list.

4 Rian Voet (1998) adds another wave to this periodization, citing the feminist struggle for citizenship at the end of the eighteenth century in France. At a time when Jean-Jacques Rousseau's ideas about women made it popular to see women as inferior to men and as useful to the republic only in their capacity as mothers, some feminists argued that gender differences should be irrelevant to citizenship. These early feminist appeals for citizenship were based on notions of equality and women's natural rights to liberty and justice.

5 Although it may have originated in the 1800s, the imagery of women using their domestic values to "clean up," or improve, political systems is still in evidence at the beginning of the twenty-first century. For example, buttons for sale at the National Women's Political Caucus at the 2000 US Democratic Party Convention read: "Clean Up Politics, Elect Women" (*Toronto Star,* 16 August 2000, A17).

6 Environmental historian Robert Gottlieb (1993, 3) argues that the history of environmentalism in general is too narrowly described and is full of unfortunate omissions. The most glaring, in his mind, is the omission of "figures not seen as engaged in *environmental* struggles because their concerns were urban and industrial," such as urbanist Lewis Mumford and the women activists involved in reforming the "dangerous trades."

7 In the Canadian women's suffrage movement of the early twentieth century, "good citizens" and "good mothers" may have been thought to be synonymous, but it is also possible that some of the suffragettes (e.g., Nelly McClung) contradicted their own campaign when they put their right to vote ahead of demands for peace. For example, some allowed their sons to go to war, despite their publicly declared opposition to it. I am grateful to Maureen Reed for suggesting that I include this point, which illustrates nicely how the politics of citizenship and motherhood, while being linked, can also clash.

8 Vera Norwood (1993), who has studied women's involvement in science (especially natural sciences like ecology) at the turn of the twentieth century, argues that these women had a more educational desire for nature than their male counterparts.

9 Gottlieb (1993) includes in his revised history of environmentalism Alice Hamilton, whom he calls America's first urban/industrial environmentalist. Hamilton's pioneering work as an urban activist anticipated the fields of epidemiology, environmental health, and occupational health and safety. This part of the history of women's community activism has been especially important to feminist urbanism in Canada, demonstrating what I believe to be an important difference between that tradition and US ecofeminism.

10 Environmental historian Donald Worster (1994) gives this credit to the German biologist Ernst Haeckel.

11 While ecofeminists like Merchant have elected to highlight the cleaning-up and moralistic aspects of progressive-era women's activism, other feminist historians have focused on the explicitly political dimensions of this work. Dolores Hayden (1981), for example, has written an excellent history of nineteenth-century women's organizing that uncovers the utopian socialist rhetoric and the practical strategies for change that were embraced by such women. Part of their vision included revaluing, redistributing, and collectivizing socially necessary labour in the name of gender equity, as evidenced in their designs for cooperative living, kitchenless houses, and communal laundries, nurseries, and kitchens.

12 For a discussion of the delineation and development of different branches of feminism, see Tong (1998).

13 See Alice Echols' (1989) history of radical feminism for one interpretation of the emergence of this perspective.

14 It was during this period that "women and environments" work, a possible distant cousin of the environmental justice movement in the United States, emerged in Canada. This work focuses on women's designs for housing and social services, and it critiques the male bias in city planning, which has resulted in woman-unfriendly suburban environments (see Wekerle, Peterson, and Morely 1980). Unfortunately, a comprehensive history of feminist environmental perspectives in Canada has yet to be written.

15 The Canadian work appears to have stronger links to socialist feminism than to radical feminism; however, this is an impression rather than an analysis (see note 14).

16 Daryl Koehn (1998) observes that Gilligan herself may have believed in extending an ethic of care to the earth because she presents Demeter, the Greek goddess of the earth, as an exemplary caregiver.

17 More recent examples: in 2000 Mother's Day was the chosen date for the "Million Mom March" against gun violence in the United States. The Aotearoa/New Zealand organization Mothers against Genetic Engineering in Food and the Environment (MAdGE) chose Mother's Day 2003 for a supermarket protest to demand the labelling of all GE foods.

Chapter 3: "Down among the Women"

1 *Down among the Women* is the title of a 1971 novel by Fay Weldon. Lorraine Code (1991, 272) makes reference to it in a comment about ecofeminism in her book *What Can She Know?*: "Its reliance on versions of an 'earth mother' stereotype that has constructed the space 'down among the women' where concern for taking care of people and things, providing nurture and support, is women's natural role, suggests a disempowering acceptance of biological determinism."

2 For a discussion of the evolution and central ideas of feminism's third wave, which includes ecofeminism alongside postcolonial and generational/youth cultures feminisms, see Mack-Canty (2004).

3 Arguably, this situation, coupled with a lag in the entry of non-elite women into academia, has caused a shift in feminist scholarship from first-person narratives, wherein the feminist theorist explores her own experiences, to scholarship in which privileged feminist academics write about the lives of non-elite women activists. In Chapter 6 I discuss the dilemmas this situation poses for feminist research.

4 The activism of working-class women and women of colour seems to receive the most attention in the feminist literature. Queer and lesbian organizing remains somewhat marginalized, although important exceptions include Phelan (1994) and Taylor and Rupp (1997).

5 The existence of this literature raises serious doubts about Mies and Bennholdt-Thomsen's (1999) and Salleh's (1997) contention that Western academic feminists have not been sufficiently interested in the grassroots survival activism of "ordinary women." I say more on this point later in this chapter.

6 As I note in Chapter 1, this was the case in Ontario, where the Progressive Conservative Party, led by Premier Mike Harris (and briefly by Ernie Eves) from 1995 to 2003, governed with a neoliberal economic agenda and neoconservative social policy platform that together constituted their so-called "Common Sense Revolution."

7 This desire is not unique to the ecofeminists to whom I am responding. It is also apparent in Gustavo Estavo and Madhu Suri Prakash's (1998, 3) *Grassroots Post-modernism*, wherein they bring the terms "grassroots" and "post-modernism" together, taking them "out of the confines of the academy [and into] far removed and totally different social spaces." They use "grassroots post-modernism" in order to "give a name to a wide collection of culturally diverse initiatives

and struggles" by "ordinary men and women" (ibid.). See also Serge Latouche's *In the Wake of the Affluent Society* (1993).

8 The term "womanism" originates in African American women's interactions with feminism (see Walker 1983). But see also Nalunnakkal (2004) for an interesting discussion of "organic womanism," a term he uses in preference to (Western, middle-class) ecofeminism when theorizing the experiences of Indian Dalit (untouchable) and Adivasi (tribal) women vis-à-vis environmental issues, particularly their struggles over land.

9 Other examples include *Women and the Environment: Crisis and Development in the Third World*, edited by Sally Sontheimer (1991); *Feminist Perspectives on Sustainable Development*, edited by Wendy Harcourt (1994); *Women, the Environment and Sustainable Development: Towards a Theoretical Synthesis*, edited by Rosi Braidotti et al. (1994); *Women Healing Earth: Third World Women on Ecology, Feminism, and Religion*, edited by Rosemary Radford Ruether (1996); and *Women Working in the Environment*, edited by Carolyn Sachs (1997).

10 It is important to note that, unlike Mies and Shiva (1993) and Salleh (1997), who tend to focus on peasant women, Merchant (1996) includes urban and middle-class professional "third world women" in her discussion of survival struggles. I follow up this point in Chapter 6. She also makes a link between women's inability to provide subsistence for others and a process of politicization leading to activism, which I follow up in Chapter 4.

11 Sturgeon (1997) provides an analysis of the race politics at the WEDO conference, which raises doubts about how well this diversity worked in practice.

12 Sturgeon's (1997) analysis focuses on two ecofeminist texts published in the early 1990s. My literature review found references to the Chipko movement in a dozen of the more recently published texts about ecofeminism.

13 As I discuss in Chapter 6, Shiva's portrayal of the Chipko movement as a women's movement has been challenged by a number of scholars. There are significant differences, for example, between Shiva's accounts and Ramachandra Guha's (1990) social history of the Chipko movement.

14 It would be nice to think that the leadership of working-class and women of colour on quality-of-life issues and in environmental justice organizations serves to simultaneously challenge the masculinism, classism, and white domination of the environmental movement. However, there is danger in assuming that this challenge happens automatically, by virtue of the very presence of such women. The domination of elite men within the mainstream green movement remains relatively unchanged, despite years of critique by ecofeminists and other "outsiders." I wonder, too, about the gender politics within the environmental justice movement in light of the privileged place of race and class within the discourse.

15 While I do not deny that children are highly sensitive to environmental contamination, I find something troubling in the idea that women/mothers should put the health of children ahead of their own. It is less common to hear women expressing concerns for their own health than it is to hear them expressing fears for the health and future welfare of children. Harriet Rosenberg (1995) makes the important observation that child protection ideology can be and has been co-opted by familist governments that have succeeded in naturalizing child protection as the sole responsibility of parents, hence justifying cuts to state services. The new right in the United States has made full use of the powerful cultural icon of the innocent, vulnerable ("unborn") child to bolster its campaigns against abortion and to police the behaviour of pregnant women.

16 The concept of "overdetermination" generally refers to the idea that a single observed effect is determined by *multiple causes at once*, any one of which might, on its own, be enough to account for it.

17 Alcoff (1988) also sees the value in identity politics but is careful to reject those deployments of identity that ground politics in *essential* identity. She believes that the most important contribution of identity politics is the problematization of the connection between politics and identity and the introduction of identity as a relevant factor in political analyses, something masculinist theory has seldom done.

18 Sturgeon also defends essentialist natures from criticism by pointing out some of the contradictions inherent in anti-essentialist positions. Elizabeth Carlassare (1994) makes a similar argument. Both Sturgeon and Carlassare draw upon Fuss' argument in *Essentially Speaking* (1989) to submit that the lines between essentialism and constructivism are not as clearly drawn as is often believed; in fact, constructivism and essentialism "imply and rest on each other" (Carlassare 1994, 222). Carlassare, following Fuss, claims that "many of the

critics of cultural ecofeminism could be guilty of resorting to an essentialist notion of essentialism, dismissing it as unconditionally 'bad' without examining the specific ways in which it is used in specific situations" (226). This seems to be one line of defence for strategic essentialism: to show that the "extreme anti-essentialists" (whoever they are) are on shaky ground because their assumptions about essentialism are essentializing in themselves.

19 This leaves aside for now (I return to it in Chapter 6) the question of whether it is even accurate, much less ethically acceptable, to represent women in this way. I think it is useful to remember Chandra Mohanty's (1991) criticism that casting "third world women" as a social category is problematic because it denies their diversity and universalizes their experiences. Moreover, the category "third world woman" is increasingly difficult to maintain within the context of a rapidly globalizing economy that brings with it transnational migration. Holding on to the "third world woman" as a distinct category protects the exaggerated contrast between North and South when, in some places (Toronto, for example), such boundaries can be blurred within a single city block.

20 It is also often based on an unproblematized notion of nature taken from the science of ecology. For a discussion of this important point, to which I have given very little consideration in this book, see Sandilands (1999a, chap. 4). See Sandilands (2002) for a useful discussion of how the environmental movement in general relies on a largely unproblematized scientific notion of nature.

21 I am partial to Monique Wittig's definition of "the operation of reduction." Reductionism works, she says, "by taking the part for the whole, a part (color, sex) through which the whole human group has to pass as through a screen" (Wittig 1992, 8).

Chapter 4: From Care to Citizenship

1 For a discussion of this distinction in ecofeminist definitions of care, see Curtin (1991); for a general discussion, see Tronto (1993).

2 Note that many of the ecofeminists to which I refer make the explicit link between care and mothering as opposed to other caring roles (such as friends or paid professionals like nurses) (Bowden 1997). It is also important to point out that the theory of mothering/caring upon which early ecofeminists drew (i.e., Chodorow's object relations) does not seem to have been replaced by another theory. The fact that Chodorow saw the feminization of caring as a problem rather than as a virtue to be celebrated is seldom acknowledged in ecofeminist texts.

3 Affirming her association with socialist ecofeminism and advising against essentializing and reaffirming women's association with caring, Merchant presents women's caring as a model upon which to build a new ethic. While she is clear that "the cultural baggage associated with images of nature as female [e.g., mother nature] means that gendering nature [as feminine] is at present too problematical to be adopted by emancipatory social movements in Western societies" (Merchant 1996, xxii), she seems less willing to apply the same proviso to the association of women with caring or mothering; rather, she celebrates women's roles in and knowledge of life-sustaining practices from ancient times to the present day as examples of earthcare.

4 Carol Gilligan herself, it has been noted, found that women often submerge their own needs and interests in order to live up to their socially prescribed roles as selfless carers and nurturers (for a discussion see Scaltsas [1992, 19]).

5 The concept (and critique) of "compulsory altruism," coined by Land and Rose (1985), is useful in further explaining this argument.

6 For a discussion of this point, see Lister (1997); Benhabib (1992); Okin (1989); and Tronto (1993).

7 Chaia Heller's (1999) exploration of erotic desire for nature is an important example of an ecofeminist perspective that moves beyond care.

8 Echoing David Harvey (1999, 128), I would question the extent to which ecofeminists' interest in care leads them "to bury conflict as a positive shaping force in human affairs," something Harvey thinks is a serious mistake on the part of certain environmentalist positions.

9 My response is that there *are* more complex and multilayered interpretations. I offer my own in Chapters 7 and 8, where I present and analyze the accounts of the thirty women activists I interviewed.

10 As I discuss further in Chapter 6, ecofeminists have been criticized by scholars who have conducted in-depth field studies of the gender relations that are observed and reported in local resource management projects (and conflicts) in developing countries like India. More

often than not, their research demonstrates that ecofeminist accounts of women's special and superior environmental knowledge are simplistic and even dangerous (see, for example, Jackson 1993; Agarwal 1998a, 1998b; Jewitt 2000).

11 It should be noted that Merchant (1996) does include greater male participation in child care in her vision of "partnership ethics." She seems at once to be valorizing women's care and calling (albeit quietly) for its redistribution. She says little, however, about the possibility of de-feminizing care.

12 Warren's treatment of care in ecofeminist ethics is interesting. In her essay "Ethics in a Fruit Bowl" (2000), for instance, she develops the notion of "care-sensitive ethics" as a universal ethic that builds on feminist ethics of care but that is not "an ethic of care" that can be separated from or contrasted to an ethic of justice. Instead, "care-sensitive ethics" is based on three conditions: an ability to care, situated universalism, and care practices. She makes an attempt to de-gender care by saying that any ethic that does not take care seriously is flawed, and she supports this position with the work of psychologist Daniel Goleman, whose book *Emotional Intelligence* (1995) argues that the ability to care for oneself and others is hard-wired into the human brain. Although I have problems with Warren's reworking of ecofeminist care ethics in this particular essay, I shall not discuss them here.

13 This echoes Elshtain's (1981) view that moral imperatives originate and are cultivated in the family. She contends that the family is the "universal basis for human culture" (quoted in Dietz 1985, 21).

14 In the language of economics, to "externalize" something is to render its value/cost irrelevant to economic calculations. For example, unpaid labour is considered non-productive, and therefore its value to society is not counted in the calculation of Gross Domestic Product. Similarly, the long- and short-term costs of air, water, and soil pollution are not subtracted from the profits of economic development (see Waring 1988).

15 In response to Reagan's Republican policies in the 1980s, the US National Organization of Women (NOW) took a stand against volunteerism on the ground that it devalues women's work and exploits their caring services. They encouraged women to seek professional careers instead (Townsend 1984 quoted in Rifkin 1995, 254). Such criticisms remain valid in the present era, although they are missing in recent feminist scholarship: I have never seen this line of argument in ecofeminist texts, perhaps partly due to a green critique of professionalization and a green embrace of active citizenship.

16 Maria Mies (1986) provides a useful explanation of the process – which she calls "housewifization" – that ensures women's essential role as consumers in capitalist societies. She writes: "to mobilize women to fulfill their duty as consumers has become one of the main strategies of capital in industrialized countries. 'Consumption work' ... is, therefore, increasing tremendously in the rich countries, and is using more and more of the 'free' time of wage-working and non-wage-working women" (Mies 1986, 125). She goes on to predict that, with the growing technological replacement of human labour, the work involved in consumption will increase even further. It is interesting that she has moved from this analysis to one that celebrates women's subsistence labour.

17 In the Canadian context, this may not be the case in the province of Quebec, where child care is still state funded and quite affordable. Although Quebec's child care policies help many families, they are also pronatalist policies that are related to official dreams of independence (and a declining birthrate).

18 Here Lister (1997) refers to the "public" sphere as a workplace. I am using a different meaning of "public" here, one that refers to a space for politics.

19 Given how important being housewives reportedly was to them, it is interesting that the women activists at Love Canal called their organization the Love Canal Home*owners* Association rather than the Love Canal Home*makers* Association. One could interrogate the class subtext of their choice. It would also be interesting to ask Lois Gibbs why she went on to call her organization the *Citizens* Clearinghouse on Hazardous Waste.

20 Ruth Lister makes the point that when women politically mobilize around their identities and concerns as mothers they seldom make lasting changes in the gender order. Of the Madres de la Plaza de Mayo she writes, for example, that "the moral power they exerted as mothers did not translate into political power as democratic structures were re-established" in Argentina (Lister 1997, 152).

21 These exceptions include: Sandilands (1999a); Plumwood (1995a, 1995b); Heller (1999); Gaard (1998). While their work is touched on only briefly here, in Chapter 5 I apply it directly to the project of critically assessing the discourse of ecological citizenship.

22 Dietz may have a very particular reading of Arendt, perhaps one that is informed by a reading of Habermasian theory, with which others would have difficulty. I am unable to pursue a discussion of this point here.

23 A valid critique of Aristotle's view of citizenship is that in the Greek polis slaves and women were not granted the status of citizen (I return to this in Chapter 5). Feminists who take a more generous approach to Aristotle argue that this exclusion is not a necessary part of his theory of politics and citizenship; rather, it is a sign of his times. It is their position that, despite its inherent sexism and elitism, the Aristotelian vision of politics and the good life is an extremely compelling one for a variety of reasons (see Dietz 1985).

24 And from ecology (or certain readings of it), Sandilands (1999a) takes it that ecofeminism should realize that it is impossible to know a "nature" that is not shaped by and filtered through human discourse, interpretation, and action. That we have no access to a prediscursive nature makes uncertainty unavoidable. I share her opinion that, in the face of radical uncertainty, the best political paradigm is democracy.

25 By saying that care should be interpreted more widely, Tronto is saying that feminists' typical association of the ethic of care with women's morality and mothering is too narrow. She believes that this narrow and often apolitical interpretation dooms care to dismissal as a serious ethico-political ideal (see Tronto 1993, 125).

26 In developing his care ethic, Curtin (1999) names (some) women's agricultural and medical practices as examples of care that are both public and political. His intention is to show that there are caring practices that are not necessarily linked to mothering. However, the extent to which these practices are gendered cannot be overlooked (after all, he uses women's rather than men's practices).

27 This is presumably an instance of the conflation of mothering and care that Tronto criticizes. While care can be generalized, motherhood cannot. But the question is, how easy is it to separate caring from mothering in order to make it a genderless or gender-inclusive practice/ feeling?

28 Salleh's concept of "holding work" is taken from Sara Ruddick (1989, 79), who writes in *Maternal Thinking* that "holding is a way of seeing with an eye toward maintaining the minimal harmony, material resources, and skills necessary for sustaining a child in safety."

Chapter 5: The Problems and Possibilities of Ecological Citizenship

1 The difference between environmental and ecological citizenship is discussed briefly in Chapter 1 (see note 2), in which I explain my decision to use the latter term. In much of the environmental politics literature, the two are used synonymously, along with "green citizenship." There are other variations that are unique to particular writers, for example Barry (2006) uses "sustainability citizenship" in a way that is similar to Dobson's (2003) use of "ecological citizenship"; that is, in order to distinguish it from the less transformative "environmental citizenship." It is beyond the scope of my present discussion to delve into the merits of these different labels.

2 To be fair, as Joni Seager (2003, 948) notes, there are many feminist theorists who also equate ecofeminism with spirituality, or with "mystical bunk, [which is] dangerously apolitical and atheoretical."

3 Echols' (1989) history of the rise of American radical feminism in the 1960s explains that, in large part, it was due to the sexism of the new left and student movements that women were mobilized to break away and form their own separate movement for gender equality. The relationship between Marxism and feminism in the 1970s and 1980s is described in detail by Heidi Hartmann (1981, 2) as an "unhappy marriage" because of "[the subsumption] of feminist struggle into the 'larger' struggle against capital," resulting in a lack of concern about sexism and patriarchy. Feminist geographer Doreen Massey (1991) offers an excellent analysis of postmodernism in which "flexible sexism" is apparent. She identifies, for example, the lack of recognition of feminist scholarship and the consigning of "minority groups" to parentheses "after the supposed universal of the white, male, heterosexual" in postmodernist writing (Massey 1991, 31). Although she made this assessment in the early 1990s, I suspect that the situation has not improved dramatically since then, at least where feminism is concerned.

4 I do not want to blame the victim here: as noted in Chapter 4, the containment of ecofeminist arguments may have a lot to do with the unfortunate fact that private-sphere concerns such as care are often "irrelevant to the moral life of the powerful" (Tronto 1993, 89).

5 As Van Steenbergen (1994) notes, however, few left citizenship theorists have paid much attention to the ecological problematique in their revisions of citizenship. This may be due, in

part, to their discomfort with the idea that ecological destruction can only be stalled by interfering with people's freedom. There is good reason to be sceptical, especially when one looks at the writings of eco-authoritarians like Hardin (1974) and Ophuls (1996), who, following Hobbes, feel that there is no time for democracy and that citizens left to make their own (inevitably self-interested) choices will not do what is needed to save the planet from collapse.

6 Bookchin also discusses the municipality and the city as sites for ecological citizenship. Curiously, while there is an extensive literature on citizenship in cities, especially "the global city" (see Isin 2000), there has been little discussion of ecological citizenship vis-à-vis life in cities.

7 Here the work of John Dryzek (1990, 1995, 1997) on discursive democracy is highly influential. Dryzek sees "deliberative designs" for increasing democratic participation in all areas of public decision making as central to the goal of "ecological rationality" (his term for sustainability). I choose not to include Dryzek in this overview of ecopolitical thought because (at the time of writing) he has not explicitly addressed the concept of green citizenship.

8 In fact Barry challenges most of the "sacred cows" of green politics: ecocentric and anarchistic ecopolitics, anti-statist positions, anti-urbanism, postmaterialism, and the bias towards direct democracy. In so doing he claims to take an immanent and "critical-reconstructive" approach that teases out the best parts of different green arguments and blends them together to make a more viable position that can appeal to the masses (in contrast to those that only an ascetic could embrace without contradiction).

9 Barry and Christoff disagree on the idea that non-humans have rights. Barry's (1999, 234) understanding of green citizenship "is not premised on non-humans having rights." This is an important debate but not one that will be pursued here.

10 The Chernobyl nuclear accident in 1986, the *Exxon Valdez* oil spill in 1989, mad cow disease in the United Kingdom throughout the 1990s, the oil spill in the Galapagos Islands in 2001, and almost daily reports of ozone depletion, climate change, and biodiversity loss are some obvious and oft-cited examples.

11 Although there is disagreement over the institutional form such a supranational environmental strategy might take, a key focus in this literature is the evolution of the environmental movement into a truly global movement that functions in a global civil society (Yearley 1996; Wapner 1996). For example, at the Rio Summit, while UN officials and heads of government were meeting, there was a parallel, unofficial proceeding called the Global Forum made up of NGO representatives and activists. There has also been a rise in transnational environmental networking, and nationally based environmental organizations have expanded into international ones (e.g., Greenpeace).

12 "Ecological space" is best conceptualized through the notion of the ecological footprint, which is "the land (and water) area that would be required to support a defined human population and material standard indefinitely" (Wackernagel and Rees 1996, quoted in Dobson 2003, 99). As I understand him, Dobson's argument is that, because there is conflict over "who gets what, when and how" (a classic definition of politics [Lasswell 1936]), this is the ecological citizen's *political space*.

13 While Dobson acknowledges the debate in feminism over valorizing women's caring versus challenging their association with caring, he never seems to take a side. And he includes "'feminine' virtue" in his description of postcosmopolitan citizenship (Dobson 2003, 39, Table 2.1).

14 Attfield (1999) notes that there are ecological theorists (especially ecocentrists) who explicitly reject the theologically based stewardship model as anthropocentric and managerial. Barry (2002) also cites its theological roots as a potential problem for the concept of stewardship but argues that it can easily be secularized.

15 Examples include: Deane Curtin (1991, 1999), who has been engaged with ecofeminist philosophy for some time; John Barry (1999), who finds much of value in materialist ecofeminist insights into the political economy of reproduction (citing Mellor 1995); Andrew Dobson (2003), who has given a central place to feminist theories of citizenship (citing Lister 1997) and some mention of feminist care ethics (citing Werbner 1999 and Sevenhuijesen 1998) in his recent work on citizenship and the environment.

16 It is well known that Israeli kibbutzim, a perfect example of small-scale communal living, have been unsuccessful in freeing women from stereotypical roles as caregivers and domestic workers (Melnyk 1985). Political sociologist George Melnyk also reports that Hutterite colonies (one of the largest and longest-surviving communal societies) are far from egalitarian: women

are solely responsible for child care and the domestic management of the collective. And while being drawn to their progressive visions, many feminist historians have noted that various communal experiments of the 1960s failed to address the gendered division of labour even though they were founded on principles of equality and cooperation (Kanter 1972). See also Taylor (1983) for a discussion of gender relations in utopian socialist intentional communities.

17 For a discussion of the "green public sphere," see Torgerson (1999). Drawing heavily on the writings of Hannah Arendt, Torgerson argues for a green public sphere as a space for *ecologically informed public discourse*. For him this depends on the acceptance of a shared meaning of citizenship as an end in itself – or, in his words, citizenship as "radically nonstrategic and noninstrumental" (14).

18 Empirical feminist research into the relationship between green practices and increased time spent on domestic work in Germany is discussed in Littig (2001).

19 The flip side of Dobson's (2003) view that private green practices should be regarded as acts of citizenship seems to be that "toiling to satisfy our material wants" in the private sphere "amounts to the production of ecological footprints which, far from removing us from the realm of citizenship, actually generates the kinds of obligations peculiar to it" (139). I wonder whether this might mean, by Dobson's logic, that those who do the most meeting of basic needs have the most ecological obligations.

20 This is not to say that marginalized groups have not found ways to actively participate in social movements in spite of the inhospitable conditions in which they live. Bickford (1996, 78) rightly points to welfare rights movements and homeless activists as evidence that "one need not have private needs met to be capable of political action."

21 For a feminist critique of the contradictions of Scandinavian welfare policies, see Hernes (1988) and Lister (1997).

22 That this ideal process of political deliberation is necessarily time consuming is of course a serious problem for feminists who embrace non-instrumental meanings of citizenship. I return to this point in Chapter 9.

23 Such arguments have inspired the proliferation of another branch of ecopolitical discourse that is wary of substantive definitions of sustainability and so advocates an ethics to guide the deliberative processes through which the concept of sustainability takes shape. Here I am referring to the work of Dryzek (1990, 1997) and Torgerson (1999), who, to differing degrees, rely on the political theories of Jurgen Habermas and Hannah Arendt.

24 http://www.on.ec.gc.ca/community/classroom/c3-understanding-e.html.

25 Something should be said about the implications for people who, for a variety of reasons, are unable or unwilling to perform their environmental duties. I am thinking here of the assumption made by environmentalists that people of colour and working-class people are not concerned with sustainability because they appear not to employ green practices to the same extent as white middle-class people (see Gosine 2003). This suggests the need for greater understanding of, among other things, the relationship between rights and responsibilities and the conditions in which ecological citizenship might be expressed/practised. Several of the women I interviewed made insightful observations about the cultural specificity of so-called green household practices (see Chapter 8).

26 For a feminist critique of Marshall's focus on class to the exclusion of race and gender inequality, see Fraser and Gordon (1994).

27 David Held notes that it is problematic that reproductive rights are ignored in mainstream citizenship literature because they are "the very basis of the possibility of effective participation of women in both civil society and the polity" (quoted in Lister 1997, 18).

28 There has also been a growing interest among feminists in "going global," or envisioning a global feminist civil society. The UN Conference on Women (and the parallel NGO forum) in Beijing in 1995 and the World March of Women in 2000 are two prominent examples. Several feminist social movement scholars have examined this topic (see, for example, Miles [1996] and Kaplan [1997]).

29 It is questionable, however, how much impact such policies have had on human-nature relationships, specifically the exploitation of nature in advanced capitalist societies in the West. As I have noted, few feminist theorists of citizenship have considered this issue. It is a lacuna that a feminist-ecological approach to citizenship should help address.

Chapter 6: Conversations with Activist Women

1 Most recent research supports the claim that women typically demonstrate higher levels of environmental concern and behaviour than men (Hunter, Hatch, and Johnson 2004). But

there are studies that find there to be no significant links between gender and environmental concern (e.g., Kaloff, Dietz, and Guaganano [2002] find that race may be more significant). Some research suggests that women are more likely than men to participate in environmental behaviour and activism (Zelezny, Chua, and Aldrich 2000), while other research has found that women tend to engage in predominantly private environmental behaviours rather than public activism (the opposite being true of men) (e.g., Tindall, Davies, and Mauboules 2003). Littig (2001) discusses the fact that it is difficult to compare these findings because of the variation in how different researchers define central concepts such as "concern."

2 Interestingly, George Nalunnakkal (2004) also criticizes Shiva's analysis of the Chipko movement for neglecting to mention that its leaders are not peasants but, rather, upper-caste Hindus.

3 I give Mies' (1986) definition of "housewifization" in Chapter 4 (see note 16). She has revisited this concept in her latest book, written with Bennholdt-Thomsen (1999), which rests on a socialist feminist theoretical analysis. But once again the union of materialism and essentialism/maternalism is apparent.

4 Greta Gaard (1998) gives the examples of Spretnak's "body parables" (i.e., women gaining insight into their connection to nature in a post-orgasmic state) and Warren's famous awakening to the earth while rock climbing.

5 Some theorists claim that, in the new "information society" (Castells 1996), the principal resource of the new citizen is "knowledge" (see also Isin 1997), while others question whether any form of knowledge can be trusted in the "risk society" (Beck 1992; see also Bauman 1993).

6 See, for example, Luke (1997), Quinby (1997), and Darier (1996).

7 It is important to note that Mellor and Salleh, along with Mies and Bennholdt-Thomsen and several others writing about ecofeminism, are intensely critical of Western/Northern feminism that has incorporated the radical (de)constructionist and anti-essentialist arguments of postmodernism. (There is little recognition of the Southern and postcolonial scholars who find these arguments useful [e.g., Spivak]). For example, Mies and Bennholdt-Thomsen (1999) reduce postmodern feminist theorizing to ideology, "political correctness," and "fashion statements," and they argue that it is tantamount to "matricide" (i.e., the murder of mothers).

8 It is worth pointing out that the appropriation of women's experiences for academic purposes is not a danger unique to white Western/Northern ecofeminist scholars. For example, as Haripriya Rangan (2000, 35) observes about Vandana Shiva: "[Shiva's] rhetoric invests her ... with the authority to speak on behalf of Feminine Nature, of Garhwali women, and for the poverty-stricken South; and it is by the constant insertion of 'Chipko women,' as she calls them, into her ... narratives that [she] reinforces her authenticity as an ecofeminist in contemporary ecofeminist discourse."

9 For discussion of the role of intellectuals and academics in processes of social change, see Gramsci (1971) and Foucault (1977).

10 With the rise of anti-globalization movements, public alliances between activists and academics have become an important strategy of resistance, as noted in Featherstone and Henwood's (2001) examination of the international anti-sweatshop campaign.

11 Negrey (1993, 25) estimates that women have a sixty-five to seventy-hour total work week if they work outside the home for fifteen hours or more per week. Bittman and Wacjman's (2000) cross-national data (collected in the late 1980s and early 1990s) indicate fewer hours than this: an average of around fifty hours per week in paid and unpaid work for all women, and around sixty hours on average for married women.

12 According to the Canadian National Survey of Giving, Volunteering and Participation, in 2000 women in Ontario participated at a slightly higher rate than men in volunteer work (27 percent versus 24 percent) and accounted for a higher percentage of total hours volunteered (53 percent versus 47 percent). However, men contributed more hours, on average, to volunteer work than did women (172 versus 160). Canada-wide, more volunteers in social service fields (e.g., child care, emergency shelters, etc.) are women (58 percent versus 42 percent), whereas more volunteers in the arts and recreation fields (e.g., sports and social clubs) are men (58 percent versus 42 percent) (http://www.givingandvolunteering.ca/factsheets.asp).

13 While I would call this "community managing" work a practice of citizenship, it is not described as such in this body of feminist literature. Note that this triple role has also been theorized by feminist researchers looking at women in developing countries. See, for example, Moser (1993).

14 Exceptions include Krauss (1997), Brown and Ferguson (1997), and Kaplan (1997), in which the impacts of women's activism on domestic relationships are mentioned.

15 In American studies it is often claimed that quality-of-life, or environmental justice, activism involves people whose everyday survival is threatened, while middle-class white people tend to be concerned with "postmaterialist" (or luxury) causes such as promoting organic foods and preserving rare plants. Di Chiro (1992) claims, for example, that the majority of activists in the EJM are working-class women of colour, while "environmentalists" tend to be white and middle class. In contrast, while there are class- and culturally informed differences in how "environment" is viewed among the women I interviewed, the fact that all thirty women from a diversity of socio-cultural and class backgrounds (including middle-class white women) are working on quality-of-life issues serves to disrupt the neat characterizations given in the US literature.

16 The "mega-city" amalgamation process was a politically charged one, inspiring the creation of a resistance movement called Citizens for Local Democracy (C4LD). Two of the women I interviewed, Kathleen Wynne and Helen Melbourne, were among the leaders of this organization, which, at one point, was attracting thousands of people to its weekly meetings.

17 Two women immigrated from the United States and one immigrated from England.

18 Toronto is one of the most energy-intensive regions in the world, according to the Royal Commission on the Regeneration of Toronto's Waterfront (1992).

19 The Conservative Party lost power to the Liberals in the fall 2003 election. I left Ontario for the United Kingdom in the fall of 2002. At the time of writing I am unable to say what effect the new government, under Premier Dalton McGuinty, will have on the province, which is still very much coping with the Harris legacy. Therefore, as explained in Chapter 1, I speak of the Conservative policies and their impacts in the present tense.

20 Feminists have argued that these cuts are characterized by a shift "from care to control" (Williams 1989) in that they are increasingly conditional on terms set by the state. This shift has also been interpreted as a shift in the meaning of citizenship: the status of citizen is granted only to those who are worthy of it by, most important, being perceived as "hard-working" and "tax paying."

21 A highlight of my time in Toronto was the 1996 Days of Action protest, at which over 300,000 citizens (myself included) descended on Queen's Park (the site of the provincial legislature), took over the streets, and shut down the city's transit system.

22 The mayor's racism was highlighted in the summer of 2001 when his comments about being reluctant to visit Kenya for fear of being "boiled in a pot of water with natives dancing around" were reported by the *Toronto Star* (and subsequently by most news media around the world).

23 During the spring and summer of 2000, Walkerton, Ontario made international headlines when E. coli bacteria contaminated its water supply, resulting in widespread illness and the death of at least seven residents. Most environmentalists contend that this disaster was the result of the Harris government's policy allowing the intensification of the commercial livestock industry and the downloading of environmental monitoring to the municipal level.

Chapter 7: The Private, the Public, and the Planet

1 See, for example, Garland (1988); Krauss (1983, 1993, 1997); Di Chiro (1992, 1998); Brú-Bistuer (1996); Seager (1993, 1996); Taylor (1997); Miller, Hallstein, and Quass (1996); Brown and Ferguson (1997); Rosenberg (1995); and Kaplan (1997).

2 Another way I could have complicated the profile is by interviewing women activists who are not mothers. I found a number of them in the process of trying to locate women to interview for this study. However, I wanted to look specifically at the implications for juggling multiple roles and relationships between motherhood and political activism within the context of the discourses of ecofeminism and ecological citizenship.

3 As I discuss in Chapter 8, some of the women were not sure they wanted to use the term "activism" to describe the work they do. Some preferred less radical labels such as "advocacy" and "volunteerism."

4 Unlike the approach of Josepa Brú-Bistuer (1996), who asked Spanish women to explain their motivations for protesting industrial waste by prioritizing a list of options she had determined (of which one was concern for family health and welfare), my questions were open-ended. Brú-Bistuer's (1996, 114) study found that "concern for family health" was the overwhelming and unanimously chosen reason women in three Spanish cities got involved in industrial waste protests "rendering the other categories [such as environmental protection] insignificant."

5 Of the six women activists working on quality-of-life issues that Kaplan (1997) interviewed for her book *Crazy for Democracy*, three are described as "deeply religious."

6 Several women of colour explained that there are cultural differences in the way "environment" is understood. Some say that treating "the environment" as a separate concern is a North American approach that is not found in their countries of origin.

7 Sadly, Ruth Morris died of kidney cancer in September 2001. A "Lives Lived" obituary was published in the *Globe and Mail* on 11 February 2002. It was only then that I learned of the many awards she had received for her activist contributions to social justice in Canada. She had received the Order of Canada six weeks before she died.

8 Frederickson (1995, 58) reports that nearly 50 percent of full-time employed mothers (aged twenty-five to forty-four) would like more time for themselves alone, whereas "the proportion for men never rises much above 25 per cent."

9 In comparison, 26 percent of married fathers with full-time employment report being time-stressed (Statistics Canada 2000, 111).

10 As I discuss in Chapters 2 and 3, maternalist (eco)feminist theorists advocate bringing the values of the private sphere into the public realm of politics (Elshtain 1981; Ruddick 1989).

11 For a discussion of why women see working at home as a way to manage the double day, see Duffy, Mandel, and Pupo (1989) and Duffy and Pupo (1992).

12 Brú-Bistuer (1996) writes that compartmentalizing tasks and fragmenting time allocation is an "androcentric" model, whereas the feminine model includes simultaneity and versatility. Although many of the women did speak of their practices of multitasking and keeping flexible schedules, they also reported that there are both advantages and disadvantages of these practices. Some wished for more flexibility, while others longed for more obvious boundaries.

13 It seems fitting that most of my interviews were conducted not in public places but in the privacy of women's kitchens (a few took place in offices and coffee shops; one was conducted in a public library).

14 In her research on women's forest activism, Maureen Reed (2003) found that women on both sides of the issue (i.e., pro- and anti-logging) criticized the allegedly inappropriate use of children to advance political aims. The documentary film *Fury for the Sound* (Wine 1997), about the women involved in the blockade at Clayoquot Sound in 1993, shows young children being put on the front lines of the protest and authorities threatening mothers that their children would be taken into state custody as a result.

15 Frederikson (1995) reports that sole-support mothers actually spend fewer hours doing unpaid work than women with spouses and children at home. It seems that, contrary to what one would expect, the presence of a (male?) partner might actually create more work rather than reduce work time through task sharing.

16 Statistics Canada (2000) reports that in 1996 15 percent of all women between twenty-five and fifty-four years of age provided unpaid care to an elderly person. This was the case for 9 percent of Canadian men in the same age range.

17 Statistics Canada (2000, 101) reports that, even though there has been an increase in the number of licensed child care spaces, the demand continues to exceed the supply by a sizable margin: "In 1996, for example, there were just over 300,000 day care spaces available to pre-school-aged children in Canada. At the same time, there were 900,000 families in Canada with at least one pre-school-aged child in which either both parents or a lone parent was employed."

18 One woman told me that she faces a clash of expectations between her own and her family's values concerning food: "I have felt a backlash at mealtimes for some of the choices I make. I've been told that I'm hysterical or that I'm silly or just not being a good mother."

19 Brown and Ferguson (1997, 257) report that "women activists in contaminated communities report high rates of conflict, separation, and divorce."

20 I do not suggest that these claims apply exclusively to women activists. Men who lack support and the resources necessary for activism must also find it difficult to sustain an intense degree of participation. I would need to do further research in order to make informed comments on which of these effects of juggling caring and activist work are specific to women. Research into the private lives of male caregivers who are juggling paid work and environmental activism has, to my knowledge, not yet been done.

21 Given the discussion of spouses and children feeling resentful about having to do more work (i.e., to "help out"), it is clear that household work is regarded as "mom's work" in some families and as a shared household responsibility in others.

22 It is important to note here that there can be discrepancies in women's and men's reporting of men's share of household labour and the actual amount and types of housework and caring

that they do. Some researchers believe that men tend to exaggerate. For a discussion of this phenomenon, see Schor (1997) and Eichler (1988).

23 Interestingly, the women did not mention the benefits of giving their daughters greater responsibility for housework, but a few talked about how their daughters had become interested in environmental and social issues partly as a result of observing and participating in their mother's activism.

24 Other time-saving strategies mentioned were cooking and freezing meals in advance, stocking up on food, and using food delivery services. Surprisingly, only two women mentioned that using information technologies, like the Internet, help them work more efficiently and save time.

25 In a follow-up question, I asked: "How would you interpret the finding that many activist women employ other women to clean their houses?" I include some of the responses here in order to show the range of opinion the women expressed:

> I would not judge activists who employ other women. I would say that they should put their energy and knowledge where it is most productive. If they pay a fair wage and use environmentally safe products and provide a safe working environment, then they are helping by employing another person.

> Volunteer activism sometimes takes a lot of time, energy, and focus. I think everyone does what they can with what they have. Some have more, some less. If activist women who employ other women pay them fairly, treat them with respect and acknowledge the dignity of their contribution – I have no problem. I personally resist the assumption that because they do, they have a bad attitude. I don't want to criticize any one's genuine efforts.

> The activist women I know do not employ other women to clean their houses. We are not activists for some people; we are fighting for social justice for everyone.

> That classism is more pervasive than other "isms."

> I wish I could as well!! I will tend to believe that those women are activists because they can afford to [be], but many of these activists are probably focused on the environment only. "The privilege of the bourgeois class" perhaps.

> I think that the activist women who can afford to hire a cleaning woman do so because they find their activism very time consuming and worthy of paying for. They are actually paying more than their time to their cause, they are putting in money from their pockets and at the same time supplying work to another woman who needs it.

> I feel that they are very lucky. Most of the people that I know that do volunteer work, volunteer in their spare time or shuffle housework and child care as best they can.

26 It would be interesting to research how women reconcile their environmental values with popular notions of household "cleanliness" constructed through marketing campaigns predominantly targeted at women. A common message is that women should protect their children from harmful "germs" by using antibacterial soaps and cleaning products. I wonder what impact, if any, high-profile health scares (e.g., E. coli in the water supply or hamburger disease also caused by a strain of E. coli bacteria) have had on women's consumer choices, household cleaning, and food preparation practices.

Chapter 8: Activist Women Theorize the Green Political

1 I argue in Chapter 6 that such methodological and/or epistemological orientations are problematic if one rejects the view that discovering "reality" is or can be the objective of research. Postmodern feminist critiques of standpoint methodologies not only question the idea that women's social identities provide a privileged vantage point from which they experience the world but also ask whether it is possible to employ "women's knowledges" for an emancipatory politics. See Haraway (1991b); Fraser and Nicholson (1990); and Butler (1992). I discuss this point again in the appendix.

2 As I note in Chapter 6, identifying women by their own names (where possible and appropriate), thereby acknowledging them for their ideas and analyses, is an important part of this stance.

3 So they are not ecofeminists, not typical environmentalists, and now maybe not even activists? While disconcerting, this question highlights the problem of fitting research participants into pre-existing categories. Sturgeon (1997) makes a similar observation about the dangers of appropriating women activists' experiences to support academic ecofeminist theories. I discuss this as a methodological problem in Chapter 6.

4 A few women said that, although it is a challenge to run an organization with no funding, accepting funds from the state would compromise their credibility in the community and so they prefer not to do so.

5 This point serves as a reminder to resist viewing a person's class status as fixed. In my study, some of the women have experienced changes in class status over time due to divorce or unemployment, while others think of themselves as "middle class" because they were raised in a middle-class environment even though they now live in poverty. I too would call myself "middle class," but as a full-time student I lived well below the poverty line, at least according to Statistics Canada's (2000) definition.

6 For a discussion of how stereotypes act as imposed "masks" that prevent what lies behind the mask from being seen and heard, see Anzaldúa (1990). Hannah Arendt, in contrast, uses "the mask" as a metaphor for a public persona (i.e., citizen) that – in the ideal sense of politics – can cover up politically irrelevant qualities, thereby allowing the unique individual ("who" we are) to sound through (Bickford 1996).

7 Temma Kaplan (1997, 44) writes: "In publicizing environmental issues, playing crazy seems to have become an important part of politics. Taking their cue from situation comedies, housewives frequently try to mug for the cameras." My research suggests that this is not always the case.

8 According to Lauren Berlant (1997), people are taught to believe that the welfare state will take care of them through the "technologies of citizenship": the activity of "national pedagogy" is carried out in popular culture (above all through television) for the purpose of creating proper national subjects and subjectivities that conform to the expectations of the powerful.

9 The same can be said of the women activists at Love Canal, who, according to Kaplan (1997), worked closely with professors Addie and Murray Levine from SUNY Buffalo throughout their campaign. Kaplan says that the Levines acted as political mentors to the women; in a sense they "became the unofficial parents of the homeowners" (40-41).

10 At least three women expressed interest in the Faculty of Environmental Studies at York University and asked about the courses offered there. I sent Julie Starr an application package soon after our first conversation. Burke Austin, Jane Smith*, and Alejandra Galvez have taken university courses in environmental studies.

11 In an increasingly self-reflexive and sceptical age, which Beck (1992, 1995, 1999) calls "the risk society," citizens not only engage in the politicization and production of scientific knowledge themselves but also work with experts who are openly critical of their own fields of expertise (whom he calls "counter-experts").

12 This point resonates with my discussion in Chapter 6 about the need to rethink the dichotomy between academics and activists that is presented in some ecofeminist texts.

13 Although it would have been an interesting question, I did not ask the women to comment on the relationship between activism and citizenship.

14 As Voet (1998) suggests, there is little feminist research on the question of how women understand and practise citizenship. The feminist literature on citizenship tends to focus on theoretical and normative aspects of citizenship.

15 Rights as opposed to responsibility did not figure prominently in the women's answers to my question. Interestingly, only Murphy Browne restricted her definition of citizenship to rights. She said: "To me being a citizen means that I should have the right to be treated the way any other citizen of Canada is treated. I should not be treated differently because of the colour of my skin."

16 Because citizenship has traditionally been about membership in a nation-state, it is an exclusionary concept. For a feminist analysis of relationships among gender, citizenship, and "the nation" (i.e., territoriality), see Yuval-Davis (2000).

17 This notion resonates indirectly with Virginia Woolf's commentary on women's citizenship in *Three Guineas*. Woolf assumed that women's moral superiority over men (whom she saw as

being inclined towards violence and war) stemmed from being "outsiders," from not being members of fascist and militarist states. Her statement that "as a woman I have no country; as a woman, my country is the whole world" (Woolf 1938, 108) is an important slogan for cultural feminists and feminist anti-war activists.

18 I discuss the use of this background questionnaire in the appendix.

19 Such confessions have an interesting precedent in green theorist Mark Sagoff's (1988) admission that he drives an oil-leaking car with an "Ecology Now!" sticker on its rear bumper. Ecological citizenship discourse could use more of these efforts to consider honestly the contradictions in trying to live green in an overdeveloped capitalist society – preferably without self-deprecating testimonials.

20 Kaplan (1997) notes that the women who lived in the Love Canal neighbourhood became suspicious of the safety of their garden produce and eventually stopped gardening altogether.

21 Precycling refers to the practice of purchasing goods that will create minimal or no waste, for example, unpackaged bulk items and fresh produce (Schultz 1993).

22 Asking the women to comment on the participation of men in their organizations is valuable because some ecofeminists have unfairly characterized certain movements as women-led when they are not (the Chipko movement is an obvious example of this problem, as I explain in Chapter 6).

23 With one or two exceptions, I did not ask the women whether they call themselves "feminists" because originally it was not my intention to comment on the degree to which their actions and ideas measure up to feminist theories. In retrospect, however, I see that this question would have strengthened my ability to comment on their political analyses and political consciousness.

24 It is interesting that Ruth Lara attributes this analysis to Maria Mies. It sounds to me more like Marilyn Waring's analysis in her 1988 book *If Women Counted: A New Feminist Economics*. Waring was mentioned in my conversations with women activists more than any other author. A close second was Rachel Carson.

Chapter 9: No Motherhood Issue

1 Lister (1997) is one non-ecofeminist exception to this observation.

2 I say this not least because of the potential for repression and abuse. We should not forget that the history of state-controlled child-rearing institutions in Canada includes the disastrous case of Aboriginal residential schools. I am grateful to Maureen Reed for drawing this point to my attention.

3 Littig (2001, 101-3) reports that, although many feminists hold out hope for them, the impacts of collective, eco-friendly services on gender relations have not been sufficiently researched. She cites one 1998 study of collective laundries in Vienna where collectivization did nothing to alter the way the work was distributed: women still did most of the laundry and had to do the extra work of coordinating the cooperation. One benefit she cites is that the work itself became more public, something about which neighbours had to converse.

4 Contrary to popular assumptions, domestic technology has not reduced the total amount of housework people do. Bittman, Rice, and Wajcman (2004) report, based on their analysis of data from the Australian 1997 Time Use Survey, that domestic appliances rarely reduce women's unpaid working time and even, paradoxically, produce increases in household labour. They also find that in those cases when domestic appliances do reduce household work (e.g., dishwashers), "it tends to be men who are the beneficiaries" (412). Unfortunately, it was not part of their study to look at relationships between domestic technology and the use of energy and other natural resources in households.

5 It is important to make space in feminist arguments for an acknowledgment that gender roles and relations have undergone important shifts since the rise of the second wave of feminism in the early 1970s, to give men some credit even though there remains considerable room for improvement. Mary Mellor's (2000, 121) statement that "not all women do women's work and much is done by subordinated men" is not quite what I have in mind, however.

6 There is something to be said here about the flip side to this position. I suspect women tend to dismiss men's forms of caring work as less valuable than women's, and in so doing tend to guard this caring work as something women do best. Perhaps this is done in order to preserve the particular kind of power that women derive from being typically more competent at caring than men. If this is true, or at least an accurate hunch, then it means that women will also need to change their approach to caring so that men and women can share it more

equally. Thanks to Maureen Reed for prompting me to think about this dimension of the issue.

7 Based on a true story: I had this very exchange with a political scientist who gave a conference paper on working-time reduction in France, in which he failed to mention anything about gender differences (Kinderman 2001). Interesting facts about how French men and women choose to spend their "free time" came out only after I asked him pointed questions on this issue.

References

Ackelsberg, Martha (1988). Communities, resistance, and women's activism: Some implications for a democratic polity. In *Women and the Politics of Empowerment*, ed. A. Bookman and S. Morgen, 297-313. Philadelphia: Temple University Press.

Acker, Joan, Kate Barry, and Johanna Esseveld (1991). Objectivity and truth: Problems in doing feminist research. In *Beyond Methodology: Feminist Scholarship as Lived Research*, ed. M.M. Fonow and J.A. Cook, 133-53. Bloomington: Indiana University Press.

Adam, Barbara (2002). The gendered time politics of globalization: Of shadowlands and elusive justice. *Feminist Review* 70: 3-29.

Agarwal, Bina (1992). The gender and environment debate: Lessons from India. *Feminist Studies* 18 (1): 119-58.

– (1998a). Environmental management, equity and ecofeminism: Debating India's experience. *Journal of Peasant Studies* 25 (4): 55-95.

– (1998b). The gender and environment debate. In *Political Ecology: Global and Local*, ed. R. Keil, D.V.J. Bell, P. Penz, and L. Fawcett, 193-219. New York: Routledge.

– (2001). A challenge for ecofeminism: Gender, greening, and community forestry. *Women and Environments International* 52/53 (Fall): 12-15.

Alaimo, Stacey (2000). *Undomesticated Ground: Recasting Nature as Feminist Space*. Ithaca: Cornell University Press.

Alcoff, Linda (1988). Cultural feminism versus post-structuralism: The identity crisis in feminist theory. *Signs: Journal of Women in Culture and Society* 13 (Spring): 405-536.

Alfaro, R.M. (1994). Women as agents of communication: Social maternity and leadership. In *Women in Grassroots Communication*, ed. P. Riano, 260-78. London: Sage.

Allen, Patricia, and Carolyn Sachs (1993). Sustainable agriculture in the United States: Engagements and silences. In *Food for the Future: Conditions and Contradictions of Sustainability*, ed. P. Allen, 139-67. New York: John Wiley and Sons.

Altvater, Elmar (1999). Restructuring the space of democracy. In *Global Ethics and Environment*, ed. N. Low, 283-309. New York: Routledge.

Anzaldúa, Gloria (1990). Haciendo caras, una entrada / an introduction. In *Making Face, Making Soul / Haciendo Caras: Creative and Critical Perspectives by Feminists of Color*, ed. G. Anzaldúa, xv-xviii. San Francisco: Aunt Lute Foundation.

Arai, A. Bruce (2000). Self-employment as a response to the double day for women and men in Canada. *Canadian Review of Sociology and Anthropology* 37 (2): 125-42.

Arendt, Hannah (1958). *The Human Condition*. Chicago: University of Chicago Press.

– (2000). *The Portable Hannah Arendt*. Ed. and introduction Peter Baehr. New York: Penguin Books.

Armstrong, Pat (1996). Unravelling the safety net: Transformations in health care and their impact on women. In *Women and Canadian Public Policy*, ed. J. Brodie, 129-50. Toronto: Harcourt Brace and Co.

Armstrong, Pat, and Hugh Armstrong (1990). *Theorizing Women's Work*. Toronto: Garamond Press.

– (1994). *The Double Ghetto: Canadian Women and Their Segregated Work*. Toronto: McClelland and Stewart.

Arnstein, Sherry (1969). A ladder of citizen participation. *Journal of the American Planning Association* 35 (4): 216-24.

Attfield, Robin (1999). *The Ethics of the Global Environment.* Edinburgh: Edinburgh University Press.

Bakan, Abigail B., and Daiva K. Stasiulus (1996). Structural adjustment, citizenship, and foreign domestic labour: The Canadian case. In *Rethinking Restructuring: Gender and Change in Canada,* ed. I. Bakker, 217-42. Toronto: University of Toronto Press.

Bakker, Isabella, ed. (1994). *The Strategic Silence: Gender and Economic Policy.* London: Zed Books.

– (1996a). Deconstructing macroeconomics through a feminist lens. In *Women and Canadian Public Policy,* ed. J. Brodie, 31-56. Toronto: Harcourt Brace and Co.

– (1996b). Introduction: The gendered foundations of restructuring in Canada. In *Rethinking Restructuring: Gender and Change in Canada,* ed. I. Bakker, 3-25. Toronto: University of Toronto Press.

Barber, Benjamin (1984). *Strong Democracy: Participatory Politics for a New Age.* Los Angeles: University of California Press.

Bar On, Bat-Ami, and Ann Ferguson (1998). Introduction. In *Daring to Be Good: Essays in Feminist Ethico-Politics,* ed. B. Bar On and A. Ferguson, ix-xix. New York: Routledge.

Barry, John (1996). Sustainability, political judgement and citizenship: Connecting green politics and democracy. In *Democracy and Green Political Thought,* ed. B. Doherty and M. De Geus, 115-31. New York: Routledge.

– (1999). *Rethinking Green Politics.* London: Sage Publications.

– (2002). Vulnerability and virtue: Democracy, dependency and ecological stewardship. In *Democracy and the Claims of Nature: Critical Perspectives for a New Century,* ed. B.A. Minteer and B. Pepperman Taylor, 133-52. Lanham, MD: Rowman and Littlefield.

– (2006). Resistance is fertile: From environmental to sustainability citizenship. In *Environmental Citizenship,* ed. D. Bell and A. Dobson, 21-48. Cambridge, MA: MIT Press.

Bartky, Sandra (1990). *Femininity and Oppression.* New York: Routledge.

Bauman, Zygmunt (1993). *Postmodern Ethics.* Oxford: Blackwell.

BBC News (2004). Profile: Wangari Maathai. Published 10 October: http://news.bbc.co.uk/2/hi/africa/3726084.stm (accessed 22 January 2006).

Beck, Ulrich (1992). *The Risk Society: Towards a new Modernity.* London: Sage.

– (1995). *Ecological Politics in an Age of Risk.* Cambridge: Polity Press.

– (1998). The cosmopolitan manifesto. *New Statesman,* 20 March: 28-30.

– (1999). *World Risk Society.* Cambridge: Polity Press.

Beder, Sharon (1997). *Global Spin: The Corporate Assault on Environmentalism.* White River Junction, VT: Chelsea Green Publishing.

Benhabib, Seyla (1992). *Situating the Self: Gender, Community and Postmodernism in Contemporary Ethics.* New York: Routledge.

Benyon, J., and A. Edwards (1997). 1997: Crime and public order. In *Developments in British Politics 5,* ed. P. Dunleavy, A. Gamble, I. Holliday, and G. Peele, 327-41. Basingstoke, UK: Palgrave Macmillan.

Berlant, Lauren (1997). *The Queen of America Goes to Washington: Essays on Sex and Citizenship.* Durham, NC: Duke University Press.

Berry, Wendell (1977). *The Unsettling of America: Culture and Agriculture.* New York: Avon Books.

Best, Steven, and Douglas Kellner (1991). *Postmodern Theory: Critical Interrogations.* London: The Guilford Press.

Bickford, Susan (1996). *The Dissonance of Democracy: Listening, Conflict, and Citizenship.* Ithaca: Cornell University Press.

Biehl, Janet (1991). *Finding Our Way: Rethinking Ecofeminist Politics.* Montreal: Black Rose Books.

– (1998). *The Politics of Social Ecology: Libertarian Municipalism.* Montreal: Black Rose Books.

Birch, Eugenie Ladner (1983). From civic worker to city planner: Women in planning, 1890-1980. In *The American Planner: Biographies and Recollections,* ed. D.A. Krueckeberg, 396-427. New York: Methuen.

Bittman, Michael, and Judy Wajcman (2000). The rush hour: The character of leisure time and gender equity. *Social Forces* 79 (1): 165-89.

Bittman, Michael, James Mahmud Rice, and Judy Wajcman (2004). Appliances and their impact: The ownership of domestic technology and time spent on household work. *British Journal of Sociology* 55 (3): 401-23.

Bookchin, Murray (1980). *Toward an Ecological Society.* Montreal: Black Rose Books.
– (1982). *The Ecology of Freedom.* Palo Alto, CA: Cheshire Books.
– (1989). *Remaking Society.* Montreal: Black Rose Books.
– (1992). *Urbanization without Cities: The Rise and Decline of Citizenship.* Montreal: Black Rose Books.
Bookman, Ann, and Sandra Morgen, eds. (1988). *Women and the Politics of Empowerment.* Philadelphia: Temple University Press.
Boserup, Ester (1970). *Women's Role in Economic Development.* New York: St. Martin's Press.
Bossin, Bob (1999). Nature made it, women saved it: Five women pull off one of the world's great environmental victories. *Homemakers,* September: 54-70.
Bowden, Peta (1997). *Caring: Gender-Sensitive Ethics.* New York: Routledge.
Braidotti, Rosi, Ewa Charkiewicz, Sabine Hausler, and Saskia Wieringa (1994). *Women, the Environment and Sustainable Development: Towards a Theoretical Synthesis.* London: Zed Books.
Brenner, Johanna (1996). The best of times, the worst of times: Feminism in the United States. In *Mapping the Women's Movement: Feminist Politics and Social Transformation in the North,* ed. M. Threlfall, 17-72. London: Verso.
Brodie, Janine (1995). *Politics on the Margins: Restructuring and the Canadian Women's Movement.* Halifax: Fernwood Publishing.
– (1996a). Canadian women, changing state forms, and public policy. In *Women and Canadian Public Policy,* ed. J. Brodie, 1-28. Toronto: Harcourt Brace and Co.
– (1996b). Restructuring and the new citizenship. In *Rethinking Restructuring,* ed. I. Bakker, 126-40. Toronto: University of Toronto Press.
Brown, Phil, and Faith Ferguson (1997). "Making a big stink": Women's work, women's relationships, and toxic waste activism. In *Women Working in the Environment,* ed. C. Sachs, 241-64. Washington, DC: Taylor and Francis.
Brú-Bistuer, Josepa (1996). Spanish women against industrial waste: A gender perspective on environmental grassroots movements. In *Feminist Political Ecology: Global Issues and Local Experiences,* ed. D. Rocheleau, B. Thomas-Slayter, and E. Wangari, 104-24. New York: Routledge.
Bullard, Robert (1990). *Dumping in Dixie: Race, Class and Environmental Quality.* Boulder CO: Westview Press.
– (1994). Environmental racism and the environmental justice movement. In *Ecology: Key Concepts in Critical Theory,* ed. C. Merchant, 254-65. Atlantic Highlands, NJ: Humanities Press.
Butler, Judith (1990). *Gender Trouble: Feminism and the Subversion of Identity.* New York: Routledge.
– (1992). Contingent foundations: Feminism and the question of "postmodernism." In *Feminists Theorize the Political,* ed. J. Butler and J. Scott, 3-21. New York: Routledge.
– (1993). *Bodies That Matter: On the Discursive Limits of "Sex."* New York: Routledge.
Caldecott, Leonie, and Stephanie Leland, ed. (1983). *Reclaim the Earth: Women Speak Out for Life on Earth.* London: The Women's Press.
Calder, Gillian (2003). Recent changes to the maternity and parental leave benefits regime as a case study: The impacts of globalization on the delivery of social programs in Canada. *Canadian Journal of Women and the Law* 15 (3): 342-66.
Canadian Association of Food Banks (2000). *Hunger Count 2000: A Surplus of Hunger.* Canada's annual survey of emergency food programs. Prepared by Beth Wilson and Carly Steinman, http://www.icomm.ca/cafb/hc-2000.pdf.
Card, Claudia (1989). Gender and moral luck. In *Identity, Character and Morality: Essays in Moral Psychology,* ed. O. Flanagan and A. Rorty, 199-218. Cambridge, MA: MIT Press.
Carlassare, Elisabeth (1994). Essentialism in ecofeminist discourse. In *Ecology: Key Concepts in Critical Theory,* ed. C. Merchant, 220-34. Atlantic Highlands, NJ: Humanities Press.
Castells, Manuel (1996). *The Rise of the Network Society.* Oxford: Blackwell.
Chodorow, Nancy (1978). *The Reproduction of Mothering.* Los Angeles: University of California Press.
Christoff, Peter (1996). Ecological citizens and ecologically guided democracy. In *Democracy and Green Political Thought,* ed. B. Doherty and M. De Geus, 151-69. New York: Routledge.
Clarke, Paul (1996). *Deep Citizenship.* London: Pluto Press.
Code, Lorraine (1991). *What Can She Know? Feminist Theory and the Construction of Knowledge.* Ithaca: Cornell University Press.
– (1995). *Rhetorical Spaces: Essays on Gendered Locations.* New York: Routledge.

– (2000). How to think globally: Stretching the limits of imagination. In *Decentering the Center*, ed. U. Narayan and S. Harding, 67-79. Bloomington: Indiana University Press.

Cohen, Marjorie Griffin (1995). Social policy and social services. In *Canadian Women's Issues*, ed. R.R. Pierson, M.G. Cohen, P. Bourne, and P. Masters, 264-84. Toronto: James Lorimer and Co.

Collard, Andrée (1988). *The Rape of the Wild*. London: Women's Press.

Collins, Patricia Hill (1990). *Black Feminist Thought: Knowledge, Consciousness, and the Politics of Empowerment*. New York: Routledge.

Cook, Judith, and Mary Margaret Fonow (1986). Knowledge and women's interests: Issues of epistemology and methodology in feminist sociological research. *Sociological Inquiry* 56 (1): 2-29.

Cornell, Drucila (1997). Gender hierarchy, equality and the possibility of democracy. In *Feminism and the New Democracy*, ed. J. Dean, 210-21. Thousand Oaks, CA: Sage Publications.

Cott, Nancy (1989). What's in a name? The limits of social feminism, or expanding the vocabulary of women's history. *Journal of Women's History* 76 (3): 809-29.

Cowan, Ruth Schwartz (1983). *More Work for Mother: The Ironies of Household Technology from the Open Hearth to the Microwave*. New York: Basic Books.

Cruikshank, Barbara (1999). *The Will to Empower: Democratic Citizens and Other Subjects*. Ithaca and London: Cornell University Press.

Cuomo, Chris J. (1998). *Feminism and Ecological Communities: An Ethic of Flourishing*. New York: Routledge.

Curtin, Deane (1991). Toward an ecological ethic of care. *Hypatia* 6 (1): 60-74.

– (1999). *Chinnagounder's Challenge: The Question of Ecological Citizenship*. Indianapolis: Indiana University Press.

Dankelman, Irene, and Joan Davidson (1988). *Women and Environment in the Third World*. London: Earthscan.

Darier, Éric (1996). Environmental governmentality: The case of Canada's Green Plan. *Environmental Politics* 5 (4): 585-606.

– (1998). Time to be lazy: Work, the environment and modern subjectivities. *Time and Society* 7 (2): 193-208.

Davion, Victoria (1994). Is ecofeminism feminist? In *Ecological Feminism*, ed. K.J. Warren, 8-28. New York: Routledge.

Dean, Hartley (2001). Green citizenship. *Social Policy and Administration* 35 (5): 490-505.

D'Eaubonne, Françoise (1974). The time for ecofeminism. In *Ecology: Key Concepts in Critical Theory*, ed. C. Merchant. Trans. Ruth Hottell, 174-97. Repr., Atlantic Highlands, NJ: Humanities Press, 1994.

– (1999). What could an ecofeminist society be? *Ethics and the Environment* 4 (2): 179-84.

DeVault, Marjorie L. (1991). *Feeding the Family: The Social Organization of Caring as Gendered Work*. Chicago: University of Chicago Press.

Diamond, Irene, and Gloria Orenstein, eds. (1990). *Reweaving the World: The Emergence of Ecofeminism*. San Francisco: Sierra Club Books.

Di Chiro, Giovanna (1992). Defining environmental justice: Women's voices and grassroots politics. *Socialist Review* 22 (4): 93-130.

– (1998). Environmental justice from the grassroots: Reflections on history, gender, and expertise. In *The Struggle for Ecological Democracy*, ed. D. Faber, 104-36. New York: The Guilford Press.

Dickens, Peter (1996). *Reconstructing Nature: Alienation, Emancipation and the Division of Labour*. New York and London; Routledge.

Dietz, Mary (1985). Citizenship with a feminist face: The problem with maternal thinking. *Political Theory* 13 (1): 19-37.

– (1991). Hannah Arendt and feminist politics. In *Feminist Interpretations of Political Theory*, ed. M.L. Shanley and C. Pateman, 232-52. Cambridge: Polity Press.

– (1998). Context is all: Feminism and theories of citizenship. In *Feminist Ethics*, ed. M. Gatens, 301-22. Dartmouth, NH: Ashgate.

Di Leonardo, Micaela (1998). *Exotics at Home: Anthropologies, Others, American Modernity*. Chicago: University of Chicago Press.

Di Matteo, Enzo (2000). Black activist says cops brutalized her. *Now Magazine*, 20-26 July: 27.

Dinnerstein, Dorothy (1976). *The Mermaid and the Minotaur: Sexual Arrangements and Human Malaise*. New York: Harper Collins.

Dobson, Andrew (1995). *Green Political Thought*. 2nd ed. New York: Routledge.

– (1998). *Justice and the Environment: Conceptions of Environmental Sustainability and Theories of Distributive Justice.* Oxford: Oxford University Press.

– (2003). *Citizenship and the Environment.* Oxford: Oxford University Press.

Donner, Wendy (1997). Self and community in environmental ethics. In *Ecofeminism: Women, Culture, Nature,* ed. K.J. Warren, 375-89. Bloomington: Indiana University Press.

Doyal, Lesley (1995). *What Makes Women Sick: Gender and the Political Economy of Health.* London: Macmillan Press.

Dryzek, John S. (1990). *Discursive Democracy: Politics, Policy, and Political Science.* New York: Blackwell.

– (1995). Green reason: Communicative ethics for the environment. In *Postmodern Environmental Ethics,* ed. M. Oelschlaeger, 101-18. Albany, NY: SUNY Press.

– (1997). *The Politics of the Earth: Environmental Discourses.* Oxford: Oxford University Press.

– (1999). Global ecological democracy. In *Global Ethics and Environment,* ed. N. Low, 264-82. New York: Routledge.

Duffy, Ann, Nancy Mandel, and Noreen Pupo (1989). *Few Choices: Women, Work and Family.* Toronto: Garamond Press.

Duffy, Ann, and Noreen Pupo (1992). *Part-Time Paradox: Connecting Gender, Work and Family.* Toronto: McClelland and Stewart.

Easlea, Brian (1983). *Fathering the Unthinkable: Masculinity, Scientists, and the Nuclear Arms Race.* London: Pluto Press.

Echols, Alice (1989). *Daring to Be Bad: Radical Feminism in America, 1967-1975.* Minneapolis: University of Minnesota Press.

Eckersley, Robyn (1992). *Environmentalism and Political Theory: Toward an Ecocentric Approach.* Albany, NY: SUNY Press.

Ehrenreich, Barbara, and Arlie Russell Hochschild, eds. (2002). *Global Woman: Nannies, Maids, and Sex Workers in the Global Economy.* London: Granta.

Eichler, Margrit (1988). *Families in Canada Today: Recent Changes and their Policy Consequences.* 2nd ed. Toronto: Gage.

– (1995). Designing eco-city in North America. In *Change of Plans: Towards a Non-sexist Sustainable City,* ed. M. Eichler, 1-23. Toronto: Garamond Press.

– (1997). *Family Shifts: Families, Policies and Gender Equality.* Toronto: Oxford University Press.

Eisler, Rianne (1988). *The Chalice and the Blade: Our History, Our Future.* New York: Harper and Row.

Elshtain, Jean Bethke (1981). *Public Man, Private Woman: Women in Social and Political Thought.* Princeton, NJ: Princeton University Press.

Elson, Diane, ed. (1995). *Male Bias in the Development Process.* 2nd ed. Manchester: Manchester University Press.

Environment Canada (Ontario Region) (2000). What is environmental citizenship? *Great Art for Great Lakes: A "Virtual" Classroom Resource for Environmental Information,* http://www.on.ec.gc.ca/community/classroom/c3-understanding-e.html (accessed 28 January 2006).

Epstein, Barbara (1993). Ecofeminism and grass-roots environmentalism in the United States. In *Toxic Struggles: The Theory and Practice of Environmental Justice,* ed. R. Hofrichter, 144-52. Philadelphia: New Society Publishers.

Errington, Jane (1988). Pioneers and suffragists. In *Changing Patterns: Women in Canada,* ed. S. Burt, L. Code, and L. Dorney, 51-79. Toronto: McClelland and Stewart.

Estavo, Gustavo, and Madhu Suri Prakash (1998). *Grassroots Post-modernism: Remaking the Soil of Cultures.* London: Zed Books.

Etzioni, Amitai (1995). *The Spirit of Community: Rights, Responsibilities and the Communitarian Agenda.* London: Fontana Press.

Evans, Patricia M., and Gerda R. Wekerle (1997). The shifting terrain of women's welfare: Theory, discourse, and activism. In *Women and the Canadian Welfare State,* ed. P. Evans and G. Wekerle, 3-27. Toronto: University of Toronto.

Faber, Daniel, and James O'Conner (1989) The struggle for nature: Replies. *Capitalism, Nature, Socialism* 1 (3): 174-78.

Falk, R. (1997). Resisting "globalization from above" through "globalization from below." *New Political Economy* 2: 17-24.

Faulks, Keith (1999). *Citizenship in Modern Britain.* Edinburgh: Edinburgh University Press.

Featherstone, Liza, and Doug Henwood (2001). Clothes encounters: Activists and economists clash over sweatshops. *Lingua Franca* March: 27-33.

Felesky, Leigh (2001). Will women save the earth? *Herizons* (Spring): 14-18.

Ferguson, Ann (2000). Resisting the veil of privilege: Building bridge identities as an ethico-politics of global feminisms. In *Decentering the Center*, ed. U. Narayan and S. Harding, 189-207. Bloomington: Indiana University Press.

Finch, Janet (1984). Community care: Developing non-sexist alternatives. *Critical Social Policy* 9: 6-18.

– (1990). The politics of community care in Britain. In *Gender and Caring*, ed. C. Ungerson, 34-58. New York: Harvester Wheatsheaf.

Finch, Janet, and Dulcie Groves (1983). Community care and the invisible welfare state. *Radical Community Medicine* (Summer): 15-22.

Folbre, Nancy (1993). *Who Pays for the Kids? Gender and the Structures of Constraint.* New York: Routledge.

Foucault, Michel (1977). The political function of the intellectual. *Radical Philosophy* 17: 12-14.

– (1984). *The Foucault Reader*, ed. Paul Rabinow. New York: Pantheon Books.

– (1989). The ethics of the concern of the self as a practice of freedom. In *Foucault Live: Interviews 1961-1984*, ed. S. Lotringer. Trans. L. Hockroth and J. Johnston, 432-49. New York: Semiotext(e).

Fox, Bonnie (1983). *Hidden in the Household: Women's Domestic Labour under Capitalism.* Toronto: The Women's Press.

Frank, Dana (1985). Housewives, socialists, and the politics of food: The 1917 New York cost of living protests. *Feminist Studies* 11 (2): 255-85.

Fraser, Nancy (1997). *Justice Interruptus: Critical Reflections on the "Postsocialist" Condition.* New York: Routledge.

Fraser, Nancy, and Linda Gordon (1994). A genealogy of dependency: Tracing a keyword of the US welfare state. *Signs* 19 (2): 309-36.

– (1998). Contract versus charity: Why is there no social citizenship in the United States? In *The Citizenship Debates: A Reader*, ed. G. Shafir, 113-27. Minneapolis: University of Minnesota Press.

Fraser, Nancy, and Linda Nicholson (1990). Social criticism without philosophy: An encounter between feminism and postmodernism. In *Feminism/Postmodernism*, ed. L.J. Nicholson, 19-38. New York: Routledge.

Frazer, Elizabeth (1999). *The Problems of Communitarian Politics: Unity and Conflict.* Oxford: Oxford University Press.

Frazer, Elizabeth, and Nicola Lacey (1993). *The Politics of Community: A Feminist Critique of the Liberal-Communitarian Debate.* London: Harvester Wheatsheaf.

Frederickson, Judith A. (1995). *As Time Goes By ... Time Use of Canadians.* General social survey. Statistics Canada: Housing, Family, and Social Statistics Division. Ottawa: Minister of Industry.

Friedman, Marilyn (1995). Beyond caring: The de-moralization of gender. In *Justice and Care: Essential Readings in Feminist Ethics*, ed. V. Held, 61-77. Boulder, CO: Westview Press.

Frye, Marilyn (1983). *The Politics of Reality: Essays in Feminist Theory.* Freedom, CA: The Crossing Press.

Fuss, Diana (1989). *Essentially Speaking: Feminism, Nature and Difference.* New York: Routledge.

Gaard, Greta (1998). *Ecological Politics: Ecofeminists and the Greens.* Philadelphia: Temple University Press.

Garland, Anne Witte (1988). *Women Activists: Challenging the Abuse of Power.* New York: The Feminist Press.

Gibson-Graham, J.-K. (1996). *The End of Capitalism (As We Knew It): A Feminist Critique of Political Economy.* Cambridge, MA: Blackwell.

Giddens, Anthony (1994). *Beyond Left and Right: The Future of Radical Politics.* Stanford, CA: Stanford University Press.

Giles, Wenona, and Sedef Arat-Koc, eds. (1994). *Maid in the Market: Women's Paid Domestic Labour.* Halifax: Fernwood Publishing.

Gilligan, Carol (1982). *In a Different Voice: Psychological Theory and Women's Development.* Cambridge, MA: Harvard University Press.

Gimbutas, Marija (1974). *Gods and Goddesses of Old Europe.* London: Thames and Hudson.

Glaser, Barry, and Anselm Strauss (1968). *The Discovery of Grounded Theory: Strategies for Qualitative Research.* London: Weidenfeld and Nicholson.

Gluck, Sherna Berger (1997). Whose feminism, whose history? Reflections on excavating the history of (the) US women's movement(s). In *Community Activism and Feminist Politics*, ed. N. Naples, 31-56. New York: Routledge.

Goleman, Daniel (1995). *Emotional Intelligence: Why It Can Matter More than IQ.* London: Bloomsbury.

Gorz, André (1993). Political ecology: Expertocracy versus self-limitation. *New Left Review* 202: 55-67.

Gosine, Andil (2003). Myths of diversity. *Alternatives* 29 (1): 12-17.

Gottlieb, Robert (1993). Reconstructing environmentalism: Complex movements, diverse roots. *Environmental History Review* 17 (4): 1-19.

Government of Canada (1990). *Canada's Green Plan: Canada's Green Plan for a Healthy Environment.* Ottawa: Minister of Supply and Services.

Gramsci, Antonio (1971). *Selections from the Prison Notebooks.* New York: International Publishers.

Grant, Judith (1993). *Fundamental Feminism.* New York: Routledge.

Greenpeace (1997). Hamilton's vinyl fire site amongst "most toxic in Canada." Press release, 25 August 1997.

Grimshaw, Jean (1986). *Philosophy and Feminist Thinking.* Minneapolis: University of Minnesota Press.

Gruen, Lori (1997). Revaluing nature. In *Ecofeminism: Women, Culture, Nature,* ed. K.J. Warren, 356-74. Bloomington: Indiana University Press.

Guha, Ramachandra (1990). *The Unquiet Woods: Ecological Change and Peasant Resistance in the Himalayas.* Los Angeles: University of California Press.

– (1994). Radical environmentalism: A third world critique. In *Ecology,* ed. C. Merchant, 281-89. Atlantic Highlands, NJ: Humanities Press.

Gundersen, A. (1995). *The Environmental Promise of Democratic Deliberation.* Madison, WI: University of Wisconsin Press.

Hall, Michael, Larry McKeown, and Karen Roberts (2001). *Caring Canadians, Involved Canadians. Highlights from the 2000 National Survey of Giving, Volunteering, and Participating.* Ottawa: Minister responsible for Statistics Canada, Ministry of Industry.

Hamilton, Cynthia (1990). Women, home and community: The struggle in an urban environment. In *Reweaving the World,* ed. I. Diamond and G. Feman Orenstein, 215-22. San Francisco: Sierra Club Books.

Haraway, Donna (1991a). A manifesto for cyborgs: Science, technology and socialist feminism in the 1980s. In *Feminism/Postmodernism,* ed. L.J. Nicholson, 190-233. New York: Routledge.

– (1991b). *Simians, Cyborgs, and Women: The Reinvention of Nature.* New York: Routledge, Chapman and Hall.

– (1996). *Modest-Witness, Second-Millennium: Femaleman Meets Oncomouse: Feminism and Technoscience.* New York: Routledge.

Harcourt, Wendy, ed. (1994). *Feminist Perspectives on Sustainable Development.* London: Zed Books.

Hardin, Garrett (1974). Living on lifeboat earth. *Bioscience* 24: 10.

Harding, Sandra, ed. (1987). *Feminism and Methodology: Social Science Issues.* Bloomington: Indiana University Press.

Hartmann, Heidi (1981). The unhappy marriage of Marxism and feminism: Towards a more progressive union. In *The Unhappy Marriage of Marxism and Feminism: A Debate on Class and Patriarchy,* ed. L. Sargent, 1-41. London: Pluto Press.

Harvey, David (1999). Considerations on the environment of justice. In *Global Ethics and the Environment,* ed. N. Low, 109-30. New York: Routledge.

Hawthorne, Susan (2002). *Wild Politics: Feminism, Globalisation and Bio/Diversity.* North Melbourne: Spinifex Press.

Hayden, Dolores (1981). *The Grand Domestic Revolution.* Cambridge, MA: MIT Press.

– (1984). *Redesigning the American Dream: The Future of Housing, Work and Family Life.* New York: W.W. Norton.

Hayward, Tim (1994). *Ecological Thought: An Introduction.* Cambridge: Polity Press.

Hekman, Susan (1999). Identity crises: Identity, identity politics and beyond. In *Feminism, Identity and Difference,* ed. S. Hekman, 3-26. Portland, OR: Frank Cass Publishers.

Held, David (1987). *Models of Democracy.* Stanford, CA: Stanford University Press.

Heller, Chaia (1999). *The Ecology of Everyday Life: Rethinking the Desire for Nature.* Montreal: Black Rose Books.

Hennessy, Rosemary (1993). *Materialist Feminism and the Politics of Discourse.* New York: Routledge.

Hernes, Helga (1988). The welfare state citizenship of Scandinavian women. In *Feminism, Identity and Difference,* ed. K. Jones and A. Jonasdottir, 187-213. London: Sage.

Hochschild, Arlie, and Ann Machung (1989). *The Second Shift: Working Parents and the Revolution at Home.* New York: Viking-Penguin Press.

Hofrichter, Richard, ed. (1993). *Toxic Struggles: The Theory and Practice of Environmental Justice.* Philadelphia: New Society Publishers.

Homer-Dixon, Thomas F. (1999). *Environment, Scarcity, and Violence.* Princeton, NJ: Princeton University Press.

Hunter, Lori M., Alison Hatch, and Aaron Johnson (2004). Cross-national gender variation in environmental behaviours. *Social Science Quarterly* 85 (3): 677-94.

Isin, Engin (1997). Who is the new citizen? Toward a genealogy. *Citizenship Studies* 1 (1): 115-32.

–, ed. (2000). *Democracy, Citizenship and the Global City.* New York: Routledge.

Jackson, Cecile (1993). Doing what comes naturally? Women and environment in development. *World Development* 21 (12): 1947-63.

Jaquette, Jane (1994). Women's movements and the challenge of democratic politics in Latin America. *Social Politics* (Fall): 335-40.

Jenson, Jane (1996). Part-time employment and women: A range of strategies. In *Rethinking Restructuring,* ed. I. Bakker, 92-108. Toronto: University of Toronto Press.

Jewitt, Sarah (2000). Unequal knowledges in Jharkhand, India: De-romanticizing women's agroecological expertise. *Development and Change* 31: 961-85.

Jochimsen, Maren, and Ulrike Knobloch (1997). Making the hidden visible: The importance of caring activities and their principles for any economy. *Ecological Economics* 20: 107-12.

Jones, Kathleen B. (1993). *Compassionate Authority: Democracy and the Representation of Women.* London: Routledge.

– (1998). Citizenship in a woman-friendly polity. In *The Citizenship Debates: A Reader,* ed. G. Shafir, 221-47. Minneapolis: University of Minnesota Press.

Kaloff, Linda, Thomas Dietz, and Gregory Guagnano (2002). Race, gender and environmentalism: The atypical values and beliefs of white men. *Race, Gender and Class* 9 (2): 1-19.

Kanter, Rosabeth Moss (1972). *Commitment and Community: Communes and Utopias in Sociological Perspective.* New York: Free Press.

Kaplan, Robert (1994). The coming anarchy. *Atlantic Monthly* 274 (2): 44-76.

Kaplan, Temma (1982). Female consciousness and collective action: The case of Barcelona, 1910-18. *Signs* 7 (3): 545-66.

– (1997). *Crazy for Democracy: Women in Grassroots Movements.* New York: Routledge.

Kapoor, Ilan (1993). Abstraction as violence and the radical democratic alternative: A political-ecological critique of India's development process. PhD diss., Department of Political Science, University of Toronto.

Kealy, Linda, ed. (1979). *Not an Unreasonable Claim: Women and Reform in Canada, 1880s-1920s.* Toronto: Women's Educational Press.

Kelly, Petra (1984). *Fighting for Hope.* London: Chatto and Windus.

Kheel, Marti (1993). From heroic to holistic ethics: The ecofeminist challenge. In *Ecofeminism,* ed. G. Gaard, 243-71. Philadelphia: Temple University Press.

Kilpatrick, K. (1997). Hamilton site called "most toxic in Canada." *Toronto Star,* 26 August: A3.

Kinderman, Daniel (2001). The emancipatory potential of modernity: André Gorz and working-time reduction. Unpublished paper presented at Postmodernism and the Environment: Critical Dialogues Conference, Congress of the Humanities and Social Sciences Federation of Canada. Université Laval, Quebec. 26 May.

King, Roger J.H. (1991). Caring about nature: Feminist ethics and the environment. *Hypatia* 6 (1): 75-89.

King, Ynestra (1988). Coming of age with the Greens. *Z Magazine,* February: 19.

– (1990). Healing the wounds: Feminism, ecology, and the nature/culture dualism. In *Healing the Wounds: The Emergence of Ecofeminism,* ed. I. Diamond and G. Orenstein, 106-21. San Francisco: Sierra Club Books.

Kirby, Sandra, and Kate McKenna (1989). *Experience, Research, Social Change: Methods from the Margins.* Toronto: Garamond Press.

Kittay, Eva Feder (1999). *Love's Labor: Essays on Women, Equality, and Dependency.* New York: Routledge.

Koehn, Daryl (1998). *Rethinking Feminist Ethics: Care, Trust and Empathy.* New York: Routledge.

Koven, Seth, and Sonya Michel, eds. (1993). *Mothers of a New World: Maternalist Politics and the Origins of Welfare States*. New York: Routledge.

Krauss, Celene (1983). The elusive process of citizen activism. *Social Policy* (Fall): 50-55.

– (1993). Women and toxic waste protests: Race, class and gender as resources of resistance. *Qualitative Sociology* 16 (3): 247-62.

– (1997). Challenging power: Toxic waste protests and the politicization of white, working class women. In *Community Activism and Feminist Politics*, ed. N. Naples, 129-50. New York: Routledge.

Lahar, Stephanie (1991). Ecofeminist theory and grassroots politics. *Hypatia* 6 (1): 28-45.

Lake, Marilyn (1993). A revolution in the family: The challenge and contradictions of maternal citizenship in Australia. In *Mothers of a New World*, ed. S. Koven and S. Michel, 378-95. New York: Routledge.

Land, Hilary (1991). Time to care. In *Women's Issues in Social Policy*, ed. M. Maclean and D. Groves, 7-19. New York: Routledge.

Land, Hilary, and Hilary Rose (1985). Compulsory altruism for some or an altruistic society for all? In *In Defense of Welfare*, ed. P. Bean, J. Ferris, and D. Whynes, 74-96. London: Tavistock.

Lasswell, Harold (1936). *Politics: Who Gets What, When, How?* Repr., London: Peter Smith.

Lather, Patti (1991). *Getting Smart: Feminist Research and Pedagogy with/in the Postmodern*. New York: Routledge.

Latouche, Serge (1993). *In the Wake of the Affluent Society*. London: Zed Books.

Li, Huey-Li (1993). A cross-cultural critique of ecofeminism. In *Ecofeminism*, ed. G. Gaard, 272-94. Philadelphia: Temple University Press.

Light, Andrew (2002). Restoring ecological citizenship. In *Democracy and the Claims of Nature: Critical Perspectives for a New Century*, ed. B.A. Minteer and B. Pepperman Taylor, 153-72. Lanham, MD: Rowman and Littlefield.

Lincoln, Y., and E. Guba (1988). *Naturalistic Inquiry*. London: Sage.

Lipietz, Alain (1992). *Towards a New Economic Order: Postfordism, Ecology and Democracy*. Oxford: Oxford University Press.

– (1995). *Green Hopes: The Future of Political Ecology*. Cambridge: Polity Press.

Lister, Ruth (1997). *Citizenship: Feminist Perspectives*. New York: New York University Press.

Littig, Beate (2001). *Feminist Perspectives on Environment and Society*. Harlow, UK: Prentice Hall.

Low, Alaine, and Soraya Tremayne, eds. (2001). *Women as Sacred Custodians of the Earth? Women, Spirituality and the Environment*. New York and Oxford: Berghahn Books.

Low, Nicholas, and Brendan Gleeson (1998). *Justice, Society and Nature: An Exploration of Political Ecology*. New York: Routledge.

Luke, Timothy W. (1997). *Ecocritique: Contesting the Politics of Nature, Economy and Culture*. Minneapolis: University of Minnesota Press.

Luxton, Meg (1980). *More Than a Labour of Love: Three Generations of Women's Work in the Home*. Toronto: The Women's Press.

– (1987). Time for myself: Women's work and the fight for shorter hours. In *Feminism and Political Economy*, ed. H. Jon Maroney and M. Luxton, 167-78. Toronto: Methuen.

McAdams, Claire (1996). Gender, class, and race in environmental activism: Local responses to a multinational corporation's development plans. In *The Gendered New World Order: Militarism, Development, and the Environment*, ed. J. Turpin and L.A. Lorentzen, 51-69. New York: Routledge.

McClure, Kirstie (1992). The issue of foundations: Scientized politics, political science, and feminist critical practice. In *Feminists Theorize the Political*, ed. J. Butler and J. Scott, 341-68. New York: Routledge.

McCracken, Grant (1988). *The Long Interview*. London: Sage.

MacDonald, Helen (1994). Heeding Rachel Carson's call: Reflections of a home-making eco-crusader. *Alternatives* 20 (2): 21-25.

McDowell, Linda (1992). Gender divisions in a post-Fordist era: New contradictions or the same old story? In *Defining Women: Social Institutions and Gender Divisions*, ed. L. McDowell and R. Pringle, 181-92. Cambridge: Polity Press.

– (1999). *Gender, Identity, and Place: Understanding Feminist Geographies*. Minneapolis: University of Minnesota Press.

MacGregor, Sherilyn (1995). Deconstructing the man-made city: Feminist critiques of planning thought and action. In *Change of Plans: Towards a Non-Sexist Sustainable City*, ed. M. Eichler, 25-49. Toronto: Garamond Press.

– (1997). Feeding families in Harris's Ontario: Women, the Tsubouchi Diet, and the politics of restructuring. *Atlantis: A Women's Studies Journal* 21 (2): 93-110.
– (2000). Fiddling while Rome burns? Sustainable communities and the politics of citizen participation. *Women and Environments International* (Summer/Fall): 21-24.
– (2001). A matter of interpretation: On the place of "lived experience" in ecofeminist research. *Women and Environments International* (Fall): 34-35.
– (2004). Reading the Earth Charter: Cosmopolitan environmental citizenship or (light) green politics as usual? *Ethics, Place, and Environment* 7 (1-2): 85-96.
Mack-Canty, Colleen (2004). Third-wave feminism and the need to reweave the nature/culture duality. *NWSA Journal* 16 (3): 154-79.
MacKinnon, Catherine A. (1987). *Feminism Unmodified: Discourses on Life and Law*. Cambridge, MA: Harvard University Press.
McMahon, Martha (1995). *Engendering Motherhood: Identity and Self-Transformation in Women's Lives*. London: The Guilford Press.
– (1997). From the ground up: Ecofeminism and ecological economics. *Ecological Economics* 20: 163-74.
Macnaghten, Phil, and John Urry (1998). *Contested Natures*. London: Sage.
Mansbridge, Jane (1998). Feminism and democratic community. In *Feminist Ethics*, ed. M. Gatens, 339-95. Dartmouth, NH: Ashgate.
Marcuse, Herbert (1966). *Eros and Civilization*. Boston: Beacon Press.
Marshall, T.H. (1950). Citizenship and social class. In *The Citizenship Debates: A Reader*, ed. G. Shafir, 93-111. Reprint, Minneapolis: University of Minnesota Press.
Massey, Doreen (1991). Flexible sexism. *Environment and Planning D: Society and Space* 9: 31-57.
Medjuck, S., M. O'Brien, and C. Tozer (1992). From private responsibility to public policy: Women and the cost of care-giving to elderly kin. *Atlantis: A Women's Studies Journal* 17 (2): 44-58.
Mellor, Mary (1992). *Breaking the Boundaries: Towards a Feminist Green Socialism*. London: Virago Press.
– (1995). Materialist communal politics: Getting from there to here. In *Contemporary Political Studies*, eds. J. Lovenduski and J. Stanyer. Belfast: Political Studies Association.
– (1997). *Feminism and Ecology*. Washington Square, NY: New York University Press.
– (2000). Feminism and environmental ethics: A materialist perspective. *Ethics and the Environment* 5 (1): 107-23.
Melnyk, George (1985). *The Search for Community: From Utopia to Co-Operative Society*. Montreal: Black Rose Books.
Mendus, Susan (1998). Different voices, still lives: Problems in the ethics of care. In *Feminist Ethics*, ed. M. Gatens, 137-47. Dartmouth, NH: Ashgate.
Merchant, Carolyn (1996). *Earthcare: Women and the Environment*. New York: Routledge.
Merriam, Sharan B. (1988). *Case Study Research in Education: A Qualitative Approach*. San Francisco: Jossey-Bass Publishers.
Mies, Maria (1983). Towards a methodology for feminist research. In *Theories of Women's Studies*, ed. G. Bowles and R. Duelli Klein, 117-39. New York: Routledge.
– (1986). *Patriarchy and Accumulation on a World Scale*. London: Zed Books.
Mies, Maria, and Veronika Bennholdt-Thomsen (1999). *The Subsistence Perspective: Beyond the Globalized Economy*. London: Zed Books.
Mies, Maria, and Vandana Shiva (1993). *Ecofeminism*. London: Zed Books.
Miles, Angela (1996). *Integrative Feminisms: Building Global Visions, 1960s-1990s*. New York: Routledge.
Miller, Vernice, Moya Hallstein, and Susan Quass (1996). Feminist politics and environmental justice: Women's community activism in West Harlem, New York. In *Feminist Political Ecology*, ed. D. Rocheleau, B. Thomas-Slayter, and E. Wangari, 62-85. New York: Routledge.
Mills, Patricia Jagentowicz (1991). Feminism and ecology: On the domination of nature. *Hypatia* 6 (1): 162-78.
Mohanty, Chandra Talpade (1991). Cartographies of struggle: Third world women and the politics of feminism. In *Third World Women and the Politics of Feminism*, ed. C.T. Mohanty, A. Russo, and L. Torres, 1-47. Bloomington: Indiana University Press.
Moser, Caroline (1993). Adjustment from below: Low-income women, time, and the triple role in Guayaquil, Equador. In *"Viva": Women and Popular Protest in Latin America*, ed. S. Radcliffe and S. Westwood, 173-96. New York: Routledge.

Mouffe, Chantal (1992a). Democratic citizenship and the political community. In *Dimensions of Radical Democracy: Pluralism, Citizenship, Community,* ed. C. Mouffe, 225-39. London: Verso.

– (1992b). Feminism, citizenship and radical democratic politics. In *Feminists Theorize the Political,* ed. J. Butler and J.W. Scott, 369-84. New York: Routledge.

– (1993). *The Return of the Political.* London: Verso.

Nagarajan, Vijaya Rettakudi (2001). Soil as the Goddess Bhudevi in a Tamil women's ritual: The Kolam in India. In *Women as Sacred Custodians of the Earth?* ed. A. Low and S. Tremayne, 159-74. New York and Oxford: Berghahn Books.

Nalunnakkal, George Mathew (2004). Towards an organic womanism: New contours of ecofeminism in India. *Asia Journal of Theology* 18 (1): 51-68.

Naples, Nancy A. (1991). "Just what needed to be done": The political practice of women community workers in low-income neighborhoods. *Gender and Society* 5 (4): 478-94.

– (1992). Activist mothering: Cross-generational continuity in the community work of women from low-income urban neighborhoods. *Gender and Society* 6 (3): 441-63.

– (1997a). Women's community activism: Exploring the dynamics of politicization and diversity. In *Community Activism and Feminist Politics,* ed. N. Naples, 327-49. New York: Routledge.

– (1997b). Women's community activism and feminist activist research. In *Community Activism and Feminist Politics,* ed. N. Naples, 1-27. New York: Routledge.

– (1998). *Grassroots Warriors: Activist Mothering, Community Work and the War on Poverty.* New York: Routledge.

Narayan, Uma (2000). Essence of culture and a sense of history: A feminist critique of cultural essentialism. In *Decentering the Center,* ed. U. Narayan and S. Harding, 80-100. Bloomington: Indiana University Press.

National Action Committee on the Status of Women (NAC) (1995). A decade of deterioration in the status of women in Canada: A summary report. Toronto, August.

Negrey, Cynthia (1993). *Gender, Time, and Reduced Work.* New York: SUNY Press.

Nelson, Julie (1997). Feminism, ecology and the philosophy of economics. *Ecological Economics* 20: 155-62.

Newby, Howard (1996). Citizenship in a green world: Global commons and human stewardship. In *Citizenship Today: The Contemporary Relevance of T.H. Marshall,* ed. M. Bulmer and A. Rees, 209-21. London: UCC Press.

Newman, Rich (2001). Making environmental politics: Women and Love Canal activism. *Women's Studies Quarterly* 29 (1/2): 65-84.

Noddings, Nel (1984). *Caring: A Feminine Approach to Ethics and Moral Education.* Los Angeles: University of California Press.

Norwood, Vera (1993). *Made from This Earth: American Women and Nature.* Chapel Hill, NC: University of North Carolina Press.

Novac, Sylvia (1995). Seeking shelter: Feminist home truths. In *Change of Plans,* ed. M. Eichler, 51-70. Toronto: Garamond Press.

O'Brien, Mary (1981). *The Politics of Reproduction.* Boston: Routledge and Kegan Paul.

Okin, Susan Moller (1989). *Justice, Gender and the Family.* New York: Basic Books.

Ophuls, William (1996). Unsustainable liberty, sustainable freedom. In *Building Sustainable Societies: A Blueprint for a Post-Industrial World,* ed. D. Pirages, 33-44. New York: M.E. Sharpe.

Orleck, Annelise (1993). "We are that thing called the public": Militant house-wives during the Great Depression. *Feminist Studies* 19 (1): 147-72.

– (1997). Tradition unbound: Radical mothers in international perspective. In *The Politics of Motherhood: Activist Voices from Left to Right,* ed. A. Jetter, A. Orleck, and D. Taylor, 3-20. Hanover, NH: University Press of New England.

Orloff, Ann Shola (1993). Gender and the social rights of citizenship: The comparative analysis of gender relations and welfare states. *American Sociological Review* 58 (June): 303-28.

Paehlke, Robert (1994). Possibilities for and limitations on environmental protection in the changing metropolis. In *The Changing Canadian Metropolis: A Public Policy Perspective,* ed. F. Frisken, 1:106-22. Toronto: Canadian Urban Institute.

Pardo, Mary (1995). Doing it for the kids: Mexican American community activists, border feminists? In *Feminist Organizations: Harvest of the New Women's Movement,* eds. M. Marx Feree and P. Yancey Martin, 356-71. Philadelphia: Temple University Press.

Pateman, Carol (1988). *The Sexual Contract.* Cambridge: Polity Press.

– (1992). Equality, difference, subordination: The politics of motherhood and women's citizenship. In *Beyond Equality and Difference: Citizenship, Feminist Politics and Female Subjectivity*, ed. G. Bock and S. James, 17-31. New York: Routledge.

Pepper, David (1993). *Ecosocialism: From Deep Ecology to Social Justice*. New York: Routledge.

Peterson, Rebecca (1979). Impacts of the conserver society on women. In *Women and the Conserver Society* (special issue). *Conserver Society Notes* 2 (1): 4-8.

Phelan, Shane (1994). *Getting Specific: Postmodern Lesbian Politics*. Minneapolis: University of Minnesota Press.

Phillips, Anne (1991). *Engendering Democracy*. Cambridge: Polity Press.

– (1993). *Democracy and Difference*. University Park, PA: Pennsylvania State University Press.

Pietila, Hilkka (1997). The triangle of the human economy: Household – cultivation – industrial production. An attempt at making visible the human economy in toto. *Ecological Economics* 20: 113-28.

Plant, Judith (1990). Revaluing home: Feminism and bioregionalism. In *Home! A Bioregional Reader*, ed. V. Andruss, C. Plant, J. Plant, and E. Wright, 21-3. Philadelphia: New Society Publishers.

Plumwood, Val (1993). *Feminism and the Mastery of Nature*. New York: Routledge.

– (1995a). Feminism, privacy, and radical democracy. *Anarchist Studies* 3: 97-120.

– (1995b). Has democracy failed ecology? An ecofeminist perspective. *Environmental Politics* 4 (4): 136-69.

– (2002). *Environmental Culture: The Ecological Crisis of Reason*. London: Routledge.

Postiglione, A. (1994). *The Global Village without Regulations: Ethical, Economical, Social, and Legal Motivations for an International Court of the Environment*. Florence: Giunti.

Pulido, Laura (1996). *Environmentalism and Economic Justice: Two Chicano Struggles in the Southwest*. Tucson, AZ: University of Arizona Press.

Putnam, Robert (2000). *Bowling Alone: The Collapse and Revival of American Community*. New York: Simon and Schuster.

Quinby, Lee (1990). Ecofeminism and the politics of resistance. In *Reweaving the World*, ed. I. Diamond and G. Orenstein, 122-27. San Francisco: Sierra Club Books.

– (1994). *Anti-Apocalypse: Exercises in Genealogical Criticism*. Minneapolis: University of Minnesota Press.

– (1997). Genealogical feminism: A politic way of looking. In *Feminism and the New Democracy: Re-Siting the Political*, ed. J. Dean, 146-67. London: Sage.

Rangan, Haripriya (2000). *Of Myths and Movements*. London: Verso.

Ransom, Pamela (1999). Women's environment and development organization. In *Sweeping the Earth: Women Taking Action for a Healthy Planet*, ed. M. Wyman, 131-40. Charlottetown, PEI: Gynergy Books.

RCFTW (Royal Commission on the Future of Toronto's Waterfront) (1992). Regeneration: Toronto's waterfront and the sustainable city: Final Report. Honourable David Crombie, Commissioner. Minister of Supply and Services, Toronto.

Reed, Maureen G. (2000). Taking stands: A feminist perspective on "other" women's activism in forestry communities of northern Vancouver Island. *Gender, Place and Culture* 7 (4): 363-87.

– (2003). *Taking Stands: Gender and the Sustainability of Rural Communities*. Vancouver and Toronto: UBC Press.

Reinharz, Shulamit (1992). *Feminist Methods in Social Research*. Oxford: Oxford University Press.

Rich, Adrienne (1976). *Of Woman Born*. New York: W.W. Norton.

Rifkin, Jeremy (1995). *The End of Work: The Decline of the Global Labour Force and the Dawn of the Post-Market Era*. New York: G.P. Putnam's Sons.

Riley, Denise (1988). *Am I That Name? Feminism and the Category of "Woman" in History*. Minneapolis: University of Minnesota Press.

– (1992). Citizenship and the welfare state. In *Political and Economic Forms of Modernity*, ed. J. Allen; P. Braham, and P. Lewis, 179-210. Cambridge: Polity Press.

Ristock, Janice L., and Pennell, Joan (1996). *Community Research as Empowerment: Feminist Links, Postmodern Interruptions*. Oxford: Oxford University Press.

Roach, Catherine (1991). Loving your mother: On the woman-nature relation. *Hypatia* 6 (1): 46-59.

Robbins, Bruce, ed. (1993). *The Phantom Public Sphere*. Minneapolis: University of Minnesota Press.

Roberts, Wayne, and Susan Brandum (1995). *Get a Life! How to Make a Good Buck, Dance around the Dinosaurs and Save the World While You're at It.* Toronto: Get a Life Publishing House.

Rocheleau, Dianne, Barbara Thomas-Slayter, and Esther Wangari, eds. (1996). *Feminist Political Ecology: Global Issues and Local Experiences.* New York: Routledge.

Romain, Dianne (1992). Care and Confusion. In *Explorations in Feminist Ethics: Theory and Practice,* ed. E. Browning Cole and S. Coultrap-McQuin, 27-37. Bloomington: Indiana University Press.

Roseland, Mark (1998). *Toward Sustainable Communities: Resources for Citizens and Their Governments.* Philadelphia: New Society Publishers.

Rosenberg, Harriet (1995). From trash to treasure: Housewife activists and the environmental justice movement. In *Articulating Hidden Histories: Exploring the Influence of Eric Wolf,* ed. J. Schneider and R. Rapp, 190-204. Berkeley, CA: University of California Press.

Rowbotham, Sheila (1986). Feminism and democracy. In *New Forms of Democracy,* ed. D. Held and C. Pollett, 78-109. London: Sage.

Ruddick, Sara (1980). Maternal thinking. *Feminist Studies* 6: 46-61.

– (1989). *Maternal Thinking: Toward a Politics of Peace.* New York: Beacon Press.

Ruether, Rosemary Radford, ed. (1996). *Women Healing Earth: Third World Women on Ecology, Feminism, and Religion.* Maryknoll, NY: Orbis Books.

Sachs, Carolyn E., ed. (1997). *Women Working in the Environment.* Washington, DC: Taylor and Francis.

Sachs, Wolfgang, ed. (1993). *Global Ecology: A New Arena of Political Conflict.* London: Zed Books.

Sagoff, Mark (1988). *The Economy of the Earth: Philosophy, Law, and the Environment.* Cambridge: Cambridge University Press.

Sale, Kirkpatrick (1985). *Dwellers in the Land: The Bioregional Vision.* San Francisco: Sierra Club Books.

Salleh, Ariel (1994). Nature, woman, labour, capital: Living the deepest contradiction. In *Is Capitalism Sustainable?* ed. M. O'Connor, 106-24. London: the Guilford Press.

– (1996). Social ecology and the man question. *Environmental Politics* 5: 258-73, http://www.cat.org.au/vof/versions/salleh.htm.

– (1997). *Ecofeminism as Politics: Nature, Marx and the Postmodern.* London: Zed Books.

– (2000). The meta-industrial class and why we need it. *Democracy and Nature* 6 (1): 27-36.

Sandilands, Catriona (1993). On "green consumerism": Environmental privatization and "family values." *Canadian Women's Studies/Les cahiers de la femme* 13 (3): 45-47.

– (1997). Is the personal always political? Environmentalism in Arendt's age of the political. In *Organizing Dissent,* ed. W.K. Carroll, 76-93. Toronto: Garamond Press.

– (1999a). *The Good-Natured Feminist: Ecofeminism and the Quest for Democracy.* Minneapolis: University of Minnesota Press.

– (1999b). Raising your hand in the council of all beings: Ecofeminism and citizenship. *Ethics and the Environment* 4 (2): 219-33.

– (2001). From unnatural passions to queer nature. *Alternatives* 27 (3): 30-5.

– (2002). Opinionated nature: Toward a green public culture. In *Democracy and the Claims of Nature: Critical Perspectives for a New Century,* ed. B.A. Minteer and B. Pepperman Taylor, 117-132. Lanham, MD: Rowman and Littlefield.

Savarsy, Wendy (1992). Beyond the difference versus equality policy debate: Postsuffrage feminism, citizenship and the quest for a feminist welfare state. *Signs* 17 (2): 329-63.

Saward, Michael (1993). Green democracy? In *The Politics of Nature: Explorations in Green Political Theory,* ed. A. Dobson and P. Lucardie, 63-80. New York: Routledge.

Scaltsas, Patricia Ward (1992). Do feminist ethics counter feminist aims? In *Explorations in Feminist Ethics,* ed. E. Browning Cole and S. Coultrap-McQuin, 15-26. Bloomington: Indiana University Press.

Schor, Juliet (1997). Utopias of women's time. In *Feminist Utopias in a Postmodern Era,* ed. A. van Lenning, M. Bekker, and I. Vanwesenbeeck, 45-53. Tilberg: Tilberg University Press.

Schultz, Irmgaard (1993). Women and waste. *Capitalism, Nature, Socialism* 4 (2): 51-63.

Scott, Joan (1992). Experience. In *Feminists Theorize the Political,* ed. J. Butler and J. Scott, 22-40. New York: Routledge.

Seager, Joni (1993). *Earth Follies: Coming to Feminist Terms with the Global Environmental Crisis.* New York: Routledge.

– (1996). "Hysterical housewives" and other mad women: Grassroots environmental organizing in the United States. In *Feminist Political Ecology*, ed. D. Rocheleau, B. Thomas-Slayter, and E. Wangari, 271-83. New York: Routledge.

– (2003). Rachel Carson died of breast cancer: The coming age of feminist environmentalism. *Signs: Journal of Women in Culture and Society* 28 (3): 945-72.

Segal, Lynne (1987). *Is the Future Female? Troubled Thoughts on Contemporary Feminism.* London: Virago Press.

Sen, Gita, and Caren Grown (1985). *Development, Crises and Alternative Visions: Third World Women's Perspectives.* New York: Monthly Review Press.

Sevenhuijsen, Selma (1998). *Citizenship and the Ethics of Care: Feminist Considerations on Justice, Morality, and Politics.* New York: Routledge.

Shiva, Vandana (1989). *Staying Alive: Women, Ecology and Development.* London: Zed Books.

– (1993). *Monocultures of the Mind.* London: Zed Books.

–, ed. (1994). *Close to Home: Women Reconnect Ecology, Health and Development Worldwide.* Philadelphia: New Society Publishers.

– (2004). Earth democracy: Creating living economies, living democracies, living cultures. *South Asian Popular Culture* 2(1): 5-18.

Shove, Elizabeth (2003). *Comfort, Cleanliness and Convenience: The Social Organization of Normality.* Oxford: Berg.

Siim, Birthe (1988). Towards a feminist rethinking of the welfare state. In *The Political Interests of Gender*, ed. K. Jones and A. Jonasdottir, 160-86. London: Sage.

Smith, Andy (1997). Ecofeminism through an anticolonial framework. In *Ecofeminism: Women, Culture, Nature*, ed. K.J. Warren, 21-37. Bloomington: Indiana University Press.

Smith, Dorothy (1987). *The Everyday World as Problematic: A Feminist Sociology.* Milton Keynes, UK: Open University Press.

Smith, Mark J. (1998). *Ecologism: Towards Ecological Citizenship.* Milton Keynes, UK: Open University Press.

Snitow, Ann (1989). A gender diary. In *Rocking the Ship of State: Toward a Feminist Peace Politics*, ed. Adrienne Harris and Ynestra King, 35-73. Boulder, CO: Westview Press.

Solnit, Rebecca (2005). The housewife theory of history: Undomestic troubles and unsung heroines. Orion online May/June, http://www.oriononline.org/pages/om/05-3om/Solnit.html (accessed 28 August 2005).

Sontheimer, Sally, ed. (1991). *Women and the Environment: Crisis and Development in the Third World.* London: Earthscan.

Sorkin, Michael, ed. (1992). *Variations on a Theme Park: The New American City and the End of Public Space.* New York: Hill and Wang.

Spain, Daphne (1995). Sustainability, feminist visions and the utopian tradition. *Journal of Planning Literature* 9 (4): 362-69.

– (2000). Black women as city builders: Redemptive places and the legacy of Nannie Helen Burroughs. In *Gendering the City: Women, Boundaries, and Visions of Urban Life*, ed. K.B. Miranne and A.H. Young, 105-18. New York: Rowman and Littlefield.

Spivak, Gayatri Chakravorty (1985). Can the subaltern speak? Speculations on widow sacrifice. *Wedge* 7/8 (Winter-Spring): 120-30.

– (1987). *In Other Worlds: Essays in Cultural Politics.* London: Methuen.

Spretnak, Charlene (1990). Ecofeminism: Our roots and flowering. In *Reweaving the World*, ed. I. Diamond and D. Feman Orenstein, 3-14. San Francisco: Sierra Club Books.

Squires, Judith (1999). *Gender in Political Theory.* Cambridge: Polity Press.

Staeheli, Lynne (1996). Publicity, privacy, and women's political action. *Environment and Planning D: Society and Space* 14 (5): 601-19.

Starhawk (1979). *The Spiral Dance: A Rebirth of the Ancient Religion of the Great Goddess.* New York: Harper and Row.

– (1993). *The Fifth Sacred Thing.* New York: Bantam.

Statistics Canada (1998). 1996 Census: Labour force activity, occupation and industry, place of work, mode of transportation to work, unpaid work. *The Daily*, 17 March, http://www.statcan.ca/Daily/English/980317/d980317.htm.

– (2000). *Women in Canada 2000: A Gender-based Statistical Report.* Ottawa: Ministry of Industry.

Stauber, John C., and Sheldon Rampton (1995). *Toxic Sludge is Good for You: Lies, Damn Lies, and the Public Relations Industry.* Monroe, ME: Common Courage Press.

Steward, Fred. (1991). Citizens of planet Earth. In *Citizenship*, ed. G. Andrews, 65-75. London: Lawrence and Wishart.

Stinson, Jane (2005). Privatization of public services: What does it mean for women? *Women and Environments International* 64/65: 5-8.

Stoecker, Randy (1992). Who takes out the garbage? Social reproduction and social movement research. *Perspectives on Social Problems* 3: 239-64.

Stone-Mediatore, Shari (2000). Chandra Mohanty and the revaluing of "experience." In *Decentering the Center*, ed. U. Narayan and S. Harding, 110-27. Bloomington: Indiana University Press.

Stone, Merlin (1976). *When God Was a Woman*. New York: Harcourt Brace.

Sturgeon, Noël (1997). *Ecofeminist Natures: Race, Gender, Feminist Theory and Political Action*. New York: Routledge.

– (1999). Ecofeminist appropriations and transnational environmentalisms. *Identities* 6 (2-3): 255-79.

– (2001). Privilege, non-violence and security: An American ecofeminist responds to 9/11. *Women and Environments International* (Fall): 7-9.

Taylor, Barbara (1983). *Eve and the New Jerusalem: Socialism and Feminism in the Nineteenth Century*. New York: Pantheon Press.

Taylor, Dorceta E. (1997). Women of color, environmental justice and ecofeminism. In *Ecofeminism: Women, Culture, Nature*, ed. K.J. Warren, 38-81. Bloomington: Indiana University Press.

Taylor, Verta, and Leila J. Rupp (1997). Women's culture and lesbian feminist activism. In *Community Activism and Feminist Politics*, ed. N. Naples, 57-80. New York: Routledge.

Teeple, Gary (1995). *Globalization and the Decline of Social Reform*. Toronto: Garamond Press.

Tindall, D.B., Scott Davies, and Céline Mauboulès (2003). Activism and conservation behaviour in an environmental movement: The contradictory effects of gender. *Society and Natural Resources* 16: 909-32.

Tong, Rosemary Putnam (1998). *Feminist Thought: A More Comprehensive Introduction*. 2nd ed. Boulder, CO: Westview Press.

Torgerson, Douglas (1999). *The Promise of Green Politics: Environmentalism and the Public Sphere*. Durham, NC: Duke University Press.

Tronto, Joan C. (1993). *Moral Boundaries: A Political Argument for an Ethic of Care*. New York: Routledge.

Turner, Bryan S. (1992). Contemporary problems in the theory of citizenship. In *Citizenship and Social Theory*, ed. B.S. Turner, 1-18. London: Sage.

– (1994). Post-modern culture/modern citizens. In *The Condition of Citizenship*, ed. B. van Steenbergen, 153-68. London: Sage.

Ungerson, Claire, ed. (1990). *Gender and Caring: Work and Welfare in Britain and Scandinavia*. New York: Harvester Wheatsheaf.

United Nations (1992). *Agenda 21*, http://www.un.org/esa/sustdev/documents/agenda21/english/agenda21toc.htm (accessed 28 January 2006).

Urry, John (1998). Globalization and citizenship. Paper presented to World Congress of Sociology, Montreal, July, http://www.comp.lancs.ac.uk/sociology/soc009ju.html.

– (2000). Global flows and global citizenship. In *Democracy, Citizenship, and the Global City*, ed. E. Isin, 62-78. New York: Routledge.

Van Gunsteren, Herman (1998). *A Theory of Citizenship: Organizing Plurality in Contemporary Democracies*. Boulder, CO: Westview Press.

Van Steenbergen, Bart (1994). Towards a global ecological citizen. In *The Condition of Citizenship*, ed. B. van Steenbergen, 141-52. London: Sage.

Voet, Rian (1998). *Feminism and Citizenship*. London: Sage.

Wainwright, Hilary (1994). *Arguments for a New Left: Answering the Free Market Right*. Oxford: Blackwell.

Walker, Alice (1983). *In Search of Our Mother's Gardens*. New York: Harcourt Brace Jovanovich.

Walkom, Thomas (2000). Laying waste. *Toronto Star*, 26 August: K1, K3.

Walzer, Michael (1983). *Spheres of Justice*. Oxford: Basil Blackwell.

Wapner, Paul (1996). *Environmentalism and World Civic Politics*. Albany, NY: SUNY Press.

Waring, Marilyn (1988). *If Women Counted: A New Feminist Economics*. New York: HarperCollins.

Warren, Karen J. (1990). The power and promise of ecological feminism. *Environmental Ethics* 12 (2): 125-46.

– (1999). Care-sensitive ethics and situated universalism. In *Global Environmental Ethics*, ed. N. Low, 131-45. New York: Routledge.

– (2000). *Ecofeminist Philosophy: A Western Perspective on What It Is and Why It Matters*. Lanham, MD: Rowman and Littlefield.

Wekerle, Gerda, and Linda Peake (1996). New social movements and women's urban activism. In *City Lives and City Forms: Critical Research Canadian Urbanism*, ed. J. Caulfield and L. Peake, 263-81. Toronto: University of Toronto Press.

Wekerle, Gerda, Rebecca Peterson, and David Morely (1980). *New Space for Women*. Boulder, CO: Westview Press.

Weldon, Fay (1971). *Down among the Women*. London: Heinemann.

– (1987). *The Hearts and Lives of Men*. London: Heinemann.

Werbner, Pnina (1999). Political motherhood and the feminization of citizenship: Women's activism and the transformation of the public sphere. In *Women, Citizenship, and Difference: Postcolonial Encounters*, ed. P. Werbner and N. Yuval-Davis, 221-45. London: Zed Books.

Williams, Fiona (1989). *Social Policy: A Critical Introduction – Issues of Race, Gender, and Class*. Cambridge: Polity Press.

Wine, Jerry Dawn, and Janice Ristock, eds. (1991). *Women and Social Change: Feminist Activism in Canada*. Toronto: James Lorimer.

Wine, Shelly (1997). Fury for the Sound: The women at Clayoquot. Documentary film produced by TellTale Productions, British Columbia, Canada.

Wittig, Monique (1992). *The Straight Mind and Other Essays*. Boston: Beacon Press.

Wolf, Naomi (2001). *Misconceptions: Truth, Lies, and the Unexpected Journey to Motherhood*. New York: Doubleday.

Woolf, Virginia (1938). *Three Guineas*. New York: Harcourt.

World Commission on Environment and Development (1987). *Our Common Future*. Oxford: Oxford University Press.

Worster, Donald (1994). *Nature's Economy: A History of Ecological Ideas*. Cambridge: Cambridge University Press.

– (1995). The shaky ground of sustainability. In *Deep Ecology for the 21st Century: Readings on the Philosophy and Practice of the New Environmentalism*, ed. G. Sessions, 417-27. London: Shambhala.

Wyman, Miriam (1999). Introduction. In *Sweeping the Earth: Women Taking Action for a Healthy Planet*, ed. M. Wyman, 13-25. Charlottetown, PE: Gynergy Books.

Yearly, Steven (1996). *Sociology, Environmentalism and Globalization: Reinventing the Globe*. London: Sage.

Yeatman, Anna (1993). Voice and representation in the politics of difference. In *Feminism and the Politics of Difference*, ed. S. Gunew and A. Yeatman. London: Allen and Unwin.

Young, Iris Marion (1990). *Justice and the Politics of Difference*. Princeton, NJ: Princeton University Press.

Yuval-Davis, Nira (1997). Women, citizenship and difference. *Feminist Review* 57 (Autumn): 4-27.

– (2000). Citizenship, territoriality and the gendered construction of difference. In *Democracy, Citizenship and the Global City*, ed. E. Isin, 171-88. New York: Routledge.

Zeff, Robin Lee, Marsha Love, and Karen Stults (1989). *Empowering Ourselves: Women and Toxic Organizing*. Arlington, VA: Citizens Clearinghouse for Hazardous Waste, Inc.

Zelezny, Lynnette, Poh-Pheng Chua, and Christina Aldrich (2000). Elaborating on gender differences in environmentalism. *Journal of Social Issues* 56: 443-57.

Index

activism: as community service, 182-84; conventional meanings of, 182-84; effects of caring responsibilities on, 161-68, 208, 260n14; gendered participation in, 5, 7, 46, 117-18, 207-10, 212-13; impact of social condition/location on, 185-90; lack of financial support for, 185-86; quality-of-life issues, 15, 16, 22-24, 44-49, 182, 223, 250n5; as a rewarding activity, 175-79. *See also* activist women; grassroots activism

activist women, 46, 64, 125-26, 133; attitudes to, 182, 187-90, 195; burnout, 167-70; difficulties in saying no, 157-58; ecofeminist representation of, 3-5, 40-44, 124-25, 129-31, 148; empowerment and, 72, 136-37, 178-79; family issues, 161-67, 171; housewife label and, 188-90; marginalized women, 137, 186-88, 193, 195, 257n20; public/private sphere boundaries, 95, 136, 158-61, 220, 260n12; scientific expertise and, 193-96; time issues, 155-58, 209-10; white middle-class, 127-28, 185, 186, 195. *See also* housewife activists; interviewees

African American activism, 36, 193

Agarwal, Bina, 40, 126

Alcoff, Linda, 19, 49-50, 252n17

Aman, Jamila, 140, 151, 153-54, 198, 205, 208

Anthony, Susan, 177, 201, 211

Arendt, Hannah, 75-76, 134, 229, 262n6

Aristotle, 75, 255n23

Austin, Burke, 160, 186, 187, 192, 194

barefoot epistemology, 4, 43, 59, 64

Barry, John, 78, 88-90, 95-96, 103, 256n8-n9, 256n15

Beck, Ulrich, 92, 114, 173, 262n11

Bennholdt-Thomson, Veronika, 39, 257n7

Biehl, Janet, 73, 78, 87

Bookchin, Murray, 86-87, 89, 98, 102-3

Bowden, Peta, 61, 63-64, 117

Browne, Murphy, 141, 144, 153-54, 188, 205, 208, 262n16, 263n21

Brú-Bistuer, Josepa, 259n4

Buck, Karen, 148-49, 185, 196

Canada's Green Plan, 108

CANE. *See* Community Action North End (CANE)

care, feminized ethic of, 61-63

care, politicized ethic of, 76-78, 234

caring, 55, 57; clash with activist activities, 161-68, 208; in ecofeminist discourse, 6-7, 8, 19, 57-70, 117-18, 130, 148, 235, 253n2, 254n12 (*see also* maternalism); eldercare, 260n16; as exploitative labour, 61-63, 67-70, 163, 212; in green discourse, 95-96; negative implications of feminized care, 7, 58, 62-63, 67-70, 155-70, 216 (*see also* gendered division of labour); as a political concept, 76-79, 220-21. *See also* child caring; responsibility

Carlassare, Elisabeth, 55, 252n18

Carson, Rachel, 48

Chaudhuri, Nita, 153-54

child caring, 260n17; for children with environmental illnesses, 47-48, 66, 252n15; effects of activism on, 156, 161-64, 260n14; as impetus for activism, 66, 148-51; men and, 233-34. *See also* responsibility; shared parenting

Chipko movement, 43, 126-27, 252n12-n13, 258n2

Chodorow, Nancy, 26-27, 253n2

Christoff, Peter, 88, 90-91, 106

citizenship, 5-6, 12, 75-76, 90, 219-20, 259n20, 262n16; constraints of gendered division of labour, 100-5, 109-10, 117-18; in ecofeminist discourse, 5-6, 7, 31-32, 73-77, 81, 97, 118; feminism and, 5-6,

22-29, 31, 81, 95, 97-115, 200, 250n4, 250n7, 251n11; first-wave feminism and, 23, 25, 31, 250n4, 250n7, 251n11; "free time" and, 101, 103, 155-56, 224, 228-32; global, 91, 92-96, 225-28; Greek polis, 87, 101, 255n23; in green political discourse, 83-96, 97; local communities, 86-88; moral duty/responsibility, 105-12, 117, 197-200; nation-states, 88-92; as performative activity (Arendt), 72, 113; performative vs instrumental, 223-25; sites/spaces for practice of, 78, 115-16, 228, 256n6; women's access to, 23, 185-90. *See also* democratic politics; ecological citizenship; feminist ecological citizenship; responsibility

civic duty, 85, 89-90. *See also* citizenship

Clayoquot Sound, 124, 125, 260n14

Code, Lorraine, 62, 113-14, 129, 133-34

Collins, Patricia Hill, 36

common good, 98, 106

communal living, 171, 230, 256n16, 263n3

Community Action North End (CANE), 145

community care, 12-13, 68, 69, 135, 152

community discourse: eco-communalism, 86-88; feminist criticisms of, 97-100, 106-7, 115

community othermothers, 36

conservation activism, 23-24

cosmopolitanism, 86, 91, 92-96, 99, 111, 112-15, 116, 225-28, 256n12

cultural feminism, 24-25, 26-29, 31, 49. *See also* feminism

cultural practices, 151-52

Cuomo, Chris, 65

Curtin, Deane, 30, 55, 77, 78, 88, 95, 99, 255n26, 256n15

Darier, Éric, 108-9

Dean, Hartley, 95

d'Eaubonne, Françoise, 20

democratic politics, 84-85, 224-25, 255n24; cosmopolitanism, 86, 91, 92-96, 99, 111, 112-15, 116, 225-28, 256n12; eco-communalism, 86-88, 97-100, 106-7, 115; ecological stewardship, 86, 88-92, 96, 115-16, 256n14; feminism and, 73-74, 81-84, 96. *See also* citizenship; radical democracy

developing countries, 127-28; ecofeminist discourse and, 40-44; re/sisters, 4, 40, 43-44, 53

Di Chiro, Giovanna, 46, 137

Dietz, Mary, 72, 74, 75, 77, 78

Dobson, Andrew, 86, 94-95, 103, 111, 116, 249n2, 256n13, 256n15

domestic work. *See* household duties

domestic workers, 69; hiring by activists, 173-74, 244, 261n25

duties discourse. *See* privatization; responsibility

earthcare, 27, 60, 83, 136. *See also* activism; green practices

eco-communalism, 86-88, 97-100, 106-7, 115

ecofeminism, 34-35; examples of practice, 30-31; experiential knowledge vs academic, 38-40. *See also* ecofeminist discourse

ecofeminist discourse, 3, 19, 34, 60; activist-academic relationships, 131-34, 215; caring concept in, 6-7, 8, 19, 57-70, 117-18, 130, 148, 235, 253n2, 254n12 (*see also* maternalism); citizenship, 5-6, 7, 31-32, 73-77, 81, 97, 118; grassroots activism in, 38-49; green political theorists and, 82-84, 95, 96; history of, 21-32; representation of activist women, 3-5, 40-44, 53-54, 124-25, 129-31, 148. *See also* experiential knowledge; maternalism

ecological citizenship: cosmopolitanism, 86, 91, 92-96, 99, 111, 112-15, 116, 225-28, 256n12; eco-communalism, 86-88, 97-100, 106-7, 115; ecological stewardship, 86, 88-92, 96, 115-16, 256n14; responsibility and, 105-12, 201-7, 216, 219, 222, 249n2, 255n1. *See also* feminist ecological citizenship

ecological degradation, 41-44, 255n5

ecological footprint, 231, 256n12, 257n19

ecological stewardship, 86, 88-92, 96, 115-16, 256n14

ecomaternalism. *See* maternalism

Eichler, Margrit, 246

EJM. *See* environmental justice movement

empowerment, 72, 136-37, 178-79. *See also* politicization

Environment Canada, 108

environmental activism. *See* activism

environmental citizenship. *See* ecological citizenship

environmental governmentality. *See* environmentality

environmental justice movement, 15, 44-49, 252n14, 259n15

environmental movements, 24, 256n11; ecofeminist discourse and, 82-84; as white middle-class movements, 45-46, 252n14. *See also* activism

environmental risks: distribution of, 15, 114-15

environmental sustainability. *See* sustainability

environmentality, 90, 108-9, 150-51

epistemology. *See* ways of knowing

essentialism, 4, 7-9, 19, 54-55, 252n18; strategic essentialism, 4, 34, 52, 112
ethic of care, 27-28, 220-21, 255n25-n26; as counter-productive discourse, 61-65. *See also* caring
Etzioni, Amitai, 107
experiential knowledge, 21, 52-53; vs academic, 38-40; interpretation of, 129-31, 147, 180-81, 261n1; privileging of, 39, 53, 78, 180-81, 193-94, 217; scientific knowledge and, 193-96; strategic essentialism and, 52-53

female essentialism. *See* essentialism
feminine principle, 6, 43-44, 58, 59, 64-65, 78-79, 126, 217
feminism, 8; citizenship and, 5-6, 22-29, 31, 81, 95, 97-115, 200, 250n4, 250n7, 251n11; community discourse and, 97-100, 106-7, 115; concept of "woman," 35; first wave, 22-24, 25, 31, 250n4, 250n7, 251n11; role of consciousness-raising, 71, 72, 79; second wave, 19, 24-29, 31, 33, 255n3; third wave (see ecofeminism); valorization of grassroots activism, 3-5, 35-37, 38-39. *See also* ecofeminism
feminist ecological citizenship, 3, 6, 79, 217-21, 236-37, 249n2; balancing goals, 221-23; inclusivity, 225-28; non-territorial, 116, 225-26; performative politics, 223-25; redistribution of caring, 228-36
feminist environmentalism, 249n2, 250n1
Foucauldian analysis, 108-9, 150, 198, 225
Friedman, Marilyn, 62-63

Gaard, Greta, 21, 127
Gallagher, Ann, 145-46, 147, 187, 188, 190, 197-98, 213
Galvez, Alejandra, 141, 151, 200, 206, 208, 211, 213
Garland, Anne Witte, 136-37
gender norms, 62-63; housewife activist label, 188-90; resistance to, 70-71, 79. *See also* gendered division of labour
gendered division of labour, 10, 67-70, 79, 100, 135, 219, 253n2, 260n22, 263n5; citizenship and, 100-5, 109-10, 117-18; green practices, 103, 105, 201; necessary labour, 70, 103, 109-10, 117, 135-36, 142-43; participation in activism, 5, 7, 46, 117-18, 207-10, 212-13; redistribution of, 104, 228-36; views of interviewees on, 212-15, 232-33. *See also* men
Gibbens, Li-Lien, 152, 153-54, 185, 206, 230
Gibbons, Vasta, 156, 162, 163, 193, 205, 213, 227, 263n21

Gibbs, Lois, 46, 47, 71, 189, 254n19
Gilligan, Carol, 26-27, 28, 30, 251n16, 253n4
global civil society, 9, 86, 92, 114-16
globalism. *See* cosmopolitanism
Goldman, Marcie, 149, 183, 186, 197, 211
governmentality: environmentality, 90, 108-9, 150-51
grassroots: definition of, 37, 251n7
grassroots activism: as authentic experience, 38-40, 64; citizenship and, 38, 227-28; ecofeminist discourse and, 38-49; negative responses to, 37-38, 182; quality-of-life activism, 44-49; valorization of, 3-5, 35-37, 38-39; women in developing countries and, 42-44. *See also* activism; interviewees
Greek polis, 87, 101, 255n23
Green, Joanne, 143, 199
green political theorists, 9-10; authoritarianism and, 78, 86, 106; citizenship, 83-96, 97; ethics and, 105-7; feminist discourse and, 82-84, 95, 96; treatment of eco-feminism by, 82
green practices, 67, 225, 257n24, 263n21-n22; gendered division of labour, 103, 105, 201; greening of household duties, 109-10, 117, 138-39, 173, 201-7, 222-23; intensification of labour and, 100-1, 202-3; interviewees, 138-39, 201-7, 222-23
Greenbelt movement, 43, 66
Greenham Common, 29
Grey, Josephine, 143, 152, 185, 195, 201, 208
Griffin, Susan, 26
Grimshaw, Jean, 129, 130
Guha, Ramachandra, 126

Hamilton, Alice, 250n9
Hamilton (ON), 145-46, 186, 187
Haraway, Donna, 160-61
Harris, Mike, 11, 141-42, 144, 163, 251n6, 259n19, 259n23
Hausfrauisierung. See housewifization
Hooker Chemical Company. *See* Love Canal
household duties, 263n3-n4; domestic workers, 69, 173-74, 244, 261n25; gendered division of labour, 103, 105, 201; greening of, 109-10, 117, 138-39, 173, 201-7, 222-23; organization of, 171-75. *See also* caring; green practices; necessary labour
housewife activists: difficulties experienced by, 66, 158-61; as a label, 188-90; relationship between activism and motherhood, 66, 148-54. *See also* interviewees

housewifization, 47, 127, 254n16, 258n3
Hypatia: Journal of Feminist Philosophy, 30-31
"hysterical housewives" label, 189-90

identity politics, 33-34, 35, 49-50, 219. *See also* strategic essentialism
India, 126-27. *See also* Chipko movement
industrial/urban environmental issues, 24, 45, 250n6, 250n9, 251n14
interviewees, 118-19, 123-24, 128, 137-38, 140-41, 147, 215-16, 236; activist concept and, 181-85; as activist/theorizers, 181; community activism, 143-44, 145-47; frustration with government, 191-93; green practices, 138-39, 201-7, 222-23; household duties, 171-75; motivation, 148-54, 197, 208-10; naming/anonymity of, 139-40, 245-46; selection, 240-42; self-neglect, 155-58, 167-70; social and cultural situations, 185-88, 240-42, 262n5; tensions between activism and private caring, 147, 154-67; views on caring and sustainability, 210-12; views on gendered division of caring, 212-15, 232-33; views on motherhood/citizenship, 197-201, 262n15; views on rewards of activism, 175-79

Jackson, Cecile, 125-26
Jones, Kathleen B., 77, 78
Jones, Laura, 162, 186, 200-1, 203, 233, 263n21

Kaplan, Temma, 38
Kennedy, Jackie, 150, 155, 203, 205, 233, 263n21
knowledge. *See* ways of knowing
Krauss, Celene, 137

Lahar, Stephanie, 30-31
Lara, Ruth, 141, 151, 153-54, 206, 212
Latina activism, 36-37
leisure time, 101, 103, 104, 155-56, 209-10
libertarian municipalism, 86-87
LIFT. *See* Low Income Families Together (LIFT)
Lipietz, Alain, 104
Lister, Ruth, 99-100
lived experience. *See* experiential knowledge
logic of domination, 34
Love Canal, 46-47, 183, 254n19, 262n9
Low Income Families Together (LIFT), 152

Maathai, Wangari, 67
Madres de la Plaza del Mayo, 36, 254n20
Marcelle, Karen, 143, 200
marginalized women. *See* non-elite women
Marshall, T.H., 110
Marx, Karl, 102

masculinism, 101-5, 102, 235-37
material feminists, 24
maternal thinking, 27, 29, 44, 62, 74, 77-78
maternalism, 4, 5, 6, 19-22, 25, 29-30, 46, 47-49, 51, 60, 148; dangers of, 6, 7, 8-9, 30, 52-56, 71-73, 74, 77, 78-80, 83, 217, 220, 253n10; historical antecedents, 8, 22-24, 51
Melbourne, Helen, 153, 187, 203, 209, 259n16
Mellor, Mary, 4, 28-29, 83, 98, 99, 257n7
men, 96; caring behaviours, 59, 125, 263n6; participation in activism, 207-10, 212-13, 257n1, 260n20; participation in caring labour, 103, 232-36, 254n11, 263n6. *See also* gendered division of labour
Merchant, Carolyn, 3-4, 23-24, 40, 60, 252n10, 253n3
Merson, Sari, 183, 200, 205, 263n21
methodological issues: activist-academic relationships, 131-34, 215; ecofeminism and, 124-34; interpreting "lived experience," 129-31, 147, 180-81, 261n1. *See also* ecofeminist discourse; methodology
methodology, 14-15, 134-37, 236-37, 238-39, 244-48; questions/conversations, 138-39, 181, 242-44, 259n4, 263n21-n24. *See also* interviewees; methodological issues
Mies, Maria, 4, 39, 43, 44, 59, 78, 127, 254n16, 257n3, 257n7
Mittelmann, Terri, 150-51, 189, 204, 233
moral mothers, 23-24
moral responsibility. *See* responsibility
Morris, Ruth, 153, 187, 199, 260n7
Mother's Day protests, 29
motherhood: and citizenship, 197-201, 250n7; meanings of, 52, 71; as political identity, 66, 71, 80. *See also* maternalism
mothering theory, 26-29, 31, 253n2. *See also* maternalism
Mothers and Others Day Action, 29
Mothers of East Los Angeles, 46, 150
Mouffe, Chantal, 106, 228-29, 235
municipal housekeeping, 22-23, 182, 250n5
Muriuki, Wangari, 141, 153, 158, 206-7, 212

Nalunnakkal, George, 126
Naples, Nancy A., 36-37
necessary labour, 102-5, 135-36; gendered division of labour, 70, 103, 109-10, 117, 135-36, 142-43. *See also* household duties
neighbourhoodism, 187
neoliberal agendas, 10-14, 107-9, 185, 220, 249n5; Ontario government, 11, 142-44, 163, 220, 251n6
new right agendas. *See* right-wing agendas

NIABY (not in anyone's backyard), 227
NIMBY (not in my backyard), 37-38, 227
non-elite women, 35, 127-28, 137, 186-88,
193, 195, 257n20; domestic workers, 69,
173-74, 244, 261n25; poverty, 135, 152,
186-87; racialized women, 36, 69, 115,
187, 188, 193, 260n6
Noonan, Maureen, 143

oikos (household), 24
Ontario: government, 141-42, 193,
259n19, 259n23; Hamilton, 145-46,
186, 187; neoliberal agendas, 11, 142-44,
163, 220, 251n6. *See also* Toronto

paideia, 88, 224-25
Patti, Nikola, 153, 162, 192, 209
performativity/performative politics, 72,
75-76, 112-13, 218, 223-24
Plastimet fire, 145-46
Plumwood, Val, 101, 109, 225, 230
polis (Ancient Greek notion of), 87, 101,
155n23
political economy: women's unpaid labour,
67-70
political identity. *See* citizenship;
motherhood
politicization, 32, 66-72, 191-93, 215-16.
See also activism; citizenship
pollution, 145-47, 149, 173, 191, 195, 204
postcosmopolitanism, 116, 226, 256n13
postmodern feminism, 39, 40, 49, 132,
258n7
postmodernism, 57, 251n7, 255n3
post-structural feminism, 19, 49
poverty, 135, 152, 186-87
private sphere. *See* maternalism; public/
private spheres
privatization, 10-14, 68-69, 109, 163, 186,
220. *See also* neoliberal agendas
Progressive Conservative Party (Ontario),
141-42
progressive era, 22, 31, 182, 198, 251n11
public/private spheres, 160-61, 184, 222;
blurring of boundaries, 95, 136, 158-61,
220, 260n12; home responsibilities vs
community work, 136, 147, 154-67. *See
also* citizenship; politicization

quality-of-life activism, 15, 16, 22-24, 44-
49, 182, 223, 250n5
Quinby, Lee, 70-71

radical democracy, 74, 103, 228-29
re/sisters, 4, 40, 43-44, 53
Reed, Maureen, 125-26, 260n14
responsibility, 109; citizenship and, 105-
12, 117, 197-200; ecological citizenship
and, 105-12, 201-7, 216, 219, 222,

249n2, 255n1; environmentality and, 90,
108-9, 150-51; vs rights, 105-7, 110-11.
See also caring; cosmopolitanism; household duties; stewardship
right-wing agendas, 249n5, 252n15;
privatization of caring labour, 10-14,
68-69, 163, 220; use of grassroots
discourse, 37-38, 80
rights, 105-7, 110-12
Riley, Denise, 54, 76
Ruddick, Sara, 27, 28, 29

Safe Sewage Committee (SSC), 146-47
Salleh, Ariel, 70-71, 74, 78, 82, 210, 236,
257n7; re/sisters, 4, 40, 43-44, 53; views
on academic feminism, 39, 40
Sandilands, Catriona, 78; views on
democracy, 74, 75-76, 112, 255n23;
views on strategic essentialism, 53, 54-55,
112
Schor, Juliet, 231
scientific expertise, 193-96
Seager, Joni, 47, 71, 189, 249n1
Segal, Lynne, 7-9, 10, 16
self-neglect, 155-58, 167-70
sewage treatment, 146-47
shared parenting, 233-34
Shinn, Karey, 146, 185, 187, 189, 195, 196
Shiva, Vandana, 4, 40, 44, 59, 82, 134;
Chipko movement, 43, 126-27, 252n13,
258n2
Shour, Cheryl, 149, 182, 190, 191-92, 199,
211-12, 213
Smith, Jane (pseud.), 154, 164, 184, 206-7,
213
social connections, 152-53, 177-78; stress
of activism on, 156-57, 163-67
sociological essentialism, 7, 208
spirituality, 26, 82, 255n2
Spretnak, Charlene, 21, 25-26
SSC. *See* Safe Sewage Committee (SSC)
Starr, Julie, 185
stewardship, 107-8; ecological stewardship,
86, 88-92, 96, 115-16, 256n14
strategic essentialism, 4, 34, 50-56, 52,
112
strategy of reversal, 62, 225
Sturgeon, Noël, 50-51, 52, 55, 252n18
subsistence perspective, 4, 43-44, 59, 64-65,
78-79, 131, 233
subsistence work, 41-44
suffrage, 23, 250n7
sustainability, 9, 84-85, 86-89, 108, 118,
210-12, 249n4
sustainable development, 108, 128
sustainable living. *See* green practices
Swallow Richards, Ellen, 24

Taylor, Dorceta, 46, 137

time, 104; citizenship and, 101, 103, 155-56, 224, 228-32; issues for activist women, 155-58, 209-10; redistribution of caring responsibilities, 228-32
Torgerson, Douglas, 82, 103-4, 257n17
Toronto (ON), 140-44, 187, 259n18, 259n21-n22; pollution, 146-47, 149, 173, 195
Tronto, Joan, 74, 76-77, 78, 255n25

United Kingdom, 10, 107, 108
United Nations Earth Summits, 4, 42, 51, 91-92, 112, 256n11
urban environmental issues, 24, 45, 250n6, 250n9, 251n14. *See also* environmental justice movement

van Steenbergen, Bart, 93-94, 95
volunteerism, 68, 185-86, 254n15, 258n12. *See also* activist women; interviewees

WAA21. *See* Women's Action Agenda 21
Walkerton (ON), 259n23
Waring, Marilyn, 263n25
Warren, Karen J., 65, 254n12
ways of knowing, 3-4, 15, 41, 47-49, 51, 60; academic vs experiential knowledge, 38-40; debate concerning masculine vs feminine, 62-63; feminine principle, 6, 43-44, 58, 59, 64-65, 78-79, 126, 217; strategy of reversal, 62. *See also* experiential knowledge; maternal thinking

WED literature, 40-44, 126
WEDO. *See* Women's Environment and Development Organization (WEDO)
Weldon, Fay, 251n1
welfare state, 103-5, 117; dismantling of, 7, 10-11, 13, 69, 107, 169; social policies for collectivizing caring work in view of its dismantling, 12, 70, 103-5, 117, 142-43, 230
womanism, 39, 40, 252n8
women: connection to nature, 3-5, 20, 24, 29, 59, 61; dangers of strategy of reversal, 62; in developing countries, 4, 40, 43-44, 53, 127-28; effects of neoliberal agendas on, 10-14, 141-43; labour, 135-36, 258n11-n12, 260n15. *See also* activist women; gendered division of labour; maternalism; non-elite women
Women's Action Agenda 21, 42, 112, 233
Women's Environment and Development Organization (WEDO), 42, 51, 112
Woolf, Virginia, 262n17
working from home, 158-61
Woudstra, Karen, 149, 153-54, 188, 189, 194, 209-10
Wyman, Miriam, 48
Wynne, Kathleen, 143, 153-54, 185, 210-11, 259n16

York Region Environmental Alliance (YREA), 149
YREA. *See* York Region Environmental Alliance (YREA)